LAND & LEISURE

Second Edition

n/a

LAND & LEISURE

Concepts and Methods in Outdoor Recreation
Second Edition

Edited by

Carlton S. Van Doren
Texas A&M University

George B. Priddle
University of Waterloo

John E. Lewis
Parks Canada

Maaroufa Press, Inc.
Chicago

Maaroufa Press Geography Series Eric Moore, Advisory Editor

Library of Congress Catalog Card Number: 77-94184
ISBN: 0-88425-010-5
Manufactured in the United States of America

Designed by First Impression

To my wife,
Sharon

ACKNOWLEDGMENTS

As my predecessors have indicated, editing a book is not a simple task but a challenge of some magnitude. I am indebted to David W. Fischer, John E. Lewis, and George B. Priddle for undertaking the original task; and I have both appreciation and admiration for their imagination and effort. I hold a similar admiration, appreciation, and professional respect for the authors that have contributed to this edition. I wish to thank my departmental colleagues at Texas A&M University for acting as sounding boards as I assembled, organized, and evaluated many excellent scholarly writings in the process of selection for this volume. Colleagues include the professors and the graduate students, who provided insights from their youthful perspectives. In addition I gratefully acknowledge the cooperation of the administrators of the Recreation and Parks Department and Texas Agricultural Experiment Station at Texas A&M University.

A final acknowledgment is due Ted Tieken, Publisher, Maaroufa Press, Seva Johnson, Editor, and Ellen Thanas, Editorial Assistant, for their trust and patience.

As general editor and compiler, I assume full responsibility for any errors, omissions, and inadequacies in this edition.

CARLTON S. VAN DOREN
Department of Recreation and Parks
Texas Agricultural Experiment Station
Texas A&M University
January 1979

Contributors

Arthur A. Atkisson, Professor and Chairman, Department of Public and Environmental Administration, University of Wisconsin, Green Bay

Malcolm I. Bevins, Associate Resource Economist, Agricultural Experiment Station, University of Vermont

Roger N. Clark, Research Social Scientist, USDA Forest Service, Pacific Northwest Forest and Range Experiment Station, Seattle

John L. Crompton, Assistant Professor, Texas Agricultural Experiment Station, Department of Recreation and Parks, Texas A&M University

Robert K. Davis, Assistant Director for Economics, U.S. Department of the Interior, Office of Policy Analysis

Michael Dower, Director, Dartington Amenity Research Trust, Dartington, England

B. L. Driver, USDA Forest Service, Rocky Mountain Forest and Range Experiment Station, Fort Collins, Colo.

Diana R. Dunn, Professor and Head, Department of Physical Education, University of Arizona

David W. Fischer, International Institute of Applied Systems Analysis, Austria

Donald M. Fisk, Special Assistant to the Assistant Secretary for Science and Technology, U.S. Department of Commerce

David E. Gray, Vice President of Administration and Staff Coordination, California State University, Long Beach

Seymour Greben, U.S. Peace Corps Director, Monrovia, Liberia, West Africa

C. A. Gunn, Professor, Department of Recreation and Parks, Texas A&M University

Harry P. Hatry, Director, State and Local Government Research Program, The Urban Institute, Washington, D.C.

John C. Hendee, Assistant Director, USDA Forest Service, Southeast Forest Experiment Station, Asheville, N.C.

Warren E. Johnston, Professor, Department of Agricultural Economics, University of California, Davis

Jack L. Knetsch, Professor, Department of Economics, Simon Fraser University, Burnaby, British Columbia

W. F. LaPage, Leader, Outdoor Recreation Marketing Research Project, Forestry Sciences Laboratory, Durham, N.H.

David W. Lime, Project Leader, USDA Forest Service, North Central Forest Experiment Station, St. Paul, Minn.

Robert C. Lucas, Principal Research Social Scientist and Project Leader for Wilderness Management Research, USDA Forest Service, Intermountain Forest and Range Experiment Station, Forestry Sciences Laboratory, Missoula, Mont.

CONTRIBUTORS

Patrick E. McCarthy, Chancellor, University of Maine

Stephen F. McCool, Associate Professor, School of Forestry, University of Montana

Eugene Mattyasovsky, Professor, Department of Urban and Regional Planning, University of Toronto

Frank W. Millerd, Associate Professor of Economics, Department of Economics, Wilfrid Laurier University, Waterloo, Ontario

Stanley Parker, Office of Population Censuses and Surveys, Social Survey Division, London

Harvey S. Perloff, Dean, School of Architecture and Urban Planning, University of California, Los Angeles

Ira M. Robinson, Professor of Urban Planning, University of Calgary, Calgary, Alberta

Mordechai Shechter, Professor and Chairman, Department of Economics, University of Haifa, Israel

George H. Stankey, Research Social Scientist, USDA Forest Service, Intermountain Forest and Range Experiment Station, Forestry Sciences Laboratory, Missoula, Mont.

Bryan Thompson, Professor, Department of Geography, Wayne State University

S. Ross Tocher, Samuel Trask Dana Professor of Outdoor Recreation, University of Michigan

E. Boyd Wennergren, Director of International Programs, Utah State University

Lowdon Wingo, Jr., Director, School of Urban and Regional Planning, University of Southern California

contents

INTRODUCTION TO THE SECOND EDITION

The first edition of *Land & Leisure* proved to be a highly successful venture. It was well received by academicians and by students training to be professionals. The original triad of editors did a masterful job of selecting articles and of tying together the excellent writings of twenty-eight authors. Five years have now elapsed since the first edition was published, and the current editor has been hard pressed to improve upon the original. In an age of rapid communication and attendant social change, however, new as well as some old problems, issues, concepts, and methods have come to the forefront. This edition is an attempt to address both the old and the new from a fresh perspective.

Leisure has come to be a vital force in our lives. It represents an opportunity for self-expression, identity, and self-actualization apart from our work. Within the larger framework of leisure, recreation is assuming a greater role. At one time or another each of us is a participant in some kind of outdoor or indoor recreation, whether actively or passively, as our tastes and whims dictate or as these opportunities present themselves. As increased amounts of leisure time contribute to our growing demands for recreation, larger amounts of resources of varying diversity and quality are required to meet those demands. With this in mind, it is clear why the planning, managing, and administration of recreational resources—particularly in urban areas—is of personal interest to everyone. Such efforts determine the quality of our recreational experiences and provide the range of opportunities available to us.

The rapid growth of recreation pursuits has led to overuse of facilities with subsequent abuse of quality to sites and recreation experiences. Losses of this nature, coupled with the demands for new recreational areas, have accelerated interest in the planning and management of recreation resources.

Interest has also accelerated into a holistic view of leisure in our lives. This view has stimulated a changing vision of what we as individuals want. Leisure has become a part of self-discovery, vital to our well-being. The individual has become the central focus of leisure commitments. Leisure and recreation are recognized as essential for our health and learning and for adopting to societal changes. Public and private providers of leisure experiences are cognizant that people are the primary concern. When the first edition of this book was published, conservation and ecology were central themes. They are still prominent, but in addition there is now a humanistic movement and awareness that cannot be ignored. The second edition of *Land & Leisure* therefore could more properly be entitled Man, Resources and Leisure, reflecting a focus on man.

The post–World War II surge in the use of recreation areas, which found the few hard-working recreation professionals unprepared to meet the demands placed upon them, has been rekindled. We have more and better trained professionals today, but we also have more people with changing leisure desires and needs. Each day is a new challenge for the trained professional. It is an exciting period and the adaptable, trained professional can be richly rewarded if he or she can respond effectively to society's leisure needs.

Our knowledge of leisure in the United States is based on the benchmark U.S. Outdoor Recreation Resources Review Commission study reports published in 1962. These first in-depth studies of recreation signaled the beginning of an era in which recreation issues would be dealt with openly and across a wide range of professional and interdisciplinary interests. The 1961 Ottawa meeting, Resources for Tomorrow, was Canada's first national recreation study. In the United Kingdom two studies, the 1967 *Pilot National Recreation Survey of Britain* by Rogers and *Planning for Leisure* (1969) by K. K. Sillitoe, provided benchmark data. In Australia a comparable national survey was initiated by Bloomfield's *The Role, Scope and Development of Recreation in Australia* (1973) and was followed by a national conference in 1975, Leisure—A New Perspective. Generalizing as to the state of recreation across cultures is risky and I will make no attempt to do so here. The point, however, is that within the English-speaking countries leisure has been addressed and analyzed with the blessing of national governments. In most countries the study of leisure/recreation needs and resources has become a profession in its own right.

The U.S. Outdoor Recreation Resources Review Commission study reports are now factually outdated. The federal government, primarily through the Bureau of Outdoor Recreation and, in 1978, the Heritage, Conservation, and Recreation Service, has supported periodic national recreation surveys and, in 1973, a nationwide plan for outdoor recreation, *Outdoor Recreation—A Legacy for America.* The Heritage, Conservation, and Recreation Service dispenses to state, regional, and local governments federal money from the Land and Water Conservation Fund.

Unfortunately, politics has played a strong role in the federal government's involvement with recreation advancement. *A Legacy for America* was originally completed in 1970 but was withheld by the Nixon administration because it was inflationary. The Department of the Interior estimated it would cost $42 billion to implement. The final published report in 1973 was much less ambitious and has been criticized by many professional organizations including the National Recreation and Parks Association.

A Legacy for America made no attempt to provide goal priorities and ignored research needs and the training of professionals. It unduly focused on land and facilities and ignored operations. It included a strong urban recreation focus but provided few suggestions for meeting growing needs in urban areas. Until a different administration makes efforts to improve the planning and development of recreation, we are saddled with an apparent de-emphasis of federal leadership. This means that professionals must assume more involvement in the development and provision of all types of recreation services.

Active professional interest is manifest at the college and university level, with increasing numbers of students selecting careers in recreation. In the United States recreation is no longer taught and studied by a handful of academics in separate departments. The educational roots of professionals in recreation and parks were originally planted in two broad educational disciplines: the social sciences and the natural sciences. This heritage helps in understanding the recreation and parks dichotomy. Recreation professionals traditionally received training in sociology, social work, education, physical education, and health sciences. The leaders of the playground movement of the early 1900s are identified with this type of training. A second group of professionals evolved from the natural sciences, primarily forestry, wildlife, horticulture, and, later, landscape architecture, engineering, and urban planning. Today academic training for professionals frequently includes a mixture of social and natural sciences.

The first edition of *Land & Leisure* was envisioned as an introduction to the student reader of the cornerstones of recreational land use—spatial, behavioral, economic, and physical analysis—in the hope that in time a dialog would be encouraged between newly graduated professionals and experienced practitioners. The book was purposefully assembled to reflect an interdisciplinary overview in order that students might develop a basic understanding of the types of problems, concepts, methods, and approaches helpful in furthering and integrating knowledge of recreation services. The second edition has of course been modified to reflect the changes in contemporary thinking regarding recreation.

Land & Leisure, second edition, has several objectives. It is designed to demonstrate some of the basic, up-to-date ideas and issues that have evolved over the last decade and a half and that have been influential in shaping decisions in recreation/leisure services. The ideas and discussions included are complex with no simple solutions. Some chapters follow a "cookbook" style, providing a step-by-step, "how to do it" presentation. But the readers are cautioned that every locale and every human interaction is different, and the "cookbook" should be considered only as a general guide. The successful cook develops his or her own recipe with unique ingredients. Emphasis in the selection of chapters has been based on writings that demonstrate challenging concepts, methods, issues, and ideas. Whenever possible the focus has also been on works that illustrate research or survey applications.

In the second edition one goal is to emphasize urban recreation and the use of resources and facilities within the metropolitan milieu. Selecting appropriate chapters to meet this goal has not been easy because interest and financial backing to study urban recreation have been scarce. Yet with a population that is highly urbanized and a current energy situation that seems to foretell a growing crisis, recreation/leisure pressures are critical in our metropolitan space.

A second goal is to underscore the increased importance of the private sector as a means to provide recreation/leisure services, whether they be urban, suburban, or rural. Public-private cooperative planning and management offer promise for meeting many of the nation's recreational needs. A third goal is to provide some new terminology and understanding for any student involved in this profession. One such holistic concept is systems analysis. A systems approach is inherently a part of most of our subconscious thinking. We are all forced to deal with complexities in order to identify a problem, consider alternative solutions, and select promising optimizations. A systems approach initially assists us in recognizing the interrelationships among all components of a problem. Issues, policies, and programs should always be considered and evaluated as interdependent parts of a total system. Systems theory offers a basis for organization and informational feedback.

Finally, the following chapters should highlight the importance of the individual. Recreation/leisure pursuits are, after all, for us. As a part of this goal that centers on the individual, emphasis will focus on the differences between the recreation manager/administrator viewpoint relative to the user and, particularly, on public input into management development decisions.

This book, like the first edition, is divided into five parts. Part 1 is designed to give the student an overview of recreation within our changing society, to highlight the importance of the individual and how each of us undergoes changing personal recreation needs. In addition the first part focuses on urban recreation and on organizational structure for providing recreation, and it includes a direct and indirect discussion of a systems analytic framework for planning and management. Part 1 overall is an assessment of where we have been, where we are, and what our future direction may be.

Planning and management are the topics covered in part 2. The physical resources, human motivations, behavior, and maintenance of the quality of the resource and the leisure experience are central to this part. The four chapters are ordered so that the concepts, methods, and theories presented increase in complexity. In addition no single academic discipline is highlighted. An interdisciplinary, integrative approach is evident.

Chapters that address the methods of recreation use evaluation comprise part 3. As in part 2 the chapters in the beginning present basic approaches, some of which are discipline based such as economics, sociology, geography, and urban planning. Most of this part addresses problems of recreational behavior; and, for the student interested in research, these five chapters are probably of most interest and challenge.

The second edition departs significantly from the first edition in part 4. There are a number of rationales for including chapters on public-private interface. One of the strongest is that this area is one of the least understood within the profession and one that receives minimal attention during a student's study and training. A second rationale is, simply, self-defense. The recent passage of Proposition 13 in the state of California may not argue well for the continued flow of public funds into recreational and other public welfare agencies. The public increasingly demands accountability for dollars invested and, as a result, some public recreation may falter and even decline. A dedicated professional may find public-private joint ventures one way to maintain some programs.

Another reason for including part 4 is to highlight an area of study that has probably been lacking in many higher education recreation and park curricula. This is the professional area of study that includes courses in business analysis, accounting, finance, management, and marketing. All of these subjects are increasingly becoming necessary for the middle to upper range of professionals in recreation/leisure services.

The recreational decision process is the theme of part 5. Regional planning is the general topic of all chapters, but public input to the planning process is paramount to successful planning.

Each of the five parts contains an overview, where the initial themes are discussed in more detail and the chapters are interrelated. Each also contains a list of further readings that should be very helpful to the serious student.

An astute reader will recognize that I have refrained from any reference to outdoor recreation and instead have referred to recreation/leisure. My original attraction to this profession stemmed from interest in outdoor recreation, but I firmly believe that the profession has now advanced beyond the use of the word *outdoor.* Recreation is the same wherever it takes place. I do not deny that many of our recreation/leisure pursuits take place outdoors, but as professionals we should be concerned with all leisure pursuits in all locations.

Land & Leisure is intended primarily for use in college curricula, although it should also be helpful to professional planners. The book has been designed for a general course in recreation, be it within a single discipline, a multidisciplinary course, or as part of a professional program in recreation and park planning or administration. The readings can be used as a basic text or as a supplement; they can also be used in conjunction with additional readings of particular interest to the instructor.

Part One
RECREATION, CHANGING SOCIAL VALUES & ASSESSMENT

OVERVIEW

An underlying issue of all recreation provision is its social value and how we assess our ability to provide it. The chapters in part 1 concentrate on the issues and processes at work within our recreation system and society. It stimulates the reader by posing questions about recreation/leisure in a contemporary context. Then the parts that follow provide the means to answer some of the questions posed.

Although since World War II and particularly in the 1960s and 1970s, heightened environmental interest and a vocal populace have been of significant benefit to the recreation and parks movement, professionals have been at times slow to respond to many social changes occurring in contemporary American society. Chapter 1 proposes a plan to develop a more responsive and humanistic approach as a basis to improve leisure services. Then, in order to provide a dynamic framework to assist us in understanding recreation/leisure values and behavior, chapter 2 gives descriptive insights as to how individuals view leisure at various stages in the life cycle.

A "systematic" approach to planning for recreation appears in chapter 3. This discussion helps us begin to answer questions concerning the total recreation system and how facts and values can be analyzed as part of the planning process. Finally, the last chapter, which is more factual and technical than the others, cogently poses some basic questions concerning urban recreation needs, and it reviews three techniques for assessing recreation.

CHAPTER 1

FUTURE PERSPECTIVES

David E. Gray
Seymour Greben

When this article first appeared in 1974, its candid assessment of the recreation and parks movement in the United States was intended to provoke introspection within the profession. Here it serves as an excellent introduction to this volume by providing an historical overview of urban recreation, commentary on its present, changing status, and speculation for its future. Though directed at the movement in the United States, the appraisal by David Gray and Seymour Greben has implications for recreation and park professionals and students everywhere.

YESTERDAY

[The United States in the 1970s] is, admittedly, an America which is perceived quite differently from [that] of 1900 by its citizens and by people around the world. It is a country that no longer is preeminently shaped by the Frederick Jackson Turner vision of a never-ending physical or geographical frontier. What remains of that type of frontier is, in the main, peripheral to the mainstream of America, and no amount of nostalgic yearning for the past in the form of citing moon, space, and undersea exploration can obliterate the reality that if America is confronted today with frontiers of preeminent consequence, they are social frontiers—not geographical ones.

In the 1930s America suffered a debilitating economic depression. A combination of war and near-war and tinkering with the country's free enterprise, sometime Keynesian economic system has since dimmed the memory of that horrible, degrading period by providing a kind of inflationary near-prosperity for a relatively large percentage of the people. (This should not be read as a walking away from the truth of large, continuing poverty pockets in the populace, [discussed below].) Only the "old" people in our society still remember the Great Depression, and even they no longer make major lifestyle decisions on the basis of those memories. If the Great Depression of the 1930s is of importance today, it is probably so for two primary reasons:

1. Having experienced it, or not having experienced it, represents one of the consequential symbols of the generation gap.

Reprinted from *Parks and Recreation,* July 1974, pp. 26–33; 47–56, by permission of the National Recreation and Parks Association and the authors.
This paper was originally addressed to members of the recreation and park movement and written at the suggestion of the General Council of the National Recreation and Park Association.

2. The depression period marked the beginning of a realization that government can, and will, play a major role in confronting the chronic problems of specifically identifiable groups within our midst. Government became involved with social reality—and quite definitely will remain involved in spite of temporal rhetoric . . . to the contrary.

Since the depression [the United States] has experienced war and near-war as a way of life; and as a by-product (fringe benefit?) the economy has received continuing, substantial governmental stimulus and control. [The United States] has been clearly established as a major world power with all the attendant pragmatism, self-righteousness, and virtues that are bequeathed to nations of this status. We have sallied forth from isolation to involvement in everyone's affairs throughout the world, and now we are flirting again with a probably unattainable goal of semi-isolation. We have begun to explore the solar system and will continue to do so, and we have become somewhat titillated with the bottom of the sea. Anticommunism has become an obsession which, unfortunately, is not usually counterbalanced by pro-*anything* of substance. Now we are doing business with the "worst" Communists—and we are pleased about it.

The social historians say that we have been involved with things and accumulation, not ideas or matters of the spirit. Those of us who are forty and [over] are mystified and often angry with those who do not seem to understand and appreciate what we feel we have accomplished. Just when we start to feel proud, they "kick us in the ass" (that is how *they* would say it), and they say we are selfish, self-centered, and inconsistent.

It is the *they* that may be a dominant theme of [the 1970s] and of the future; *they* are all the people [of the United States] who no longer can be fitted under the traditional umbrella of American majority opinion and culture, the ones who have been shaking us and threatening us and challenging us and *changing us* . . . [in the recent past].

[Currently] in America, we are visibly affected by the reality of old people, hippies, blacks, teenagers, women, American Indians, migrant poor, Chicanos. It is true that . . . it is becoming stylish to say that the antiwar movement, the youth movement, and the women's rights movement, as examples, are all passing fancies. They have won no elections, they have had no long-term effect on our national thought process, and they will pass on like dance marathons, goldfish swallowing, green stamps, and other fads.

This is patent nonsense, a kind of wishful thinking to go back to a stability that never really existed. The "movements" which we have experienced—and they can all be recognized as social movements—have truly revolutionized society; they have brought about profound, lasting change and they continue today. Their rhetoric and their style have infuriated us at times, but their noise and fervor must not cause us to lose sight of their deep significance. Who can deny the reality and permanent significance of these changes?

1. Government can no longer . . . dictate what is right and desirable. Government, at all levels, is absolutely dependent upon maximum

citizen participation if it is to succeed in accomplishing the classical functions of a democratic government.

2. Ethnic, religious, and other minority cultures must participate equally in the mainstream of life. Abject, unadulterated bigotry cannot and will not be tolerated, legally or socially, and the more socially sophisticated forms of intolerance are passing from the scene.
3. No public institution can function on the basis of a dual standard; i.e., this is what we say we stand for, but it has no relationship with the way we operate (e.g., [U.S.] colleges and universities teaching about democracy but, in the minds of their students and faculty, functioning as an oligarchy, or worse, a dictatorship).
4. No longer can industry or government or individuals plunder the physical environment in the names of development and progress and growth. The new laws that are now on the books—and, more important, the attitudes of our people—will simply not allow for further despoiling of the environment. Perhaps the most astounding reality [today] is that somehow industry does accommodate itself to newly formulated controls which protect the environment. Industry continues to survive in spite of new zoning laws and legislation which control utility placement, billboards, and signs and which establish standards for open space and park dedication and even [in spite of enacted] . . . laws say what can be developed when.
5. [In the United States] our conscious and acknowledged attitudes toward social behavior, particularly relationships between the sexes, have taken a whole new dimension, perhaps most typified by a beginning of a diminishing of hypocrisy. Many of us would disagree as to which of the many changes in this category is most significant and lasting, but the changes are real and positive. They have been inspired largely by young people's insistence on honesty and acknowledgement of what is real. Again, this is not to be confused by the distraction of style and rhetoric—or four-letter words—when the main value is one of shock therapy.
6. We must recognize that to be old or to be a female in [U.S.] society provides a separate experience, a separate environment from all who are not old or female. We must recognize that the old and the female (and how many other groups?) will no longer allow themselves to be despised or ignored or legislated against.
7. The majority culture must recognize that the job of creating a healthy society requires a conscious and ethical responsibility to share with all of the minority cultures the equal opportunity to participate in the mainstream.

This, then, is a partial, selected view of [the United States in the 1970s], the America in which the recreation and park profession functions and serves. [As professionals], our task now is to attempt to define . . . the state . . . of the recreation and park movement today, so that we can evaluate our potential to provide productive services to the [United States] which will emerge [at the turn of the century].

TODAY

Unfortunately, even as late as [the 1970s], recreation and parks [professionals] attempt to remain all things to all people. We have many spiritual parents, and perhaps our most honorable parentage stems from the fact that some of the thinkers who caused us to come into existence conceptualized our role as a part of the total quest for the "good life." Early progressive movements in [the United States]—the historically significant ones that dealt with pure food and drug laws, working conditions, and humanized immigration laws—also paid attention to protection of natural resources and productive use of leisure time. Since early in the twentieth century, these recreation and park issues have been a part of the total progressive movement and ethic in the United States. As a result, government throughout the United States has come to accept recreation and parks as a basic in the list of services which citizens should receive; and all facets of local government—city, county, and special purpose district—share the responsibility for the function.

With this acceptance has come the development of a formalized recreation and park movement which has tended to emulate other governmental services in formulating goals, organizational patterns, and symbols of professionalism. Nationally known leaders have emerged (at least they are nationally known in our recreation and park world); and, to simplify communication and understanding in our world, we have created our version of a party line complete with words and phrases defined with consistent meaning by most of our colleagues. We have, in the best traditions of our country, formed a variety of different professional groups based upon political subdivision, geographic regions, specialized interest, and profession. And we attempt regularly to evaluate ourselves.

Therefore, in attempting to chronicle what we might aspire to in the ... next thirty years for recreation and parks, it would seem reasonable to attempt to evaluate the recreation and park movement today. How we have functioned historically, our perceptions of the world around us, should give reasonable insight into what might be expected in the future.

Unfortunately, based upon a measurement of leadership in social movements, there is not much reason for optimism. This is not to say that the recreation and park movement has not made important contributions to the well-being of [the United States] or that certain individuals within the movement have not made singularly brilliant contributions which are viewed in an aura of great public acceptance. Rather, what we are saying is that our contribution has been somewhat minimal in terms of providing leadership for the main current of social progress in [the United States] and somewhat marginal as to where the action is.

... [I]n terms of what is important in our world (achievements, problems, etc.), it appears that we are not yet in the foreground of dynamic change and that typically we have been followers, not leaders. How do we arrive at this conclusion?

1. In most [U.S.] cities, publicly supported recreation and park budgets are an embarrassingly small portion of the total—at a time when many, perhaps most, [persons in the United States] would agree that the dual tasks of preserving and protecting the physical environment and providing constructive, useful leisure time experiences rise to the top of our national list of needs. This conceivably results from our own inability to define our role beyond narrow, often parochial boundaries.
2. In most [U.S.] cities, it is difficult to identify any great overall community interest and knowledge [of the recreation and parks] movement or of our local leaders. (Compare this with concern for law and order, public education, etc.)
3. During the past ten years, when change has symbolized American life, we have not kept pace and hardly ever have we led. Examples?

   Relationship with minority communities. There are few or no examples of our movement introducing innovative, constructive ideas which would lead to a greater sense of equality of opportunity. Within [the National Recreation and Park Association], we have been publicly embarrassed by the emergence of first a black caucus and later a minority caucus as an expression of disappointment on the part of minority groups and individuals that we are not responsive. If we fail to make an appropriate place for minorities in our own organization, how can we presume to succeed in our local minority communities?

   Relationship with environmental organizations. There are exceptions . . . but generally we have rejected or have been unreasonably slow in establishing common cause with the environmental movement. Hardly ever have we provided substantive leadership for this vital movement which should, in truth, be our natural ally.

   Relationship with women. A vital new movement has emerged in America, and its existence until now has had little consequence to our own movement and received no creative leadership from us. We still announce jobs for which only males can qualify (although we do not know why), and we continue to announce program offerings such as girls' dance class and boys' craft class, even though these specially distinguished classes serve no need and are repugnant to an ever-growing segment of society. Often, our only reason for continuing these classes results from a fear that what we perceive as a dominant male majority culture will oppose any change to nonintegrated classes.

   Community participation. Our rhetoric and public statements now support the idea of community participation, but look how long it took us to reach this point and how little relationship there is between the generalization of philosophical support and the actuality of real support and leadership in the specific situation. How often the comment is heard in our meetings, "We believe in community participation and we are working on it, but we have a long way to go yet." A kind of "absolution" technique has emerged as a substitute for actual commitment; so long as we say we are working at achieving a desirable goal, [we are relieved] of any responsibility to do anything.

   Understanding and support for the disadvantaged. It is a relatively simple task to create a sense of "busyness" at most parks or recreation centers. There is a certain percentage of children and adults who would show up to play basketball and picnic regardless of whether any staff [were] present. But while we revel in this semblance of success, we often are guilty of overlooking the disadvantaged, whether they be so because of physical, spiritual, economic, or other factors. The people who need us the most are often ignored or, worse, made to feel unwelcome. We did not, on our own, redesign our facilities so that they could be used comfortably and with dignity by handicapped persons. We were *forced* into design changes by the special interest groups who must look out for the welfare of the blind, the lame, the old, and the retarded. We still have not developed programs which provide positive answers to the problems generated by the drug culture, even though we know that a considerable percentage of our young people are confronted by this culture.

4. Lastly, we are not identified with the major problems which confront [U.S.] society. In 1900, 60.3 percent of our population lived in rural areas and 39.7 percent lived in urban areas. By 1970 the situation was reversed—rural 26.5 percent and urban 73.5 percent. And yet we still persist in debating whether urban needs will be our primary concern. In today's world, we face the reality of a mounting anger often typified by rising violence, terrorism, and antisocial behavior. Instead of coming forth with new, substantive predelinquency solutions (one reason for our existence), we are "copping out" and joining in the push for more police and more police protection (postdelinquency) as the answer. Today when one speaks privately to the creative leaders in the movement, the real "shakers" and "movers," they inevitably describe their sense of isolation because they dare to be innovative and because they defy the party line. How similar this is to Ibsen's *Enemy of the People,* who became concerned with the polluting of the town's water supply by the major industry—and who was kicked out of polite society for his attempts at reform.

This is one view of [the United States] and the recreation and park movement today. It is a pessimistic summary, one filled with deep concern and disappointment. It does not attempt to overlook the accomplishments; but, in all candor, it is our view that the next thirty years must be an era of solid achievement and leadership if the movement is to fulfill our hopes and dreams and if we are to assume a major role in building a [United States] which is rich in human and spiritual blessings.

THE FUTURE OF AMERICAN SOCIETY

Today change is occurring in response to visions dimly grasped but widely and powerfully felt that deal with who we are, what we might do, and what we can be in light of the limits and potentials we see in the human dimension. There is a broad and growing humanistic ethic permeating [the United States]. It sees the great need of our nation in human terms. It would not rank improved technology or an improved economy as central needs in our national life. It would see as central the primary social needs: human development, improved processes of human interaction, and protection and restoration of our environment. It is precisely in these fields that the recreation and park movement must operate. It is in these fields the movement finds its mission and identity.

In [the United States] there is a rapidly changing vision of what we want our lives to be. At the root of the great change in self-perception that is now evolving is the way we feel about ourselves and the way we conceive of ourselves as human beings. Our sensation of being alive, our sense of individual existence, and our vision of identity are all being revised. In short, our whole concept of what it means to be human is undergoing profound change. [The United States] is turning inward. We are reexamining our thoughts, our ideals, our motives. Our method is introspection and our goal is self-discovery. The new frontier is the exploration of inner space. The motive is a deeper participation in life. The really significant problems in our country lie in the area of human interaction. It is in these relationships that human destruction or human development takes place. It is precisely here that a new society will be created, if there is to be a new society. Something important is happening, and it is possible that those of us who devote our lives to the recreation and park movement may have a part in it. If we recognize what we are about, it may be a significant part.

The American Institute of Planners in its Fiftieth Year Consultation expressed the national purpose as: "To assure the primary importance of the individual, his freedom, his widest possible choice, his access to joy and opportunity, his impetus to self-development, his responsible relation to his society, the growth of his inner life, and his capacity to love." This glowing vision of our potential future we have not yet attained. One of the things swift social and technological change is demonstrating is that our cultural heritage mutates faster than our physical and biological heritage.

Abraham Maslow has suggested that human motives are arranged in a pyramid that ranges from "physiological" needs at the bottom through "safety," "belongingness and love" (or social needs), "esteem" (including self-respect and feelings of success), to "self-actualization," which has been attained when the individual has become all he or she is capable of becoming. A growing number of Americans are no longer content with the physiological and security base of that structure. They have set out to climb the pyramid. They seek experience at the center of existence—not the experience of escapism but a deeper participation in life.

Health

As a nation, we are beginning to perceive that health is more than the absence of disease. There is a great national debate going on over the goals of health care. The growing concept is the idea of health as well-being, and the debate centers on the issue of keeping people well versus curing them after they are sick. The recreation movement has a stake in that debate. As therapists, recreation personnel have a role in curing the sick; but as members of the recreation and park movement, we all have a role in developing a society that will help keep people well.

The World Health Organization has defined health as "a state of complete physical, mental, and social well-being, and not merely the absence of disease and infirmity." To be free of illness, discomfort, and disability is of itself highly desirable, but the absence of these conditions is not the highest expression of human potential. The individual who lives constructively and creatively beyond a level of ordinary effectiveness is beginning to fulfill his or her potential and is approaching the full state of health. That individual will be making the most of life. Health is not an end in itself; it is a state of being that permits people to make the most of themselves. Health improves the vitality of mankind and releases people for the creative life. Recreation is one aspect of that life. It is a cliché to talk of poor adaptation to the freedom granted by increasing free time; but cliché or not, it is true; and the results of maladaptation have significant human consequences. Poor adjustment shows itself in various kinds of sociopsychological disturbances. Sando Ferenczi, in a classic study published in 1926, identified a pattern of "Sunday neurosis" now being reconfirmed in a study in England that shows an increase in psychosomatic phenomena—including depression and suicides—during holidays and vacations. Other reactions to free time are excessive guilt, compulsive work, and self-alienation.

Mobility and Transience

Mobility has been widely discussed as a significant social phenomenon for several years, but we have recently come to realize that *mobility*, which suggests movement from place to place, is inadequate to indicate the pervasiveness and social consequences of the conditions we are experiencing. The word recently adopted for that is *transience*, which may be defined as the rapid turnover of relationships with people, places, and things. The current high rate of mobility in the United States produces relationships of short duration and low intensity with other people, with places, and with things. Motion, which was originally a means, has become an end. For many, transience is the essence of life. We see it in the mobility of habitation, in the "Dixie Cup" approach to possessions, in the "serial monogamy" of marriage. Transience is evident all around us. Cars are rented, dolls are traded in, dresses are discarded after a single wearing, friendships come and go, marriages last for a few months or years. In a transient society where there are no long-term commitments, there must be a feeling for the temporary that makes something as good as it can be, while it lasts.

The small group is the essential vehicle and unit of learning and of life support. The forces at work in our culture are tearing apart the old small groups that have been central in our society. Groups based on family, work, and friendship decline. New forms like collectives, communes, liberation groups, "growth centers," and ecology and consumer action organizations have evolved to replace them. These groups are not random; they are attempts to bring people together into an organization capable of coping with the world in flux. If we are to help mitigate the human toll of transience, it is our task to develop nuclei around which small groups can form and to speed up group process so that the benefits of group membership can be experienced before transience tears it apart again.

Learning

Learning is a lifetime enterprise. It begins with the first breath and ends with the last. It is the central activity of life; in a very real way, it is life. It varies in pace and intensity, but it goes on day and night, year after year. Learning expands awareness, stores information, develops conditioned responses, establishes identity; it governs perceptions, regulates human interaction, influences health. Learning determines who we are and how we behave. The most significant kinds of learning do not take place in school. Education as we are coming to know it goes beyond developing skills. The new emphasis is on development of individual human capabilities to enhance the quality of life in all its aspects and to enhance individual and social well-being. Developmental psychologists have established beyond any doubt the intimate relationship between playing and learning. A child's learning is best centered on the child's own experience. For most children, play experience is the thing life is made of. If people are not learning, they are probably not enjoying recreation. We must be deeply involved in learning. We have learned to sustain life; and now we want to enhance it.

Urban Recreation

Our cities do not work as they should. In the typical suburban neighborhood today there is no commons, no public meeting place where the people of the neighborhood can interact. The predilection of the city planner for sorting land use by functions and putting all like uses together has segregated residential areas into compounds which include only houses. These sterile areas often do not provide even a corner store where one might pass the time of day with a neighbor.

Recreation activities operate *within* the social environment and *form a part of* the total social environment of the community and the nation. In many communities they are a conspicuous part of the pattern of social interaction. In areas where the neighborhood has lost its social significance as an organizing device for human association, recreation activities are the primary arena beyond work and kinship. In communities with high rates of mobility, recreation may be more effective than kinship as a social nucleus. Open space is social space. In the great urban parks of the nation a daily open house takes place that brings together people of the neighborhood in a no-host social event. An essential task is to provide the commons where the people of the city can interact.

Social Change

It is tempting but unsatisfactory, when one considers the impact of change on the recreation and park movement, to concentrate on technological change, which has a physical embodiment and is, therefore, easier to perceive. It is unsatisfactory because, in spite of the widespread influence of technological change, it is not the most significant force impacting the movement. That force is social change. That illusive combination of changes in technology, economics, politics, philosophy, environmental perceptions, and religion is remaking mankind's view of the universe and what it means to be human. We only dimly perceive how pervasive social change is and what it may portend. Even that dimly lit vision confirms that things cannot remain as they are.

The recreation and park movement and the agencies that administer programs exist in a political and social environment that is increasingly complex. The state and most communities are politicized to a degree we have not experienced before. Concurrent and interwoven into this increase in the tempo and intensity of political activity are technological and social developments that are changing the social environment dramatically. It is in this rapidly changing social environment that the recreation and park movement must operate. The magnitude of social change is so great it defies description; it may defy comprehension until it is seen in the framework of history, but some trends can already be seen as highly influential. Among them the changing pattern of family relationships, deterioration of the sense of neighborhood, the development of an urban individual, altered conditions of work, the changing role of women in society, race relations, sorting of society on the basis of age, and revolutionary changes in our system of values appear to be highly significant.

Failure of the recreation and park movement to deal with change continually will inevitably lead to crisis. An adaptive mechanism that denies change or denies the significance of change can lead only to major crisis in place of a whole series of more-or-less manageable problems that will permit incremental adaptation. Adjustment to change requires flexibility and a short response time. Managing change requires a preferred vision of the future. We need images of potential tomorrows, conceptions of possible tomorrows, and identification of our probable tomorrows.

The central concepts of the recreation and park movement are ideas whose time has come. The concern for people that has been and is the primary theme in the philosophical foundations of the recreation movement has become the major thrust of contemporary life in this country. It is apparent in the humanistic movement that is sweeping the nation and the world. We see it in humanistic psychology, attacks on the abuses of technology, the peace movement, empathy for the poor, the drive for improved medical care, the move to reject possessions as the symbol of identity, the effort to improve education, women's liberation, race relations, and in a thousand other [areas]. These ideas are being acted out in programs and demonstrations and individual efforts all around us.

The fundamental themes of the park movement are also a major national obsession. *Conservation* and *ecology* are the watchwords of the age. The realization that human beings are not independent of nature but a part of it has seeped into the national consciousness. The few that have been concerned about survival of the endangered species are now joined by the thousands who are deeply concerned about the survival of people in today's urban environment. We now see mankind as an endangered species. It is a frightening prospect.

Future of the Movement

Alvin Toffler has suggested, "No serious futurist deals in prediction." It is not our purpose to predict the future; rather, it is our intent to examine some of the alternatives and to suggest some elements of the preferred future for the recreation and park movement. It is time for us to devote increasing thought to the role recreation services should play in the community and what recreation should mean to the individual. We can begin to rethink the content of recreation programs by noting the nature of the promise of the human species. Contribution to fulfillment of that promise is the reason for recreation and park programs. A central purpose of community recreation programs is to help improve the quality of living. A great many park and recreation people have not made the connection between parks and the environment or recreation and the quality of life.

We must give more attention to the recreation concept and improve our definition of it. Current definitions ignore or give little attention to the psychological implications of recreation. They are activity centered. Definition in terms of activities is unsatisfactory because a given activity may provide recreation for one individual and not for another; worse yet, it may provide recreation for a person at one time but not at another. Current definitions work within a time frame—leisure—but recreation may occur at any time. They hold out for inherent reward, but many recreation responses are dependent on feedback from others, and it is not clear why acceptance of material reward invalidates the experience. Some mandate social acceptability. A little introspection will reveal the absurdity of that criterion.

We should have discovered long ago the nature of the business we are in, but we have not. Only now are we beginning to rethink what recreation is. In the emerging view it is not activities or facilities or programs that are central; it is what happens to people. Recreation is not a specific event, a point in time, or a place in space; it is a dimension in life, a state of being. The proposed definition is:

> Recreation is an emotional condition within an individual human being that flows from a feeling of well-being and self-satisfaction. It is characterized by feelings of mastery, achievement, exhilaration, acceptance, success, personal worth, and pleasure. It reinforces a positive self-image. Recreation is a response to esthetic experience, achievement of personal goals, or positive feedback from others. It is independent of activity, leisure, or social acceptance.

Following that definition, recreation is feeling good about yourself. It is a peak experience in self-satisfaction. It stems from esthetic experience—the sense of being a significant part of a vast and mysterious whole; it comes from establishing a personal goal and achieving it—the higher the standard, the more intense the recreational experience; it comes from favorable reactions of others—the kind of support that builds a self-image of personal affection and competence. Recreation has nothing to do with leisure; it can occur at any time. It has nothing to do with activity; it can occur in tennis or accounting. It has nothing to do with social acceptance. In short, our traditional definitions of recreation do not advance our understanding of it. For thirty or forty years or more the recreation and park movement has been deluded by a false perception of recreation. This has warped our services, given us false priorities, prevented effective evaluation of results, and inhibited our ability to interpret what we do. Worst of all, it has prevented us from developing an understanding of our goals and methods. The popular understanding of recreation in our field cannot sustain further development. The concept is bankrupt.

Recognition of recreation as an internalized emotional response is comparatively easy. Acting on that knowledge in recreation and park agencies will be far more difficult, but it is necessary if we are substantially to improve our services. Adopting the suggested definition or something like it is the first step toward improving our contribution to the quality of life. Developing the methods of implementing the definition is the second.

Some implications of this proposed new definition are already clear:

1. We must alter our programs and the way they are conducted to emphasize human development, well-being, and development of a positive self-image.
2. We must enhance the possibility that people can experience the peak experience described in the definition—in short, the opportunity for esthetic response, achievement of personal goals, and positive feedback from others.
3. We must rethink competition and the way it is used in recreation programs.
4. We must accept the responsibility for the human consequences of what we do.
5. We must evaluate everything we do in human terms. The critical questions are not, How many were there? or Who won? The critical question is, What happened to Jose, Mary, Sam, and Joan in this experience?

Services

We must reorient our approach to services to think not only in terms of activities and programs but also in terms of human experience. The recreation program should help each individual extend his or her intellectual and emotional reach. The three-dimensional person is the person who is a participant in the creative process, one who has something to say, a way to say it, and someone to listen. Recreation improves awareness, deepens understanding, stimulates appreciation, develops one's powers, and enlarges the sources of enjoyment. It promotes individual fulfillment. It encourages self-discovery. It helps give meaning to life.

Leadership

People who grew up on the frontier a century or two ago were isolated because of physical separation; today people in the cities are isolated because of emotional separation. Factors which inhibit self-expression through recreation may be physical, social, or economic. They may be inherent in the social or political system, but the more severe limitations are often self-generated. Lack of skill, insecurity, little knowledge of opportunity, fear of failure, and a variety of other internalized factors can limit or destroy motivation. Overcoming these inhibitions often requires competent leadership. Learning to serve in this way is a very personal process. It is a matter of extending one's experience by sharing it with others, assimilating it, and eventually drawing on it. It is a search for attitudes rather than methods. It is more a matter of being than a matter of doing. The highly personal patterns of human interaction that are at the root of successful service in this field are not established procedures. They are expressions of experience and attitudes. What one thinks and feels about oneself and other people comes through. The recruitment and training of personnel who can give adequate leadership will require methods we have not yet invented.

Planning

We must have better planning processes. Critics argue that much planning is antihuman, and in many cases they are right. It is easy to lose social, cultural, and psychological values in the overwhelming desire to maximize economic efficiency. The answer to the criticism is not to act without a plan; that approach generates its own tyranny. Rather it is to devise a planning method that embraces these values. We desperately need a method of planning that permits social cost-benefit analysis. Lacking such a system, we are turning control of our social enterprises over to the accounting mind. The accounting mind reaches decisions by a method in which short-range fiscal consequences are the only criterion of value. Recreation and park services will not survive in that kind of an environment. Most of the great social problems that disfigure our national life cannot be addressed in a climate dominated by that kind of value system.

We do not need irrationality, rigid traditionality, passive acceptance of change, despair, or witless revolution. We need a powerful, rational strategy for the management of change. We need planning based on an accurate assessment of the world and our place in it. We need an understanding of purpose. We need a consensus broad enough to sustain united action. We need programs that provide essential human services; and we need informed, articulate spokespersons who can help create a climate in which agencies can prosper.

Human needs are met through experiences; the method of providing experience is program; participation in program is based on interest. The interests to be met, the programs to be conducted, the experiences to be provided are determined by organizational goals. Organizational goals must be immediately responsive to the needs and wishes of those the organization was created to serve. Since different people experience physical and social conditions in different ways, it is imperative that facilities and programs be designed with particular clientele and particular reference groups in mind. The idea that "universals" of human behavior and human response exist is the idea that produces stereotyped programs and stereotyped facilities. There may be a few near-universals like the physical and esthetic response to water, but even here the response to water is expressed in different ways by different people. The imperative is that persons planning programs and parks must know intimately the culture, wishes, social patterns, and lifestyle of the people who are to use them; the park or program must fit those conditions. There is no such thing as a universal person, and there is no such thing as a universal park or universal recreation. There is an individual emotional response by an individual person in an individual park.

Programming

We must recognize the potential role of recreation in the development of people. The goals of organized recreation programs are to provide people with opportunities for exercising their powers, for recreational experience, and for developing a positive self-image. Any program that receives a participant whole and sends that person back damaged in self-respect, self-esteem, or relationships with others is not a recreation program. The fact that it may be a basketball program with games played during leisure is irrelevant. Such a program is not a recreation program unless the emotional response of the participant is positive.

We have need for challenge and risk taking in recreation programs. Such elements must be regulated to assure the penalties for failure are not too high. They can be graduated to all levels of skill and risk, but they are an essential element that has great relevance to self-discovery, self-development, and self-enhancement. Risk and challenge are not present only in physical activities; they can be an ingredient in social activities also. Challenge is present in a broad range of pursuits, from skydiving to sailing and from acting to angling.

Recreation programs can offer a chance for experiencing the joys of mastery. In modern life it is a rare experience to prove oneself or to exhibit mastery. To run a risk, meet a challenge, to see the results of one's own effort—all are important means of developing a positive self-image. To be competent, confident, and recognized is a powerful feeling. Recreation pursuits are often the only arena where such a feeling can be experienced.

Open Space

How we feel about things is enormously important. Open space, for example, is usually justified because it provides recreation opportunities, conserves scenic and natural resources, and gives form to metropolitan communities. None of these reasons says much about how open space serves people. It implies much but says little because it does not communicate the human needs served by open space and how we feel about it. The study *Open Space for Human Needs* provides some insights on the contributions open space can make to the people of the city. In the view of those who completed the study, open space in a metropolitan area provides psychic relief from the urban landscape. It provides choices not otherwise available. It gives perspective, changing vistas, orientation. It permits other perceptions of the relationship between the world and self. It aids exploration of other facets of one's identity. Open space generates a different psychological response than does a strictly urban landscape. We feel differently about it. The benefits of an open space system identified in the above study are: manipulating material directly, exhibiting mastery, meeting a challenge or running a risk, opportunity for low-level stimuli as a release from the density of personal encounter in the urban world, relaxation, contrast, social contact free of the usual restraints of city living, the opportunity to try new social roles, achievement of a sense of being part of the natural order of things, and extension of one's intellectual and emotional reach. This is not the typical list of the landscape designer or the activity specialist. What is being explored here is the meaning open space has for the user. The list helps define psychological need and intellectual and emotional response.

The Human Element

The recreation movement must draw on its own independent research and on the social sciences, particularly sociology, psychology, and social anthropology. We need the concepts and theories these disciplines can offer to rationalize, extend, and improve the services of recreation agencies. We must evaluate and select what we use in terms of human need. We must interpret what we take in terms of human values and the development of human effectiveness. To carry out this kind of a mission we will need to be able to measure not only participation in recreation events but also perceptions and emotional reactions to these events.

Institutional Change

Every social agency in the nation is under test. Either the [agencies] will adapt to the new time now developing or they will die. Drawing all the wagons in a circle and defending the status quo will not keep out the night. Educational institutions, churches, youth organizations, recreation agencies, fraternities, women's clubs, and many other institutions are substantially out of phase with the wishes and perceived needs of their intended clientele. Organizational obsolescence is widespread and growing. Social and technological change is overwhelming most institutions because the processes of change are more rapid than the processes of adaptation. What is needed is a continual process of organizational renewal that updates the agency's values, programs, and procedures at a pace equal to the process of social and technological change. None of us knows how to do that precisely, but we must learn to do it.

A very live question in today's society is whether institutions *can* change. The nation retains the hope that its institutions are capable of generating the will to change internally. Park and recreation agencies have not yet been the object of intense criticism the way the educational system, the police, the church, and lately the prison system have been because [they] have not been important enough in national priorities. As a result [they] have not had the enormous external pressure for change some other institutions have had. Therefore, the question of whether [they] can change of [their] own volition is a significant one.

Citizen Involvement

We are moving toward greater citizen involvement in community affairs and in local government. Many programs supported by the federal government require it and the times demand it. We ought to foster that principle. One way to involve more citizens in a useful way is to form an advisory council for each center. Some administrators are reluctant to do that. There is a fear of citizen participation that centers around loss of control, but when such councils are formed properly and utilized skillfully, the benefits far outweigh any liabilities. We must learn to work successfully with large numbers of citizen groups.

Our vision of appropriate government demands participation of *all* the people because it is right and because it is more effective. An adequate set of goals for a recreation agency cannot be set by a few people. As the number of social components grows and change makes the whole system less stable, it becomes less and less possible to ignore the demands of political minorities. Goals set without consultation of those who are affected will be increasingly difficult to execute. We must find a way to involve hundreds of people in each community in the question that is so rarely asked, What kind of a community do you want in ten, twenty, or thirty years?

It is time we addressed the all-important question of what our goals are. What kinds of services do we wish to render and to whom? What are the social benefits of those services? How will we know whether these goals are being reached? If we are short of resources, as we probably will be, what are our priorities?

The recreation and park movement cannot be an effective political force until it is unified, aware, willing to pursue its ideals in legislation, and skilled in the political arena. We must gain legislative support for the movement and for our individual agencies.

The vehicle that holds us together nationally is the recreation and park movement. The movement requires nurture, too. It needs mass, a sense of mission, renewal, leadership, ideas, identity, goals, political sophistication, and a social conscience. Collectively we must give it what it needs. Without the movement, we are a collection of disconnected parts.

There is the fear, and it may not be unfounded, that the forces in [U.S.] society are centrifugal. Our aspirations for a more humanistic society rise faster than our progress in developing such a society. This aspiration gap is a source of much frustration. The world is far from perfect, but it is not unalterable. There is progress. The fact that our perceptions of a quality life exceed our ability to make it a reality should not be a cause for despair. It produces frustration, of course, particularly in the "now generation," but the dream always precedes the reality. It is significant that we can now dream of a better society. There is a chance the dream may become the reality, and that is the promise that makes the social turmoil we are now going through worthwhile.

We in the recreation and park movement are now caught with a vast conceptual attic filled with ideas that are no longer useful but are too good to throw away. To adjust to our future it will be necessary to discard some facets of the past. We often perceive our institutions as change agents, but evidence suggests otherwise. Many social institutions are created to control and inhibit change, and they are often effective. Even among those not specifically organized to preserve tradition and manage the status quo, a generally conservative approach is common. Whether we can generate the will to change and the sense of direction necessary to adapt to our changing environment is a question we must now face.

Many people feel powerless in the swift-flowing stream of change. They feel swept along by currents and they feel they cannot steer. In reality it is not the future that is beyond our grasp and beyond our ability to influence; it is the present that cannot be mastered. A common reaction to "future shock" is to seize the present and try to hold it. More common still is an attempt to turn back to a time that looks in retrospect more orderly, more pleasant, less threatening. These are the responses that are beyond control. One cannot hold today; one cannot regain yesterday. It is only tomorrow that is subject to planning and control.

We are all engaged in the struggle to make an imperfect society work. There is the distinct possibility that [U.S.] society and the recreation and park movement are on divergent courses. If we fail to deal effectively with the future, it may be because we have none. It is time we devoted ourselves to the complex question of what our purposes are, and it is time we devoted ourselves to the achievement of those purposes. Here is an action program to begin these tasks.

AN ACTION PROGRAM FOR THE RECREATION AND PARK MOVEMENT

To reorient the primary thrust of the movement and to accelerate the processes of change, we recommend that the National Recreation and Park Association (NRPA) and the agencies and individuals active in the park and recreation field undertake accomplishment of these goals:

1. Using this statement as a working paper, rethink the future of the movement in terms of its meaning for the people of the local community, the nation, and the world.
2. Adopt a humanistic ethic as the central value system of the movement.
3. Develop and act on a social conscience that focuses park and recreation services on the great social problems of our time and develop programs designed to contribute to the amelioration of those problems.
4. Develop a set of guidelines for programs that emphasizes human welfare, human development, and social action.
5. Foster integration, coherence, and growth in the recreation and park movement because [it] represents a major potential in the worldwide thrust for positive life experience.

6. Reorganize and reorient our agencies in a way that will renew their energies, improve their sense of mission, and make them more responsive to human need and social change.
7. Establish common cause with the environmentalists and other social movements that embrace a value system similar to [that of the recreation and park movement].
8. Establish a substantial research effort designed to investigate the nature of the recreation experience, to improve our understanding and definition of it, and to strengthen our ability to stimulate it.
9. Develop evaluation methods capable of measuring the contribution of park and recreation experience to human welfare which can make us accountable for the human consequences of what we do.
10. Develop an effective interpretation program capable of articulating to a national and worldwide audience the meaning of park and recreation experience in human terms.
11. Revise recreation and park curricula to emphasize development of a social mission, a humanistic ethic, the processes of human development throughout life, the psychology of park and recreation experience, group processes, and human ecology.
12. Take the data, values, and concepts thus assembled and promote them as central themes in a comprehensive in-service training effort in recreation and park agencies throughout the nation, an in-service training effort which is clear about where we are and where we wish to proceed.
13. Organize the members of the recreation and park movement as an effective political force capable of affecting local and national political processes.

In support of the goals, we recommend that the NRPA:

1. Accept responsibility for stewardship and leadership of the recreation and park movement.
2. Create an organizational structure and a program which can attract to the association and successfully involve thousands of lay and professional members. Lay membership must be encouraged, and the association must frontally attack a situation in which the large majority of our "professionals" do not see any reason for joining their own association. This is a commentary on the commitment of the personnel and a judgment of the effectiveness of the NRPA. As historically constituted, the association has failed to prove to its prospective members that there is a viable purpose for membership. The hopeful signs of change already visible must be pursued vigorously. The association must draw the bulk of its support from its own members.
3. Promote recognition of intelligent use of our leisure as a national issue which has enormous implications for [U.S.] society; move quickly to define the issue, suggest appropriate responses, and elicit the national attention the issue deserves.

4. Take the lead in developing broad understanding and acceptance of these concepts:
   a. Participation, not winning, is the legitimate goal of leisure utilization and participation; not merely watching is basic to health and development.
   b. Working together rather than working alone to provide fulfillment and recognition is a legitimate goal of leisure activities.
   c. The function of leisure is unrealized when the participant receives no real sense of gratification from an experience or when gratification is achieved as an antisocial, destructive phenomenon associated with another person's discomfort or disgrace.

   There is urgent need to accept these concepts and act upon them, beginning with the park and recreation profession.
5. Take the lead in integrating recreation and parks into a single entity with an appropriate name which encompasses both recreation and parks and reflects concern for productive living in a healthy, creative, leisure life.
6. Provide national leadership to the environmental movement which enlists the forces of park and recreation personnel in the cause of restoring and preserving our natural environment; begin to formulate immediately a national strategy that will make the move for a better environment local and urban, as well as rural.
7. Develop and advocate an open space policy for America that articulates the meaning of open space in human terms.
8. Become a leading participant in the major social movements of our day with specific emphasis on the need for equal opportunity for all [persons in the United States], including racial minorities, minorities based on age, and minorities based on sex; begin this task by increasing its sensitivity and responsiveness to its own minority membership.
9. Extend and improve the excellent work already begun in providing the national government with information required to help our leaders formulate effective legislation; formulate annually an NRPA legislative program.
10. Take action to reduce and hopefully eliminate the pattern of internal and persistent bickering which has been so much a part of the relationships among the branches, the state organizations, the National Council, and other units of the association.

To further these goals, we recommend that local governmental units, including counties, cities, and special districts:

1. Closely identify with the total planning process commitment to planning—not only to the obvious factors of open space requirements and total park acreage based on population density but also to matters of set-back ordinances—requirement for underground utilities, sign and billboard regulation, control over automobiles and truck traffic through greenbelts, noise abatement, and street tree planting. As an immediate

goal, recreation and park agencies should be represented regularly and assume leadership roles on the local planning body and should develop, publicize, and support a comprehensive master plan for the community.

2. Carry out a regular legislative function, symbolized specifically by development annually of a legislative program which it actively pursues and which becomes the primary basis for program implementation.
3. Develop a statement of goals and objectives which is known and understood by the total staff of the organization, the community, the citizens, and government leaders; the statement must be ever-changing, dynamic, and a reflection of our highest ideals. It must also include reference to:
    a. Our belief in, and identity with, community leadership and citizen participation: not "lip service" to community participation but true joint planning and operating involving the energy and resources of the people in the communities and the park and recreation staff.
    b. The responsibility of our total staff to know and understand what we mean when we refer to "positive leisure experience." There must be recognition that this can be accomplished only if we are completely committed to this ideal and are willing continually to communicate these ideals.
    c. Support of the aspirations of the many subcultures in the community and our conviction that we must assume a leadership role in assuring equal opportunity and participation for all our citizens.
    d. Our deep commitment to the preservation of a healthy environment and our definition of the specific responsibilities which must be assumed by the staff in making this goal possible.
    e. Problems that must be confronted, priorities, and commitment to seeking workable solutions.
4. Recruit, develop, and support individuals to lead recreation and park agencies who are capable of occupying positions of community leadership, who are seen as leaders by the members of the community, who represent the ideals of the movement, who are strong enough to fight for an unpopular cause without losing the ability to lead, and who are skillful enough to accomplish the agency's goals.
5. In individual departments, there are specific goals that we can and should start achieving now. A partial list would include the following:
    a. The total staff, and particularly those responsible for individual centers or activities, must understand the concept of recreation as a positive and pleasurable experience for the participant and as a means of emphasizing human development.
    b. The total staff must be committed to the importance of its mission. It is when we settle for minimum commitment that we achieve minimum response from our communities; and it is when we lack commitment that we assume a low priority of importance in our communities.

c. Employees must stop being parks *or* recreation staff members and recognize a oneness that is defined by the recipients of our services, not by the emptiness of our internal conflicts. We should aim to eliminate organizational definitions such as "parks division" or "recreation branch"; for the nomenclature is no longer relevant and its continued existence tends to perpetuate an expensive, outdated fiction of the past.
d. Begin now to eliminate all artificial restraint from program participation based upon sexual and ethnic distinctions. These bars are useless and arbitrary and they help to perpetuate a condition in our society that is repugnant.
e. Develop an affirmative action program intended to offset the limitations on employment that have historically hampered minorities and women; eliminate job requirements which discriminate in any way against individuals or groups because of race, sex, or any other irrelevant factor.
f. Define a set of responsibilities for community participation, for each facility or activity director, and a timetable for achieving the increments of this participation; community participation should be viewed as including evidence of an active, viable, representative community support group which participates in major decision making including land acquisition, development, program planning, budgeting, and program scheduling.
g. Assign environmental and planning responsibilities for [the] entire field staff, particularly those staff members who minimize their environmental role by thinking only in terms of recreation programs. These assignments should include at least some of the following:
    1a. Development of an active environmental organization at each center, well supported by the total staff.
    2a. Organization of programs which improve the environment of the center and the environment of the community. These should include tree planting (and maintenance) programs, painting, cleanup campaigns, improvements of drainage, mural painting, organized community action in combatting vandalism, and participation in community action to protect the environment against undesirable physical intrusion.
    3a. Presentation of lectures and other programs in conjunction with local schools and environmental groups to elevate awareness of environmental matters.
    4a. Maintaining facilities with concern for maximum use and esthetics.
h. Ascertain that individual centers and activities function at times most convenient for the public, not the staff. This may mean expanded evening and weekend schedules, and it may demand innovative experimentation with various types of flexible work schedules.

In pursuit of these goals, we recommend that colleges and universities:

1. Reexamine the scope of their commitment to the park and recreation movement to think through the nature and goals of the movement, its potential contribution to American life, the kind of education candidates for careers in the field should have, articulation and improvement of research efforts, and organization and extension of the literature.
2. Undertake a systematic investigation of the outcomes of park and recreation experience and develop a taxonomy of human benefits.
3. Establish contacts with park and recreation agencies that will strengthen in-service and reentry education services.
4. In concert with other segments of the movement, develop an interpretation program for recreation and park services that focuses on the contribution these services make to human development and welfare.

To achieve these goals, we recommend that individuals in the recreation and park movement:

1. Develop a commitment not only to the agencies of local service but also to the movement and to the organizations that sustain it.
2. Provide ideas, financial and political support, and leadership to the NRPA.
3. Develop a national perspective, an understanding of the forces of social change, appreciation of the potential of the movement, and avenues of professional service through study of the field, participation in professional meetings, and interaction with others active in parks, recreation, conservation, and public affairs.
4. In local and national arenas, aid the processes of change and the improvement and expansion of park, recreation, city planning, public administration, and conservation services.

CHAPTER 2

LEISURE IN THE LIFE CYCLE

Stanley Parker

This chapter by Stanley Parker describes the many characteristics and meanings of leisure for the different stages of the life cycle. We will see that leisure has no single form or expression; it changes for individuals as their social roles change.

This chapter will look at the role of leisure in the lives of individuals at various ages and in different family circumstances. First we shall examine the ways in which children experience play as leisure, paying particular attention to sex, age, social class, and cultural differences. Our understanding of leisure during the period of youth depends on how we view the process of adolescence, and there are various theories to guide us here. During adult life there are changes taking place in most individuals' family responsibilities which affect their experience of and attitudes toward leisure. Finally, in the "third age" there are special problems for both men and women who have to cope with a period at the end of their lives which is sometimes too easily thought of as "all leisure."

CHILDREN, PLAY, AND LEISURE

It is doubtful whether we can sensibly use the concept of leisure at all for preschool children, since time for them has not become institutionally divided between obligatory activity (at school) and nonobligatory activity.[1] For school children the notion of leisure becomes more appropriate, although the choice of leisure pursuits is normally restricted by parents and by the usually limited amount of pocket money children are given to spend. For pre-adolescent children the term *play* has normally been used to describe activities which there is no obligation to undertake and which serve as ends in themselves—what for other groups we would call "leisure."[2] In practice, the play and leisure of pre-adolescent children amount to much the same set of activities, since such children generally play in their leisure time.

There are three broad types of theory about play which are relevant when considering the question of children and leisure: physiological, biological, and psychological.[3] *Physiological* theories are mainly in terms of the expenditure of surplus energy (Herbert Spencer saw parents as providing for the basic needs of their young, whose energies had consequently to be expended on purposeless activities) or recreation (Lazarus believed that when a child is tired he can recuperate by expending energy on vigorous play). As the Childs

Reprinted from Stanley Parker, *The Sociology of Leisure* (London: Allen & Unwin, 1976, 1977), pp. 51–63, by permission of the publisher and the author.

remark, these physiological theories fail to explain most of the variations in play behavior.

Biological theories divide mainly into the concepts of prepractice play and recapitulation. Karl Groos defined *play* as the " 'generalized impulse' to practise those instincts necessary for survival in adult life"; and thus, unlike Spencer, he viewed play as highly purposeful. Stanley Hall argued that at each stage of development the child reenacted the experiences of his race at a defined stage in its history (thus children climbing trees recapitulate the ape stage in man's evolution). Of these theories, there is something to be said for Groos, especially in relation to children in pre-industrial societies, but little to be said for Hall.

Psychological explanations of children's play are mostly associated with Sigmund Freud and Jean Piaget. Freud saw play as having two main functions: the reenactment of unpleasant events in order to master them ("repetition compulsion") and the modification of events in play as one would like them in reality ("wish fulfillment"). For Piaget, play was similar to learning and imitation and [it] featured the process of assimilation—digesting and integrating cultural materials and signals in order to make them the child's own. Again, while these theories account to some extent for children's motivation to play and their attitudes toward adults and other children, they cannot cope with variations in play behavior which are found in practice.

Some of the major variables which help to explain differences in children's play are those of sex, age, social class, and culture. Many writers on children's play have noted the effects of sex differences. Some have discussed the different activities enjoyed by boys and girls, while others have singled out their different ways of playing. In the United States greater emphasis is given to achievement in the upbringing of boys, and American schoolboys play more games of physical skill.[4] With girls there is more emphasis on obedience, and they tend to play more games of strategy. However, recent evidence is that girls are increasingly coming to prefer what were formerly boys' activities. Thus traditionally male games such as baseball and camping today show less-marked differences between the sexes. The change represents not so much a convergence between the play roles of the sexes as an expansion in the scope of girls' leisure activities.

At different ages boys and girls tend to prefer different types of play. These may be divided into physical (including games of skill), creative, and imaginative. A study by Elizabeth Child showed that girls took part in all three types, though at different ages.[5] At about three years their play is mainly creative; for example, painting. Later imaginative play increases; and from six to twelve years, physical play is popular. In contrast, boys of all ages from three to twelve took part in physical activities most of all, with creative play second and imaginative play a poor third. Other studies show that children of both sexes with high IQs tend more often to engage in imaginative play.

Social class has a significant effect on type of play. The two main factors here are availability of play space and style of upbringing. Working-class children, as compared with middle-class children, generally have less play space inside the home and poorer facilities in their neighborhood, so they more often play in the streets. The restrictiveness of an urban environment is particularly evident if children live in tower blocks, since they often have to make a considerable journey to the play area below. This is most unfortunate for preschool children, since there is often little room indoors for them to play and parents are unwilling to let them go outside on their own.

Style of upbringing or socialization, which is linked with social class, also affects children's play. Although style of socialization—strict or permissive, concerned more with discipline or with freedom—may vary from time to time within broad class groups, most children will be subject to parental influence which encourages one type of play rather than another. Working-class parents are likely to encourage their children to fight their own battles and thus to exhibit more overt aggression in their play. By contrast, children of middle-class parents are more likely to have their disputes arbitrated by their parents and to play with less-apparent aggression in their own houses or gardens. Attendance at grammar or secondary modern school, which is correlated with class membership, has been found to result in differences in reading habits, club membership, and favorite activities outside school.[6]

Perhaps the most pervasive differences [among] types of children's play [occur] because of the different cultures in which they are raised. Roberts and Sutton-Smith have put forward a "conflict-enculturation" hypothesis to account for cross-cultural variations in play.[7] In societies which stress success as an important goal, children will play games of physical skill and use success in these games to assuage their anxiety about achievement. In these cases the basis of involvement in games is the need for relief from inner tensions which the socialization process has brought about. Children in other cultures have quite a different set of motivations to play instilled in them. Thus the play of Hopi Indian children in general imitates the activities of adults: the girls play house and the boys build imitation corrals.[8]

ADOLESCENTS AND LEISURE

The periods of childhood and of full adult status are separated by something called "adolescence," though other nouns for this period of life include "teenager," "youth," "young person," and so on. In some cultures, this period is short or even nonexistent: individuals pass more or less straight from childhood to adulthood. Even in [English society], adolescence may be said to last longer for the middle class than for the working class. To understand the role of leisure at this stage in the life cycle it will be helpful to bear in mind the three perspectives on adolescence suggested by Cyril Smith: as a period of socialization during which the knowledge and attitudes appropriate to certain adult roles are internalized; as a period of various transitions in status and role; and as "youth culture" having an autonomous influence which may conflict with adult values.[9]

During the period of adolescence the individual is socialized into leisure habits and attitudes through two main agencies: his family and other institutions (chiefly schools and voluntary organizations) with which he comes into contact. The influence on a young person's leisure that his family has will depend on a number of factors, among which two of the most important are being in or out of full-time education and living with or apart from parents. A boy or girl at school or college and living with parents is subject to a considerable limitation of his or her leisure activities. While modern parents tend to feel the obligation to let their teenage nonearning children choose their own friends, the amount of pocket money allowed determines the possibilities of turning free time into leisure, at least of the consuming kind. A young person who is either living away from his parents or has a job (or both) is in a much better position to enjoy a wide choice of leisure activities and be relatively free from adult supervision of these. For most urban and financially independent youngsters the processes of dating and courtship take place in an atmosphere of commercialized recreation over which parents have comparatively little influence.[10]

. . . [B]oth educational and religious institutions play a part—though probably a decreasing one—in socializing young people into leisure habits and attitudes. To "reach" young people, such institutions (including civic and other organizations aiming to cater to the needs or solve the problems of youth) have to effect a compromise between the "fun" expectations of their clients and the more "serious" expectations of their leaders. Some of the best work is being done where the gap between these two sets of expectations is least.

The second, transitional perspective on adolescence directs our attention to the successive small shifts in status and role which help to explain why juvenile behavior so often appears uncertain and the young person, at a loss as to how he or she should behave. Progression from primary to secondary school and perhaps university involves successive improvements in status which normally carry with them greater command over resources and greater freedom of movement. Whereas the "socialization" perspective lays emphasis on the change in parental supervision when the young person enters employment, the "transitional" perspective is more concerned with actual changes in the pattern of life and leisure. Towards the end of his school life the student will be under increasing pressures of competition for examination success and for entry into higher education, which will limit the time available for leisure.

For a young person who does not enter higher education, starting full-time work usually means much less time available for leisure. He is likely to set off for work earlier than he did for school and return later, probably more fatigued. Although his weekends will not be much affected, his holidays will be much shorter. To compensate for this, he is likely to have a sharp increase in income, making it possible to exercise more choice in leisure activities. Whether or not they go out to work, girls usually have a greater obligation to perform household duties than boys. Surveys show that teenage girls less often go out in the evenings than boys, though this difference is less marked in the later years of adolescence. There is also a social class difference: "adolescent daughters of middle-class working mothers engage in much organized and unorganized leisure activity. . . . By contrast the daughters of lower-class working mothers report heavy home responsibilities and fewer leisure activities."[11]

The third perspective on adolescent leisure is that of youth culture. Wherever young people have gathered together, apart from adults, they have tended to develop their own style of life, and the marked segregation of adolescent boys in working-class communities has produced the typical "corner boy" culture. This segregation is now more common among all classes, and the pattern is shared by girls as well as boys. The expansion of the mass media has made it possible for the young to achieve a symbolic unity which does not need ([but] clearly is enhanced by) physical association. At the same time, adolescence is a period when the individual's involvement in family life is weak. In deciding how to use their spare time, young people in contemporary society are much more strongly influenced by the views of their peers than by those of their parents.[12] They are keen to develop new tastes and they are willing to experiment, with the result that their leisure is extremely colorful and varied in contrast to the more stable and conventional pursuits of their elders.

Youth culture is closely identified with the world of entertainment and, more recently, with protest. Indeed the two are linked, since some entertainers have become leading figures in social protest. The emergence of youth culture has led not only to commercial exploitation of this popular market but has also presented a more fundamental challenge to the nature of industrial society by stimulating both protest and withdrawal movements. Protest has been especially concerned with race relations but more recently also with nostalgia for a simpler and purer way of life in the communes. David Marsland sees youth culture as to some extent "the necessary structural matrix of contemporary counter-cultural developments, and the seedbed of structural transformation to a new societal type."[13] Youth culture has changed the character of "pop" music and entertainment for adult audiences and has altered clothing and hairstyles for age groups other than teenagers. However, the impact of the leisure styles of the young upon their elders should not be overestimated. Adults still form the larger part of the market for most forms of entertainment, and it is only with their support that these remain economically viable.

LEISURE IN ADULT LIFE

Between the pre-employment "first age" of childhood and adolescence and the "third age" of retirement there is a substantial period of the life cycle during which most adults are either working for a living or raising a family or both. There are exceptions to this broad generalization—some adolescents and some persons beyond retirement age have a paid occupation—but for most of us the adult years from about twenty to sixty-five are more active than those before or later.

As Max Kaplan points out, a static view of the family is being increasingly discarded in realistic studies, including those of leisure.[14] "The family" is many families as changes take place in the ages of the children, father's career, or mother's work in the home and outside it. Consequently, we may review the experience of leisure by individuals at different adult ages and with varying responsibilities to other members of the family.

When dealing with a span of the life cycle which embraces forty or more years, age is clearly a factor influencing changes in patterns and preferences for leisure activities. But chronological age is not by itself enough to explain all the differences. We need to take into account also that at any given age some people will be married and some single and that some of the former will have no children, some young children, and some older children. The concept which includes all four dimensions—age, sex, marital status, and children—has been called "domestic age." Researchers have found this concept useful in analyzing and interpreting the results of surveys into leisure behavior, and we shall find it similarly useful in summarizing some of their results.

In 1965–66 in a sample of urban areas in Britain, a major leisure survey was carried out which provided much data on the recreational patterns of domestic age groups.[15] Although for the sample as a whole television viewing ranked as the most time-consuming leisure occupation, this was not so throughout the life cycle. Among young single people (aged 15–22) the greatest emphasis was given to physical recreation. In fact for young men this continued as their outstanding leisure interest into early married life, and it was only when they became fathers that it fell to second place below television. Changes in leisure habits took place more swiftly among women: at marriage their participation in physical recreation dropped to fourth place below crafts and hobbies, television, and social activities. For men, gardening, decorating, and other do-it-yourself tasks became significant only after marriage. At 46–60, after their children had grown up, men tended to spend fewer leisure periods watching television, and there were signs of a slight revival of interest in physical recreation at this time. Women's crafts and hobbies (mainly knitting) were most often mentioned as chief leisure activities by married women between the ages of 23 and 45. At all ages, women mentioned social activities more frequently than men.

Another, smaller study concentrated on the leisure activities of the 17–32 age group . . . in one community just north of London.[16] It confirmed some of the findings of the larger survey and added others. Single people were found to take part in a much wider variety of activities outside the home than married people, and it is when they are single that there exists the greatest degree of similarity and equality in the leisure practices and preferences of the sexes. Social class had a bearing on leisure behavior within each of the domestic age groups: for example, more people from white-collar and professional backgrounds participated in formal clubs, groups, and organizations of all kinds than did those from blue-collar backgrounds. The researchers believe that their findings lend support to the picture of a well-defined and somewhat conventional pattern of leisure activities in the community studied. These are said to arise in the context of the life cycle rather than [to] be caused by any new factors which obtain today but were nonexistent in the past.

Let us look more closely at the experience of leisure at various stages of the "second age." In recent decades the age of marriage has become lower and many more young couples find themselves parents in their early twenties than used to be the case. Before they were married, the young couple probably spent much of their free time together. Much tension may result if the young husband wants to spend most of his leisure time with friends from his single days.[17] Equally, the young bride may want to spend all her spare time with her mother.

More importantly, a young couple's decisions on how to spend their leisure will be partly determined by whether the wife is working. If the desire to start buying a house is the main reason for the wife working, then leisure expenditure will probably take second place. Other young couples who are content with modest accommodation may wish to spend more on leisure, including perhaps expensive holidays.

Parenthood brings about quite dramatic changes in the leisure habits of young people.[18] Their domestic responsibilities increase with the result that the amounts of time and money available for leisure interests diminish. Such free time as is left tends to be spent in the home, and pursuits previously centered upon the peer group are often dropped. Few new leisure interests are acquired after marriage with the exception of gardening, an interest which is consistent with a home-centered life. Marriage counselors are concerned that some young married people are so tied down by small children that they practically become prisoners in their own homes, never getting out together in the evening and losing many of their former friends and interests. To some extent, babysitting—whether cooperative among a group of mothers, paid, or volunteered by grandparents—is an answer to this problem, but it is one that is not available to all couples.

As people grow into middle age and their children leave home, the domestic responsibilities of the couple become lighter. Household chores are less demanding and more money is available for leisure. During this phase of life, leisure interests might be expected to be rejuvenated and people, to engage in more activities outside the home. For the wife, in particular, release from the obligations of parental responsibility provides an impressive amount of free time.[19] Actually (as noted in the surveys) very little increase in participative leisure takes place. Some people do develop an active interest in community-based organizations—such as the church and civic associations—during their middle years, but this is not typical. The general trend is for leisure interests and activities increasingly to become restricted with age despite decreased responsibilities.

Kenneth Roberts offers two explanations for this decline in leisure interests.[20] One is that during middle life the individual's physical and mental vigor declines, which may account for a reluctance to cultivate new interests. People may feel no inclination to do more than drift along in the routine to which they have become accustomed during their earlier years of married life. The second possible explanation is that so many of the leisure industries aim to capture the interest of younger age groups: an adolescent image has become attached to the ideas of having fun and seeking amusement, an image with which older people are reluctant to identify. Roberts suggests that it is probably this combination of social inhibitions and a lack of personal inclination that accounts for the widespread failure of people to fill their free time with new interests once their family responsibilities have diminished.

In the previous paragraphs we have been discussing the situation of married people. We must not, however, forget the substantial minorities of single people, including those who do not remarry. In terms of financing their leisure, single people are generally the lucky ones. They can afford more expensive holidays and more frequent outings than married couples on the same income. But many single men and women suffer from loneliness in their leisure hours, which in some cases results in neurotic conditions and even suicide.[21] This is particularly true in big cities, where life can be alien and impersonal. Just getting away from the city is not always a solution. Many single persons, especially women, take their loneliness with them on solitary holidays; or they may prefer to immerse themselves in work, including voluntary work, rather than face the emptiness of "play" leisure.

LEISURE AND THE ELDERLY

Owing to improved medical science and social welfare, more people are living past retirement age, and for longer periods, than formerly. The elderly are often thought of as having a great deal of leisure but only because it is assumed that they are no longer working and are in reasonably good health. Both these assumptions, however, are untrue for significant minorities of older people. Cross-cultural research in Britain, the United States, and Denmark shows that between 24 and 31 percent of men are still working at seventy and between 15 and 19 percent, at seventy-five.[22] Other studies show that some 5 percent of the elderly are in residential homes or hospitals, and the proportion who are either bedridden or housebound is 8 to 13 percent.[23]

Health and mobility have an important effect on both the amount of leisure available to the elderly and the quality of its enjoyment. Satisfying use of leisure cannot substitute for poor health, lost family and friends, or an inadequate pension. Nor can it take the place of the feelings of usefulness and purposefulness which are probably the greatest needs of the aged.[24] For those in good health and able to move about freely, retirement can bring new opportunities to take up, or have more time for, a wide range of leisure pursuits. But for the elderly who are not in good health the problem of filling the empty hour is partly solved in that things take longer to do, anyway. A report on a study of the handicapped and impaired showed that elderly men frequently had to give up participating in sports and gardening: elderly women most often had to give up handicrafts, walking, and shopping.[25] The picture emerging from this study was one of a population with above-average amounts of disposable time but frustrated physically, mentally, environmentally, and financially in its enjoyment of this extra free time.

Retired persons as a whole face the problem of what to do with extra time available. The problem particularly affects men, since women may well find that retirement from their job or from responsibilities connected with their own children is filled to some extent by activities connected with their grandchildren. There is a considerable difference between the social classes in the impact of retirement and the ways in which it is coped with. Men in professional and senior management occupations are often able to continue some form of work after official retirement age; this is less often possible for those in manual and many business occupations. Middle-class older women are more likely than working-class women to be already members of one or more voluntary organizations, and unless they have a paid occupation which ends at an arbitrary age they will not notice much change in their lives.

So far as participation in leisure activities is concerned, the process of withdrawal which we saw as frequently starting in middle life tends to continue into old age. This is no doubt due in some cases to changed financial position: some elderly people have to stop going out to places of entertainment or other events because they cannot afford it. There is some suggestion that hobby activities tend to increase after age fifty, but after the early seventies, with the diminution of sensory functions, they decrease again.[26] The major survey quoted earlier shows that the pattern of leisure of the elderly differs from that of younger people in several marked respects.[27] Whether in full-time employment or not, men aged 61 [and] over spend more time on gardening, while among the retired group park visits and walks increase sharply. Single women aged 61 [and over] spend much more time on social activities than do other women.

At present there are more than 7,000 social clubs for elderly people in England and Wales.[28] They vary from monthly socials held in a church hall to quite elaborately equipped day centers. The clubs themselves are not always welcomed by elderly people. Less than 7 percent of old people attend a club in any given week, and it has been estimated that only 15 to 20 percent of those entitled to use the clubs ever do so.[29] The clubs are generally more popular with women than with men, and men more often prefer clubs unrestricted by age. The question of whether clubs are a good thing is part of a broader issue of whether active leisure is something to be encouraged in preference to passive leisure. While there is every reason to seek to provide more adequate facilities for those who wish to take part in club activities, it is questionable whether people who show no signs of needing more social contact should be pressured to "join in."

Although the question of leisure for the elderly should by no means be identified with the question of adjustment to retirement, there are substantial grounds for seeking to understand the changing content and functions of leisure in the context of changed role status on retirement. One of the foremost contributions to thinking in this area has been the "disengagement theory" of Cumming and Henry. According to this theory,

> Ageing is an inevitable mutual withdrawal or disengagement resulting in decreased interaction between the ageing and others in the social system to which he belongs. The process may be initiated by the individual or by others in the situation. The ageing person may withdraw more markedly from some classes of people while remaining relatively close to others. His withdrawal may be accompanied from the outset by an increased preoccupation with himself; certain institutions in society may make this withdrawal easy for him.[30]

The theory has led to a large number of research studies . . . [both supporting and refuting it]. It has been extensively criticized, chiefly on the grounds that there is no reason to suppose that its propositions apply outside contemporary [U.S.] culture. It has also been suggested that, though it may be an adequate description of aging as experienced by many fairly healthy and economically secure old people, it is not acceptable as a picture of aging among other important groups of old people such as the poor, the house bound, or the extremely isolated.[31] The concept of "activity within disengagement" has been suggested by Streib and Schneider to account for the trend and countertrend.[32] They divide such activity into two main categories: the leisure role (which involves seeing the later years of life as "leisure years") and the citizenship-service role (programs by private and governmental agencies, including activity as foster grandparents and manning "dial-a-friend" services).

We need to appreciate the extent to which the disengagement theory in particular, and the prevailing ideas about retirement in general, are class based. It is significant that Marion Crawford found a *change* rather than a cessation of anticipated involvement after retirement by most groups.[33] Middle-class men in her study anticipated less interaction as friend and worker and more as leisure time user; working-class men felt the same, apart from substituting "parent" for "friend." Middle-class women anticipated less interaction as worker and more as leisure time user; working-class women anticipated less interaction as neighbor and worker and more as parent. There is thus no question of "disengagement" for most working-class women. Their lives have been embedded in an extended family and neighborhood network, and they have probably never thought about separate activities or time called "leisure." But for other elderly women and most elderly men there is a real problem to be faced after the involuntary loss of one role and the difficulty of finding another.

A FRAMEWORK FOR ANALYSIS OF CHANGE

To the extent that static categories such as age, sex, and marital status are insufficient for understanding people's leisure behavior and values, a framework is required that is amenable to the analysis of change and variation. The Rapoports have explored the utility of the family life cycle framework for this purpose.[34] Individuals change their preoccupations, interests, and activities as they develop in the course of their own life cycle and as they move through social roles in relation to the family life cycle and family structure. . . . Particular preoccupations may be present all through the life cycle, but they often tend to become more salient at certain of its phases. Interests are formed, sustained, or changed by the interaction between an individual's preoccupations and his social environment at any or all of the stages of his life cycle.

NOTES

1. E. Child and J. Child, "Children and Leisure," in M. A. Smith et al., eds, *Leisure and Society in Britain* (London: Allen Lane, 1973), p. 135.
2. A. Giddens, "Notes on the Concepts of Play and Leisure," *Sociological Review*, March 1964.
3. Child and Child, "Children and Leisure," pp. 136–38.
4. R. R. Sears et al., *Patterns of Child-rearing* (New York: Harper, 1957).

5. Child and Child, "Children and Leisure," pp. 142–43.
6. M. Stewart, "The Leisure Activities of Grammar School Children," *British Journal of Educational Psychology* 40 (1970).
7. M. Roberts and B. Sutton-Smith, "Child Training and Game Involvement," *Ethnology*, April 1962.
8. S. A. Queen and R. W. Habenstein, *The Family in Various Cultures*, 4th ed. (Philadelphia: Lippincott, 1974), p. 59.
9. C. S. Smith, "Adolescence," in Smith et al., eds., *Leisure and Society*.
10. W. Waller, *The Family—A Dynamic Interpretation* (New York: Dryden, 1951).
11. W. J. Goode, *The Family* (Englewood Cliffs, N.J.: Prentice-Hall, 1964), p. 76.
12. K. Roberts, *Leisure* (London: Longman, 1970), p. 45.
13. D. Marsland, "Youth and Leisure," in S. Parker et al., eds, *Sport and Leisure in Contemporary Society* (London: Polytechnic of Central London, 1975).
14. M. Kaplan, *Leisure in America* (New York: Wiley, 1960), p. 62.
15. K. K. Sillitoe, *Planning for Leisure* (London: HMSO, 1969), p. 17.
16. N. C. A. Parry and D. Johnson, *Leisure in Hatfield, Stage II*, Department of Psychological and Social Studies, Hatfield Polytechnic, August 1973.
17. E. T. Ashton, *People and Leisure* (London: Ginn, 1971), p. 48.
18. Roberts, *Leisure*, p. 46. See also S. Parker, "Professional Life and Leisure," *New Society*, October 10, 1974.
19. W. E. Thompson and G. F. Streib, "Meaningful Activity in a Family Context," in R. W. Kleemeier, ed., *Aging and Leisure* (New York: Oxford University Press, 1961), p. 184.
20. Roberts, *Leisure*, pp. 47–48.
21. Ashton, *People and Leisure*, p. 57.
22. E. Shanas et al., *Old People in Three Industrial Societies* (New York: Atherton Press, 1968), p. 292.
23. A. Harris and S. Parker, "Leisure and the Elderly," in Smith et al., eds., *Leisure and Society*.
24. C. K. Brightbill, *The Challenge of Leisure* (Englewood Cliffs, N.J.: Prentice-Hall, 1960), p. 73.
25. C. R. W. Smith, "Leisure Activities of Impaired Persons," in A. Harris, *Handicapped and Impaired in Great Britain* (London: HMSO, 1971), p. 93.
26. O. von Mering and F. L. Weniger, "Social-Cultural Background of the Ageing Individual," in J. E. Birren, ed., *Handbook of Ageing and the Individual* (University of Chicago Press, 1959), p. 321.
27. Sillitoe, *Planning for Leisure*, p. 174.
28. Harris and Parker, "Leisure and the Elderly," p. 175.
29. Ashton, *People and Leisure*, p. 64.
30. E. Cumming and W. E. Henry, *Growing Old* (New York: Basic Books, 1961), p. 14.
31. J. Tunstall, *Old and Alone* (London: Routledge, 1966), p. 240.
32. G. F. Streib and C. J. Schneider, *Retirement in American Society* (Ithaca, N.Y.: Cornell University Press, 1971), p. 182.
33. M. P. Crawford, "Retirement and Role-playing," *Sociology*, May 1972.
34. R. Rapoport et al., *Leisure and the Family Life Cycle* (London: Routledge, 1975).

CHAPTER

3 URBAN GROWTH AND THE PLANNING OF OUTDOOR RECREATION

Harvey S. Perloff
Lowdon Wingo, Jr.

Originally published in 1962, this article appeared in the landmark publication of the U.S. Outdoor Recreation Resources Review Commission. Time has not detracted from its message. Harvey Perloff and Lowdon Wingo, Jr. promote the systems analysis framework as suitable to organize all recreational planning and research, to determine the relevance of a particular study, or to suggest critical gaps as resources and social needs change. Systems thinking, then and now, is a prerequisite to understanding recreation and leisure.

The future of outdoor recreation in the United States is closely bound up with the forces which are shaping our metropolitan civilization. Our material wealth proliferates; our genius for innovation augments our leisure; our numbers and our wants press upon the land; and in measure appropriate to these, our collective search for recreation intrudes itself among our major national purposes. New problems have emerged, some from the special requirements inherent in the nature of recreation, others from the changing characteristics of urban living—the concentration of people and activities in great urban regions, the spilling out of urban development over the land, the needs for psychic renewal generated by the tempo and environment of urban life. Called for is a special brand of tough-minded planning based on a new perspective of outdoor recreation and its interconnections with other important areas of national concern.

What is the "problem" of outdoor recreation? It is something quite different today from what it was two generations ago, when the main concern of government was to secure for the public and posterity a magnificent endowment of irreplaceable landscape resources. This concern fathered not only the national parks system[1] but also Chicago's Lake Front, San Francisco's Golden

---

Reprinted from U.S. Outdoor Recreation Resources Review Commission, *Trends in American Living and Outdoor Recreation*, Study Report no. 22 (Washington, D.C.: Government Printing Office, 1962), pp. 81–100, with permission of the authors. This article has been extensively edited for this volume and the notes renumbered.
The authors wish to acknowledge a large debt to Irving K. Fox and Marion Clawson, their colleagues at Resources for the Future, Inc., at the time this article first appeared, for their helpful comments and criticisms.

Gate Park, and the Charles River Park in Boston; it is manifest today in the political tug of war over the proposed Chesapeake and Ohio Canal Park along the Potomac River.

By contrast, today's problems do not center on the acquisition of the unique and dramatic resources for the public but on the broad availability of outdoor recreation for frequent enjoyment by everyone; nearby open areas for weekend visits by moderate-income urbanites are more characteristic of our recreation needs than the annual trip to a faraway area of unforgettable beauty by the fortunate persons who can get there.

In one sense, the existence of the problem is a measure of the achievement of the material utopia toward which Western civilization has been moving for two centuries. Freedom and wealth have made vast populations demanders after space, sun, air, water, and the simple grandeur of nature, and we are increasingly conscious that the supply of things—brought together in a recreation environment—is painfully limited.

Future historians may find that the most enduring property of this metropolitan civilization is congestion—an increasingly awkward relationship between space in its many guises and our demands upon it. This is true of transportation and of buildings; it is no less true of outdoor recreation.

The central dilemma of outdoor recreation planning is how to ameliorate its special forms of congestion so that the regenerative qualities of nature in the open can be enjoyed without discrimination by those who possess the appetite for its rewards.

Planning for recreation is an extraordinarily difficult intellectual and political task. It would be demanding enough if we could concentrate our attention and our efforts on the building of recreation into a sensible scheme of environmental planning for the metropolitan region; here we would face all of the usual problems associated with the fragmentation of government in the metropolitan region and, expressly, with the lack of technique for broad-scaled, regionwide planning. But this parochial view is no longer tenable: in their search for opportunities for recreation, urban dwellers now travel across states with the same ease with which a generation ago they crossed counties. Geography is no barrier, and the demand for recreation spreads out across the national landscape from all of the urban regions. One dimension of affluence and leisure is mobility, and it is the mobility of the urban populations across the nation which elevates outdoor recreation to the status of an important national problem. The current picture of outdoor recreation as a national problem is one of unsatisfied demands and satiety side by side, of a capricious patchwork of facilities whose performance when measured against the needs of a great urban civilization is melancholy, indeed.

How should a problem of this sort be tackled? Our experience has made it clear that the hallowed processes of planning by bits, spurts, and crises can achieve little. We need new tools not only to cope with the problems but especially to expand and deepen our understanding of outdoor recreation as a systematic form of behavior in our society. One of these tools, which has come to be known as "systems analysis,"[2] promises to throw some light on the kinds of problems which one encounters in recreation planning. In the pages that follow, we have tried to think through in a very general way how to apply a systems approach to the problems of outdoor recreation, in the hope of saying something useful about how planning for outdoor recreation might be improved. . . .

THE BIG ISSUE IN PLANNING OUTDOOR RECREATION

Outdoor recreation has a number of inherent properties which make its planning very difficult: some are typical of the planning of any community service or facility[3]; others relate more to the character of regionwide services, such as drainage, water distribution, sewerage, and transportation; still others develop simply because of the differences in scope and complexity between planning for urban populations and the planning that goes on within the urban community. The difficulties encountered at each level tend to amplify the rest in a way that makes the planning of outdoor recreation a complex exercise, indeed. . . .

The initial dilemma for the outdoor recreation planner is posed by the lack of guidelines for decisions. No market mechanism exists by which public preferences can direct the allocation of community resources into recreation, or among the various recreation alternatives. There is no more consumer sovereignty here than in public education or public health—if anything, there is probably less. He is thrown back on budget making as the allocating mechanism—a political process where ultimately ballots rather than dollars vote. Political allocation is probably more egalitarian than the market—its decisions are not weighted by income distribution—but it can be so erratic and imprecise that the final allocation may be only a distorted parody of what the community wants and needs. Services depending on long-range public investments are especially sensitive to these imperfections, a circumstance which has been one of the most persuasive warrants for long-range comprehensive planning in urban areas. Given the prime objectives of all general governmental services, a basic investment program dimensioned over the long run can be laid out to permit political allocation against an orderly background of information and programs. The long-range comprehensive plan is essentially a device for organizing and ordering the investment claims upon the public purse without which political allocation can be largely a result of mere reaction to "squawk" and brute power.

However, the potentialities of long-range planning are currently not being realized. There are many reasons for this. One of the central reasons has to do with the manner in which city planning is handled. The relationship of comprehensive physical planning to the needs, wants, and demands of urban populations has always been a special issue for the city planner. But his actual scope has fallen far short of "comprehensiveness." His responsibility has been partial in the sense that he has been expected to plan the physical facilities without having any role in specific functional programs. At best he can only assure that the capacity to produce a given output will be available. A tendency to exclude the variability of functional programs from his considerations has been a direct consequence of his separation from the operating end of the public services. Having, on the other hand, no direct mechanism, such as a market indication, to inform him about what people want has led him to make assumptions about objectives. This condition, in which he has only limited responsibility for the services produced and few direct and intimate links with what people want and need, has impelled him to rest his case on what people ought to want, such as the orderly, the efficient, the beautiful.

Now, however, we are beginning to understand that the performance of governmental programs can be measured only in terms of what people want of them. We are beginning to see public programs as behavioral systems—with key elements grounded in continually changing views of what is desirable and needed and with public pressures building up around what is available as against what is expected and aspired for—a constant back-and-forth flow of action and reaction. Such a viewpoint calls for particular kinds of information—the kinds of information which are rarely available at the present time. At the most general levels, the special frameworks of economists, sociologists, and psychologists are essential to identify the characteristics of behavior systems. At the level of data we need information of a special sort on the wants, needs, demands, behavioral patterns, and responses of the various population subgroups, since it follows that we are more likely to be concerned with program effectiveness than with simple concepts of efficiency. . . .

The freedom with which people move about the region in pursuit of outdoor recreation greatly complicates its planning: meeting recreation needs may begin with the urban community, but sooner or later the planning horizon must stretch far beyond the city limits. The effective production of a public service depends on a responsible relationship between the government producer and the private consumers. By these terms the modern metropolitan area—with its alkanized suburbs and its penchant for ignoring state boundaries—is in an impossible position. Nowhere is there lodged responsibility to cope with such transcendent needs of the region as transportation, water and sewerage, air pollution, and, now, outdoor recreation. Numerous solutions have been experimented with, ranging from metropolitan government through special purpose authorities; and though such solutions may have had beneficent consequences for some kinds of metropolitanwide public services, there is no showing that the problem of outdoor recreation has proven amenable to these approaches. . . .

It is evident that outdoor recreation cannot be viewed purely as a local matter. The nature of the demands and the distribution of the resources virtually compel the local community to act irresponsibly with respect to the interests of the larger community. The real challenge is the design of a broad system of recreation facilities which will exploit each region's resources for outdoor recreation for the kinds of demands which will confront it. This involves overcoming jurisdictional barriers, but it also requires a clear view of the equities involved—if arbitrary restriction is to be struck down as a legitimate device, equal care must be taken to assure that the costs and deprivations are distributed in some rough correspondence to the benefits. Certainly the problem is not laid to rest merely by penetrating the jurisdictional barriers, but to penetrate them—or to rise above them—is an essential condition for the planning of outdoor recreation for the latter part of this century.

Thus, the planning of outdoor recreation involves problems which transcend even the difficult issues of modern city planning. Where the planning of urban services generally encounters its most severe difficulties, there also the planning of outdoor recreation will meet with special problems. However, the overcoming of these problems for city planning generally is no assurance of an effective recreation program. There are special problems—unique to and innate in outdoor recreation as a human and social activity—which must be overcome. The solution of the problems that it has in common with city planning is necessary, but it is not sufficient for an effective program of outdoor recreation services. The content of recreation behavior involves us in one of the most complex and difficult areas of public policy. Why this is so is suggested by a more detailed look at some of the demand and supply features of outdoor recreation.

The relationship of recreation users on the demand side to recreation resources on the supply side, as already noted, is anything but direct. Mobility is the hard fact in the problem of political jurisdiction, but it has a more important dimension, also. The geographical range of people pursuing their recreation inclinations is great and growing, not only because of more time and money but especially because new recreation appetites have been stimulated. For example, skin diving was once the exclusive property of a small number of daring underwater explorers; in the seaboard cities today, one can purchase skin diving equipment in the better stocked drugstores. Certainly a crucial effect of mobility is its propensity to bring into range of the individual's curiosity new recreation alternatives and new experiences. The inverse of this, however, is that the clientele for any activity or facility tends to become more and more geographically diffuse.

Demand has another dimension also. The problem for the planner is not only how many people, as a case in point, propose to spend time camping this summer but also how many people propose to camp, for example, in Yosemite Park on July 4. The potential market for Yosemite's limited services is nationwide, and, depending on how millions of people make their vacation decisions, the demand on any one day can be crushing. So far, it seems that aggregate recreation behavior may be somewhat more unstable than most forms of consumption simply because the market is so vast; the alternatives have high degrees of substitutability for consumers; and fad, fashion, and the "snowball effect" can exert decisive effects at any one moment.

The increasing tenuousness of the relationship between the users and the providers of outdoor recreation facilities has special policy requirements. The great burdens which this vast and mobile demand for recreation opportunities can thrust upon unusually desirable resources and facilities immediately raise questions about how to ration them so that they can be used at a level which will still offer a valuable recreation experience to the user and at the same time protect them from the permanent damage or destruction which consistent overexploitation would impose. Under these circumstances there is always a danger that the rationing techniques will be injudicious—that they will be inordinate and so waste valuable services, that they will be discriminatory and leveled against groups whose needs are great, that they will be irresponsible and unresponsive to the needs of the large community. The prospects for such behavior are sufficiently great to evidence a need for a new definition of public responsibilities in the field of outdoor recreation. An effective system of recreation will require a consistency of policy which current arrangements seem incapable of achieving.

One other complication needs to be recorded—the relationship between activities and facilities. If outdoor recreation were a basically uniform public service, such as the distribution of water or the provision of fire protection, it would involve a comparatively simple set of policy problems. Actually, what we call "outdoor recreation" is an extremely heterogeneous bundle of activities whose relationships to recreation facilities are likewise imprecise. The questionnaire used in the *National Recreation Survey*[4] lists some twenty-three activities ranging in generality from "playing outdoor games or sports" to "water-skiing," but in fact the list is almost endless. Some of these activities depend on very specialized facilities, such as "mountain climbing with gear" or skiing; others can be engaged in with facilities of a more general character. This complex and slippery relationship of facilities to activities is amplified by the fact that most users tend to be recreationally unspecialized; they may not only engage in any of a number of activities but may substitute among these with considerable freedom. The technical characteristics of production among the services of outdoor recreation are complicated enough, but the characteristics of demand, given the extremely elastic behavior of a large fraction of the consumers, are even more complex. To plan a system of facilities around demands of this sort will most certainly tax existing techniques and viewpoints to their limits.

Finally, space compounds the complex relationships between the demand for outdoor recreation services and the facilities supplying them. Facile substitution among kinds of facilities and among different kinds of recreation activities is complicated by the ease with which the consumer can make locational substitutions—another consequence of mobility. If facilities in one area are congested and unappealing, one can gain access to more desirable facilities in other areas. To the extent that facilities are easily accessible, high-quality facilities are likely to experience excessive demands, while lesser facilities go underutilized. The natural consequence of this is a gigantic propensity for "peaking." How to satisfy this or to rearrange it is a strategic problem facing the planner.

For all of these reasons the long-range planning for outdoor recreation is extraordinarily difficult. Where it is comprehended in the planning of cities and metropolitan regions, it partakes of all of the main problems to which they are heir. Beyond this, the very nature of outdoor recreation itself as a form of individual and social behavior not only defies conventional policy approaches but eludes conventional forms of analysis. A proper ordering of these issues would undoubtedly begin with repairing the deficiencies in the analytical framework, so that a probing of the main features of outdoor recreation quite properly follows.

OUTDOOR RECREATION CONCEIVED IN "SYSTEMS" TERMS

All the difficulties described above, coupled with the evident shortcomings of the present approaches to planning outdoor recreation, argue the need for a new planning and policy framework—a system, if you will—which brings into perspective the recreation behavior of urban populations, the evolving needs and demands, and the requirements and potentialities on the supply side. Hopefully, such a systematic analysis and resynthesis will define some of the indispensable specifications for the planning of outdoor recreation. To carry out such a procedure requires that we specify the key elements and describe how they interact. If we can identify the casual relationships between the system and the environment-at-large which may affect the operation of the system, we can seek out interventions to achieve the kinds and levels of performance we want. Fully aware of all the pitfalls, we attempt here to suggest some central features of such a "systematic" approach to outdoor recreation. While some rather obvious things need to be included to describe the elements, there is a gain in trying to see the picture whole.

The Elements: Recreation Publics, Activities, Facilities

The core elements of outdoor recreation can be viewed in terms of people—or, more specifically, various recreation "populations"—the outdoor recreation activities in which they participate, and the inputs from the public sector—the facilities—which make their activities possible. In this context, people are seen as possessing characteristics which are associated with common features of their recreation behavior: populations can be broken down into groups, homogeneous in large degree, and exhibiting consistent recreation tendencies, or propensities. These recreation propensities are the basic links between populations and the outdoor recreation activities which are available to them. In fact, the demand at any moment for outdoor recreation—as a public service—can be construed as the summing of the recreation propensities of the population. Activities and outdoor recreation facilities are related by the degree to which the technological requirements of activities can be met by the characteristics of the facilities. Two steps, then, need to be taken: first, to investigate the nature of the elements of the system—population groups, outdoor recreation activities, and the facilities for outdoor recreation; then to explore the interactions among them.

Population groups as elements. Analysis of the total population in terms of reasonably consistent groups[5] can isolate the major variables in the system; "mix" effects can be distinguished from structural effects in the recreation behavior of large groups. We know, for example, that the recreation behavior of the wealthy is different from that of the poor, that the young engage in activities shunned by the elderly, that males enjoy uses of their leisure time having little appeal to females. Any shuffling of the proportions of rich and poor, young and old, male and female, will show up as changes in the aggregate recreation behavior of the community without anyone actually changing at all. On the other hand, some kinds of changes do result from alterations in the recreation patterns of large groups in the population; these are structural effects, which can be isolated by eliminating "mix" as the source of variation.

The first step, then, is to disaggregate the population into groups which are reasonably homogeneous by criteria discussed below. These outdoor recreation groups are the basic units of the system and are drawn so as to exhaust the population: every member of any population will fall into one of the boxes. Under this condition any change in group behavior identified by the criteria can be described as a shift among outdoor recreation classes and structural changes are defined out of the problem. The prediction of recreation behavior is then achieved by the process of assigning the members of a population to the outdoor recreation groups through estimates (1) of the characteristics of the new population increments and (2) of the probabilities that individuals will shift among the outdoor recreation classes in the interim.

The classifying criteria must, of course, be significantly associated with recreation behavior, otherwise the reliability of the forecasts will be no greater than that associated with random choice. The predictive power of this framework, hence, depends on analysis of the factors dominant in the patterns of recreation behavior. Position in the life cycle, socioeconomic status, subjective preference patterns, and location appear to be the influential factors in recreation behavior, although we would do well to keep our eye on a residual, or "all others," class of factors.

Certainly one's position in the family or life cycle has a substantial influence on the outdoor recreation activities in which he is likely to engage. Families with small children tend to exploit recreations in which all can jointly participate; young, single males are predisposed toward more active, more challenging, and perhaps more competitive activities; elderly retired couples frequently seek reasonably passive but gregarious recreation activity. In this sense where one stands in life has an important effect in setting out the bounds within which recreation behavior is likely to take place.

Socioeconomic status is equally obvious as a variable in how people make choices about the use of leisure time.[6] This variable has a number of dimensions: an income effect is clearly distinguishable—rich people can simply afford more expensive forms of recreation than the less affluent; there is also a class effect—certain recreations have prestige associations which influence recreation behavior; education effects, leisure time effects, and a number of others are present, but these elements will tend to be strongly intercorrelated so that the broad differential of socioeconomic status has an importance of its own.

The subjective preference patterns of individuals are effective determinants, also. This includes all of those personal proclivities we refer to as *tastes*, ranging from inscrutable psychic predispositions to physical endowment. Personal history, especially of one's youth, conditions later uses of leisure. It is also a fact that one enjoys doing the things he does well, so that training and skills are big factors in personal preferences for outdoor recreation.

Location in its broadest sense has a special set of effects depending on the level of interest. At the regional level, uniquely local patterns in the use of leisure are apparent. To some extent they stem from tradition, but in greater degree from major differences in regional endowments—it is no accident that winter sports are more popular in New England than in the Southwest. At another level, the influence of location results from conditions of accessibility: location determines the time-and-money costs of gaining access to facilities, a major factor in the total costs for some types of activity. Other important criteria could be used to disaggregate the population, but a set of outdoor recreation classes built on these criteria would go far toward a reliable framework with which to predict recreation behavior.

Activities as elements. The second set of elements is the broad array of outdoor recreation activities which people will pursue when opportunity permits. These reflect the output of any system of recreation and so exhibit a significant difference between recreation and the other sectors of public production. Most public services are produced for instrumental reasons; they are actually intermediate inputs into other production processes. Fire protection and transportation systems are most certainly oriented to sustaining the complex of production activities in the community. Here the government is playing its role of investment in social overhead to improve the efficiency of the city as a vast productive plant. Another set of government products are not intermediates but are enjoyed as final goods. Outdoor recreation, like education and cultural preoccupations, is an end product which is wanted, needed, and demanded for its own sake. Its consumers view it as a crucial ingredient in the total quality of life, as providing a tone to experience which infuses day-to-day living with a special individual quality. Outdoor recreation has as many forms and is as complex as human play and esthetic satisfaction are capable of being. This quality of diversity and complexity is essential to outdoor recreation and needs to be kept central in plans and policies. To meet some concept of demand by pruning away the luxuriant opportunities for individualism generally inherent in recreation would be a spurious solution.

In the system we are describing, activities are the fulcrum which fixes the overall relationship of the recreation propensities of outdoor recreation groups to the array of facilities which are in different degrees available to users. They relate in specific ways to the behavior patterns of the outdoor recreation groups and each has certain requirements for the nature of the facilities that support it. To make these relationships clear, outdoor recreation activities can be classified by some specific criteria.

Skill requirements set apart some activities from others in signal fashion. Some make strong demands on the physique, skills, and experience of their devotees. Mountain climbing is an extreme example, but this is true of skiing and swimming, also. Participation in (and demand for) such activities will be limited to those properly equipped to participate in them. Others require little of participants, such as picnicking or walking, and their potential demand is limited only by other factors. Certainly skill requirements do distinguish in an important way among these activities.

The role of group participation is a useful differential, also. Some activities are basically solitary. Trout fishing is an excellent example; nothing is more superfluous than a second fisherman at a trout pool. Other activities invite joint enjoyment, and some—group games—positively require it.

Personal expenditure requirements are likewise significant in their variation among activities. At one extreme, yachting and polo require tremendous investments in the appropriate paraphernalia; at the other, walking and picnicking require virtually none.

Seasonal and climatic orientations differentiate among activities in ways that influence the distribution of demand throughout the year and among the regions. Winter sports and hunting are clear examples of seasonal specialization. Others, not directly limited by seasonal conditions, nevertheless tend to be modified by climatic conditions. Fewer people probably hike in winter than in summer, and open swimming and sunbathing are abandoned when temperatures are below 70 degrees.

Many activities are highly specialized in terms of the kinds of facilities they require, while others are quite undifferentiated in this respect. Hunting depends on an unimproved natural environment; pleasure boating requires the construction of marinas. Some activities can be enjoyed under conditions of extreme density, as in the intensive use of public beaches on hot summer days; others, such as hunting, are essentially space-extensive. Many activities have special resource requirements to be met by the native endowment of a facility. Mountain climbing needs mountains; but even hiking needs a natural endowment of topography, flora, and fauna to absorb and stimulate the hiker. Each activity has its own requirements which must be met by facilities before the activity can be carried out. The nature of these requirements is an important link between those activities which people are likely to want and those which can be provided.

Other features characterize the differences between outdoor facilities, but the ones set forth have the virtue of being highly selective in terms of who participates, when, where, and how much. These activity classes have the role in the system of linking the demand side of the picture—populations, outdoor recreation groups, and their recreation propensities—to the supply side, consisting of the array of facilities which public policy provides.

Facilities as elements. From the policy point of view, facilities for outdoor recreation have several key characteristics which influence the manner in which the system operates. A facility may be highly specialized in use, so that one, or at best, a few activities can be carried on in it. Unspecialized facilities permit several activities to be enjoyed concurrently by different users, where the activities are themselves unspecialized. A facility may be "multiple purpose" in the sense that it is arranged to permit a number of specialized and unspecialized activities to be carried on simultaneously. The facility can be viewed as an intermediate product in the production of outdoor recreation services, which are consumed when the facility is used. Since the technology of this product is an essential feature of the system, it is useful to examine the nature of the inputs.

The concept of land is too gross for our concern because two aspects of land have unique consequences for the use of facilities: space, in a simple geometric sense, and the resource endowment that goes with it. Space as the effective quantity of the land input frequently involves some complex dimensions: length more than area is important in the recreation capacity of a public beach and, similarly, of streams for canoeing and fishing; unobstructed area is crucial for space-extensive games, and other spatial features may influence the way in which we measure the input of space into a facility. Whatever the resource endowment of the facility, however, simple area has an important relationship to capacity for most activities. Resource endowment—all of those features which especially suit an area for specific kinds of outdoor recreation—is the qualitative dimension of the space input. Scenic qualities and the availability of bodies of water or of game and fish relate to activities for which the land might be used.

A second type of input embraces capital investment in improvements. Capital inputs have special significance for facilities which are not highly endowed with natural resources and for those adapted to some highly specialized recreation activities. Cities have, on occasion, developed parks from old sanitary fills with heavy expenditures for compacting, topsoil, and landscaping, for example, and so have substituted capital for deficient endowment. Golf courses are highly specialized facilities involving a substantial investment in reshaping the topography, in landscaping, and in the special installations which the sport requires. Capital investment frequently substitutes for space where land prices are high: Chicago reclaimed much of its recreation lake front from Lake Michigan at great cost, for example. Finally, capital is often used to increase the intensity with which parks of high demand or limited area can be used. In general, investment in recreation capital has the effect of increasing the degree of specialization of a facility and may involve a wide range of projects from hiking trails to artificial lakes.

Although location does not fit the role of an input, it is so critical a factor affecting the ability of a facility to produce services valued by a recreation clientele that its omission here would leave the analysis incomplete. The primary effect of location (or accessibility) is exhibited in the intensity with which a facility is used. In the following section, we examine the special role of location in greater detail.

Interactions Among the Elements: The System at Work

A systems analysis approach to a problem requires a focus on the relationships which connect the elements of the system and which are the pathways by which changes are communicated among the elements. Effective public policy must work its purposes through these relationships. If the problem is seen to be one of relating a set of demand conditions to a set of supply conditions, these interactions stand in the place of the market. If the problem is basically construed as a matter of minimum standards of welfare, the interactions are the mechanism by which such an objective must be achieved. Both views might, of course, be applied.

The outstanding feature of a system is the interdependence of its parts, and interdependence is abundantly apparent in the complex array of outdoor recreation demands, activities, and facilities across the nation. This can best be seen in terms of the spatial features of the interactions. The demand for Yosemite's extraordinary services begins in Boston, Little Rock, Sioux Falls, and Coeur d'Alene just as effectively as in Los Angeles or San Francisco, and when urban Californians preempt its services for their local recreations, they clearly do so at the expense of its ability to serve the vacationing Bostonian. In the same way in which the national economy can be described and analyzed in terms of its subnational parts, so the total production and consumption of the services of outdoor recreation in the various parts of the nation constitute a unitary system whose facilities extend from the great western national parks down to the local park systems in the cities. The thread which knits this system together is the demand of recreation[7]—its magnitude, its mobility, its variety.

If this is—as is suggested here—a vast, interdependent behavioral system, there are some rather revolutionary implications for public policy in outdoor recreation. In the first place, substantial elements of the demand for local facilities may actually arise outside of the community—a large proportion of local recreation services may actually be exported. Then, because of the leakages to the rest of the system, local recreation objectives may be very difficult to achieve. But the obverse is true also; parts of the system outside of the community may absorb so much of the local demand for outdoor recreation that a modest local program might easily meet the unsatisfied wants in the community. The central conclusion is unavoidable—the performance of any local outdoor recreation program is strongly conditioned by the performance of the total system of outdoor recreation. How this system works and how performance levels evolve and change require some exploration before planning and policy requirements can take form.

Location, intensity of use, and quality in outdoor recreation. People engaging in outdoor recreation use space. How much they use—and what kind—depends on the characteristics of the specific activity. Picnickers use a small area around a table or fireplace; hikers occupy that much of a trail which permits comfortable walking; hunters preempt virtually all of the area within easy range of their weapons. In addition, the space actually used is surrounded by a penumbra of space which, varying with the activity and the user, plays an important role in the evaluation of the recreation experience. At one end of the scale the amount of space may be so restricted that the conduct of the activity and the value of the recreation experience are seriously impaired; at the other the marginal value of additional space to the user for the activity is negligible. Family picnicking may be a frustrating experience if strangers are similarly picnicking ten feet away, yet a family exclusively occupying an acre of ground for its picnic would probably not value an additional acre very highly. At some point within this penumbra of accessory space a point exists where the quality of the experience will begin to decline very rapidly with any further reduction in the amount of space available to the user for the activity in which he is engaged. The relationship of this point to the core, or minimum, space requirements varies greatly among activities and among individuals; nevertheless, its existence is the crucial fact, suggesting a positive relationship between the quality of the recreation experience and the amount of space—within these limits. Further, since the amount of space per unit is the reciprocal of density, the relationship between the density of use of a facility and the quality of the individual experience is negative within these limits: as the number of persons using the facility at any one time increases, at some point the quality of the "product"—the recreation experience—will begin to decline very rapidly. This is the congestion effect in outdoor recreation—a key factor in the performance of the system and its parts.

Density—the number of users employing a facility for a given activity simultaneously—is related to the broader concept of intensity of use. A high intensity of use is associated with a high volume of demand; a high density of use is associated with the peaking characteristics of demand as measured by "load factor," the ratio of average to maximum demand. Density and intensity are loosely related; neither necessarily implies the other, but in reality the characteristics of demand for most activities are such that little violence is done to truth to assume that high intensity implies high density.

Intensity is introduced here because of its relationship to a more general concept of demand, and our objective at this point is to indicate the manner in which demand, the nature of the facility, and performance are intimately interrelated. Two characteristics of a facility determine its level of output: the first involves the kinds of services which a facility is equipped to produce, such as canoeing, hiking, and swimming. A double-pronged effect is apparent here. The space requirements, capital investment, and natural endowment establish a set of capacities for the facility (where capacity is anchored to the concept of minimum space requirements for an activity). Then, this output addresses a specific market, a group of users whose recreation propensities can be served by it. The nature of the product, in short, identifies the output in its quantitative and qualitative terms.

The second dimension is embraced by the concept of location—where the facilities are located with respect to their consuming publics. Location affects the performance of a facility because distance influences the recreation decisions of the consumer. Normally, a consumer will use a given facility at a rate related to its distance from his home: the more remote it is, the less he will tend to use it. Or, given several comparable facilities, all other things being equal, he will use the nearer more frequently than—or to the exclusion of—the more remote.

Although these relationships seem simple and straightforward, they are actually quite complex in practice. Distance is the prime barrier to the consumption of outdoor recreation services, many of which are free goods in situ. In order to enjoy these services, the user must overcome this barrier; he must transport himself to the facility, and this involves him in cost calculations. It not only costs money to make the trip to the facility and return, but it takes time. Since his supply of both is not unlimited, he must always measure the satisfaction of the anticipated experience against the values of other experiences which alternative uses of his time and money would have made possible. In short, distance is a measure of the dominant private costs confronting the consumer of outdoor recreation services. Transportation costs are not necessarily the only costs to a user of a given activity, but they do distinguish between the facilities producing the activities in an important way—particularly when the key element of time is weighed in the balance.

If all of the persons demanding the services pertinent to an activity can be accommodated at the near facility at a density consistent with an unimpaired satisfaction from the experience, the other facilities may not be used at all. The case is more likely, however, that the capacity of the facility or the volume of demand would result in congestion; i.e., densities at which the quality of the service is substantially impaired. For any user there will be a point in the decline of the quality of the experience where its value to him will be less than the private costs, or opportunity costs, of realizing the experience. When this happens he will cease to be a demander.

The preceding case will hold only in the absence of effectively competing facilities. Where alternative, if more remote, facilities are available, the user will tolerate the decline in quality only to the point where the value of the differential in quality between the nearest and the next nearest is equal to or greater than the increment in the distance costs associated with the more remote of the two. For any number of facilities located in specific ways with respect to a market or clientele, this relationship will hold. Thus, given the nature of the demand side of the market for an activity, as well as the number, sizes, and locations of facilities producing the relevant services, there is an equilibrium distribution of users among the facilities such that the quality of the service at any facility is valued by the user at the private costs associated with it. If all users valued the quality of service in the same way and had common sets of private costs, there would be no economic problem; and where the number of users exceeded the capacity constraints some form of rationing would be required. As is more realistically the case, private costs vary tremendously, and uniformity in the manner in which people appraise and evaluate quality in the recreation experience is an untenable assumption. The aggregate of demand is a summation across a mix of demanders who vary with respect to the private costs of the experience and quality valuation, so that, although the equilibrium condition is pertinent, it is also subject to the nature of the demand "mix."

The simple case of uniform facilities and a single activity does not really restrict the system, for the conclusions are easily expanded into the whole system by the competition among activities for space among the facilities—especially in the long run—and by the ease of substitution among activities which characterizes the consumer. It is true that some activities have very tenuous interconnections in the system—the demand for participation in polo probably has very little impact on the system—but these are at the margin of the problem and need not concern us greatly.

The central conclusion here is that all outdoor recreation facilities are tied together in a system in which changes, general or localized, tend to have impacts on many or all of the other facilities in the system. In the short run, the expansion of one facility will set in motion a wavelike set of impacts in the system. In the first instance, those facilities for which it is an easy substitute will experience a reduction in the intensity with which they are used or, obversely, an appreciation of the quality of the services produced. In the second instance, more remote facilities which are easy substitutes for the first set will have the same experience, and in this fashion the effects of the change are propagated throughout the system. There is a qualification of this process, since it assumes that all facilities operate within congestion ranges initially: the rise in quality of the services at the one location induces an appropriate consumer response. Where the quality of service is not materially affected by the expansion, no consumer can materially improve his position by changing the place at which he consumes his services, and the impact is dampened, or even totally absorbed, by the excess capacity.

These then are some of the central economic characteristics of the system of outdoor recreation. It consists of facilities which produce the services of outdoor recreation, services whose quality declines (or whose implicit prices rise) with increasing density and, hence, with intensity. These facilities turn out specific products at given locations. Further, the system includes a set of consumers with propensities to engage in certain kinds of recreation, budgets in both money and time, knowledge of alternatives, and an inclination to act rationally to maximize their net satisfactions. The location of all of the facilities and the residential locations of the users determine the distance costs, which relate the behavior of the consumers to the nature of the products of the various parts of the system. The scale of consumer behavior here is dominated by the severe peaking of demand and the extremely low load factors.[8]

The policy problem now becomes somewhat simpler in the overall. The government is the producer of a service which it may not always care to price but generally prefers to offer as a free good. However, the use of the service carries with it private costs which exert something of a price effect on the behavior of the consumer. How can an investment-allocating mechanism be constructed for such a system?

The nature of consumer demand for outdoor recreation. Since it is the behavior of consumers which powers the system, some of its main features are worth exploring for a clearer picture of how this behavior is likely to change in response to external developments and especially to changes elsewhere in the system, such as those induced by changes in public policy. *Demand* in the economic sense refers to the manner in which people in an aggregate will use their resources to satisfy their subjective preferences. . . .

The peculiarity, then, of outdoor recreation as a province of economics is that the consumer must engage in "double budget" calculations; he must spend a time income and a money income, the sizes of which are determined by the wage bargain. There are, accordingly, private costs associated with every form of recreation, no matter how free it is in money terms; at the very least an activity "costs" the amount of time necessary to engage in it. This peculiarity produces some special characteristics in individual demand. At one extreme, one may have a very large money income and a very limited amount of leisure time to allocate, so that the real constraint on his demand is the availability of time; at the other, an unemployed laborer may well have a large leisure time income but virtually no money income, so that his consumption possibilities among outdoor recreations are limited by the amount of money he can afford to spend. When one sums up these possibilities across the population, the aggregate demand for outdoor recreation will have its own dynamics compared to other demand sectors and will tend to respond to secular changes in the economy in a quite different way. . . .

The accounting framework has provided an indispensable technique for assembling and organizing our information about the money economy, and it seems clear that for purposes of outdoor recreation it needs to be expanded to take into consideration the "time economy." We not only need information about how many people will have incomes between, say, $5,000 and $10,000 per year at any given time, but we also need the distribution of leisure incomes within this class and how each is arranged in time. In its simplest form, this accounting system might take the form of a set of boxes organized by income class along one axis and by "leisure class" along the other. Each box would contain the number of consuming units, or users, within that income and leisure class. Summed across one axis the accounts would produce income distribution; summed the other way, the distribution of leisure. Because the accounts are exhaustive, it will require all changes to be completely accounted for—there are no leaks in the data system. . . .

We now have before us the operating characteristics of the system of outdoor recreation. Turning toward the facilities, or the supply side of the system, we observe that the quality of the services and the intensity with which a facility is used are closely linked together and these, in turn, are linked to the accessibility characteristics of the facility. The demand side is built on the significance of time as a cost dimension and on access costs as the parameters integrating supply and demand. . . .

Guidelines for Planning and Policy

A soaring demand for leisure time activities and the systemic character of outdoor recreation are the dominant ingredients of this new challenge to the ingenuity of planners and decision makers at every level of government. By the criteria of our social wants the invisible hand of the market is a defective guide; short-run political decision making, however, too frequently disregards critical interdependencies so that policy is dissipated in execution or vitiated by side effects so negative that sought-after social benefits are swallowed up by uncounted social costs: What is needed then is a carefully designed process for planning the development of the outdoor recreation system which can meet these tests:

1. It must perform a market-type function of investing the consumer with a more effective sovereignty over the allocation of the resources that go into the system.
2. It must equip the system with a mechanism to assure the realization of the appropriate social benefits.
3. It must exploit fully the internal interdependencies of the system as well as its interconnections with other sectors of public and private activity.

In the final section of this essay we set down some tentative suggestions on the type of approach which might be appropriate for the development and performance of such a process.

The most conspicuous issue emerges from the very nature of the growing demand, its scope, and its origins. The rate of growth is truly remarkable, and it takes its basic character from the processes of urbanization which gave it birth. Contrast these considerations with a public policy in outdoor recreation which has been distinguished by a preoccupation with the natural resources of the landscape to the extent that the development and distribution of the elements of this system bear only a fortuitous relationship to the geography of demand. This bias has by implication chosen the kinds of activities to be supported and the publics to be served without admitting the proliferating demand and the pressing social needs to any primacy in the setting of objectives and in the choice of means; policy formulations which begin—and frequently end—with the delimitation of areas of extraordinary landscape qualities are from the very beginning ill-adapted to serve any concept of popular recreation needs. Measured against demands and needs of urban populations, these resources are generally in pitifully short supply; furthermore, the intensity at which they are used frequently requires regulation to avoid ecological damage to the resource itself.

The dimensions and character of demand strongly assert the need to shift our basic policy in outdoor recreation away from its excessive emphasis on resource-based activities and in the direction of a dominant role for user-oriented forms of recreation. The evolving need is not so much for more Yosemites, Grand Canyons, and Okefenokees as it is for millions of acres of just plain space, endowed in many cases with only perhaps modest landscape and topographical interest but richly and imaginatively developed—this is the basic shift in approach that is called for by the logic of the present-day situation. Without this, it is hard to see how outdoor recreation facilities are to withstand the deluge of demand building up in our cities. Conserve our national recreation and landscape resources, yes; but do not confuse this conservation objective with the powerful objective of meeting the recreation needs of the nation. What is needed is a new strategy for recreation policy which is urban oriented—that is, oriented toward serving the great majority of the national population—in its articulation with urban needs, developmental in its constantly improving levels of performance, and carefully integrated with the whole array of public activities which afford a joint payoff for the production of recreation services. . . .

In short, the emphasis of an urban-oriented system of recreation rests heavily upon an extensive supply of space permanently located within comparatively easy access of its market.[9] It requires policy coordination among such urban functions as transportation and open space programs. Finally, it requires institutional devices and information flows to permit a continuing adjustment of the supply of recreation opportunities to the changing dimensions of demand.

That a recreation program should be developmental is merely another way of saying that it should have some special dynamic qualities. In the first place, it must be capable of responding smoothly to changes in demand. As the region grows, so should the capacity of the system; as the mix of outdoor recreation groups undergoes alteration, so should the system permit the fulfillment of new demands and wants. As there is no ceiling on the absorption of education, of spiritual self-fulfillment, or culture, so recreation needs ever-expanding horizons if it is to serve its humanizing function well. Hence, such a system should be developmental in the sense that it attains progressively higher levels of performance and proliferates the kinds of recreation opportunities available to all groups within the region. . . .

The nature of the national system of outdoor recreation imposes responsibility on government at all levels to respond to this general problem in a large-scale, integrated way. Mechanisms by which consumers can register their wants, by which consumer horizons can be expanded and enriched, by which the government, with its sights fixed on long-run developmental goals, can respond sensitively and smoothly to changes in user demands need to be developed. It is not sufficient, however, for the public to key its programs solely to tracking demand. It must more and more take on the creative role of being an imaginative risk taker along the whole developmental front of outdoor recreation; failing this, our system of facilities a generation from now could consist almost exclusively of scenic views from highways, 60 million picnic facilities and campgrounds, and very little else. In short, the institutions which we need must have a dual capacity of informing themselves about—and responding to—what people want and need, and of building into their programs an increasingly rich array of opportunities for recreation diversification and individuation. . . .

NOTES

1. Cf. John Ise, *Our National Park Policy* (Baltimore: Johns Hopkins Press, 1961).
2. A concise description of systems analysis and its role in decision making can be found in the National Academy of Sciences—National Research Council, *Conference on Transportation Research* Publication 840 (Washington, D.C., 1960), pp. 61–63. Our "systems approach" seeks to identify the strategic relationships, not to quantify them. It is the logical exercise which must precede systems analysis.
3. See especially Herbert J. Gans, "Recreation Planning for Leisure Behavior: A Goal-oriented Approach" (Ph.D. diss., University of Pennsylvania, 1957). Gans' dissertation is possibly the most thoroughgoing study of the role of public policy in the production of public recreation services. Although it centers on recreation as a problem for the city planner, its insights have illuminated many aspects of the role and responsibility of government in the provision of recreation services.
4. U.S. Outdoor Recreation Resources Review Commission, *National Recreation Survey,* Study Report 19 (Washington, D.C.: Government Printing Office, 1962), prepared by the commission staff on the basis of data collected by the Bureau of the Census (Form Rec. IV-4).
5. One approach to the analysis of demand by characterizing "user groups" is described in National Advisory Council on Regional Recreation Planning, *A User-Resource Recreation Planning Method* (Loomis, Calif.: National Advisory Council on Regional Recreation Planning, 1959).
6. See especially Eva Mueller and Gerald Gurin, with Margaret Wood, *Participation in Outdoor Recreation: Factors Affecting Demand Among American Adults,* U.S. Outdoor Recreation Resources Review Commission Study Report 20 (Washington, D.C.: Government Printing Office, 1962).
7. Marion Clawson has pioneered in the development of demand analysis in outdoor recreation in his *Methods of Measuring the Demand for and Value of Outdoor Recreation,* rep. no. 10 (Washington, D.C.: Resources for the Future, 1959).
8. A *load factor* is the ratio of average demand for all periods to peak price demand.
9. For the New York metropolitan region alone in 1985, and by conservative standards, it is estimated that 1,100 square miles of permanent open space will be needed to add to the existing 600 square miles, the total of which comprises 25 percent of the region's total land area. See Regional Plan Association, *The Race for Open Space* (New York: Regional Plan Association, 1960), p. 9, tab. 1.

CHAPTER 4

RECREATION, OPEN SPACE, AND SOCIAL ORGANIZATION

Diana R. Dunn.

This treatise is stimulating because it questions the "conventional wisdom" of evaluating urban leisure needs and encourages critical introspection. Professor Dunn recommends that before we monitor in the traditional fashion, we first identify our societal leisure goals. Public social services demand accountability; recreation services to be accountable require systematic monitoring.

URBAN RECREATION NEED

... The history of urban recreation need assessment in the United States is both short and spasmodic. This is due in part, of course, to the relatively new phenomenon of urbanization in this country. As cities grew and their attendant problems began to emerge, a fundamental philosophical question surfaced for those concerned with [city] recreation and open space. In its simplest form, [this question] is, Equal recreation opportunity for all? or more (or different) recreation for some? In oversimplified measurement terms it is, General standards? or comparative need?

Should the nation, or any political body within it, subscribe to one of these alternatives; or, if both are to be used, should they be based on differentiated groups or geographic areas? More important, should the public and voluntary sectors subscribe to the same philosophy, or should they differ in this regard? Perhaps most fundamental, who decides, and how? These questions have relevance not only for those in recreation but for all those involved in providing or receiving local public and voluntary services.

Until the 1960s there was a reasonably clear-cut division of responsibility between public and voluntary sectors at the local level. The public sector provided generalized services to all; the voluntary sector sought to provide compensatory services to some. Then came the federal War on Poverty, with its identification of Model City areas; the passage of considerable legislation aimed at helping specific target groups, and categorical grant programs designed to further particular services or facilities. All of this swung the national pendulum toward the "comparative need" side of the scale, with need condition and need fulfillment mechanisms and programs determined largely at the national level. In 1973, however—weighted by the enactment of general reve-

---

Reprinted from Betty van der Smissen, ed., *Indicators of Change in the Recreation Environment—A National Research Symposium*, Penn State HPER Series no. 6 (University Park: The Pennsylvania State University, College of Health, Physical Education, and Recreation, 1975), pp. 259–300, with permission of the author. The article was considerably condensed for this volume.

nue sharing and the current consideration of special revenue sharing—the pendulum swung back to the "equal opportunity for all" position, as determined at the local level.

Basic to the provision of any service to the general public is the assumption of the existence of a condition of need. The concept of recreation need has both an individual and a societal dimension. It is considered a basic desire but not a primary survival need. It is similarly considered an amenity; and its provision, not a first-level responsibility of the social order (i.e., public *or* voluntary sector). Recreation is generally recognized as being a need spread evenly over the population. It is not specific to atypical individuals or groups.

The challenge of allocating public and voluntary resources for recreation in an urban context is essentially that of any community organization dilemma: to attain and maintain a balance between needs and resources in the geographic area to be served. The task is one of determining resources, determining variances, and finally determining priorities. Given the fragmentation of agencies providing recreation—and the philosophic debate attending it within the heterogeneous American urban population—the task is not easy.

The recreation movement was born in the era of reformers and child savers who believed in close supervision of an adolescent's recreation and leisure. The settlement house was the first bulwark against the evils lurking for youth in the slums of a rapidly urbanizing and industrializing nation. Recreation need was equated with the amelioration of social pathologies, especially for the underprivileged, and more particularly for youth.

Initially, recreation opportunities were supported by philanthropic interests or private groups. Early in the present century, however, recreation also became a municipal government function, first because of citizen demands for parks, then for organized recreation services. Soon the idea that recreation is a fundamental and universal human need and that all people need recreation became the commitment and rallying cry of the newly minted public service profession. Meeting the needs and interests of all people became the motto: "The program should provide equal opportunity for all, regardless of race, creed, social status, economic need, sex, age, interest, or mental or physical capacity."[1] More succinctly, "The comprehensive program of recreation should be based upon the needs, interests, and abilities of all the people."

In the 1960s, the influences of the War on Poverty, federal categorical funding, public opinion, the civil rights movement, and urban unrest—all had tremendous impact on public and voluntary recreation services in the metropolitan areas of the United States. The public park and recreation profession responded (at least rhetorically) to its original concern for the disadvantaged in urban America. The modification in commitment reflected a renewed emphasis stressing that while all people need recreation, "people are unequal in their need for community-supported recreation services."[2] Indeed, it was no longer heresy to observe that a great many people had no need at all for public or voluntary recreation services.

The measurement of the extent of a specific social need condition, and the measurement of the degree to which a particular public or voluntary service alleviates the condition seem elementary. A rational basis for the allocation of resources to meet variances in need condition across subunits of a vast metropolitan complex also seems essential. Trusting taxpayers assume that police, fire, transportation, recreation, and other municipal services have provided or developed such measures and means to evaluate and allocate resources. In reality, it was not until the late 1960s that, under the leadership of the Urban Institute, systematic measures of local government effectiveness were developed. The element of need, or how much is enough or too much, has still not been approached. Cities have operated on a budget of scarcity, so the possibility of too many fire hydrants, public health nurses, drug clinics, or swimming pools has never been very real. The consideration of need, then, has always been from the standpoint of the problem of distribution of too few resources or the battle of priorities by advocates of one kind of need against those pushing another; that is, "playgrounds for the north end versus the south" or "playgrounds versus squad cars."

Several techniques for assessing local recreation need have emerged during the history of the urban recreation movement. The most obvious deals with the playgrounds-versus-squad-cars issue and may be called the "grass-roots technique." In its purest form, individual citizens assess their need for recreation services (and, very likely, competing services) and voice their decision via the ballot, as in a bond referendum.

Two other techniques for assessing local recreation need are philosophical opposites, yet both speak to the issue of whether to place new resources in the north end or the south end of town. The "equality technique," based on the position that local recreation should be equally provided to residents, uses space and facility standards (commonly based on population density) to provide the basic measure required for resource allocation. The "social concern technique" is based on the belief that people are *not* equal in their need for local recreation services and that various social, economic, and environmental characteristics in addition to population density are critical to a realistic assessment of recreation need.

Grass-Roots Technique

From the time of the transition from the philanthropic provision of recreation for the underprivileged to the municipally provided recreation services for all, the voter has been a powerful determinant of the need for recreation and its primary grass-roots spokesman. Two pertinent generalizations emerge from a review of recent studies of local referendum elections. First, socioeconomic status is directly related to how an individual votes. Second, while it is clear that a vote cast on a local issue is conditioned by a wide range of factors, one of these is the voter's implicit perception of self-interest and need for the service.

In reviewing reports from cities around the nation, the number of bond issues for parks and recreation passed by municipal governments in 1969 was barely 60 percent of the number passed one year earlier. The number of bond issues which failed increased more than 20 percent in the same year. Both measures reversed slightly in 1970, but data for subsequent years are not available. The amount of the bond issues passed declined from $140 million in 1967 to less than $50 million in 1969, then moved up slightly to $52 million in 1970.[3] A coincident dramatic decline in bond issue passage occurred in many other public service areas, such as libraries and educational institutions, during this same period.

One might speculate that municipalities ceased putting all their eggs in the bond issue basket as federal categorical funds became more and more available for land acquisition and development. However, capital outlay by municipalities for parks and recreation declined by nearly half ($153 million to $80 million) between 1967 and 1969. Clearly, supplemental funds were not forthcoming to make up diminishing bond revenues. Another conjecture which might be forwarded is that, as federal funds (which often required state and local matching funds) increased, bond efforts decreased, since (1) localities did not need as much local input because of the federal matching funds and/or (2) localities were reluctant to commit the matching funds *in advance* because the federal dollars might never be forthcoming.

Unfortunately, citizens usually cannot affect directly voluntary or public revenues designated for operating expenditures. They may defeat a city income tax proposal or neglect the United Fund, but it is difficult to determine whether their rejection is issue-specific. When they *do* have a select-in-or-out choice, however, the waters are not so muddy. Unless a dramatic reversal has occurred since 1970, grass-roots citizen support for major park and recreation bond packages is declining, and no new bonanza has taken its place.

A fundamental dimension of recreation grass-roots approaches to understanding the recreation needs and interests of constituencies is the citizen survey. Recent work by the Urban Institute has examined this technique as it can be used to obtain information about a number of measures of effectiveness of local recreation agencies. Citizens, the institute determined, can play a vital role in evaluating facilities, staff, crowdedness, accessibility, safety, and other important aspects of local recreation. Telephone interview is the technique advocated by the institute after examining possibilities including self-administered and face-to-face interview methods with regard to cost, response rate, representativeness of respondents, interview attention span, man-hour requirements, and ease of work load scheduling.[4]. . .

Equality Technique

Standards—commonly based upon population density—provide the basic measure for the equality technique to determine local recreation needs. No general provision is made in any space or facility standard for adapting practice or priority because of the presence or absence of any other factor included in a broad community survey. The primary virtue of this tradition appears to be that the equal distribution of recreation resources based on the distribution of population is easy to compute and, more appealingly, easy to interpret, defend, and sell. Historically, when local needs were locally determined and responded to by mobilizing local resources via the public purse, these last-mentioned attributes were of enormous consequence. They should not be understated today.

Although they have been disparaged in recent years, standards still offer the most common approach to comparative need assessment for many public services. The park and recreation profession has expended considerable energy throughout this century to devise and publicize minimum space and facility standards for urban populations. Regrettably, the efforts of the profession have resulted in but a single, undifferentiated set of standards; and community leaders across the nation have been admonished to "adjust the standards to fit the local situation." Thus, minimum standards for adequate open space are the same for Newark and Oklahoma City, although their respective population densities are 576 and 16,273 persons per square mile and their climates and ethnic compositions are among other great differences. Despite extensive efforts to halt the practice, however, "standards" have frequently been adopted as the ideal rather than the minimum.

Standards historically evolved without regard for what actually existed. This was not because standard setters were arrogant but rather because they did not have quantitative information about what in fact *did* exist in urban areas across the nation.[5] A 1970 study provides information about the quantity of open space and noncommercial recreation resources and services in twenty-five U.S. cities and their inner city areas.[6] (Unfortunately it did not go far enough; it did not provide data for more affluent or less densely populated city areas or for suburban areas, so that they might also be compared with the national minimum standards as well as with what exists in the inner cities. Nor did it include an accounting of commercial open space and recreation resources or services in the inner cities.) The materials below compare statistics from these study cities and inner city study areas with national minimum standards.

Table 4-1 presents national minimum standards for several facilities included in the study. Figure 4-1 shows five selected facilities in the study cities and inner city study areas as a percentage of the national minimum standard as derived from table 4-1 and adjusted to the units of analysis available to the study. It may be seen that in 1970, there were three categories of facilities which met or very nearly met the national minimum standards both in the cities and in the inner city study areas: (1) parks, playgrounds, tot lots; (2) pools, splashboards, etc.; and (3) ball diamonds. (It should be remembered that the city percentage was derived from information submitted by the local public park and recreation agencies in 1970, whereas the inner city study area percentage was obtained by field research leaders during the same year and included facilities in the public, private, and voluntary sectors.) Two categories of facilities—tennis courts and basketball and volleyball courts—were drastically underrepresented in both the study cities and inner city study areas when compared with the national minimum standards. A reexamination of the minimum standards for these facilities is clearly desirable.

Information[7] about one of these facilities [parks, playgrounds, playlots] in terms of the minimum standard, the number existing, and the surplus/deficit for the twenty-five cities and inner city study areas showed great variances occurring: . . . Philadelphia needed 9,664 acres of open space for playgrounds, playlots, and parks in order to meet the national minimum standard, whereas

	Standard (1,000 persons)
Baseball diamonds	1/6,000
Softball diamonds (and/or youth diamonds)	1/3,000
Tennis courts	1/2,000
Basketball courts	1/500
Swimming pools (25 m)	1/10,000
Swimming pools (50 m)	1/20,000
Open space	
Playlots	1/500-2,500
Vest pocket parks	1/500-2,500
Neighborhood parks	1/2,000-10,000
District parks	1/10,000-50,000
Large urban parks	1/50,000
Regional parks	Serves entire population

TABLE 4-1. *National Minimum Standards for Selected Facilities*
Source: National Recreation and Park Association, *National Park and Recreation and Open Space Standards* (Washington, D.C., 1970).

Phoenix exceeded the minimum standard for the same open space by 12,880 acres. Similar variances occurred in other study areas: Milwaukee and Philadelphia were 552 and 932 acres, respectively, below the national minimum standard, whereas the study areas in Denver and Los Angeles exceeded the minimum standards by 328 and 1,100 acres, respectively. It should be observed that only four study areas—Boston, Denver, Seattle, and Los Angeles—exceeded the minimum standard of open space for playgrounds, playlots, and parks. Many questions suggest themselves after an examination of the data and the standards, including the following:

1. How important are traditional standards or the facilities they assess to the health of a city?
2. If a city meets or even exceeds substantially every minimum space and facility standard, is it "recreationally advantaged" compared with others which do not?
3. Is a neighborhood which has a surplus of open space or facilities automatically superior to one with difficiencies?
4. Are there other measures which may reveal far more about the "recreational health" of a city or a neighborhood?
5. Is there sufficient rationale for pursuing these standards—for mounting a national or local effort to raise all urban areas to meet these somewhat arbitrary minimums?
6. If publicly supported recreation should be a means to ameliorate social pathology in large cities, are these measures related to social health or its absence?

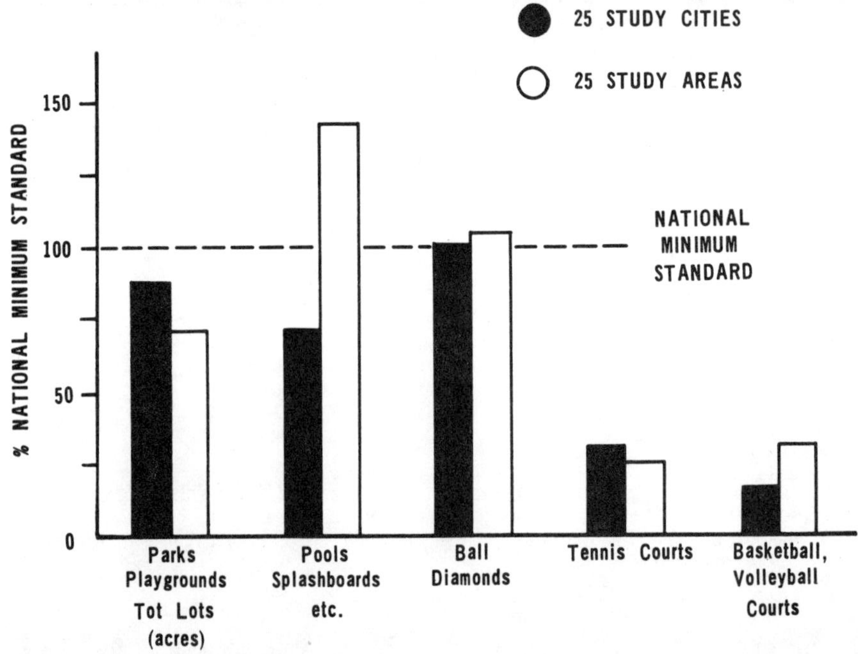

FIGURE 4-1. *Selected Space and Facilities in Study Cities and Study Areas as a Percentage of National Minimum Standard*
Source: U.S. Department of Housing and Urban Development, Office of Community Planning and Development, *Open Space and Recreation Opportunity in America's Inner Cities* (Washington, D.C., 1974), p. 91.

7. If publicly supported recreation should be an end in itself, are these measures the ones which should be commonly financed in every city?

Social Concern Technique

A significant part of the public conscience reawakening of the 1960s was the reversal of a quarter of a century of maximizing centralization in local public service administration. Decentralization, accessibility, and participation became legitimatized goals for the first time since the 1930s—at least in theory at the local level. Subunits of urban areas were brought into focus to create an awareness that the parts which make up the whole city may be quite dissimilar and, more important, that the needs of the parts may be very different.

Precedent for recreation and park studies evolved from the social welfare field, where the assessment of need priority among geographic subunits and among social services has been a part of many metropolitan-area social planning studies. The approach was first employed prior to World War I in studies undertaken in Portland, Maine, and in other eastern cities. A long lull in such efforts ended with a group of post–World War II studies.[8] . . . In these, subunits ranged in number from 183 census tracts averaging 5,000 population in Indianapolis, to 74 neighborhoods averaging 104,000 population in New York, to 12 welfare planning areas averaging 48,000 population in south-central Los Angeles, to 38 social planning areas averaging 55,000 population in Boston. Most important is the concept that both social need and recreation resources must be quantitatively determined and the differences between need and resource, measured for each study area. The variances were so determined and ranked, thus placing each study area in relation to the others, based on a simple greater-lesser bifurcation.

Methodology ranged from verbal description to graphic presentation to elementary statistical techniques. . . . Need variables used in the selected studies were, in the order of most often utilized: age, juvenile delinquency rate, population density, income, housing, population stability, occupation, education, race, mortality rates, employment rates, and percentage of foreign born. Resource variables used, in the order of frequency, were: acreage, facility, leadership, attendance, costs, and programs.

The study . . . completed in Los Angeles in 1969[9] utilized basic concepts and techniques of an instrument developed by the Recreation and Youth Services Planning Council of Los Angeles for determining the comparative need for recreation services among geographic areas.[10] The approach was employed by the council as part of a study of recreation needs in south-central Los Angeles after the 1965 riots in Watts.[11] Subsequently it was adopted by the Los Angeles City Planning Department and Los Angeles City Recreation and Park Department, and it was used in the development of the recreation element of the City of Los Angeles Master Plan.

The council proceeded from three assumptions:

1. There are measurable social characteristics and neighborhood recreation resources which indicate comparative need for recreation and youth services by areas, communities, or neighborhoods in an urban setting.
2. All citizens have important basic needs for recreation services; but, due to different socioeconomic characteristics and interests, their needs can be met in different ways.
3. Priorities in community-subsidized recreation services should go to those experiencing maximum social pressures from density of population, number of youth, low income, and evidence of social disorganization. . . .

As with the preceding space standards section, because data are available, the following materials compare statistics from study cities and study areas using the "social concern technique." For modifications made on the Los Angeles system, see note 6.

Cities

This section contains summary information regarding the computation of the resource index, need index, and comparative priority of need index for the twenty-five study cities.

Resources. . . . C-Scores[12] calculated from three variables, the resource index for twenty-four study cities (Tampa was not included due to lack of citywide resource data), and the ranking of the cities with respect to their resources [yielded the following results][13]:

1. Milwaukee had the highest per capita park and recreation operating expenditure; New Orleans, the lowest.
2. Denver and Phoenix had the largest number of acres of open space per 1,000 population; Oakland, Atlanta, Philadelphia, Detroit, Birmingham, and Houston had the fewest.
3. Milwaukee had the highest number of park and recreation full-time personnel per 1,000 population; Houston and New Orleans had the lowest.
4. Overall, Milwaukee ranked number one with respect to resources, and New Orleans and Newark were twenty-third and twenty-fourth, respectively.

Need. Need index computation for the twenty-five cities showed . . .[14]:

1. Newark, Boston, and Philadelphia tied for the highest need with respect to population density; Oklahoma City had the lowest.
2. New Orleans had the highest index score with respect to percentage of families below the poverty level; Seattle had the lowest.
3. Newark had the highest need index score with respect to the percentage of children eighteen years of age and under living with both parents; Kansas City had the lowest.

Overall, Newark ranked number one with respect to need, and Portland and Kansas City were twenty-third and twenty-fourth, respectively.

[As for] the comparative priority of need for recreational services in twenty-four study cities as computed through a determination of the comparative difference of the resource index and the need index, Newark and New Orleans were first and second, respectively, with respect to comparative priority of needs, and Milwaukee and Portland were lowest in comparative priority.[15] . . .

The study cities and the inner city study areas were ranked by comparative priority of need for recreational services.[16] . . . Although there are differences in rankings between the cities and their respective study areas, a rank order statistical procedure revealed that the rankings were nonetheless significantly positively correlated. Nevertheless, it is clear from this data that substantial differences do occur. For example, the city of Oakland ranks fourteenth in rank priority of need, but the inner city study area of Oakland ranks seventh. Further, the city of Detroit ranks third in rank priority of need, but the inner area of Detroit ranks 17.5. These variances indicate clearly that inner city need cannot necessarily be equated with or inferred from citywide recreation need.

Rhetorical questions similar to those which concluded the previous section (standards) suggest themselves with respect to comparative need measurement. Most crucial is the dilemma of factor selection and its corollary, factor weighing. What is important in determining comparative recreation need among cities or neighborhoods? Who should decide, and how? Is there sufficient rationale upon which to base persuasive arguments on behalf of recreation facilities and open space in the arena of urban austerity? Will the same values obtain in all cities as priorities are determined by those making decisions regarding resource allocation?

NATIONAL AND STATE APPLICATIONS

Other agencies with related concerns involving the assessment of recreation need or the establishment of priorities for resource distribution in an era of scarcity have sought to use comparative need techniques.

The U.S. Department of the Interior Bureau of Outdoor Recreation developed COMPARE—A Computer Oriented Method of Program Analysis, Review, and Evaluation—for assessing applicant priorities nationwide.[17] The COMPARE system is an effort to provide a "common denominator" for evaluating projects, and all proposed projects are assigned a cost-effectiveness ratio based on measured cost, capacity, and need for recreation. The system may be expressed by the formula:

$$\text{cost-effectiveness} = \frac{\text{output capacity} \times \text{recreation deficit}}{\text{total public costs}}$$

This ratio is expected to give highest rankings to projects which (1) meet the greatest needs; (2) last the longest; (3) are efficiently constructed; and (4) can be efficiently operated and maintained. The system uses OTUs (one time use) as the recreation deficit measure, which reflects recreation capacity in terms of total number of people that can be accommodated at any given moment. Cost factors are amortized over the life of the project, and annual operation and maintenance costs are considered, along with user fees. . . .

Internationally, some efforts have been initiated to obtain data for comparison with cities in this country in order to assess similarities and differences between European and North American cultures. Language, cultural history, geographic differences and other confounding variables complicate greatly these efforts and make difficult learning useful lessons from our European neighbors in the problems of high-density urban living.

MISSING LINKAGES

The previous discussion points out the *technical feasibility* of determining needs or comparative priorities *after* assumptions have been established and accepted. Regrettably, most of the underlying assumptions are based on "conventional wisdom," "seat-of-the-pants intuition," or some manifestation of "common sense." It is perhaps late, but still important, that we turn attention to assessing the *conceptual desirability* of these assumptions. Only such scrutiny will permit us the luxury of knowing how to do more of what is right and how to eliminate those activities which make doubtful contributions to the populations we profess to serve but which in fact sap our resources and may be but generously termed "pork barrel programs."

Implicit . . . is the belief that relationships do exist between recreation opportunity, open space, and social organization. Clear, however, is the fact that the nature these relationships is not known. Even more apparent is the necessity of achieving and understanding these relationships—in order both to do good and to do well.

For heuristic purposes, selected data from the twenty-five-city study has been treated to uncover relationships between recreation opportunity, open space, and social organization. Few important relationships were found. . . .

[The analysis] shows that city population density is related positively to eight selected study variables (study area refers to inner city high-density, low-income section of each city):

1. study area population;
2. study area population density;
3. study area units serving the entire core area;
4. city multifunctional buildings;
5. city park and recreation capital expenditures in 1970;
6. number of study area recreation programs;
7. study area median family income;
8. study area and city percentage, nonwhite population.

Thus, as the city population density increases, more recreation and open space units serve the core areas of the cities, more multifunctional buildings are found in the cities, more recreation programs are observed in the inner city areas, and more money is spent for city park and recreation capital expenditures.

. . . [City] population density is related negatively to eight study variables:

1. city land area;
2. study area vacant lot acreage;
3. study area open space;
4. number of study area units serving neighborhoods;
5. number of study area multifunctional buildings;
6. evaluation of study area units;
7. city percentage of population over twenty-five and high school graduates;
8. city percentage of children under eighteen living with both parents.

As the population density increases in the cities, decreases occur in open land space, number of units serving the entire core area, study area number of multifunctional buildings, and the condition of study area open space and recreation units.

Perhaps as important, however, city population density had no significant relationship to many study variables, including the number of outdoor recreation facilities, city park and recreation operating expenditures in 1970, park and recreation personnel levels, and citizen participation.

Those concerned with recreation services in cities have a professional responsibility to seek answers and to initiate changes—perhaps dramatic ones—where they are indicated. With the increasing data available and growing public demand for accountability, abrogation of this duty will only postpone the day when others do it for us. The choice of action or reaction may not long be open to us.

[CONCLUSIONS]

As is the case with any review article on past efforts, this discussion is very likely obsolete. Threaded through this paper run several themes which deserve examination in light of this possibility:

1. Data on some measures of recreation, open space, and social organization are becoming increasingly available.
2. This data may be inadequate and inaccurate or may otherwise mislead the uncautious user.
3. Data manipulation capabilities are becoming better and more widely available.
4. Assumptions about the relationships of measures of recreation, open space, and social organization are unsubstantiated, possibly erroneous.
5. A goal structure upon which data should be gathered, organized, and utilized is nonexistent.
6. Traditional recreation open space and social indicators may have minimal relevance to the quality of community life.

The lack of commonly held, measurable goals and objectives looms as the greatest challenge facing recreation. This assertion is not new or revolutionary; it is simply a paraphrase of much prior literature, such as [this] passage . . .

> Many years ago John Collier, a great friend and critic of recreation, charged the recreation leaders in this country with "conducting pigmy programs, seeking pigmy results, amid giant opportunities." Collier's criticism still [is valid]. A critical weakness of the recreation profession is that at present its people do not have great purposes which they are united in wanting to achieve.[18]

Intuitively, [the present author] finds inadequate the notion that the goal of recreation is to give people what they want, or to achieve minimum space or facility standards, or to equalize the provision of selected recreation opportunities across neighborhoods, cities, states, or the country. Increasingly [the author] prefers larger purposes as starting points, such as those suggested by Gray and Greben:

> A central purpose of community recreation programs is to help improve the quality of living.
>
> The primary goal of recreation and park services is human development.[19]

[They] have identified two challenges which flow from such goal statements, pointing out that we must:

> Develop evaluation methods capable of measuring the contribution of park and recreation experience to human welfare which can make us accountable for the human consequences of what we do.
>
> Undertake a systematic investigation of the outcomes of park and recreation experience and develop a taxonomy of human benefits.[20]

These are indeed important challenges. The alternative is to continue to gather data virtually randomly on what is easy to measure or has been measured traditionally and to assume that what is difficult to measure or has not been measured before is unimportant. Hopefully, we will be able to benefit from and transfer much of the knowledge accrued in the past as we move toward the development and refinement of goal-specific measurement systems. In any case, we must strive in the future to identify first what our goals are and then to determine measures and techniques useful in determining the degree of goal attainment. To continue present practice will perpetuate a situation where the tail is wagging the dog.

There is danger in quantitative effort without quality control: mindless computers can mislead rather than enlighten. Awareness of this may prevent dramatic error as enormous amounts of data become available for manipulation by newly minted computer virtuosos probing recreation matters. It behooves pioneers to interpret findings judiciously and report conclusions with humility and generous amounts of common sense.

We must reason before we calculate or risk the possibility that our indicators and our field may have little real relationship to the quality of community life.

NOTES

1. Reynold E. Carlson, Theodore R. Deppe, and Janet R. Maclean, *Recreation in American Life* (Belmont, Calif.: Wadsworth, 1963), p. 14.
2. David E. Gray, "The Case for Compensatory Recreation," *Parks and Recreation*, April 1969, p. 23.
3. *Parks and Recreation*, August 1971, pp. 17–31.
4. Harry P. Hatry and Diana R. Dunn, *Measuring the Effectiveness of Local Government Services: Recreation* (Washington, D.C.: Urban Institute, 1971); U.S. Department of the Interior, Bureau of Outdoor Recreation, *How Effective Are Your Community Recreation Services?* (Washington, D.C., 1973). See also chapter 13 of this volume.
5. For extensive discussions of the history and development of standards in the United States, three documents are recommended: Robert D. Buechner, ed., *National Park, Recreation and Open Space Standards* (Washington, D.C.: National Recreation and Park Association (NRPA), 1971, pp. 6–8; Seymour M. Gold, *Urban Recreation Planning* (Philadelphia, Pa.: Lea & Febiger, 1973),

pp. 143–81; and Edwin J. Staley and George Hjelte, *A Profile of Recreation and Youth Services in the Pasadena-Foothill Area* (Los Angeles, Calif.: Recreation and Youth Services Planning Council, 1969), pp. 100–106.
6. U.S. Department of Housing and Urban Development, Office of Community Planning and Development, *Open Space and Recreation Opportunity in America's Inner Cities* (Washington, D.C., 1974).
7. Ibid., p. 92.
8. Ibid., pp. 99–101.
9. Ibid.
10. Edwin J. Staley and George Hjelte, *A Profile of Recreation and Youth Services in the Pasadena-Foothill Area* (Los Angeles, Calif., 1969), pp. 132–145, app. G; Edwin J. Staley, "Determining Neighborhood Recreation Priorities: An Instrument," *Journal of Leisure Research*, winter 1969.
11. Edwin J. Staley and David E. Gray, *Study of Recreation Needs and Services: South Central Los Angeles* (Los Angeles, Calif., 1966).
12. Staley, "Determining Neighborhood Recreation Priorities;" J. P. Guilford, *Fundamental Statistics in Psychology and Education*, 4th ed. (New York: McGraw-Hill, 1965).
13. *Open Space*, p. 105.
14. Ibid., p. 107.
15. Ibid., p. 108.
16. Ibid., p. 113.
17. U.S. Department of the Interior, Bureau of Outdoor Recreation, *COMPARE: A System for Optimizing Federal and Federally Assisted Recreation Programs*, Phase II, *General Report* (Washington, D.C., 1970).
18. American Association for Health, Physical Education, and Recreation, *Goals for American Recreation* (Washington, D.C., 1964), p. 5.
19. David E. Gray and Seymour Greben, "Future Perspectives," *Parks and Recreation*, July 1974, pp. 26–33; see also chapter 1 of this volume.
20. Ibid., pp. 47–56.

FURTHER READING

Recreation, Changing Social Values & Assessment

Bloomfield, J. 1975. *The role, scope and development of recreation in Australia.* Canberra: Australian Government Publishing Service.

Cheek, N. H., Jr., and Burch, W. R., Jr. 1976. *The social organization of leisure in human society.* New York: Harper & Row.

Leisure—A new perspective. 1975. Canberra: Australian Government Publishing Service.

Loy, J. W., and Kenyon, G. S. 1969. *Sport, culture and society.* New York: Macmillan.

Mercer, D. 1973. The concept of recreation need. *Journal of Leisure Research* 5 (winter): 37–50.

National urban recreation study. 1978. USDI, Heritage Conservation and Recreation Service and National Park Service. February.

Perloff, H. S., ed. 1969. *The quality of the urban environment.* Baltimore: Johns Hopkins Press.

Proceedings—Resources for Tomorrow Conference. 1962. 3 vols. Ottawa: Queens Printer.

Rogers, B. 1967. *Pilot national recreation survey.* British Travel Association Report no. 1. University of Keele.

Sillitoe, K. 1969. *Planning for leisure.* London: HMSO.

The recreation imperative: A draft of the nationwide outdoor recreation plan prepared by the Department of the Interior. 1974. Printed at the request of Henry M. Jackson, Chairman, Committee on Interior and Insular Affairs, United States Senate. September.

U.S. Department of the Interior. Bureau of Outdoor Recreation. 1973. *Outdoor recreation—A legacy for America.* Washington, D.C.: Government Printing Office.

______. *Outdoor Recreation Resources Review Commission reports.* 1962. Washington, D.C.: Government Printing Office.

Study Reports:

3. Wilderness and recreation—A report on resources, values and problems.
5. The quality of outdoor recreation: As evidenced by user satisfaction.
10. Water for recreation—values and opportunities.
19. National recreation survey.
20. Participation in outdoor recreation: Factors affecting demand amongst American adults.
21. The future of outdoor recreation in metropolitan regions of the United States.
22. Trends in American living and outdoor recreation.
23. Projections to the year 1976 and 2000: Economic growth, population, labor force and leisure, and population.
26. Prospective demand for outdoor recreation.
27. Outdoor recreation literature: A survey.

Van Doren, C. S., and Hodges, L. 1975. *America's park and recreation heritage—A chronology.* Washington, D.C.: Government Printing Office.

Von Bertalanffy, L. 1968. *General system theory.* New York: Braziller.

Part Two

RESOURCE UTILIZATION: PLANNING & MANAGEMENT

OVERVIEW

Part 2 has a threefold objective: (1) to present some of the concepts and methods that have been developed to assist the recreation planner and manager in analyzing the physical environment and the impact of man's recreational activities on the resource; (2) to highlight the value of the recreational experience to man, to identify the psychological, physiological, and social needs that recreational experiences can satisfy, and to show how the planner/manager can identify and accommodate people's values and attitudes; and (3) to continue to identify and recognize the organization system in operation, particularly the elements involved.

Knowledge about the character of recreational resources is useful in planning and management: it helps define and limit the mix of recreation opportunities that can be supported and provides insights into possible costs of providing these opportunities. The first chapter in this part is a simple, direct, and basic review of the physical elements in the natural resource system.

The next chapter focuses on man and the recreational experience; the complicated treatise deals with a conceptual framework involving the behavior of the recreator. The third chapter then provides an integrative view of the physical resource and the recreation experience from a management viewpoint. Finally, the last chapter describes the complexities of man/resource leisure interactions with the use of a simulation model; models, as representations of reality, help to introduce consistency in planning and management.

CHAPTER 5

RECREATION AREA PLANNING: SOME PHYSICAL AND ECOLOGICAL REQUIREMENTS

Eugene Mattyasovsky

This chapter serves as an excellent introductory statement and overview of the complexities associated with recreation and the physical environment. It outlines some of the basic physical and biological concepts that the recreation planner must consider. As with many studies, the concepts take on added meaning because Eugene Mattyasovsky presents them in conjunction with a case study.

SCOPE OF THE PROBLEM

Our rapidly growing cities, with their varied land use demands, create a complex planning task in the selection and provision of suitable land for these uses. *Suitable* can mean different things. The criteria used in determining the effectiveness of various uses change over time in response to changes in technology and ideals.

Among these land uses outdoor recreation is increasing rapidly in significance. The demand is growing much faster than the population because the per capita demand is also increasing. According to some U.S. experts, by 1987 four times as much area will be needed per capita as was required in 1967.

The "planning" of these areas has many aspects: sociological, ecological, economic, legislative-administrative, transportational, and so on. All are important; we need the help of all of these perspectives for selecting, developing, and maintaining outdoor recreation areas.

Research sponsored by the Canadian Council on Urban and Regional Research and conducted by the present author concentrates on the problem of "establishing physical and ecological criteria for site selection and maintenance" of outdoor recreational areas outside a city. To translate this into everyday language, the research tries to provide answers in the areas following:

1. the basic physical and ecological criteria for selecting and planning regional recreation areas;
2. specific ecological questions connected with water;
3. multiple uses, compatibility of different uses;

Reprinted from *Plan* of the Town Planning Institute of Canada 8, no. 3 (1967): 91–109, by permission of the Town Planning Institute of Canada and the author. This article has been extensively edited for this volume.

4. positive steps such as erosion control, flood control, preservation of vegetation covering, and so on;
5. establishment and maintenance of a so-called "partial ecological balance" or at least a "natural state" within the areas;
6. "intensity" or "use density" of the various uses to be permitted.

As an experimental research area for studying the questions on the "ground," the outer areas of a fifty-mile radius from Toronto were selected. The existing and potential recreation areas in this belt were examined, excluding city parks, high-density-use recreation areas, sports fields, and other specific recreation uses. Outdoor recreational areas of fifty acres and above in extent with at least partly natural settings and mixed active and passive uses were identified for research purposes. . . .

A necessary first step was to obtain an overall picture of the present situation in the fifty-mile radius belt, including the more-or-less accepted proposals of the different authorities. Unfortunately no such compilation was available in comprehensive form, so a map had to be made showing all those categories which have any outdoor recreational significance, such as provincial parks, "conservation areas," larger private and municipal parks, hunting and fishing preserves, and so on.

The data of the map and inventory were compared with the existing and expected 1980 population. Without going into details, what is really interesting for us is the overall picture: how the existing recreation areas relate to the users and what the picture will be in, say, 1980, adding proposed (and more-or-less accepted) future recreation areas, and relating to the projected 1980 population. . . .

To identify or criticize whether [recreational area] is quantitatively adequate was felt to be outside the scope of the research. We omitted it because to determine the measure of adequacy is a question of the standards we apply. These standards are rather arbitrarily determined on assumed bases which include consideration of existing habits and trends in the kind of recreational uses. In other words, they are determined in a cultural, economic, and legislative-administrative context, as well as by ecological considerations. To analyze the standards from all of these different points of view would lead us far from our present task.

Also we feel that—admitting the importance of the quantitative side—the focus should be shifted to the qualitative aspects.

There is a new trend that emphasizes these aspects, such as:

1. the differentiation of their suitability for different recreational uses;
2. esthetic, historic, scientific value of the land;
3. physical and ecological aspects of the outdoor recreation areas.

This research concentrated on these qualitative aspects, with particular emphasis on the last one.

In a selected natural setting the following aspects can be considered relevant from physical and ecological points of view:

1. size
2. physiography, soil, geology
3. water
4. vegetation covering
5. animal life
6. management, maintenance practices, recreational demand sought by the public, and so on, insofar as they are connected with points 1 to 5.

THE "PROPER SIZE" OF RECREATION AREAS

. . . It appears reasonable to approach the physical and ecological consequences of the size by attempting to establish either a minimum or an optimum size. The minimum size would be an area where a more-or-less complex biological community, characteristic of the original setting, can be preserved; and optimally where this community can be preserved in a "balanced" or "self-maintaining" state. Unfortunately, the term ecological "balance" may be only vaguely defined and does not answer the question of whether there should be a "balanced" state at all; the concept cannot be used at the present time as a precise basis to determine size. . . .

So our attitude should be: many differently sized areas have to be accepted for practical reasons, and the ecological considerations should be adjusted to the actual size. This implies a very far-going compromise. But to create a possibility for this compromise, "ecological balance," or rather "natural state," is one of the goals of the research.

Of course, even if we accept, in principle at least, that all sizes are acceptable, there are important items to consider.

Certain 40- to 120-acre lands needed for facilities and so on are not easily reducible, which means that in a less than 400-acre area the remaining "natural" part becomes so small that it is nearly impossible to maintain as "natural." The relative length of boundary with adjacent areas becomes proportionately so great that it is increasingly difficult to protect the land from outside threats.

With smaller than 400- to 600-acre areas it would seem better policy to change the character rather than force compliance with a general pattern of providing these areas with all the conventional outdoor recreation facilities in a reduced space. . . .

VEGETATION COVERING IN RECREATION AREAS

Usually the most conspicuous feature of an outdoor recreation area is its vegetation. . . . The vegetation covering of an existing or prospective recreation area can be examined from the following aspects:

1. general character as it stands;
2. the interest, or "demand," of the visiting public and its relation or effect to certain recreational uses—wildlife, fishing, hiking, and so on;

3. management practices: possibility of manipulation; policy of management.

The first two can be seen together, or the first can be examined from the point of view of the second.

In a passive-type outdoor recreation area the public is looking for a varied, scenic vegetation which gives a natural appearance. The aim is to be "with nature" or to have the illusion of being with nature.

Varied vegetation implies variation in coverage. Open areas vary with patches of dense forest, scattered trees and bushes, some water-edge vegetation, and so on. Also the differences in age and size of the trees can add to the variation and the scenic value. This variety of coverage actually exists in many of our areas; the problem is one of preservation rather than of conscious manipulation.

The case is different where previously cleared, farmed land is to be integrated into a recreation area.

Variety in floral composition also adds to the variety of appearance and general scenic value. The following criteria and general management policies can be formulated in this respect:

1. preservation of the flora found on the establishment of the recreation area in whatever serial stages they are, with a minimum apparent sign of manipulation;
2. specific consideration of plants with value as food for wildlife or other unique importance for the whole ecology of the area;
3. preferably, avoidance of the introduction of too many exotic species;
4. specific consideration (or exception in the above consideration) of strongly diseased or susceptible trees (elm and so on) and some water vegetation.

MANAGEMENT PRACTICES AND VEGETATION

There are different views as to the extent to which the natural vegetation should be manipulated within a recreation area.

Extreme "noninterference" can be a workable policy in certain types of recreational parks with an expressed intention of preserving a piece of undisturbed biotic community, although noninterference is an ideal rather than an achievable reality. Some compromise has to be made when human access is allowed.

In other kinds of recreational areas the degree of manipulation of the vegetation varies with the type and intensity of use.

Generally speaking, management practices regarding interference with the natural state or development of plant cover are less conspicuous in large passive types of recreation lands. On the other hand it can be rather artificial in some "high-density" city parks. Some observations connected with the management practices in existing recreation areas would be germane:

The predominantly natural vegetation is interspersed with manipulated, "trimmed" sections providing picnic areas, playgrounds, and so on for the public. Though it is sometimes strongly criticized it is a necessity, and a certain degree of artificiality in appearance is unavoidable. One of the most conspicuous interferences is the establishment of lawn or grass covering with its corresponding permanent mowing. Unfortunately the public is inclined to forget that without this mowing the same area would be covered by aster, solidago, and so on—"weed" jungle—in only a few years. For these areas the interference is a necessity, the only consideration being how far it should go.

Besides mowing, the use of herbicides can be questioned. This objection is sometimes justified: it depends on the kind of herbicide. Their use may have far-reaching consequences which are sometimes not fully understood. This would suggest a policy of avoiding their use as much as possible.

Another problem is the question of what to do about diseased trees and plants, parasites and plants that are harmful or not desirable from a recreational point of view. It is a subtle question, depending for an answer on how we define our goal. The standard treatments (for example, DDT for elm diseases) can save the tree but at a certain expense to the whole biotic community. To define the desirability of their application is not as easy as in forestry practice. There is much to be said for the view that the removal of the diseased trees rather than the saving of them by chemicals is, in most cases, the proper policy to pursue.

The removal of fallen or dead trees and branches is strongly objected to by those interested in animal life. They are important elements of the habitat. The distribution and density of certain animals is strongly affected by this seemingly simple operation of keeping the area "neat."

On the other hand, barren branches extending out of green healthy vegetation can disturb the esthetic and scenic value of the area, especially in a conspicuous spot. A proper compromise could be to remove the dead trees or branches in exposed places (picnic areas, edges of open meadow) but to leave the fallen trees where they are in other places with some exceptions for nature trails and highly used areas or areas adjacent to pools and streams.

Probably the most important plant management problem is how to establish or reestablish a "proper" covering in previously cleared or other barren areas such as graded or eroded banks. There are many areas of this kind and some are quite extensive. They arise from previous agricultural use or for other reasons.

Some considerations and guidance for correcting or reestablishing vegetation covering are:

1. similarity or harmony with the original vegetation, "natural" appearance;
2. fast-growing, undemanding components;
3. variety, coverage, floral composition, "skyline";
4. food plants for animal life;
5. scenic value;
6. in some cases, erosion prevention;
7. specific questions of water and water-edge vegetation;
8. and—where it exists—preservation and accentuation of the natural historical interest of some feature.

We do not have too much experience with this kind of planting. Foresters, landscape architects, recreation area planners can jointly work out some measures. These measures should fit the specific conditions of the area. On the other hand, if worked out individually, in all cases there will not be a widely applicable measure. The ideal solution would be to work out a few general patterns; and the choice, with perhaps some modification, would be left to the expert applying them in a specific recreation area. No such general patterns or measures were found in the literature presently available. There are such well-proved forestry patterns as erosion protection, wildlife cover, landscape architectural patterns, and so on, but none filling all the above requirements has been yet developed. Perhaps many of the forestry patterns should be integrated in recreation areas.

Some suggestions can be offered for achieving this integration:

1. A "natural landscape plan" should be worked out beforehand.
2. To achieve the above plan, more expensive methods and material can be justified, such as: (a) use of trees or bushes of more advanced age at transplanting and (b) application of soil cultivation, fertilizer, irrigation, or other cultivation practices of kinds normally never used in typical extensive forestry practice because of much higher initial costs. The application of other cultivation methods would accelerate the growth rate of trees.

ANIMAL LIFE IN RECREATION AREAS

The questions connected with animal life in the existing parks can be discussed from the following aspects:

1. faunal (species) composition;
2. their permanency in the area (permanent, transient, migratory, etc.);
3. their ecological role, density, fluctuation, and so on;
4. habitat and other factors affecting their existence, natural and man-made;
5. desirable policy of management (to encourage, discourage, their increase or presence, and with what measures);
6. game animals.

The composition of "species present" is the easiest and most frequently found "check list" in the published conservation studies. This check list sometimes also briefly refers to permanency or migratory habits and so on. We never know how reliable these lists are. Are they really checked or is this just a list of animals that "should" be there?

The "check lists" give an interesting but limited picture of animal life. We are equally, or even more, interested in their relative density, there role in the biotic community, and so on. Also very interesting, for the same reason, is the role of some prominent insects or other "lower" animals.

The ecological role, density, and fluctuation of numbers of different animals in our parks are to be viewed for our present purpose as an animal ecologist sees them but modified with some comments on the recreational aspects. In other words, the park can be viewed as a piece of undisturbed nature—actually this is what the visitor seeks—or, if disturbed, the degree and direction of disturbance may be acknowledged. Some of these disturbances are unavoidable for the maintenance of our parks but fortunately can be managed in a way that does not appear "disturbed" or "unnatural."

The most important representatives of animal life in the parks are the "small" animals. They are present in the greatest numbers and it is easy to interfere with their density, at least with small mammals, but to a less degree with birds.

There is very strong interest in the larger animals—the deer—on the part of visitors. Unfortunately they are, in many cases, transient.

The role of the nature trail is partly to give an opportunity for animal watching. The opportunity for the visitor to watch animals is much less than their actual frequency or density would suggest. Only diurnal animals can be observed by the average visitor; and, as many of the mammals are nocturnal, the impression is that there are fewer animals in parks than there actually are.

Another reason why the users of nature trails are disappointed in their contact with animals is the behavior of those users who are less interested. On the other hand the animals are surprisingly quick in adapting to the presence of man. It is questionable, however, whether in small parks this "taming" of animals should be encouraged. As a result, nonterritorial species or species of wide range, such as deer, become easy victims of hunters in lands outside the parks. With properly regulated use, the nature trails are also the best places to give opportunity for bird watching.

The factors affecting the population density of different animals inside the parks are similar to those outside the parks. Some of these factors are:

1. use of chemicides within the parks;
2. danger of irruptions in the case of certain species;
3. prohibition of hunting;
4. effect of adjacent lands;
5. effects connected with management practices and recreational use.

The danger of population irruptions of certain animals always increases in an area highly protected from external interference where the usual regulating factors are disturbed and the area is limited.

Considering the complex, interdependent, and mutually regulating character of biological communities, what is actually more interesting, from an ecological point of view, than the few observed irruption cases is the lack of these irruptions.

There is some increase in deer population but nowhere similar to that in some larger parks in the United States. Only in a few exceptional cases has damage caused by deer to foliage been observed.

1. The intensive temporary use of parks (weekend use) apparently does very little damage to habitat. No evidences of adverse effects were 'observed.
2. The food sources of the habitat are scarcely used up in any trophic level in the southern Ontario parks (as compared to some cases in the U.S. parks). The observations show just the opposite.
3. One very efficient habitat manipulation observed in many parks was the synchronizing of hay or other plant cutting in open areas with the breeding and nesting time of certain mammals and birds.

Other observations of park personnel and ourselves pertaining to factors affecting animal life within parks were collected. Most of them point to direct threats to animal life. Some of these are:

1. farm practices in adjacent areas;
2. boys with an inclination to disturb birds or, as "conservationists," just collecting birds' eggs, and so on;
3. stray cats, especially where the land is immediately adjacent to residential areas;
4. stray dogs, mostly in remote areas not adjacent to residential areas;
5. highways with considerable traffic adjacent to outdoor recreation areas;
6. hunting in adjacent areas;
7. vandalism, frequently mentioned by park personnel.

WATER

Every recreation survey emphasizes the importance of water. It was found that in most U.S. and Canadian parks some form of water proved to be the most critical single factor used or enjoyed by 70 to 80 percent of park visitors.

To provide water in a recreation area implies many requirements about its physical, chemical, and biological conditions.

The following aspects can be examined:

1. "forms" of water for recreation areas (flowing water, ponds, reservoirs, and so on);
2. quantity of water;
3. quality of water for different recreational uses such as swimming, fishing, boating, and wildlife habitat;
4. pollution (though it is a "quality" question, for practical purposes it has to be dealt with separately);
5. compatibility of the above uses;
6. manipulation, regulation, and so on for the above purposes.

"Forms" of Water for Recreation

... Of the different categories the following aspects have recreational significance:

1. The quantity and seasonal distribution of water flow. In the case of lake water tables: permanency and other seasonal changes.
2. Quality of water. Chemical and biological characteristics from a recreational point of view. Question of temperature.
3. Characteristic shore or bottom features, not directly water characteristics but relevant for the potential recreational use of the water itself.

These quality and quantity aspects can be discussed only in the broadest outline, characterizing mostly the differences among the different "forms" of water.

The *rivers* emptying their water into the Great Lakes are relatively short water courses with small to medium flow.

Although all have some potential recreational value they differ greatly according to:

1. seasonal and minimum water flow;
2. temperature of water;
3. chemical and biological properties of water;
4. degree and kind of pollution affecting the above properties.

The Lakes (Other than the Great Lakes)

There is hardly any other great city on the North American continent better endowed with lakes than is Toronto. Not only lakes but all kinds of lakes, of every imaginable size and quality, are available within a 100-mile radius of Toronto, and all have some kind of recreational relevance.

An evaluation of them for recreational use implies a review from two approaches: from the point of view of what is appropriate for both the lakes themselves and the users of the lakes.

The user side, here, means the subjective evaluation of preferences, biases, what body of water should be, and so on. These preferences and biases can be dealt with when evaluating the different lakes.

What kinds of lakes are there in southern Ontario, and how can they be evaluated for recreation?

The ecologist makes a convenient distinction between "oligotrophic" (poor in life) and "eutrophic" (rich in life) lakes. This categorization explains many things, but needs amplification.

1. The oligotrophic lakes are mostly outside our 50-mile radius but their recreational value is so important that they cannot be neglected here. These are the typical lakes of the Shield. Their characteristics are: transparently clear, cold, deep water, generally poor in nutrients and life. Their further characteristics and dynamisms are thoroughly described by pertinent literature. Nearly all of their main characteristics have recreational relevance, such as:
   a. Their real and apparent clearness appeals to those swimmers who are enthusiasts of the "crystal clear" waters.

b. Temperature affects their value for swimming in a negative way (being usually cold, warming up late in the season, and localization of warming to shallow bays, and so on).
c. Their characteristics do not affect boating practices but do have some effect on water skiing (as for swimming).
d. The natural low productivity of the water adversely affects fishing. (Although some favorite sport fish species such as trout and small-mouthed bass thrive well in these waters, their numbers per acre of surface water are necessarily low.)

2. The lakes within the 50-mile radius mostly belong to the eutrophic group. Their assets or disadvantages are roughly the opposites of the "oligotrophic" category. Swimmers frequently criticize their apparently "unclear" water (opaque because of microscopic algae or other organisms); fishermen object to their excess of coarse fish; and boaters dislike their frequent shallowness and dense water vegetation. On the other hand, the water is warmer, warms up earlier in the season, and potentially can maintain a much higher fish population.

Great Lakes

There is extensive literature on the Great Lakes which deals not only with general lymnological, ecological, and physical aspects but also their recreational value. The last mentioned has become especially prominent in recent years due to new attention directed toward them as a source of great, barely tapped, recreational potential.

Here are only a few general comments to be made:

1. They show great differences not only in their general characteristics but also in their recreational value. Temperature, degree of pollution, productivity, shore features, and so on make Lake Ontario, Lake Erie, and Georgian Bay quite different for recreation.
2. There are great differences of opinion about their recreational value. These range from the highest enthusiasm to the most pessimistic view, expressed by authors of different papers.
3. There is an unquestionable trend toward a continuing deterioration of recreational value of waters, mostly in Lake Erie and near great population centers in other lakes; for example, Lake Ontario around Toronto.
4. The most prominent recreational problems are temperature and pollution.

The whole "deterioration" problem of the Great Lakes is one of the main concerns of the surrounding areas. In spite of the tremendous efforts of different institutions, commissions, and government agencies, there seems to be an irresistible trend toward decline. One cannot even say that the problems are not thoroughly studied (sufficient evidence may be assembled through reference to the extensive literature: *Lymnological Survey of Lake Erie*, technical reports of other authorities, and so on). But even where the processes are rather well understood it is difficult to improve them, all the more difficult because the "use pressure" on these waters will rapidly increase in the next few decades. On the other hand, with proper technology the harmful effects can be greatly reduced. The relatively satisfactory situation in the Ruhr Valley waters shows what can be achieved—if we really make the effort.

Reservoirs

We previously pointed out how well endowed the Toronto area is with lakes. Knowing this, it sounds curious that so many reservoirs are planned partly or mostly for recreational purposes. Quite a few reservoirs of considerable size are planned within the 50-mile radius. They are flood control reservoirs, with about equal emphasis on recreation. Many are double reservoirs, the upper one acting as a regulator for the lower one. They are not—at least the lower ones—draw-down reservoirs; the levels are kept adequately high even in the late summer when other reservoirs are usually at their lowest.

On examination of the visitor statistics and their trends, there can be little question that these reservoirs are needed and will be well patronized. They are also flood control reservoirs, but their multiple use aspects are not discussed here.

From a recreation point of view a reservoir has many advantages:

1. The quality of water can be manipulated.
2. The temperature also can be well manipulated.
3. In the case of a non-draw-down reservoir the shoreline is more or less stabilized and can be developed for recreational purposes.
4. The whole biota can be manipulated.

The most important possibility for manipulation is connected with sport fishing. By a small change of water level the whole species composition can be affected.

The Quality of Water; Swimming Requirements

The ideal "swimming water" is clear, has equable pleasant temperature, is the proper size, and has comfortable bottom and shore conditions. These requirements can be found only in an artificial swimming pool. Many of these qualities, such as clear, sterile water, are not compatible with other recreational uses. Consequently swimming water is always a compromise, defined by minimum requirements rather than absolute criteria. These minimum requirements are mostly connected with health hazards to the user. Unfortunately there does not exist an overall well-defined set of standard criteria. Most authorities, municipalities, and health departments follow different "standards." Water is generally considered unsuitable for swimming if the count of coliforms is in excess of 2,400/100 ml or if any coliform samples show raw sewage discharge in the water and five-day BOD does not exceed 4 ppm.

This is a somewhat meager and debatable standard. "Coliform" refers only to the form of the organism, and does not necessarily imply pathogenic qualities. Even less a count than 2,400 coliforms/100 ml may contain virulent pathogenic organisms. There is no escape, as all natural water contains coliform bacteria and can be used without much health risk. Other criteria of such publications as the "Objectives of Water Quality Control" are rather imprecise and undefined. It puts only in general terms what should not be present in the water such as "highly toxic wastes" or "deoxigenating wastes" (whatever they are). Exceptions are "phenolic type wastes," where exact criteria are given by not exceeding an average phenol content of 2 ppb and a maximum of 5 ppb.

There is usually no consideration of the condition of the bottom (broken glass, metal sheets, and so on) or speed of current and other health hazards except sometimes around dams.

Possible proposals are:

1. More uniform standard requirements should be worked out and generally accepted.
2. The artificial swimming areas should be handled independently from the natural ones, applying a much stricter system of standards.
3. Other criteria and "minimum requirements" should be applied also in addition to the coliform bacteria count made by the authorities.

Requirements for Boating

The quality of the water itself is less important for boating considerations. The boater's interest connected with water is rather (1) the size of the body of water, (2) certain bottom features (rock reaching the surface, and so on), (3) water vegetation conditions, (4) interference with other users, and (5) existence of certain features necessary for the use of boats. These requirements are of a higher order in the case of powered boats than hand-propelled boats.

The basic problem with boating, with particular emphasis to power boating, is the question of its compatibility with other recreational uses. Boating is a space-demanding use. Its claim for water, where the area of water is limited, can interfere seriously with other users. This and many other aspects of boating, especially motor boating, make the recreation area planner less concerned with providing the needed space than with protecting other users from interference caused by boats; more correctly, with establishing a fair equilibrium between the different demands.

All observations would seem to justify the adoption of policies for the different types of boating in recreational water to be held to well-defined *zones.* This means that high-density uses of water such as swimming must be given preference, and boating should be confined to areas where it interferes less with these uses. In some cases where water sources are limited, power boats can be excluded altogether.

Sport Fishing and Ecological Criteria of Water Used for Sport

According to statistics, approximately 17 to 22 percent of recreation area users are fishermen.

But there are different kinds of fishing. Their physical and ecological requirements also differ widely.

To provide and maintain this habitat we have to know our goals. There are also many prejudices, preferences, and so on involved. The so-called "quality" fishing, "coarse fish," and similar notions already express something of this prejudice. To make it more complicated, these prejudices and preferences are most strongly held by those who manage and direct sport-fishing activities.

To choose the right habitat or to manipulate the available ones to provide the most satisfying sport fishing, outdoor recreation area planning has to consider:

1. the water quantity, quality, and temperature requirements of fishing intended to be established in the area and its relation to the available water;
2. the bottom, shore, and other physiographic features of the water course or lake bed;
3. the manipulability of the water;
4. access to the water;
5. compatibility of other uses, including other recreational uses, using the same source of water.

It is extremely difficult to define "water quality requirements" for sport fishing generally. We know a lot about the specific requirements of different sport fish, especially about some of the preferred ones such as trout. A logical approach would be to provide these conditions and assume that everything will be all right. Unfortunately the problem is much more complicated. What can be done with great effort and expense is not always the most desirable. Certain changes and trends are going on irresistibly as consequences of intensive use of the environment. To reverse them is getting more and more difficult and eventually will be practically impossible.

These changes in the fish habitat are not only due to pollution but also to many other factors which we cannot reverse. The best policy would be to recognize this and reckon with them. They probably create a constellation of conditions where different policies can be accepted, such as

1. circumstances where the improvement of conditions for certain desirable fisheries are feasible and will be the right policy;
2. other situations where there should be strong efforts made to improve or reclaim conditions to a certain degree but at the same time to adjust sport fishery to a changed environment;
3. where the main concern is to adjust the fishery to the changed conditions and make the best of them.

At the present time point (1) is the general attitude. This is right so far as it is aimed at improving existing waters, fighting against pollution, and so on, where there are reasonable hopes of achieving these goals.

The first attitude is perfectly well justified in many cases, such as middle and upper sections of streams, recreating or preserving the habitat for cold water fish, fighting pollution, and so on. In many cases proper management of these waters needs only stricter implementation of existing legislation or some very inexpensive improvements, and proper measures to control the use of these waters....

It is, of course, outside the scope of the study to try and debate technical questions. These are the fields of lymnology, fish management, and so on, a well-worked-out area (although never adequately) and well known by the responsible authorities.

The water requirements differ according to the species of fish and are connected with the quality, quantity, oxygen content, and temperature of the water. In spite of some uncertainty, some generalizations can be risked:

Temperature. The requirements are very different. Some fish tolerate a wide range (so called eurythermal); others, only a narrow (stenothermal) range. In the case of sport fishing this is a problem only in the colder side, in other words, fish such as the so-called Salamonid group. An important indirect effect of the temperature is that it is connected with the amount of dissolved oxygen.

Another aspect is the temperature requirement for spawning. This can be used in reservoir water level manipulation to influence the fish species composition. For example, pike spawn when the temperature reaches 10° C; perch, 12° C; carp, above 18° C.

What are the criteria relating to water quality requirements of water organisms, primarily for sport fish? It sounds incredible that after concentrated and substantial pertinent literature one cannot give a definite numerical figure about these requirements. Even more discouraging is the summing up of the situation by one of the most authentic experts, Clarence M. Tarzwell, in 1962 in the publication "Development of Water Quality Criteria for Aquatic Life." Although he himself risked giving some criteria in 1956 he later appeared to be less sure, emphasizing rather the uncertainties of their selection. He states: "There is a need to know more about the maximum concentrations of dissolved toxicants and the minimum concentrations of dissolved oxygen that fish and other aquatic organisms can withstand for short periods and to what level water temperature may be raised for short or extended periods without adversely affecting aquatic life."

A very generalized set of criteria can be suggested in the following form:

Oxygen content. Dissolved oxygen should not be less than 5 ppm. Some warm water fish tolerate even 2 ppm for a considerable period of time. An overall level of 5 ppm can be suggested as a minimum.

Carbon Dioxide. In lakes, reservoirs, and other more-or-less standing waters the free CO_2 concentration can be toxic and at least temporarily harmful for certain organisms. The tolerance here again varies with the species. Generally 5 cc/l can be considered as maximum. Other sources give 3 cc/l as the higher limit.

Ammonia. The decomposing organic matter—the main source of nitrogen compounds or, rather, the recirculation of nitrogen—contains a considerable amount of ammonium compounds. One of these ammonium compounds, ammonium carbonate, has a relatively high toxicity to many aquatic animals. In natural circumstances in unpolluted water, the ammonium carbonate is well below the toxic level.

Suspended solids. The two main sources of the most frequent inorganic suspended materials are erosion and effluents from earthworks and other industrial enterprises. The latter appear to be a growing danger which can—and actually does—destroy aquatic life on considerable sections of water courses.

Consequences of Pollution for Recreational Uses of Water

The general term *polluted water* covers a wide range of quality conditions, according to the causes of the pollution, the so-called pollutants. Their effect on aquatic life is also widely different.

Possible categorization by origin of the wastes can show the direction of necessary measures. These may include the following:

1. domestic sewage;
2. industrial wastes, chemicals;
3. industrial wastes, suspended inorganic material;
4. hot water from power plants, boilers, or other sources;
5. washed-in chemicides from adjacent agricultural use;
6. chemicides used in the water for mosquito control;
7. oil products from motorboats;
8. washed-in toxic materials from dumped wastes along the water course. . . .

CONCLUSION

In this brief summary, we have tried to find the necessary physical and ecological criteria for the outdoor recreation area planner.

The planner's task in these fields is extremely complex and needs the contribution of specialists and special knowledge. This in itself is not new. Nearly all planning tasks are complex by their very nature. In this case the importance of biological sciences such as ecology came out with strong emphasis. The problem is that most of our planners are not too well prepared in this field. In many respects the best outdoor recreation area "planners" are at present some of the members of the pertinent authorities (Metropolitan Toronto Conservation Authority, Department of Lands and Forests, River Valley Authorities, and so on). This is "right" to a degree and not unexpected, but as recreation areas are becoming one of the most important land uses around metropolitan areas, their development and control cannot be separated in a vacuum from the overall planning view.

CHAPTER 6

Toward a Behavioral Interpretation of Recreational Engagements with Implications for Planning

B. L. Driver

S. Ross Tocher

This chapter by B. L. Driver and S. Ross Tocher assists the recreationist who wishes to embark on behavioral investigations in recreation by providing him with a most effective conceptual framework for his studies. Discussed are the importance and nature of considerations such as motivation, satisfaction, and need. Recreation is viewed as an "experience," and the nature of that experience is carefully examined.

The purpose of this paper is to present a conceptual framework within which the conventional activity approach to recreation planning is supplemented by a behavioral interpretation of recreation. Framework is used within the context of a logical and cohesive structure within which tests can be made to evaluate the phenomena of recreation. As with all concepts, the following are neither true nor false; they are only more or less useful.

RECREATION DEFINED

What is recreation, outdoor or indoor? This is a question not infrequently asked of recreation planners or by them.

Webster defines *recreation* as "a refreshment of strength and spirits after toil; diversion or a mode of diversion; play." Webster's definition is rather complete, intuitively acceptable, and semantically useful for purposes of communication. It includes the notions of nonwork activity, replenishment, change from the routine, pleasure, and all the other ingredients commonly attributed to recreation. But how useful is the definition to recreation planners? Obviously, it has general usefulness, but it offers few, if any, specific guidelines for planning and investment scheduling. What criteria does it provide for recommending action? Can we plan for pleasure or for the refreshment of spirits? If so, how do we project the demand? What "spirit-refreshing" facilities do we provide? It is difficult to imagine that agency budgets will include line items for such things as 500 units of play!

Perhaps the definitional problem is not as great as suggested. Private and

Reprinted from B. L. Driver, ed., *Elements of Outdoor Recreation Planning* (Ann Arbor, Mich.: University Microfilms, 1970), pp. 9–29, by permission of the University of Michigan and the authors.

public recreation agencies have established guidelines for action. Further, they have realistically and pragmatically interpreted their important individual responsibilities. Nevertheless, problems associated with defining recreation have helped cause recreation planners to view recreation as *participation in activities* which, seemingly, are recreational to the participant. Through this approach, fishing becomes recreation, swimming becomes recreation, exercising becomes recreation, and so on.

The activity approach has many advantages, such as the ease of identifying who participates in what activity, when, where, and for how long. However, it suffers disadvantages because it does not make explicit the need to consider other relevant questions: Why is the recreationist participating in the activity?[1] What other activities might have been selected if the opportunities had existed? What satisfactions or rewards are received from the activity? How can the quality of the experience be enhanced? In other words, the activity approach frequently assumes that supply defines preferences (and sometimes that supply will generate demand), but it does not question what latent.preferences are not being met. It causes recreation planners to focus on supply and give too little attention to demand, which is frequently appraised in terms of past consumption. In summary and somewhat contradictorily, the activity approach is rather passive. This is especially true when projections of demand (participation) are made based on past types and rates of participation.

Even though the activity approach has many practical advantages, is it the only way to conceive of recreation? Perhaps it would be useful to view recreation not as an activity but instead as a psycho-physiological experience measured in terms of recreational responses and/or a mode or process of responses. Under this behavioral approach, recreation will consist of more than participation in an activity.[2]

To develop the proposed behavioral approach, we will make and explain five postulates about recreation.[3] These non–mutually exclusive postulates are:

1. Recreation is an experience that results from recreational engagements.
2. Recreational engagements require a commitment by the recreationist.
3. Recreational engagements are self-rewarding: the engagement finds pleasure in and of itself, and recreation is the experience.
4. Recreational engagements require personal and free choice on the part of the recreationist.
5. Recreational engagements occur during nonobligated time.[4]

The first postulate states what recreation is. The remaining four serve as descriptors or criteria to differentiate recreational behavior from other forms of human behavior. For this differentiation, *all* of the last four descriptors must be applicable if the action or event (response) is to be considered recreational.

The postulates are arranged in a numerical order of increasing specificity. Number one is a rather generic descriptor with applications to a wider array of human behavior than is number five. The key words are nonobligated time, personal choice, and rewarding (not punishing) engagements. Notice the word *engagement*, rather than *activity*, is used to incorporate better the psychological dimensions. We might be mentally engaged, only.

At the risk of causing confusion we will point out that recreation stands in opposition to work if work is defined as occurring during obligated time and/or is not, in and of itself, (positively) rewarding. For many people, *work* (as commonly defined), is recreational. It is recreational if these people are not obligated to "work" and if the "work" is, in and of itself, rewarding.

Each of these descriptors will now be briefly expanded, explained, and related to recreation planning.

RECREATION IS AN EXPERIENCE

There are analytical and conceptual advantages in viewing recreation behaviorally. Psychologists define *behavior* as any observable action (response) of a person or thing (19). (See reference list.) Also, it is commonly accepted that most human behavior is goal directed or goal guided and that *a person's responses are instrumental in obtaining some goal object or need satisfaction.*[5] Thus, although we are not always aware of the goal objects being pursued, it is relatively safe to say that most of what we do is done in the pursuit of a goal object. These behavioral pursuits, which are observable as instrumental responses, are underlaid by motivations to obtain the goal object; that is, to consummate or to receive gratification for the need leading to the goal. We can now state that participation in recreational engagements (activities, if the reader prefers) are instrumental in experiencing recreation. Further, it is being postulated that humans are motivated to recreate, that there are psychological and physiological forces, motives, drives, etc., which cause the recreationists to pursue the recreational goal object(s) and to experience recreation. Implicitly, it is being suggested that motives to recreate can be identified. Let us expand the first descriptor and postulate that recreation is an experience that exists to *the extent to which* the needs or desires to recreate are gratified. It is the experience of attaining special recreational goal objects. The level of the experience is a function of the goal state of the recreationist—his condition or situation with respect to attaining the goal object.

Laing (13) explains the basic concept being developed in simple language:

> We see other people's behavior, but not their experience. . . .
>
> Experience is man's invisibility to man. . . . Experience as invisibility of man to man is at the same time more evident than anything. *Only* experience is evident. . . .
>
> If, however, experience is evidence, how can one ever study the experience *of the other?* For the experience *of the other* is not evident to me, or it is not and never can be an experience of mine. . . .
>
> . . . I wish to define a person in a twofold way; in terms of experience, as a center or orientation of the objective universe; and in terms of behavior as the origins of action. Personal experience transforms a given field into a field of intention and action; only through action can our experience be transformed. . . .
>
> People may be observed to sleep, eat, walk, talk, etc., in relatively

> predictable ways. We must not be content with observation *of this kind alone.* Observation of behavior must be extended by inference to attributions about experience. . . .
>
> In a science of persons, I shall state as axiomatic that: behavior is a function of experience, and both experience and behavior are always in relation to *someone or something other than self.*

Records of participation in recreational activities are simply recorded observations of behavior. But, "We must not be content with observations of this kind alone. Observations of behavior must be extended by inference to attributions about experience. . . ." Actually, we need inferences about recreational experiences supported by data.

Before we attempt to identify some specific motivations to recreate, we will raise a few basic questions: From where do these motivations to recreate come? How do they arise, and why do they take the directions they do? These are difficult questions to which an oversimplified answer will be given. They come primarily from learning based on past experience. To elaborate, the two basic sources of human behavior are instinct and learning. Instinctive behavior stems from inherited characteristics that cause us to perform, respond, or act in a certain manner. Learning, the second source of behavior, is defined as a *relatively permanent change* in behavior that is the *result of past experience or practice of the individual* (19). It is now commonly accepted that most human behavior is learned behavior. Even those behavioral patterns which are generally considered to be underlaid by instinct, such as sexual drives or motivations to eat (prompted by hunger pains), are overshadowed by man's sophistication in learning. Taboos on sexual behavior, eating for self-love or for the demonstration of affluence, and the scheduling of meals at a convenient time are examples. That learning and skill development are important aspects of recreational behavior is conventional recreation wisdom. Changes in tastes and preferences for different recreational engagements must be explained by learning. It is also important in the following discussion of specific motivations to recreate.

Motivations to Recreate

To begin this discussion of specific motivations to recreate, imagine that recreation occupies a bipolar behavioral continuum with needs to escape temporarily or to disengage passively situated at one pole and motivations to engage actively listed at the other pole. Further, imagine that the extent to which either of the polar goal states is realized is measured in terms of the types and amount of information received externally or generated internally during the recreational experience. Information is used here as a measure of the ability of an individual to make decisions and to discriminate meaningfully among different values, with these additional degrees of freedom being gained either from the external (sensory) stimuli received or the internal inferential and reflective cognitive processes enacted during the engagement.

The motivation to escape—to disengage, re-engage, or engage randomly—would then underlie the *re*creational aspects of recreation. Rather loosely, it can be said that such motivations constitute drives or priming forces which "push" the recreationist from a rather structured (nonrandom) life space he wishes to avoid *temporarily* into a recreational life space in which he anticipates he can *re*plenish his adaptive energies. For example, he might be escaping an information overload situation and desire a change in stimuli (information) orientation solely for restorative purposes. At the other pole, the motivations to engage actively would underlie the creative aspects of re*creation.* More positive or "pulling" forces attract the recreationist to learn and gain *new* information rather than to escape to change his external informational environments.

The notion of informational environments being both external and internal to the person was presented to point out that the information received must somehow be processed. This processing, at least in part, requires that the new information be related to information that has been received during prior perceptual (learning) activity. This associative process is an ongoing cognitive activity of information categorization and storage (5). These associations help us to develop our mental images (representations or maps of ourselves and our external world). The representations are not dependent on just the environmentally monitored data our perceptors feed to our brain. They are formed and changed in a complex, not well-understood, and interactive process of reception, association, classification, categorization, reflection, and prediction. Thus, the internal environment is important, and each recreationist will process and appraise the information from his engagement according to his individual cognitive style and for his own purposes.

The above bipolar conceptualization is perhaps useful. However, it is too simplistic and provides limited knowledge for functional planning. Let us develop a slightly different conceptualization of human behavior, so we can leave the bipolar scheme and view recreation as a response to a multitude of motivating forces which may exist independently or in some combination simultaneously. To do this we will use Gutman's (10) and Maslow's (16) hierarchies of human behavioral responses.

Gutman differentiated human responses into six classes defined by the complexity of the behavior. The classes, which are not mutually exclusive, are:

1. vegetative
2. reflexive
3. conditioned
4. learned
5. problem solving
6. creative.

Vegetative behavior refers to basic physiological behavior, such as the intake of food and excretion of wastes. Reflexive behavior is a relatively rapid and consistent unlearned response to a stimulus, ordinarily not conscious or subject to voluntary control, lasting only so long as the stimulus is present. An example would be the doctor's tap of a hammer on the knee and the well-known response. A conditioned response is produced by a conditioned stimulus after learning. The best example is Pavlov's dog, which salivates with no food present when hearing a bell (the conditioned stimulus) if the bell has previously been paired with the presentation of food for some period of time. Learned behavior is as defined before. In addition to conditioned learning, it would include instrumental and perceptual learning. Problem solving is an even more complex type of learned behavior. It occurs when a situation exists which constitutes an obstacle to need gratification and requires cognitive processes of the individual to arrive at a solution. According to Gutman, creative behavior is the most complex form of human behavior. He defines it as any activity by which man imposes a *new order* upon his environment, frequently his mental environment. It is an organizing activity. More specifically, it is the original act by which that new order or organization is first *conceived* and given expression.

Gutman's schema complements Maslow's hierarchy of man's "lower-to-higher" needs. Maslow's listing includes physiological needs, safety needs, "belongingness" and love needs, esteem needs, and the need for self-actualization. Maslow argues that as the lower needs are satisified, we seek gratification of the next higher need in the hierarchy.

Gutman's and Maslow's ideas are useful in developing a behavioral interpretation of recreation. Both make explicit the multidimensional aspects of behavior. Maslow's conceptualization helps explain increasing demands for luxury items and recreational experiences in an economy that is quite rapidly removing constraints on gratification of lower level needs. Both hierarchies, along with judgment, permit us to postulate that in recreational pursuits, we find interesting opportunities to engage in the most complex and "highest" forms of human behavior—learning, problem solving, creativity, and self-actualization.[6] Especially relevant to recreation planning is the possibility that these types of behavior might be useful in defining functions of such planning. To follow this thought, let us leave our bipolar continuum, add to our list of motivations to recreate, relate these motivations to different types of behavior, and make inferences about how recreation planning can either help constrain or facilitate the realization of the goal objects toward which the motivations lead.

What are some other possible (and at this stage of theory development, speculative) motivations to recreate? Desires that one's children may experience certain recreational and/or learning situations can be considered a motivation. Parents and others, such as close friends, may feel motivated to recreate to share those experiences with loved ones. Or people may recreate to *affiliate* themselves with a group. The motivation in this case could be to maintain a social identity or a source of esteem.

Skill development would appear to be another important motivation to recreate. For such engagements, the amount of satisfaction (however scaled) of the recreationist should be positively correlated with the extent to which he felt he was able to apply or develop the relevant skill(s). Such satisfaction can possibly be interpreted in terms of *needs to achieve*, which appear to be important human needs (18).

The *pursuit of status*, especially the collection of status symbols (such as trophies, rocks, or even photographs), seem to motivate many people into engagements which they find recreational.

Research in psychology suggests that individuals are motivated to recreate in order to satisfy *exploratory needs*, which would contain elements of problem solving (2). Or the exploratory behavior may primarily serve a *creative function*, the rewards of which are the realization that we have established a new order in our environment.

Is the conceptualization thus far relevant to recreation planning? It should be for several reasons. Much is read in our literature about the need to provide a wide array of real opportunities for personal choice. Hopefully, the conceptualization contributes to a better understanding of why different opportunities are pursued and why the array is important. Possibly more relevant is the insight provided about the relationships between motivations, opportunities for engagement, and drive consummation, or need gratification. To illustrate, opportunities to escape, to explore, or to collect status symbols—all imply environmental arrangements which differ one from the other. Or the opportunities to gain status might differ from those to create. For example, does not Old Faithful Inn in Yellowstone Park primarily, but not totally, serve the function of providing opportunities to gain status? To be sure, it is an architectural curiosity and has many historical values. But the question still remains, Should scarce funds be allocated through public recreation agencies for the attainment of status in a unique area if other opportunities, possibly of higher value, are foregone in the process? The problem is one of determining and ranking the mix of opportunities to be provided.

Several other comments relevant to recreation planning can now be made. First, much behavior is related to the simultaneous pursuit of several goal objects. These may be complementary and mutually supportive, or competitive and conflict introducing. Thus, we can find learning (a possible goal object) and recreation happening together and frequently impossible to differentiate. Or we can find the recreationist, especially the tourist, rushing as he recreates.

The planner should recommend the enhancement of opportunities for supplemental or complementary engagements, such as the provision of interpretative and other informational facilities. He should aim to help reduce points of conflict, such as recommending the provision of certain services (lodging, food, etc.). The mix will vary for different types of engagements (i.e., for different motivations to recreate and for different recreational goal objects being pursued). Second, it might be useful for the recreation planner to view different classes of uses as having different "goal packages." The goal packages of an elderly person could differ significantly from those of a teenager.

The Recreation Experience Continuum

It was stated that the recreational planner has impact on recreational experiences through his influence on the provision of opportunities to pursue recreational goal objects. But he can also affect the experiences in other ways. To elaborate this statement, let us view the recreationist as receiving value (utility) from the experience—from goal object attainment. The magnitude of this utility is determined by several interacting factors. The most important ones are the antecedent conditions, which give rise to and determine the strength(s) of the need(s) to recreate; the attractiveness of the goal object(s); and the nature and consequences of the intervening variables which the recreationist encounters during his pursuit of the goal object.

To make more explicit how the recreation planner can effect these values, let us elaborate these sources in tabular form. See figure 6-1.

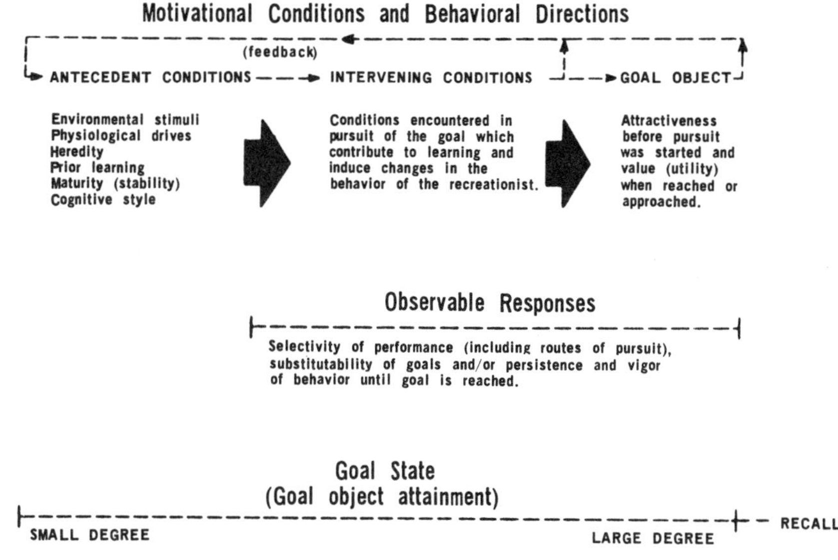

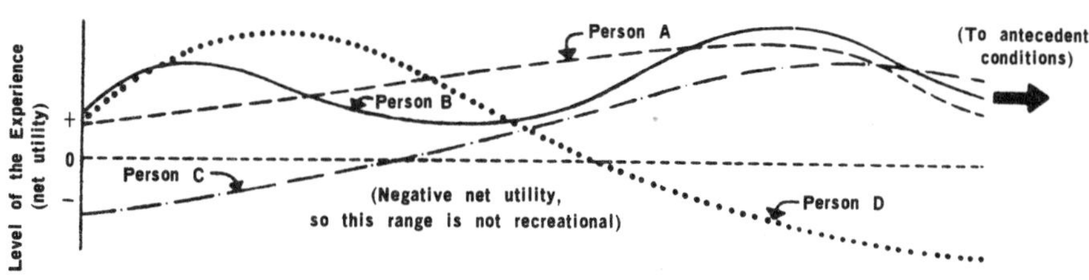

FIGURE 6-1. *Schematic Presentation of Recreation Behavior*

The antecedent conditions are those which give rise to motivations to recreate. They are not mutually exclusive and can be considered as priming forces which lead to pursuits of the goal objects. Environmental stimuli are the conditions or things to which an individual is exposed (e.g., to which he is sensitive) in his ordinary life space(s). These stimuli are varied and would include among others those measured by variables like density, environmental pollutants, pressures of the job, ethnic "place," and status incongruity. Physiological drives are self-explanatory and refer to such conditions as the need for exercise. They can find their source either in heredity or learning. Hereditary factors also are self-explanatory and refer to conditions, such as differences in neurophysiological makeup or in body structure, which could change the ability of the individual to engage in certain activities, such as strenuous ones. Prior learning has been discussed before. Particularly relevant is the fact that prior learning determines the relative attractiveness of the goal object—the level of utility expected to be realized from goal object obtainment. *Maturity* is here used to mean stability of behavioral characteristics reflected in the differences in latitudes of variation between children and the elderly (4). The elderly have rather stable and fixed behavioral patterns and less flexibility for *basic* changes in these characteristics. Cognitive style refers to the different approaches various individuals will take in a problem situation.

The intervening variables are those which the recreationist encounters en route to his goal object. They can cause changes in expectations of accomplishing the goal, and through feedback and learning, changes in the antecedent conditions for subsequent and concurrent motivational states.

The observable consequences serve as measures of behavioral responses. They are appraised in terms of selectivity of performance (such as the activities engaged in and how engaged), the vigor of the response, the persistence in the pursuit of the goal (how long engaged and with what persistence and intensity, etc.), and the substitutability of goal objects (changes in activity, etc.).

Attainment of the goal object will consummate the drive for a given motivational state. An example would be reaching the top of a mountain being climbed. The attractiveness of the goal object relates to the expected value to be received from attaining it. Expected values and actual utility received might differ significantly in either a positive or negative direction. For example, if there is a low level of anticipation but a very rewarding on-site experience, the difference is positive. Similarly, if the on-site experience is lower than anticipated, the difference will be negative. In either case, the utility from the experience becomes a component of the antecedent conditions for subsequent behavior. Net utility (utility minus disutility) is received from either approaching or attaining the goal object. It is conceptually possible that net utility might be at its peak before the drive is consummated. For example, we might find the anticipation of and preparation for a fishing trip more rewarding than facing the elements at the stream.

One aspect of the recreational behavioral continuum is not clear in the tabular schema. This is the element of recall, memory, or reminiscence. As we see it, this form of recreational engagement may take one or more of three forms. First, it can best be considered as a distinct recreational pursuit with its goal object(s), at least in part, being reminiscence. This would be the case when we show our trophies or slides to friends. In these situations, the recreational goal object would be associated with other, socially determined, goal objects. Second, the memories may put us on a new recreational continuum in a slightly different way. They may enter as antecedent conditions (not goal objects) which prompt us in the pursuit of another goal object similar to the one which gave us the satisfactory memories. Alternatively, the memories might be unsatisfactory and reduce our motivations to engage similarly again. Or the memories might crop up as intervening variables to increase or weaken the strength of a drive state. In both of these two forms or modes of recall, we are on a new continuum if the four differentiating descriptors can be applied. The third form of recall requires that the recreational-behavioral continuum be extended past goal object attainment, as indicated by the dashed line at the bottom of figure 6-1. In this case, the recall need not be associated with a new goal object and is usually a spontaneous engagement to which the separate application of the four differentiating descriptors have little meaning. It would seem that elements of all three of these forms usually exist—they strongly emphasize the educational or learning aspects of recreational behavior.

Based on the above statements, it can be seen that there is a difference between a goal object, a goal state, and a recreational state. The goal object (the trophy, skill development or application, a different environment, etc.) is that with which the recreationist relates to determine the direction and to gauge the progress of his pursuit. His changing perceptions of its relative value affect the strength, persistence, and consistency of responses emitted. These perceptions are determined by the nature of the reinforcement (positive or negative) he receives en route. Attainment of the goal object dissipates the drive for that particular motivational state and some other drive takes over.

The goal state refers to where the recreationist finds himself at any point in time with respect to goal object attainment. There are a variety of possible goal states extending from anticipation (defined in terms of the antecedent conditions) to recall.

The recreational state is the state or level of the experience. As defined early in the paper, this experience exists to the extent to which the needs or desires to recreate are gratified. Thus, *recreation itself is a state of mind.* This explains why it is so easy for us to engage in certain forms of recreation by doing nothing more than thinking. The level of the experience is determined by many variables which are influenced by factors both under the control of the recreationist and not under his control. Therefore, although recreation is highly personal, it can be significantly affected by the actions of others. Being highly personal, the level of the recreational experience will vary from person to person even though they might be subjected to the same external conditions. Further, the level of the experience can vary from goal state to goal state. Some people may "peak" during anticipation, others at the point of goal object attainment, and others during recall. Or the level of the experience may vary at essentially the same goal states for the same person during different but essentially the same type of engagements.

It is realized that this conceptualization, especially the "dynamics" of the recreational experience continuum at the bottom of figure 6-1, is an oversimplification of several aspects of human behavior as it is currently understood. Problems associated with the pursuits of subgoals and the complex and more dynamic nature of reinforcement responses emitted have not been adequately considered. For example, the importance of feedback has not been covered sufficiently. Also, the notion of net utility, at any point in time, does an injustice to the cumulative effects of memory on the level of the experience at that point in time. Although these additional dimensions are important, we feel that for the purposes of this paper they cannot and should not be considered. They would require much time and space to elaborate, would make the structure unreasonably complex and would, thereby, increase the probability of misunderstanding. The structure is reasonably consistent with existing theory and, as an introductory conceptualization, should be both meaningful and applicable as it is presented.

Relevance to Recreation Planning

What roles do, or can, the recreation planner play in enhancing the experience of the recreationist? There are many situational contexts within which the planner directly or indirectly enters the "experience continuum" of the recreationists. He enters at the *antecedent condition level* in several ways. Studies of user responses show that recreationists generally have at least partial information about the nature of the experience expected. Frequently this information comes either from prior on-site experiences of the recreationist or of his friends. The recreation planner also strongly influences other decision makers responsible for the design and provision of facilities, for educational programs, and so forth. Thus, they indirectly affect the amount of information conveyed and received and, concomitantly, the expectations of the potential users of these landscapes and facilities. Further, if outdoor recreation planners could work more closely with other environmental planners in the creation and/or maintenance of more *harmonious and compatible everyday* life spaces and in the development of such programs as environmental education, these interactions might alter antecedent conditions in a manner favorable both to the planners and to the recreationists. Perhaps we would then create and maintain environments which are more livable and from which certain people would not need to escape temporarily to the degree postulated. Recreation for these citizens, especially those in the inner cities, would not be offered as a monofunctional bandaid but instead as part of an integrated multifunctional program. If this is too utopian we should at least attempt to provide readily available opportunities for meeting basic recreation needs—opportunities within or near those environmental settings which have superordinate influence on the antecedent conditions.

In addition to the recreation planners' effects on the *antecedent conditions*, many examples can be given of how the recreation planner and developer *intervene* during the recreationists' goal pursuits. For example, the type of on-site information provided affects the extent to which a goal can be realized. So do the type and arrangement of facilities; the restrictions, such as rules and regulations; and the learning environment within which the recreationist is "placed" by the designer. Each of these is significantly influenced by recommendations of the planners. As a specific example, what recommendations should the planner make with respect to the programs to bus city children to the parks? Should recommendations be made that programs be established to provide learning or orientation sessions prior to the journey to the park, at the park, on the bus back to the city, or all three? Or, as another specific example, does the planner always recognize the constraints he might be indirectly imposing on certain age groups, especially the elderly? His studies of use rates should disclose that many of our trails are too steep or otherwise inaccessible to our older adults. These constraints are significant intervening variables.

The above discussion of recreation as an experience includes the fundamental elements of the conceptualization. The remaining discussion of the other four descriptors is geared primarily toward differentiating recreational behavior from other types of human responses.

RECREATION REQUIRES A COMMITMENT

Our proposition that recreation behavior is goal directed implies that psychological commitments are present. We pointed out earlier that they may be at the subconscious level. Most of them, however, appear to be more overt.

It is difficult to give an explicit definition of *commitment.* The one offered is that commitment is an assignment of energy, time, and other personal resources, including money. An assignment means a decision and, as with all decision situations, this implies a course or even a program of action. Energy, as used here, includes both psychic and physical energy. Psychic energy means a personal identity or association with a cause, object, or event, such as one's identity with a team in the World Series. Physical energy is self-explanatory and is related to an assignment of time. Time means personal cost, either in real or opportunity terms. For example, the time allocated to recreation could be allocated to the acquisition of additional income. The commitment will vary by type of activity engaged in, will relate to the goal objects being pursued, and will be reflected in the expenditures made on equipment, the level of skill development, and other factors. The recreationist can be committed as an active participant or as a spectator. It is difficult to be more explicit because there are gradations in intensities and/or magnitudes of commitments.

The notion of commitment has some interesting implications for recreation analyses. For example, would comparative degrees of commitment provide rough measures of the ordinal values placed on different recreational experiences? Do commitments to weekend engagements differ from those for vacations? Are commitments to "disengagement" (to temporary escape) different from those to active engagement, and do responses vary accordingly? Are commitments to wilderness engagements stronger than those to swimming locally? Can the recreation planner expect the wilderness user to expend more energy than the user of a national recreation area? Can he expect the user to walk some distance for certain services? Do some users find the quality of their experience to be increased if they expend a little additional energy? If so, how willing are they to do so? Also, are there identifiable constraints (information, income, etc.) which need to be removed before certain commitments can be made?

RECREATIONAL ENGAGEMENTS ARE SELF-REWARDING

Two criteria are offered in this descriptor. First, the gratifications received from attainment of recreational goal objects are of a nature such that these objects are pursued for their own sake and not primarily for their effects on or contributions to the attainment of other goal objects. Contrasted with work, which is pursued for income to be used to meet other goals, *recreation is an end in itself.* Second, recreational experiences are rewarding, not punishing. The experiences have net positive values: utility exceeds disutility. Together the criteria state that recreational engagements find utility in and of themselves. This does not mean that we *cannot* recreate with secondary payoffs in mind. It means only that we *need* not do so, if we are recreating as defined.

RECREATION INVOLVES PERSONAL AND FREE CHOICE

This descriptor is closely related to the one above and should be relatively self-explanatory. Several brief comments are: it is difficult to conceive of recreational engagements as *self*-rewarding if not made as a free choice, and recreational activities might best present the opportunity for man to be free. By our definition, engaging in recreational pursuits (especially with respect to obligations of time) is the only opportunity for many people to be completely free, if pure or complete freedom is defined as existing when an individual's action reflects his personal intentions, and his intentions are self-determined (11). Obviously, the problem of determinism enters, and man "as a social entity" with all his roles, expectations, identities, and ambiguities is seldom—if ever—free to determine personally his intentions. As with commitments, there is a gradation or continuum of freedom going from complete constraint to pure freedom. It is suggested that recreation lies at the end of the continuum where constraints are minimal and opportunities for spontaneity are the greatest.

Again, the implied question is whether environmental designs are constraining or facilitating. Implied in the descriptors are these three criteria of importance to recreation planners: (1) that an array of *opportunities exists* from which to make a choice, (2) that the individual is *free* and able *to choose*, and (3) that he is *free* and able *to do.* There is a difference between available and real opportunities. Many individuals can *choose* to do something, but their plan of action associated with this commitment and decision cannot be implemented because the individuals are somehow constrained from following through on their choice. These constraints could exist because of low income levels, racial discrimination, information deficiencies, or other factors which make available opportunities unreal.

RECREATION OCCURS DURING NONOBLIGATED TIME

It is difficult to define the word *obligation.* The task becomes even more difficult when the temporal dimension is added—when obligated time is being defined. *Oblige* stems from the Latin meaning "to bind," which gives one a feeling for the concept of obligated time. Another way to explain the concept is that obligated time refers to time spent during which the allocation is accompanied by a sense of urgency. We are temporally obligated to the extent which we are not free now and in the future to do something other than that which we are doing. The problem of definition is made difficult because we experience gradations in the degree to which we feel obligated with respect to time. We do because we vary in our commitments to those things which bind us temporally. These things in turn require different amounts and scheduling of time. Some are highly structured and require relatively large blocks of time while others permit more discretionary scheduling in small blocks. For example, we feel a greater temporal obligation to our work and to our school activities than we do to our household chores (such as painting the house). There is a greater sense of *urgency* with fewer opportunities for discretionary scheduling. Further, we feel less obligated to certain social commitments and to engagements in nonplay type of recreation such as a hobby activity. Finally, we feel fewer and perhaps no temporal obligations in true play type activities in which there are fewer rigid structures, greater personal freedom of choice, and few (or no) feelings of being time bound. The point is that during recreational engagements we feel a reduced obligation or no sense of obligation, urgency, or boundness with respect to time. All parents have experienced this "unconsciousness of time" of children playing before dinner—"Will they never learn to get to the table on time?" Based on a limited sample, these feelings of the parents are not as intense (or even present) when they too are playing, such as on a camping trip.

It was stated that time allocated to recreation is unobligated. This allocation can occur during time which is allotted to means and ends other than recreation but is not being fully used for these other ends and means. Examples could be reflecting on a happy event while driving, enjoying the roadside amenities while en route to work, or mentally developing a hobby while performing a routine work task. However, in most cases the time during which recreation is pursued would appear to be time allocated to recreation.

Much information is needed on personal time budgets before many prescriptive statements can be made about the significance of this descriptor to recreation planning. However, it can safely be said that in our society time is a resource, perhaps a unique resource, and should be considered as such in planning studies.

In most planning reports time is considered to be an independent variable and is generally quantified in terms of the length of the workweek, the workday, or the vacation. If we really desire ours to be a leisure society defined in terms of creative and self-fulfilling uses of nonwork time (and all the psychological and sociological implications associated with the possible demise of the Protestant Ethic), should we as planners not give serious consideration to viewing time allocated to recreational engagements as a dependent variable? By viewing time as an independent variable, we tend to accept the idea that recreation is a *residual* rather than the important social input it is. Recreation planners have much to learn about the facilitating and constraining effects of uses and psychological perceptions of time on recreational behavior and about the effects of this behavior on general welfare.

It appears that a structuring of time is necessary before recreation takes on social significance. This structuring, which became more discernible after the Industrial Revolution, makes words like nonobligated, leisure, and discretionary time more meaningful. Recreation planners must question their role in resolving any social problems being created by increasing "structured" leisure time. Viewing leisure time as a residual hardly seems the best approach. Perhaps we should encourage more social rewards for leisure behavior to balance those for work.

At first, commitments and allocations of time seem to be one and the same. But this is not the case. Allocations of time can help define the extent of a commitment, but we can be committed to a goal without feeling "time bound" while pursuing it. Both of these dimensions (postulates) offer interesting possibilities for gaining a better understanding of what recreation is.

CONCLUSION

Certain implications of the behavioral interpretation of recreation planning have been considered above. At this stage of the development of the "science of recreation," recreation planners will adopt those approaches which are useful in getting the job done. Hopefully, the behavioral interpretation will be a useful supplement to the conventional activity approach. Perhaps the primary usefulness is the raising of specific questions in a slightly different manner within a different comparative structure. Perhaps we can now find a little more meaning in such frequently asked questions as, Are we providing appropriate opportunities to recreate? The question can now be reworded to ask, Are we providing those recreational opportunities which will elicit those responses in the user that are most instrumental in satisfactorily meeting his needs and desires? These responses (the engagements in activities), the needs of the recreationist (reflected in his goal objects), and his satisfaction (the level of the experience) can all be associated within the conceptual structure presented. Admittedly, we need greater objectivity and better quantification, but progress is being made in that area too. Perhaps someday we will have a general theory of recreation behavior.

Recreation Behavior and Recreation Demand

Another possible way in which the conceptualization might be useful to recreation planning is that it requires us to go beyond the four conventional causal factors of demand (mobility, leisure time, population, and income). What are the positive (and negative) forces (the antecedent conditions) which shape our needs and desires? What causes and gives vigor and direction to our motivations to recreate?

Ours has been called the age of anxiety. If true, could this be a causal factor in rapidly increasing demand for recreation? Also, is this demand of a type that will best be met through the provision of particular types of opportunities, say, for jogging? If an increasing number of people are recreating as a form of stress mediation or reduction (as there is strong evidence to support), are we providing appropriate opportunities for the venting of the frustrations and anxieties which accompany high stress levels? Perhaps we should have punching bags, more do-it-yourself wood piles, or other modes of creative destruction in our parks and recreation areas.

The authors are convinced that many of our recreational engagements are underlaid in large part (and others to a lesser degree) by our desires to escape temporarily—to disengage, to leave the structured and the nonrandom. These recreationists are "pushed" from their everyday life space, by that life space, at least temporarily, into a restorative ecological behavioral setting—into an environment that is less demanding, into one that is remedial and one that is in many ways more predictable and less threatening.

Studies of user attitudes, especially reasons for recreating, support the argument that disengagement from the routine is an important reason for engagement in certain forms of outdoor recreation. The high frequencies of answers like "tranquility," "peace and quiet," "leave the city," and so on suggest that escape is an important motivation and that replenishment of adaptive energies is an important goal.

Researchers in physiological and psychological stress (actually the two cannot be separated because of complex feedback mechanisms, especially endocrinal activity)[7] agree that the human organism, (including his "psyche"), seeks diversion, escape, locomotion, isolation, disengagement (the terms vary from writer to writer) as modes of coping with stress, frustration, or other threats to the biological or psychological integrity of the individual.[8] Although it is tenuous to postulate relations between recreation as a form of stress mediation and reductions in conflict, hostility, and aggression, the existence of such relationships is just as difficult to disprove.

The frequently heard argument that recreation, generically conceived, is *not necessary* for mental health is misleading. What is mental health? It is appraised differently by each individual. It is not an absolute and appears to have few difinitive requirements before complete breakdown. Are sexual relations (one of our most important forms of recreation) *necessary* for "mental health"? Probably not, but most adults find such relations satisfying, plan to continue to engage in them, and would be somewhat disturbed if they were told they could not. The point is that many people find certain forms of outdoor recreation to be personally satisfying and useful to them for normal functioning. This is mental-health-reason enough without giving too much concern to the spillovers to society (which in the judgment of the present authors are, at the margin, frequently equal to or greater than the external effects of other forms of social capital, including education and national defense). We are not advocating that the recreationists should not ever pay to engage. Rather, we are saying that before specific recommendations can be made we need to consider which types of recreation needs are being met. Opportunities for temporary escape, which we conjecture have marginal utility curves with nonnegative slopes, would logically provide more spinoff benefits to society than would opportunities for skill development, the maintenance of a self-image, or the collection of status symbols.

Recreation Planners as Innovators

Another question being raised is, Are recreation planners weather vanes of current styles of life, social conditions, and tastes, or are they reflectors of past conditions? Using only the activity approach recreation planning must, by necessity, be based on past responses, which unfortunately might not satisfy current or future needs or tastes. The reader might ask, Is it being suggested that the recreation planner become an innovator as well as a provider? The counter offered is, Are the risks really much different? Certainly we can afford the risks of recommending more experimentation and innovation in design and management. If the *primary* task of the recreation planner is to plan to provide an appropriate array of real choice opportunities, should we not know more about the latent demands not being supplied? Are the opportunities provided as rewarding as would be alternative opportunities, and how can those opportunities which are provided lead to more rewarding experiences? Lastly, with regard to the function of recreation planners, are we concerned with large blocks or with marginal (incremental) units of utility? It would seem that, in a relatively affluent society, our concern is increasingly being devoted to enhancing welfare in small bits rather than in a lump-sum manner. If so, the questions being raised have even greater relevance.

Based on the previous comments, it is submitted that the demand for or supply of recreation, as defined in this paper, can never be predicted or projected. Can we project the demand for love, the supply of hostility, the future magnitude of society's greed or happiness? It is realized that we need measures of the extent to which recreational goals are being satisfied, but are we using the most appropriate measures? Certainly surrogates, such as rates of use (including numbers of visitors and visitor days), willingness to pay, resource supply and capacity, and other conventional measures must be used. But these measures tell us little about the output of recreation systems. We have better measures of the productivity of other social service systems like health and education. Few of us would accept counts of users of schools and hospitals as sufficient indicators of the effectiveness of investments in these facilities.

We make estimates of short-run participation in selected recreational *activities*, and these are too frequently taken as demand projections. But should we not attempt to measure also the meanings that people attach to their recreational experiences? Should we not know what types of constraints are being imposed on the application or development of user skills, and will participation rates give us the answer? Since most human behavior is learned behavior, can we as planners in our data acquisition gather any information on what is desired to be learned, explored, or escaped into, what status symbols are collected, why, and with what personal and social benefits?

Recreation as a Social Service

Finally, it is suggested that through a behavioral approach to recreation, the provision of recreation services will be more appropriately viewed as a social service system or subsystem (like education and health services), which provides *important and necessary inputs* to the total social system. These inputs can help *maintain the integrity* or homostasis and/or *promote the growth and development* of individual members of society.

The inputs to any system consist of matter, energy, and information—with *matter* being defined as anything having mass, such as picnic tables, *energy* being defined as the ability to do work, and *information*, in general systems theory, being defined as messages, signals, or symbols containing meaning which enhance the operants of the system to discriminate and to make decisions. It would seem a fruitful area of inquiry for recreation planners to attempt to appraise the informational value of recreation. The authors are convinced that the degree to which an experience is recreational or not is *best* reflected in the information transformations which occur from the time the user "enters" any recreation system to the time he "leaves" such a system. It is doubtful whether he ever really enters and leaves, but the conceptualization is useful. What is being suggested is that the recreationist, with all his learned behavioral patterns, including his norms, values, and expectations, enters a recreation system and during the throughput process of the system's operation experiences information changes.

These information transformations occur when the participant interacts with other components of the recreation system, such as the producers or suppliers, other participants, the facilities, and the landscape, within this different ecological behavioral setting. The transformations could be of a learning nature and enhance the ability of the recreationist to discriminate. They may be of a buffering type and enhance his adaptive capacities through a change in stimuli orientation (such as would be the case when there is a motivation to escape temporarily information overload). It is contended that these changes in the information of the participant *best* measure the extent to which his experience is recreational or not.

Admittedly, there are important energy transformations which occur in many highly active forms of recreation. Part of the experience from these engagements is feeling better physiologically. But the feeling is still based on information processing, either strictly in a physiological sense or including cognition. Accompanying the relaxed physiological state, following the burning up of excessive hormones and other biochemical constituents, is our knowledge that we feel better. The conceptualization does not permit that exercising in and of itself is recreation. Rather, exercise is a response which is instrumental to experiencing a recreational state.

In conclusion, it is suggested that the above conceptualization helps make more apparent the types of information necessary for successful recreation planning. Admittedly, much of this information is difficult to obtain, but current progress is encouraging.

Finally, it is hoped that the discussion in this paper has helped establish a psychological set in the mind of the reader which he will find useful in the ongoing process of pursuing a better understanding of recreation phenomena —a goal pursuit that is not always recreational!

NOTES

1. *Recreationist* in this paper refers to the person seeking a recreational experience and not to the recreation planner, developer, or administrator, as the word is sometimes used.
2. Several authors have pointed out these broader implications of recreation, but they have all tended to emphasize activities in their analyses and discussions. Cf. Neumeyer and Neumeyer (20) and Clawson and Knetsch (7). (See numbered reference list, below.)
3. Elements of the ideas expressed in these postulates are found in several works. Cf. Larrabee and Meyersohn (14) and Huizinga (12).
4. These criteria can be combined to define recreation as a human experience which finds its source in voluntary engagements which are motivated by the inherent satisfactions derived therefrom and which occur during nonobligated time. This definition is similar to the one adopted by Gray (9).
5. The exceptions to goal-directed behavior would be expressive behavior, such as the way we carry ourselves when we walk.
6. As an aside, the authors would advocate that the *ultimate* objective of recreation planning is to promote self-actualization. But we have a way to go before even the simpler forms of recreational behavior are readily and easily experienced. This is especially true for the poor and for certain minority groups.
7. See Christian and Davis (6).
8. See Biddle and Thomas (3); Festinger (8); Lazarus (15); Mayer and Van Gelder (17); Selye (21); and Speilberger (22).

REFERENCES

1. Atkinson, J. W. 1968. *An introduction to motivation.* Princeton, N.J.: Van Nostrand.
2. Berlyne, D. E. 1960. *Conflict, arousal and curiosity.* New York: McGraw-Hill.
3. Biddle, B. J., and Thomas, J., eds. 1966. *Role theory: Concepts and research.* New York: Wiley.
4. Bloom, B. S. 1965. *Stability and change in human characteristics.* New York: Wiley.
5. Bruner, J. S. 1957. On perceptual readiness. *Psychological Review* 64: 123–52.
6. Christian, J. J., and Davis, D. E. 1964. Endocrines, behavior and population. *Science* 146: 1550–60.
7. Clawson, M., and Knetsch, J. 1966. *Economics of outdoor recreation.* Baltimore: Johns Hopkins Press.
8. Festinger, L. 1958. The motivating effects of cognitive dissonance. In G. Lindsley, ed. *Assessment of human motives.* New York: Grove Press.
9. Gray, D. E. 1961. Identification of user-groups in forest recreation and determination of the characteristics of such groups. Ph.D. dissertation, University of California.
10. Gutman, H. 1967. The biological roots of creativity. In R. Mooney and T. Razik, eds. *Explorations in creativity.* New York: Harper & Row.
11. Hampshire, S. 1965. *Freedom of the individual.* New York: Harper & Row.
12. Huizinga, J. 1966. Homo ludens: *A study of the play element of culture.* Boston: Beacon.
13. Laing, R. D. 1967. *The politics of experience.* New York: Random House.
14. Larrabee, E., and Meyersohn, R., eds. 1958. *Mass leisure.* Glencoe, Ill.: Free Press.
15. Lazarus, R. S. 1966. *Psychological stress and the coping process.* New York: McGraw-Hill.
16. Maslow, A. H. 1954. *Motivation and personality.* New York: Harper & Row.
17. Mayer, W., and Van Gelder, R., eds. 1963. *Physiological mammalogy.* Vol. 1. New York: Academic Press.
18. McClelland, D. C. 1961. *The achieving society.* New York: Van Nostrand.
19. Morgan, C. T., and King, R. A. 1965. *Introduction to psychology.* New York: McGraw-Hill.
20. Neumeyer, M. H., and Neumeyer, E. S. 1958. *Leisure and recreation.* New York: Ronald Press.
21. Selye, H. 1956. *The stress of life.* New York: McGraw-Hill.
22. Speilberger, C. D. 1966. *Anxiety and behavior.* New York: Academic Press.

CHAPTER 7

CARRYING CAPACITY: MAINTAINING OUTDOOR RECREATION QUALITY

David W. Lime
George H. Stankey

The utilization of our outdoor recreation resources has grown at an increasing rate worldwide. To maintain the quality of the resource and concurrently to provide a quality experience for the user are not easy tasks. In this well-prepared article David Lime and George Stankey discuss: (1) what is meant by *recreational carrying capacity;* (2) what is known about capacities in terms of how both resources and experiences of visitors are affected by recreation use; and (3) what alternative procedures an administration can use to manage both resources and visitors for capacity.

Recreation resource administrators, planners, researchers, and citizen groups are continually groping for strategies that will tell them how to manage the growing numbers of Americans participating in outdoor recreation activities. We . . . are keenly aware of the attractions of outdoor recreation, the rapidly growing needs for recreational services, climbing use figures, hazards to the resource resulting from intensive visitor use, and other barometers of a "crisis in the making."

These topics frequently lead to questions such as, What is the appropriate level of use for any given recreation area? What steps can management take to increase an area's capacity without sacrificing quality? At what point must responsible administrators say, "That's enough; we're full; no more can come in"?

CARRYING CAPACITY

Few topics in recreation management are discussed as widely or as loudly as carrying capacity. The term is a perfect example of conventional wisdom: everyone talks about managing our recreation resources within their carrying capacity; but when you get to specifics—how many, what kinds, when, for whom—the discussion bogs down.

Reprinted from *Recreation Symposium Proceedings*, Northeastern Forest Experiment Station, USDA Forest Service (1971), pp. 174–84, with permission of the authors. For an extensive bibliography relevant to carrying capacity decision making, see George H. Stankey and David W. Lime, *Recreational Carrying Capacity: An Annotated Bibliography*, USDA Forest Service General Technical Report INT-3 (Ogden, Utah, 1973).

We might start with a statement of what carrying capacity *is not.* There seems to be real value in this approach because the term is often used in a misleading fashion. For example, many *space standards* have been popularized (24). Basically, these standards define the maximum number of use units (people, vehicles) that can utilize the available recreational space at one time for some activity while providing a "satisfactory" experience for the user.

For the most part there is little evidence to suggest how the "satisfactory experience" factor was arrived at and used in determining various space standards. Also, these space standards have generally failed to incorporate the level of use the physical environment can tolerate over a given time period before serious damage results. Most space standards have developed from intuitive judgments and trial-and-error experiences rather than from quantitative evidence from controlled research.

Recreational carrying capacity is not a simple, single, absolute value. There is no fixed figure we can point to for a particular recreation area and say, "This is the carrying capacity." The recreation manager is faced with a complex set of conditions. He must consider a wide range of activities, many of which are in conflict. . . . He must also provide for many different kinds of users: old, young, active, passive. And he must provide opportunities for a wide range of values, many of which are incompatible. . . .

What then *is* recreational carrying capacity? We define it under the assumption that the principal goal of recreation management is to maximize user satisfaction consistent with certain administrative, budgetary, and resource constraints. The *recreational carrying capacity* is the character of use that can be supported over a specified time by an area developed at a certain level without causing excessive damage to either the physical environment or the experience for the visitor. Thus capacity is a multidimensional and dynamic concept capable of manipulation by the manager consistent with administrative, budgetary, and resource constraints.

There are three basic components of carrying capacity: (1) management objectives, (2) visitor attitudes, and (3) recreational impact on physical resources. These are not independent considerations, of course, but rather are closely interwoven ones.

Management Objectives

Capacity can be judged only in light of the particular management objectives for a given area. These objectives must define what type of recreational opportunity or opportunities the area is going to provide. For example, will the goal of the area be to provide camping in a near-natural setting with a low level of development, or will the emphasis be on high-density use with well-developed facilities for both comfort and activities? A person interested in a camping experience in a near-natural setting with few others nearby will not enjoy camping in a state park with many other people camped close by. But this is not evidence that the area is being used beyond capacity. Rather, this individual's desires are inconsistent with the management objectives for this particular area.

At some point it may become evident that management objectives need to be reevaluated, perhaps changed. With new objectives, management practices may be substantially altered and, to the extent they are consistent with the new objectives, the manager is on safe ground. Without definite objectives, however, trying to manage any location for its carrying capacity will be an exercise in futility.

The goal of maximizing user satisfaction for a given geographic area such as the New England states can be met only if we provide a spectrum of opportunities that meets the diverse and often conflicting tastes of the public.

Burch (3) has noted that although there is a wide range of recreational tastes, certain kinds of activities tend to be associated with one another. These "activity aggregates" place certain demands on the resource and relate in certain predictable ways to other users. Thus, regionwide planning may be needed to meet the diversity of recreational tastes. However, "no one recreation supplier need feel obliged to meet all demands. Each public agency could aim clearly at a part of the demand, and refer people who want something more, less, or different to a more appropriate area" (13).

Today, developed camping facilities occupy only about 1/20 percent of National Forest land. Although much of the land is unsuited for recreational developments, the notion that we have used up the capacity of our national forests to provide for recreational demands is simply invalid. We do face a problem in establishing the appropriate mix of the many kinds of recreational opportunities we might develop, and it is here that an understanding of what the recreationist seeks becomes invaluable to management decision making. By making sure that a full range of opportunities exists (regardless of the agency or organization that provides them), we will then be in a position to match visitor needs with opportunities rather than try to develop recreation areas for the mythical "average user" (20).

Visitor Attitudes

Perception refers to the process whereby an individual receives information from the social and physical environments in which he operates, interprets it in light of his experience and attitudes, and then reacts. We know that all recreationists do not perceive the environment in the same way; what is a quality recreational experience to one may be entirely undesirable to another.

But perhaps of more importance is that what the recreationist perceives as acceptable or desirable may be quite different from what the manager perceives (23; 14; 7). In a study of National Forest campgrounds, Lucas (15) found that visitors ranked recreational site quality much differently than Forest Service administrators did. Sites ranked by managers as only "fair" were almost all ranked higher by users. Consequently, what the manager judges to be a pleasing recreational environment may be entirely different from what the recreationist seeks.

Defining recreation standards and objectives requires the consideration of *values.* Because values are subjective, to evaluate them is particularly frustrating for managers. Whose values are to count most—the managing agency's or the public's? If public values are to be relied upon, which "public" values? There are so many of them!

The answer to this dilemma is found in how visitor objectives relate to management objectives. As we suggested earlier, the needs and motivations of recreationists vary considerably; so do recreational areas. We must strive to match the two; if we fail to do so, individual recreation areas will tend to become homogeneous, lacking the variability and diversity needed in a recreational complex. We cannot please everyone everywhere. "It seems misleading to give equal weight to evaluations by people who are seeking a different type of area or experience. By analogy, a Chinese restaurant would do well to ignore the opinion about the food expressed by someone who ate there by mistake while seeking an Italian restaurant" (15).

Although management cannot rely solely on public opinion in formulating decisions, visitor attitudes are valuable in doing so. . . . They help define the spectrum of opportunities needed and the mix of these opportunities, and they shed light on how visitors might respond to specific management actions. Knowing who may oppose a given management action and taking measures to explain why their preferences cannot be met may be as important as deciding for whom the area will be managed (12). Surveys of public attitudes can give objective, unbiased feedback not otherwise available to the manager on a variety of questions.

Impact on Physical Resources

How much wear and tear of the resources should the manager permit before he says, "That's enough"? This recreational impact on physical resources is the third component of carrying capacity.

Any use of an ecosystem results in some change. Frissell and Duncan (5) found that only light use of camping sites in the Boundary Waters Canoe Area (BWCA) resulted in a loss of over 80 percent of the ground cover at the campsite. Even in locations where the management objective is to maintain a natural or near-natural setting, we immediately compromise total achievement of that goal simply by allowing use of the location.

Some might argue that the capacity of an area is the amount of use that area can support without serious damage to the resource. But what is "serious" damage? A portion of the damaged site will recover after a brief rest if use is kept low enough to allow the site to recuperate. On the other hand, certain techniques can be used by the manager to "harden" the site: he can irrigate, fertilize, rotate use, or pave, thereby making the site more resistant to change. But the action the manager takes is based on how change relates to management objectives rather than directly on change itself.

In an activity-oriented, high-density-use campground, the manager would be free to use a variety of techniques to offset problems of resource damage; for example, paving or planting hardy species. However, in a campground where the objective is to provide a camping opportunity in a fairly natural setting, the amount of resource change permissible would be comparatively small. To maintain the natural setting, the manager might have to resort to restrictions on use (numbers of people, kind of use) rather than on techniques that "harden" the site.

What the manager needs to know about recreational impacts upon the resource is (1) the character of change that will occur under specific levels and types of use and (2) how the predicted change in the physical environment relates to the management objectives for the area. Decisions about how much change is to be accepted will be more viable and defensible if we know more about how people perceive and respond to changes in the physical environment. The final decision will rest with the manager, but he can greatly narrow the range of uncertainty in decision making through active dialog with the interested public as well as with planners, engineers, academicians, and researchers.

EFFECTS OF RECREATIONAL USE ON PHYSICAL RESOURCES AND VISITOR ENJOYMENT

As . . . noted earlier, the management objective set for a recreation area is the controlling factor in determining carrying capacity. In setting management objectives, the physical resources of the area and the attitudes of users must be considered. Both of these variables are affected by increasing loads of recreationists and may together or singly establish constraints on the amount of use the area may sustain.

Impact on Physical Resources

We have considerable documentation of the effects of recreational use on soil, vegetation, and other physical components of the resource base. Damage to ground cover occurs not only because of direct bruising and crushing of vegetation but also because of soil compaction due to trampling by visitors. Root growth is impaired and tree stability is affected. Vegetation sensitive to use may be replaced by more resistant species (9). Marked changes occur in hydrologic conditions, such as a reduction in available soil moisture. Substantial amounts of protective plant litter may also be lost, further increasing the chances of soil erosion.

Water is the focus of considerable recreation use. As a consequence, problems of water pollution will represent a growing concern for the recreation manager. Oil and gas pollution from outboard motors is an especially serious problem. Between 10 and 33 percent of outboard fuel is discharged into the cooling-water exhaust stream as unburned wastes—and it may be as high as 40 percent (17). Think of the impact of those 7 million outboard craft that were using our inland waters in 1966. . . .

Related problems stem from the discharge of human wastes into water bodies, creating not only potential health hazards but also touching off problems such as algal blooms (1).

Wildlife plays an important role—sometimes as the primary one, sometimes only as an incidental source of enjoyment—in many recreational activities. Regardless of how wildlife meshes into the recreationist's objectives, however, its abundance, behavior, and survival is often influenced by recreational activity.

Impact on Visitor Enjoyment

Only a few studies have been made on how change in site quality affects a visitor's enjoyment or how the amount of recreational use affects the quality of a visitor's experience.

The Outdoor Recreation Resources Review Commission (18) found that visitors to a wide range of recreational areas were satisfied with the number of other people they encountered. In fact, the study indicated that one out of five persons felt that meeting more people would have been all right. On the other hand, nearly one out of four National Forest visitors in the study felt that use levels were excessive.

One method of reducing the feeling of crowding is to provide a certain minimum spacing between campsites. In a study of New England state parks, Shafer and Burke (21) found about one out of three persons desired a spacing of 250 to 400 feet (the sites were only 50 to 100 feet apart). In a study of National Forest campers in Minnesota, Lime (11) found that nearly all parties preferred to be well separated and screened from their neighbors. On the other hand, many recreationists prefer and even seek areas that afford opportunities to be close to others (4).

The most substantive work on crowding has been conducted in wilderness. In the BWCA, Lucas (14) found that canoeists objected to encountering others more than motorboaters and motorcanoeists did. Canoeists defined crowding not only in terms of numbers of people but also in types of use (motorboats). On lakes where total season use was less than 300 groups of canoeists, they felt that crowding was no problem. Where motorboats were found, however, canoeists felt crowded sooner. In another study in the BWCA, as well as in three western wildernesses, Stankey (22) found that tolerance to crowding was a function not only of the level and type of use encountered but also of where and when the encounters took place and the destructive behavior of visitors.

Thus unrestricted recreational use will eventually lead to soil compaction, alteration in plant species composition, increased erosion, and dissatisfaction among visitors—regardless of whether we are talking about a state park campground or a wilderness area. Since these areas have different objectives, the decisions a manager might make and the alternatives he may wish to consider are different.

TECHNIQUES FOR MANAGING THE PHYSICAL RESOURCES AND VISITORS FOR CARRYING CAPACITY

All too often we view carrying capacity in an "either/or" context: either we allow use to continue unchecked or we drastically restrict numbers. Although both of these actions are alternatives that the manager may at some time decide to adopt, there is a wide variety of alternatives and techniques available to management that will help insure the goal of maximizing user satisfaction while protecting desirable resource characteristics before it becomes necessary actually to restrict numbers. We must reemphasize that the option or combinations of options a manager may consider for any area depend primarily on the management objectives prescribed for that area. The specific goals of the area limit the character of options the manager can use.

The manager should try to accomplish the following—much of it based on Wagar's (25) discussion of managing for carrying capacity—depending on the area and its management objectives: reduce conflicts among competitive uses; reduce the destructiveness of people; increase the durability of the physical resource; and provide increased opportunities for visitor enjoyment. These goals can be achieved by three overlapping courses of action: (1) site management; (2) modification of visitor behavior through direct regulation; and (3) modification of visitor behavior by means of indirect and subtler measures.

Site Management

Imaginative site design, landscaping, and engineering can effectively increase the carrying capacity of some sites by channeling the movements of visitors, thereby limiting the area they damage, providing surfaces that withstand intensive use, and providing access to areas that are otherwise unused or very lightly used.

The movements of recreationists often can be guided by the design and arrangement of facilities and barriers. Posts, logs, rocks, and, in more critical places, fences or guard rails can be used to keep vehicles in parking spots and out of campsite and picnic areas (16). Paths, elevated walkways, and bridges can similarly channel movement.

Care should be exercised in selecting the route of paths. Routes that are picked simply because they happen to be the cheapest or easiest place to put a path probably will do little to enhance visitor satisfaction. On the other hand, letting visitors choose their own routes around the campground and then hardening these paths could result in an unnecessarily large amount of ground being paved. We need more information about the factors that influence pedestrian traffic flow.

Several techniques can be used to increase the durability of the biotic community. Sites that have been damaged by overuse will eventually recover, given enough time. The demand for recreational space is such, however, that most managers cannot afford to have a substantial proportion of the areas under their administration tied up in natural restoration. As a consequence, managers will generally need to assist natural recovery processes.

Irrigation, fertilization, and reseeding can greatly accelerate the recovery of sites. Herrington and Beardsley (8) found that an application of water, fertilizer, and seed would revegetate 70 percent of the cover at campgrounds in central Idaho in only three years, a percentage unattainable through the application of seed alone.

Where recreation use is heavy, managers may wish to convert the natural vegetative cover to more hardy species. Ripley (19) has listed a number of conifers and hardwoods that demonstrate considerable resiliency in the face of heavy recreation use. Thinning the overstory also can increase the resistance of trees and understory vegetation to abuse (26). Judicious thinning could be done to protect soil-moisture values while not appreciably reducing the amount of shading for visitors.

Recreational use can be redistributed and capacity can be increased by providing access to previously underused areas. This means not only additional roads and trails but also construction of facilities. The installation of trails, lights, elevators, etc., at some of the United States' more spectacular caverns (Carlsbad, for example) has unquestionably disturbed the cave's ecosystems. Few of us, however, would enjoy these areas had they not been altered to increase their carrying capacity. It is important to recognize that providing access not only effectively increases capacity, but it can also quickly alter the type of recreational opportunity offered.

Regulating Visitor Behavior

Through direct regulation of where visitors may go, how long they may stay, and when they may enter the area, management can attain a desired intensity of use for a particular site. Regulatory procedures include zoning, rotating use, limits on party size, and reservations. Implicit in these techniques is a trade-off between the loss in the recreationist's freedom of choice and the gain in ability of the site more nearly to meet the visitor's needs and objectives.

More visitors competing for the same amount of recreational space will frequently mean that they interfere with each other's activities. For example, water-skiing and fishing in the same area just do not go together. Mechanized trail travel (snowmobiles, trail bikes, ATVs) is largely incompatible with foot travel. Allowing high-intensity bike use in the immediate vicinity of an important nesting area for eagles could create a serious conflict.

Separating or zoning conflicting uses accentuates the need for careful and deliberate planning, but the benefits to be gained will generally outweigh the costs. Perhaps most important, zoning can assure the perpetuation of a range of recreational opportunities in an area. It assures the user's right to a free choice among alternative forms of recreation. In winter, setting aside separate trails for snowmobilers and snowshoers or cross-country skiers seems especially warranted if management wants to maximize enjoyment for both groups. In the BWCA, outboard motors and snowmobiles are banned from about one-half of the total area to reserve this part of the region for more primitive forms of recreation and travel.

In Alaska, the State Fish and Game Association has instituted a zoning plan in controlled-use hunting areas that will restrict use to primitive travel (foot, dog team, or horse) in some areas, while only foot travel would be permitted in others. Also planned is time zoning, where only so many people are permitted in a certain area at a time.

Rotating use among available sites and relying on the inherent resiliency of the resource to accommodate use is another means for reducing permanent damage caused by concentrated use. Temporary recuperation periods after watering, seeding, and fertilizing probably would be most desirable. Developed recreation areas could be designed so that sites are rested one year in three. In camping areas and picnic grounds, for example, this could be accomplished by constructing three distinct areas with separate access roads and closing off a different one each year. This would require that areas be overdeveloped by at least one-third; but, coupled with a continuing maintenance program, the results might be very rewarding.

Limiting the size of parties is an important management tool for alleviating damage to the resource. Large groups are excessively destructive of resources not only because of the large amount of space they require but also because of the intensive nature of the use. For example, ten separate parties of three horses each who use an area over a two-month period undoubtedly will have a less-detrimental impact on the trail and campsites than if all thirty horses traveled as a single group.

The noise and congestion often associated with large groups is another reason to limit party size. Although we as yet do not know how visitors react to large groups in developed recreation areas, Stankey's (22) research in wilderness showed that large parties are strongly disliked by others. Even though large groups constitute only a small proportion of total use for most recreation activities, they may well cause a disproportionate loss of enjoyment.

Requiring recreationists to obtain reservations is one way to control both the level and character of use at any given area. Complete switchover to a reservation system might create some formidable administrative problems as well as negative reactions on the part of some of the recreating public. A limited reservation system may be very useful, however.

For example, the state of Oregon has put some of its large state parks on a reservation system for the summer use period. A central clearinghouse with a toll-free telephone number maintains information regarding available camping locations. Reservations are made by phone or mail with each individual park. Although difficulties have been encountered with the program (people not showing up for their reservations, for example), the system seems well accepted. One result of the reservation program has been a shift in the makeup of use at different camps; Oregon residents tend to use the reservation parks more, while nonresidents fill the nonreservation camps.

Modifying Visitor Behavior

By understanding the factors recreationists consider in making decisions about where to go and what to do, managers can modify visitor behavior in subtler and less-obtrusive ways. By doing so, the manager does not interfere directly with the visitor's freedom of choice, yet he influences the user to make choices that produce desired changes. Visitor behavior can be modified by (1) communication and interpretation services and (2) fees or other eligibility requirements. Techniques to maintain the site also fall into this category because the way in which facilities are managed can influcncc a uscr's decision on whether to visit the site . . . and how long to stay.

It is our opinion that the dissemination of information to the public is one of the most fruitful tools administrators have available to modify visitor behavior. By increasing contact with the public (both visitors and potential visitors) managers can probably solve many current problems and help avoid others.

Communication and interpretative services for recreationists are many and varied. Organized services and personal contact include illustrated talks, movies, slides, nature walks, tours, and campfire programs. Other services include self-guiding trails and roads, museums, brochures, maps, and guidebooks. Communication between one public agency and recreationists could be increased by greater dissemination of information through other public agencies, local businessmen and chambers of commerce, newspapers and magazines, and radio and television.

Another approach is to build some visitor information centers in metropolitan areas so users can more efficiently plan trips in advance. This also would provide an opportunity to educate them about appropriate behavior, rules, etc. Because many users find recreation areas by just driving around, it is essential to have an adequate number of effectively placed roadside information signs. A study in Utah showed recreational use of an area could be changed substantially by signing (2). Finally, there undoubtedly are countless imaginative communication techniques being utilized in other fields of public relations that can be applied directly or modified for use in recreation management.

What are the by-products for both managers and recreationists of an effective communication or interpretation program? First, increasing . . . contact with visitors can help them find out what the range of recreation opportunities and attractions is in a given geographic area. They can then route themselves to those areas that match their interests. Recreational experiences may also be enhanced if visitors can be taught to . . . understand basic concepts of ecology and other outdoor values. This in turn should increase their awareness of some of the subtler attributes of an area (geology, wildlife, vegetation, archeology, and anthropology). By deepening their sense of appreciation and awareness for the natural environment, more recreationists could take better advantage of an area's recreation potential.

Second, we hope that increasing the flow of educational information to the public would result in a reduction in the destructive behavior of some persons. We assume here that much of their destructive behavior is simply the result of not knowing what is right rather than of overt maliciousness.

Third, better communication with the public gives the manager an opportunity to explain to those visitors who object or are opposed to certain management actions why their preferences cannot be met. Not only should management try better to understand the needs of their clientele, but they have an obligation to help the public understand the needs and goals of recreation management. Ultimately, this two-way process can do much to win public acceptance and support of many management procedures.

Finally, increasing the flow of information that the recreationists use in making decisions is another way to change patterns of use. More uniform and efficient use among sites should be possible. For example, people seeking solitude should be informed where use is lightest. This would . . . make use of sites more uniform and . . . also help people to maximize their enjoyment. Snowshoers and skiers would probably appreciate very much knowing on which trails they could least expect to encounter snowmobiles.

Various aspects of visitor behavior—especially use patterns—can also be modified in both space and time by the use of entrance fees, particularly differential fees. Where there is wide variation in the intensity of use between similar recreation sites (campgrounds, trails) in a given area, differential fees could produce a more even distribution of use. In much the same way that airlines and hotels use off-season rates to attract tourists, both public and private recreation suppliers could employ differential charges to shift some use to off-peak times (10). Managers of camping areas, for example, could lower or perhaps eliminate entrance fees altogether when use is traditionally low—on weekdays, during Indian summer, and so on. Some managers will be in a position to promote winter camping and extend special rates in an effort to spread use to other seasons. For those recreationists seeking an escape from the normally crowded summer campgrounds, these opportunities could be especially appealing.

Requiring recreationists to demonstrate a certain minimum level of knowledge or skill before they are eligible to participate in an activity or enter an area is another means of maintaining recreational quality where there is limited capacity and high demand. The "hunter safety" program is similar to what we have in mind; young people are required to show a certain level of proficiency in firearm safety and game-management principles before receiving a hunting license. Because of potential crowding in wilderness, "entrance exams" may some day be desirable to maintain the quality of such areas (6). While these actions of management are regulatory to a point, they do not interfere directly with the recreationists' freedom of choice. Once he has demonstrated his ability, a person is essentially free to do as he pleases, consistent with certain rules of safety.

Eligibility requirements could also be established differentially to shift use from one place to another and from one time period to another. Inexperienced canoeists, for example, might be excluded from certain streams at certain times until they reach an acceptable level of proficiency. Snow skiing is another activity where an individual could be required to demonstrate a minimum level of skill before he could use certain slopes.

We hasten to add that law enforcement also has its place in managing for capacity. Regardless of what the land manager does to protect the resource and enhance visitor enjoyment, some people simply will not get the message. To protect the site as well as the rights of the careful visitor, the responsible administrator may at times have to rely upon legal sanctions.

SUMMARY AND CONCLUSIONS

Our efforts to explore the topic of carrying capacity have left us with five conclusions.

1. There are many possible carrying capacities for a given recreation area. These capacities can be defined only in light of the objectives for the area in question. These management objectives must consider: (a) the type of recreational opportunities the area itself is going to provide and (b) the recreational opportunities other recreation suppliers in the immediate area provide. As a result, managing agencies should work closely with each other in regional planning so their individual areas function as part of a whole.

Providing a wide range of opportunities to choose from in a region will help visitors maximize their enjoyment. Use patterns should more closely parallel the goals of management, and the efficiency of management should be more nearly optimized.

2. Determining carrying capacity ultimately requires the consideration of human values. Because of the subjectivity of these values, it is essential that managers carry on an active dialog with a variety of publics. In this way management objectives and capacity guidelines will be more viable and defensible against public criticism.
3. The resistance of an area's resources to use is an important constraint on carrying capacity. Yet knowing how the resource is affected by various levels and types of use does not by itself tell the manager what is an acceptable amount of change to permit. There are many possible standards of acceptable change that the manager could employ. It is important to remember that the objectives for the area are the controlling factor for these standards. Managers must consider the opinions and concepts of a variety of publics before they act. Although administrators cannot manage by public opinion alone, these opinions can help the manager narrow the range of uncertainty in the decisions he makes.
4. There has been considerable research about the effects of recreational use on resources and recreationists. Our knowledge of the adverse effects of use on soil and vegetation resources is relatively good; knowledge about the effects on other resources—especially water and wildlife—is much less definitive.

   Our knowledge of how various levels of use, types of use, and site design affect the experiences of users is still less understood. We have learned, however, that recreationists who appear superficially similar do not have identical needs and do not perceive the recreation environment in the same manner. Nor do managers perceive the recreation environment in the same way as recreationists. Because of differences in people's tastes, it is essential that leisure behavior be thoroughly understood.
5. Managing an area for its carrying capacity can be accomplished in many ways. Numerous procedures are available to the manager before it is necessary to ration total numbers of recreationists. The aim of these techniques should be to: reduce conflicts among competing uses; reduce destructive behavior; increase the durability of sites; and provide increased opportunities for visitor enjoyment.

Procedures for postponing the rationing of use include: (1) site management—barriers, paths and trails, roads, artificial surfaces, irrigation, fertilization, and hardy species of vegetation; (2) regulating visitor behavior—zoning, rotating use, party size limitations, and reservations; and (3) modifying visitor behavior—communication and interpretation services, fees (especially differential fees), and other eligibility requirements. The *best* technique or combination of techniques to use depends primarily on the particular recreational opportunity the area is meant to provide.

Regulations, direct or indirect, are useful tools for the recreation manager. But they must be applied thoughtfully, with careful reasoning underlying their implementation. A campground filled with signs saying what a person *cannot* do will not go very far toward meeting the underlying objective of recreation management—maximizing user satisfaction. Regulations should be viewed as means to an end rather than as an end in themselves. All of us, administrators, managers, researchers, and the recreating public, need to remember that. To the extent that a regulation helps meet management objectives, it is useful. Beyond that, it is simply an encumbrance to all parties concerned. More importantly, indefensible regulations will make it more difficult to institute needed rules at some later time.

REFERENCES

1. Barton, Michael A. 1969. Water pollution in remote recreational areas. *Journal of Soil and Water Conservation* 24, no. 4: 132–34.
2. Brown, Perry J., and Hunt, John D. 1969. The influence of information signs on visitor distribution and use. *Journal of Leisure Research* 1, no. 1: 79–83.
3. Burch, William R., Jr. 1964. Two concepts for guiding recreation management decisions. *Journal of Forestry* 62: 707–12.
4. Burch, William R., Jr., and Wenger, Wiley D., Jr. 1967. The social characteristics of participants in three styles of family camping. USDA Forest Service Research Paper PNW-48. Pacific Northwest Forest and Range Experiment Station, Portland, Ore.
5. Frissell, Sidney S., Jr., and Duncan, Donald P. 1965. Campsite preference and deterioration. *Journal of Forestry* 63: 256–60.
6. Hardin, Garrett. 1969. The economics of wilderness. *Natural History* 78: 20–27.
7. Hendee, John C., and Harris, Robert W. 1970. Foresters' perception of wilderness—User attitudes and preferences. *Journal of Forestry* 68: 759–62.
8. Herrington, Roscoe B., and Beardsley, Wendell G. 1970. Improvement and maintenance of campground vegetation in central Idaho. USDA Forest Service Research Paper INT-87. Intermountain Forest and Range Experiment Station, Ogden, Utah.
9. LaPage, Wilbur F. 1967. Some observations on campground trampling and ground cover response. USDA Forest Service Research Paper NE-68. Northeastern Forest Experiment Station, Upper Darby, Pa.
10. ———. 1968. The role of fees in campers' decisions. USDA Forest Service Research Paper NE-118. Northeastern Forest Experiment Station, Upper Darby, Pa.
11. Lime, David W. 1971. Factors influencing campground use in Superior National Forest of Minnesota. USDA Forest Service Research Paper NC-60. North Central Forest Experiment Station, St. Paul, Minn.
12. ———. 1972. Behavioral research in outdoor recreation: An example of how visitors select campgrounds. In *Environment and the social sciences: Perspectives and applications.* Ed. J. F. Wohlwill and D. H. Carson. Washington, D.C.: American Psychological Association.
13. Lucas, Robert C. 1963. The status of recreation research related to users. *Society of American Foresters Proceedings,* pp. 127–28. Boston, Mass.
14. ———. 1964. Wilderness perception and use: The example of the Boundary Waters Canoe Area. *Natural Resources Journal* 3, no. 1: 394–411.
15. ———. 1970. User evaluation of campgrounds on two Michigan national forests. USDA Forest Service Research Paper NC-44. North Central Forest Experiment Station, St. Paul, Minn.
16. Magill, Arthur W. 1970. Five California campgrounds . . . conditions improve after 5 years' recreational use. USDA Forest Service Research Paper PSW-62. Pacific Southwest Forest and Range Experiment Station, Broomall, Pa.
17. Muratori, Alex, Jr. 1968. How outboards contribute to water pollution. *N.Y. Conservationist* 22, no. 6: 6–8; 34.

18. Outdoor Recreation Resources Review Commission. 1962. *The quality of outdoor recreation: As evidenced by user satisfaction.* Washington, D.C.: Government Printing Office.
19. Ripley, Thomas H. 1962. Tree and shrub response to recreation use. USDA Forest Service Research Note SE-171. Southeastern Forest Experiment Station, Asheville, N.C.
20. Shafer, Elwood L., Jr. 1969. The average camper who doesn't exist. USDA Forest Service Research Paper NE-142. Northeastern Forest Experiment Station, Upper Darby, Pa.
21. Shafer, Elwood L., Jr., and Burke, Hubert D. 1965. Preferences for outdoor recreation facilities in four state parks. *Journal of Forestry* 63: 513–18.
22. Stankey, George H. 1971. The perception of wilderness recreation carrying capacity: A geographic study in natural resources management. Ph.D. dissertation, Michigan State University.
23. Stone, Gregory P., and Taves, Marvin J. 1958. Camping in the wilderness. In *Mass leisure,* pp. 290–305. Ed. Eric Larrabee and Rolf Meyersohn. Glencoe, Ill.: Free Press.
24. U.S. Department of the Interior. 1967. *Outdoor recreation space standards.* Washington, D.C.: Government Printing Office.
25. Wagar, J. Alan. 1964. The carrying capacity of wildlands for recreation. *Forest Science Monograph* 7, no. 23.
26. ______. 1965. Cultural treatment of vegetation on recreation sites. In *Society of American Foresters proceedings,* pp. 37–39. Detroit, Mich.

CHAPTER 8

A Recreation Visitor Travel Simulation Model as Aid to Management Planning

Robert C. Lucas
Mordechai Shechter

The sophistication of modern electronic computers has ushered us into an era of realistic, utilitarian simulations of the world. This interesting article by Robert Lucas and Mordechai Shechter describes a simulation model for dispersed recreation areas. The model provides a means for experimenting with modifications of use or of area conditions to determine the effects on use patterns and encounters between visitor groups. Described are the model, the results of a test using it, and potential applications.

Numbers of people visiting most kinds of outdoor recreation areas continue to grow. This growth often creates problems for management, with the nature of the problems depending on the type of area and the management objectives established for it. In the United States, growth in use of dispersed recreation areas has been rapid (2), and the resulting problems of congestion and resource damage have been difficult for managers to solve. These problems have been particularly severe on lands established as wilderness. A wilderness, by law, is to be managed both to permit natural ecological processes to operate without alteration by man and also to provide visitors with "outstanding opportunities for solitude."

Growth in the number of visits to wilderness increased about fifteenfold from 1950 to 1975, threatening both natural ecosystems and the experience of solitude. Poor distribution of use, both in space and time, is common and accentuates the problems of congestion and ecosystem damage. Studies of the distribution of wilderness use show that very uneven patterns are the general rule; use is heavily concentrated on certain portions of each area, while larger portions are lightly visited. Similarly, a few summer weekends usually experience sharp peaks. Redistribution seems to offer considerable hope for reducing the adverse effects of heavy use.

Research has shown that visitor satisfaction is influenced substantially by types of encounters with other visitors and that visitors report strong prefer-

---

Reprinted from *State-of-the Art Methods for Research, Planning, and Determining the Benefits of Outdoor Recreation*, Pacific Southwest Forest and Range Experiment Station, USDA Forest Service General Technical Report PSW-20 (1977), pp. 31–35, with permission of the authors. Note: Dr. Shechter was affiliated with the Resources for the Future, Inc., of Washington, D.C., at the time that work described in this paper was done.

ences for low levels of encounters (7). Therefore, managers of wildernesses receiving heavy use are beginning to take actions to modify or control it. In the United States, both the national parks and the national forests are rationing use of some areas. In some cases, this is done by limiting the numbers of visitors permitted to enter each day at various access points. In other areas, managers set nightly capacities for all camping areas and require visitors to establish and adhere to rigid itineraries that will not result in the campsite capacities being exceeded. If this restriction is impossible, the party is not permitted to visit the area at that time. In a few other areas, managers have attempted to influence visitors voluntarily to shift their use to other areas or times through educational pamphlets and personal contacts.

All the managerial actions, except the establishment of rigid itineraries (which have other problems discussed below), however, suffer from a major flaw. The manager's objective is to reduce use at overused locations and to avoid excessive levels of various types of encounters (on trails, at campsites, etc.). However, there has been no way to relate changes in total use or redistribution of use to the number of encounters per party or to the amount of use of particular places within a wilderness. The complexity of travel routes, which characteristically overlap and intertwine, and the variability in travel decisions are so great that neither intuition nor analytic solutions are helpful predictors of the variables of interest for a given amount of use.

The rigid itineraries do provide a more determinate result, at least for use of key locations and encounters between camping parties, but not for encounters between parties while traveling on the trails. For many reasons (weather, illness, overambitious planning, etc.), not all parties adhere to their itinerary, so results are not as determinate as they seem. More important, such close control of movements seems to detract from the visitors' experiences of adventure, exploration, and spontaneity and to transplant the structure of modern urban life to the wilderness setting intended to offer release from civilization's pressures. In general, research has indicated that a desire to escape civilization is a major motivation for wilderness visits. Furthermore, most visitors feel assigning itineraries is a highly undesirable approach to use control (7).

If use pressures and encounters resulting from any given use level and pattern cannot be predicted, experimentation through trial and error is an apparent alternative. However, trial and error is not an effective approach. It is very time consuming; managers would have to try a policy for a year or more to see how it worked. Results for any one year could be heavily influenced by uncontrolled outside factors such as weather. Detailed information on use patterns and encounters would be available only if special studies monitored the area. It would not always be possible to create the use pattern the managers desired to test. For example, if managers wanted to know the effect of a doubling in use, there probably would be no practical way to cause this much use in the short run. At least three sorts of high costs could also result from a trial-and-error approach to use management: First, serious, long-lasting or even irreversible damage to resources might result from tests of heavy use. Second, many visitor benefits could be sacrificed, either through testing excessive use levels that seriously reduced the quality of visitors' experiences or through testing low levels of use that resulted in many people being denied entrance. Finally, frequent, major changes in use policies could lead to controversy and severe public relations problems.

Systems that are too complex for analytic solutions and that are not suited to real-world experimentation are often approached by simulation modeling (3). Therefore, a wilderness travel simulation model was developed to provide a better way to formulate and evaluate use management policies. It provides a practical way to test use patterns quickly. Variability in visitor behavior is incorporated in the model; but, in just a few minutes, use can be simulated for an entire season or a number of seasons. The model records and displays in appropriate formats all the desired information on use and encounters. Because the experimentation takes place in the computer instead of the real world, we avoid the high social costs. Even the most extreme patterns can be tested without damage to precious resources.

Travel simulation models are common, but the requirements for the wilderness model were quite different. In particular, the interest in encounters was unique. Therefore, the U.S. Department of Agriculture Forest Service entered into a cooperative research agreement with Resources for the Future, Inc. (RFF), complementing ongoing research at RFF, to develop a general use simulation model for wilderness-type areas. RFF involved specialists from International Business Machines, Inc., in the project. The model has been developed, modified, refined, and field tested. This paper describes the model and results of the field tests, and it presents conclusions about future applications.

SIMULATION MODEL

All simulation models are simplified abstractions of complex, real-world processes. However, the wilderness travel simulator quite realistically embodies the main characteristics of wilderness visitor movements and interactions. The computer program for the model generates data on visiting parties who arrive at the area at various simulated dates and clock times, enter at particular access points, select routes of travel, and move along these routes. The simulated parties may overtake and pass slower parties moving in the same direction (overtaking encounters), pass parties moving in the opposite direction (meeting encounters), or pass by parties camped in areas visible from trails or other travel routes such as rivers (visual encounters). Parties that stay overnight select campsites which they may or may not share with other camping parties (camp encounters are recorded when they occur). On an ensuing day, camping parties leave the campsite and continue on their chosen routes, and eventually they leave the area.

The model consists of four important components:

1. *Route network.* This consists of entry points, segments of trails or other travel routes, and camping areas.
2. *User characteristics.* Simulated parties have been differentiated by size and method of travel (hiking or horseback in one application and by

type of boat in another). Arrival timing patterns, travel speed, etc., can vary depending on the type of party.

3. *User-route interactions.* Route selection can vary among party types, as can travel time in each direction over different trail segments.
4. *User-user interactions.* These are the three types of encounters described above.

To make the model operational, data are needed on the area and its use. The travel network must be known as well as something about how different types of visitors behave within it: their patterns of arrival, various routes followed and relative popularity of each, travel speeds, and so on. This information is supplied to the model in probabilistic terms.

The simulator provides detailed output information for each individual simulation of a particular use situation or *scenario.* Since part of the input data is of a probabilistic nature, the model has the facility of producing summaries of a series of replications of any such scenario, providing average values of various performance measures such as the amount, character, distribution, and timing of use. For example, the number of parties of each type using each trail segment is provided (if desired, even on a daily basis in one of the three versions of the model). Additional information is available on the number of encounters by type of encounter, by type of party (classified by mode of travel or by length of stay), and by individual trail segments and campsites (again, in one version, on a day-to-day basis).

The model is coded in the IBM-originated language GPSS (General Purpose Simulation System), version V. The model to date had been successfully operated on IBM's 360 and 370 series of computers as well as on Control Data Corporation's 6600 computer. A user's manual (4) is available.*

RESULTS OF FIELD TESTS

The model has been field tested in two areas: (1) the Desolation Wilderness on the Eldorado National Forest in California and (2) Dinosaur National Monument (a National Park Service area) in Colorado and Utah. The Desolation Wilderness is a high, mountainous, lake-dotted area of about 26,000 hectares that is very heavily visited. The Green and Yampa Rivers in Dinosaur National Monument are fast-flowing, "white-water" rivers that visitors float in boats, kayaks, and rafts. Use is much lighter than in the Desolation Wilderness.

Special sample surveys provided the needed input information on use and visitor behavior. In the Desolation, visitors kept travel logs; while in Dinosaur, visitors and professional boatmen on commercially guided trips kept logs to supplement National Park use data. In both studies, information was recorded on encounters.

---

*Single copies are available from the National Technical Information Service, United States Department of Commerce, 5258 Port Royal Road, Springfield, VA 22151, U.S.A. Order no. PB 251 635. Program Tape Order no. PB 251 634.

In both areas, the first scenario was the existing situation, or "base case." One week of peak use was simulated. A one-week initialization period achieved a realistic starting condition. Simulation results were compared with data from the user surveys as one check on model validity, both for use patterns and encounters. Agreement was good, particularly in Dinosaur National Monument, where more precise information on use characteristics and travel routes was collected and used in the model. In the Desolation, encounters were, for a variety of reasons, somewhat higher according to the model than according to visitor reports. Several minor simplifications or departures from reality had compounded effects, but probably the most important reason was that the limited number of visitor travel routes (210) used in the model fell short of reflecting how variable visitor movements really were. As a result, slight overconcentrations of parties increased encounters. On the rivers, where there were fewer entry points and possible variation in routes was less, the problem was less severe.

Next, a variety of scenarios were tested. Use was increased and decreased by varying amounts, and uneven distributions were made more even by shifting use from popular entries to less-used access points, and from heavily used weekends to weekdays. Some clear relationships, not all expected, emerged. Changes in total use (all other things remaining the same) produced proportionate results. That this would be true for use patterns is probably obvious; if total use doubles, use of any specific location doubles, on the average. Encounters, expressed in per-party-per-day terms, also would double in this example—something not entirely expected.

This predictable, proportional relationship provides a convenient base for comparing results of more complex scenarios in which use is redistributed with an across-the-board change with the same total use. The use-redistribution scenarios produced lower average encounters per party per day than the same total use without redistribution. This was especially true for trail encounters (up to one-third fewer encounters than comparable across-the-board total use). Camp encounters dropped only a little below comparable unmodified use, presumably because campsites were somewhat limited; and most parties camped in about the same areas out of necessity, even though they arrived by different routes or at different times.

Average encounters do not tell the whole story, however. The frequency of extreme encounter levels (very high levels, especially, but sometimes also very low and zero levels) changed substantially. A manager probably would be more concerned about reducing or eliminating experiences of unsatisfactory quality than altering averages. In addition, changes at key trouble spots were even more pronounced. This would also probably be more relevant to a manager's evaluation of the results of a scenario than overall averages.

POTENTIAL APPLICATIONS

We conclude that the simulator is a useful tool for the manager of a wilderness or similar area. The model does not, of course, make decisions for the manager. It does, however, allow him to compare carefully the likely results of various possible alternatives before he decides to implement a management plan. This makes it much more likely that the plan chosen will achieve management objectives and that public benefits will be maximized. It also appears to us that it provides a practical way to achieve desired conditions in terms of the amount of use of key areas and the quality of visitor experiences with regard to congestion or solitude, but without requiring tight control of visitor itineraries.

We feel that the simulator should be applicable to many other sorts of dispersed recreation systems besides U.S. wilderness. In fact, we suspect imaginative applications to some very different situations might be possible and useful. The elements in the model are perfectly general. For instance, what we have named "trail segments" are, in general, "transportation linkages" and could represent any type of movement; for example, traffic on park roads or bicycle paths. The model provides for six types of "transactions" (the general GPSS term for the entities whose behavior is simulated). We have usually named them large, medium, or small hiking or horseback groups of visitors, but any designation is possible. Perhaps one type might even represent some kind of wildlife (say, elephants), if their movement could be described in probabilistic terms; and "encounters" would become "wildlife observations" and the manager's goal might be to increase, rather than decrease, encounters.

Certainly, the model is clearly applicable to any type of dispersed recreation area where visitor flows are of concern, where there are capacity constraints, where visitor encounters are significant, and where it is desired that visitors be allowed substantial freedom to move about flexibly. In such situations, the model is particularly well suited to management planning to modify use; that is, to alter numbers of visitors entering at different places and times. The model can also be used to test, within the area, effects of alterations such as new access points, closure of some travel routes, addition of campsites, and so on. However, to simulate such changes, a basis for specifying how visitors will respond to the new conditions is needed. Observation of current behavior cannot directly provide this basis, and other kinds of special information or assumptions based on expert judgment would be required.

The use of computer-based simulation modeling in outdoor recreation management planning may arouse fears of depersonalization. On the contrary, it may help make it possible to maintain the traditional values of recreational visitor independence, flexibility, and spontaneity as well as to protect resources and preserve the quality of experience in the face of growing demands on limited resources.

REFERENCES

1. Fisher, A., and Krutilla, J. V. 1972. Determination of optimal capacity of resource-based recreation facilities. *Natural Resources Journal* 12, no. 3: 417–44.
2. Lloyd, R. Duane, and Fisher, Virlis L. 1972. Dispersed versus concentrated recreation as forest policy. Seventh World Forestry Congress 7CFM/C: 111/2G(3)196. Buenos Aires.
3. Shechter, Mordechai. 1971. On the use of computer simulation for research. *Simulation & Games* 2, no. 1: 73–88.
4. ______. 1975. Simulation model of wilderness-area use: Model-user's manual and program documentation. Revised and expanded. Washington, D.C.: Resources for the Future.

5. Smith, V. K., and Krutilla, J. V. 1974. A simulation model for management of low density recreational areas. *Journal of Environmental Economics Management* 1: 187–201.
6. Smith, V. K.; Webster, D.; and Heck, N. 1974. Analyzing the use of wilderness. *Simulation Today* 24: 93–96.
7. Stankey, George H. 1973. Visitor perception of wilderness recreation carrying capacity. USDA Forest Service Research Paper INT-142. Ogden, Utah: Intermountain Forest and Range Experiment Station.

FURTHER READING

Resource Utilization: Planning & Management

Crompton, John L. 1977. A recreation system model. *Leisure Sciences* 1, no. 1.

Driver, B. L., ed. 1968. *Elements of outdoor recreation planning.* Ann Arbor, Mich.: University Microfilms.

Fabos, J. G. 1971. An analysis of landscape assessment techniques. In An analysis of environmental quality ranking systems, *Recreation symposium proceedings,* pp. 40–55.

Isard, W. 1972. *Ecologic-economic analysis for regional development.* New York: Free Press.

Jubenville, A. 1978. *Outdoor recreation management.* Philadelphia: W. B. Saunders.

Litton, R. B., Jr. 1968. Forest landscape description and inventories. USDA Forest Service Research Paper PSW-49.

McHarg, I. L. 1969. *Design with nature.* New York: Doubleday.

Reid, Leslie M. 1973. Planning the recreation and park system. In *Managing municipal leisure services.* Washington, D.C.: Institute for Training in Municipal Administration, International City Managers Association.

Rutledge, A. J. 1971. *Anatomy of a park.* New York: McGraw-Hill.

Wright, J. R. 1974. Urban parks planning: A systems approach. *Recreation Canada* 32: 35–44.

Young, Lawrence F. 1972. The systems model approach to urban policy planning. *Journal of Environmental Systems* 2, no. 1 (March): 71–85.

Part Three
METHODS OF RECREATION USE EVALUATION

OVERVIEW

The demand for recreation is determined in much the same way as the demand for other goods and services. Recreation/leisure demand is, however, unique because it frequently involves intangibles with no market price. Satisfaction is not measured monetarily but on the basis of personal experience.

This part, unlike the previous ones, focuses on concepts, methods, and techniques that assist in understanding and providing services; there is less emphasis on current issues. The first two chapters introduce economic and social concepts commonly used to evaluate recreation resources and recreation behavior. The third chapter provides a detailed description and application of the basic economic concepts and some of the social concepts involved in measuring the economic value of the recreation/leisure experience for planning purposes. Demonstrated in the fourth chapter are some of the geographers' methods for analyzing not only the travel experience but the effect of the location on visitor use; it also includes a discussion of systems theory relative to recreation travel.

The next chapter is somewhat less complex, a relatively straightforward description of the measures useful for evaluating urban recreation resources and programs. This "how-to-do-it" method will hopefully be adopted in evaluating such services. The most complex and certainly one of the most advanced in terms of research methods is the final chapter: it considers a variety of activities that collectively comprise the recreation experience and recognizes that these activities may be quite different from those envisioned by the management system.

CHAPTER 9

ECONOMIC CONCEPTS RELEVANT TO THE STUDY OF OUTDOOR RECREATION

E. Boyd Wennergren
Warren E. Johnston

This paper basically describes the economic nature of outdoor recreation and serves as a basis for more detailed discussion. Boyd Wennergren and Warren Johnston emphasize that public recreation is not market priced and is not a free good. Their review of economic valuation concepts serves to introduce demand theory to the analysis of outdoor recreation resources. Demand estimates and value approximations are primary to efficient public and private investment decisions, and more importantly they are necessary to maximize society's economic and social returns.

During the last decade and a half, economists have given considerable attention to the economic analysis of outdoor recreation issues, including the nature of demand and the valuation of outdoor recreation. Beginning with the early work of Marion Clawson in 1959, following Hotelling's seminal idea a year earlier, economists have asserted the analytical capability of economic reasoning to assist investigative and policy processes related primarily to the allocation of public funds and outdoor recreation development and management issues.

In this paper, we discuss the economic characteristics of outdoor recreation that facilitate the application of economic theory to its study. In the process, we consider selected economic concepts and principles that are meaningful to economic analysis of outdoor recreation, rather than just describe the economic characteristics of outdoor recreation. In this way, we hope to provide an appreciation for the underlying economic nature of outdoor recreation and a general basis upon which to pursue more detailed inquiry.... Throughout, the frame of reference for the examination of outdoor recreation is on those activities traditionally provided outside the private sector through development and management decisions of public agencies.

INTRODUCTION

The need to subject activities like outdoor recreation to economic analysis is not always obvious to noneconomists. Therefore, let us first turn briefly to a discussion of some basic questions.

Reprinted from *Outdoor Recreation—Advances in Application of Economics,* USDA Forest Service General Technical Report WO-2 (March 1977), pp. 3–10, with permission of the authors.

The problems of economic organization are important to any society and involve decisions with respect to: (a) what types and quantities of goods and services will be produced; (b) who will produce the goods and services and by what processes; and (c) who will receive the goods that are produced. Decisions are required about the allocation of scarce resources (both public and private) because possible resource uses in our society exceed the quantity of resources available. . . .

In order to decide the proper allocation of scarce resources among alternative resource uses, informed decision makers must know the values of the limited (scarce) resources as they are applied in alternative uses. Without such value estimates, the allocation process cannot function properly. Economic theory suggests that such allocation is most efficiently accomplished when the benefit gained per unit of a resource used in given productive or distributive activities is equal among all activities.

Generally, economists recognize two ways of attempting to achieve economic efficiency in the allocation of scarce resources. For market goods and services, the mechanism of the market and the prices that result from the free operation of supply-and-demand forces provides one basis for determining value. Prices determined in markets are indicators of value and provide a basis for resource allocation. For example, investment flows toward the provision of commodities with higher economic returns and away from those with lower returns. Likewise, the purchase of commodities with higher prices suggests higher assigned values for those commodities by consumers (and vice versa). As consumers express their market preferences, consumer demands, in essence, express "willingness to pay" for market goods and services.

Conscious effort by analysts to derive implied values in the absence of appropriate market prices is the second means for achieving economic efficiency. Many times markets cannot or do not express appropriate allocative values because either market pricing does not exist or the existing pricing mechanism does not account for all benefits and costs related to the transaction process. In these situations, economic efficiency in resource allocation must rely on the planning process and forms of collective action which presume the expertise of governmental technicians.

It is the fundamental need to achieve efficient allocation of scarce resources that leads us to require value estimates for alternative resource uses such as investments in the public provision of outdoor recreation. If we are content to permit ad hoc resource use and allocation (perhaps on the basis of political power or "least friction" administrative decisions) and have no need to demonstrate productivity or contribution to social or individual welfare, then the concept of economic efficiency is irrelevant. If, however, we require some order and rationality to the allocation process, then value estimates are essential to achieve efficient allocation of scarce resources.

An important distinction must be made between *exchange values* and *use values* in the estimation of relevant values in which allocative decisions can be properly made. Exchange, or market, values reflect how much consumers will pay to have ownership rights to the use or consumption of a given commodity. They do not always reflect the value in use to the consumer.

Exchange and use values obviously can vary markedly and are conceptually very different. For example, a consumer may pay an exchange value of $20 for food items to sustain his life; but that expenditure, which reflects, among other things, the value of resources used in food production, does not accurately reflect the value of the consumer's life, which is sustained by food. Other classical examples are diamonds—which have a high exchange value but relatively low use value—and air, which has an extremely high use value but a very low exchange value (at least before the days of excessive pollution, when air was considered a free or nonscarce good).

We are, therefore, interested in the derivation of exchange values (whether they be real or implied measures of willingness to pay) as the basis for making efficient allocative decisions. It is important to recognize the difference in the two types of values, since people often revert to the articulation of use values when expressing their position relative to outdoor recreation; i.e., How can we possibly value the feeling one gets from seeing a beautiful sunset or even the thrill of "shooting" the rapids of the Colorado River? Both may be deemed to be "good" and desirable. But the array of possible public investments exceeds available resources and, therefore, decision makers need to assign exchange values in order to allocate resources efficiently.

Now . . . let us (1) describe the economic characteristics of outdoor recreation, a commodity not traditionally subject directly to market forces in the United States, and (2) introduce the fundamental conceptual bases for analytical procedures that have been developed to estimate exchange values for use in allocating scarce resources among competing demands. The competing public demands might be either between alternative outdoor recreation investments or between those in outdoor recreation and other areas of public expenditures; say, flood control, watershed management, timber management, power, and the like.

ECONOMIC CHARACTERISTICS OF OUTDOOR RECREATION

If one accepts the concept of consumer sovereignty, the logic of economics suggests that consumers allocate their time and money resources among goods and services in a way so as to maximize their satisfaction. Outdoor recreation is but one portion of the consumption bundle for which time and money resources are expended. As such, it possesses characteristics normally ascribed to other economic goods purchased by consumers.

Outdoor recreation activities *satisfy individual wants.* People recreate to satisfy needs, whether they be physical, social, or psychological, just as they engage in other forms of activity or as they consume other want-satisfying commodities. Therefore, outdoor recreation has the ability to satisfy individual wants, a requirement of all goods and services of economic consequence.

Outdoor recreation is *subject to the law of diminishing marginal utility.* This economic law posits that additions to total utility are successively smaller as additional units of a good or service are consumed. (We shall return to this concept shortly.)

Lastly, outdoor recreation can be appropriated or acquired within the economic system and is in relatively scarce supply. The latter characteristic is critical to the existence of value and, as one learns in an introductory course in economics, scarcity is the central issue of economics.

Recreation is a commodity that is basically esthetic in its attributes. One does not consume sightseeing, hiking, or fishing as he or she does steak; nor does one use recreation in the same manner as he or she uses a new suit or hat. There are those who consider the intangibles of esthetic experiences immeasurable and apart from economic inquiry. Our previous reference to the valuation of a sunset is a case in point. But any special consideration given to the esthetic properties of outdoor recreation is unjustified when we consider that many economic commodities also possess esthetic properties and differ from outdoor recreation perhaps only in degree. Style-conscious Americans purchase more than warmth and body cover in their apparel; a steak dinner consumed at a restaurant satisfies more wants than mere physical [ones]. Attendance at a movie, theater, or athletic performance may be more closely akin to outdoor recreation, since it involves "consumption" that is entirely esthetic in nature. Therefore, the esthetic properties uniquely attributed by some to consumption activities are not sufficient to dismiss economic analysis of issues pertaining to outdoor recreation.

Perhaps the most unique economic characteristic of outdoor recreation is its lack of a market price. Most athletic contests, movies, and theater performances are market priced by the forces of supply and demand. Consequently, these prices can be used efficiently to allocate resources among alternative activities. The presence of market prices explains lesser concerns about valuation and allocation decisions related to forms of recreation or entertainment with high degrees of esthetics and subject to market forces of supply and demand. In the absence of a market price, indirect systems of valuation commensurate with those used to plan investments for the provisions of market goods are necessary if resources are to be allocated efficiently.

Although it lacks formal market pricing, outdoor recreation is *not a free economic good.* While the market price may be zero, or near zero, all goods and services compete for the time and money resources of consumers. The choice process requires not only weighing the direct expenditures of time and money, but it also implies attention to the economic concept of opportunity cost. One measure of the cost of any activity is the value of the most valuable foregone alternative sacrificed by choice. While available at a zero—or very low—market price, consumption of recreation is limited by the alternative choices of the recreator, including the need for gainful and remunerative employment. Therefore, a form of economic constraint effectively regulates the consumption of outdoor recreation, even in the presence of a zero market price. If this were not the case, why would a pleasure boater ever leave the lake or a fisherman, the stream?

Finally, the consumption of outdoor recreation is subject to time and money constraints and the same law of diminishing marginal utility as any other economic good. To illustrate this last point, consider figure 9-1. The

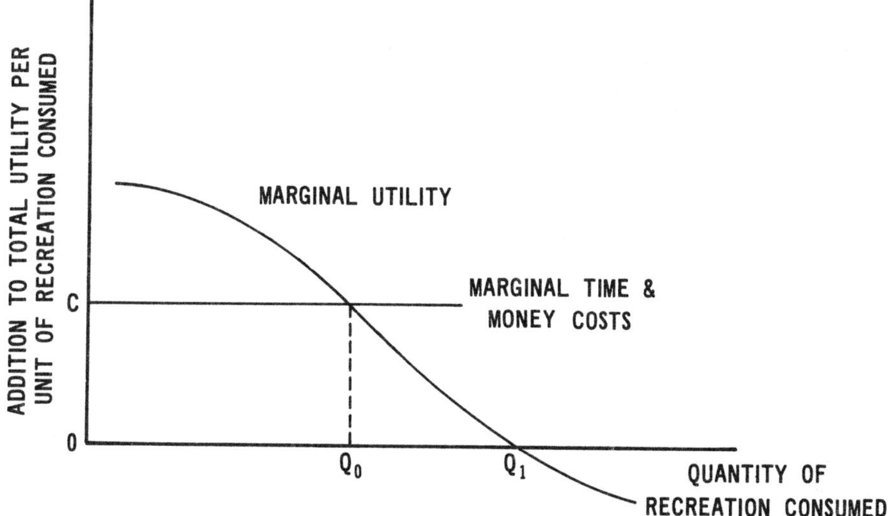

FIGURE 9-1. *Marginal Utility and the Consumption of Increasing Quantities of Recreation*

marginal utility curve indicates additions to total utility as additional units of recreation are consumed. The marginal cost line reflects per unit time and money costs associated with increases in the consumption of recreation activity. In the absence of any time and money constraints, the recreationist would choose a large quantity of recreation (Q_1), since all increments of consumption up to that quantity add to total utility, or satisfaction. In the presence of time and money costs, however, consumption is limited to a lesser quantity, Q_0. At that level of consumption, the added satisfaction obtained from the last unit of recreation consumed is equal to the cost expenditure required for that last additional unit of recreation.

THE DEMAND FOR OUTDOOR RECREATION

Attempts to derive empirical estimates of exchange values for outdoor recreation have been significantly complicated by the absence of a formal market-pricing mechanism. These efforts have, however, recognized outdoor recreation as an economic commodity and applied the conceptual logic of the economic theory of demand, modified to recognize the absence of explicit market prices.

Economists define *demand* as "a schedule of quantities that an individual or group of individuals will purchase at various prices." Stated briefly, the quantity of a given commodity demanded by an individual is a function of the price of the commodity and demand determinants such as the income of the individual, his tastes and preferences, and the prices of alternative goods.

Three demand functions are graphically shown in figure 9-2. The first demand curve, D_1, represents quantities demanded for alternative levels of price and given levels of the demand determinants indicated above. It incorporates, as do curves D_2 and D_3, the concept of quantities demanded at alternative levels of price. For example, we observe that quantity Q_1 will be demanded at price P; that at higher price P′, quantity demanded falls to Q_1'; and that at lower price P″, quantity demanded increases to Q_1''.

Changes in demand determinants shift demand curves. For example, as income increases or as tastes and preferences change toward favoring the commodity, the demand curve shifts to the right. This means that at a stable price, P, consumers will buy successively greater and greater quantities (Q_1 to Q_2 to Q_3) as demand shifts.

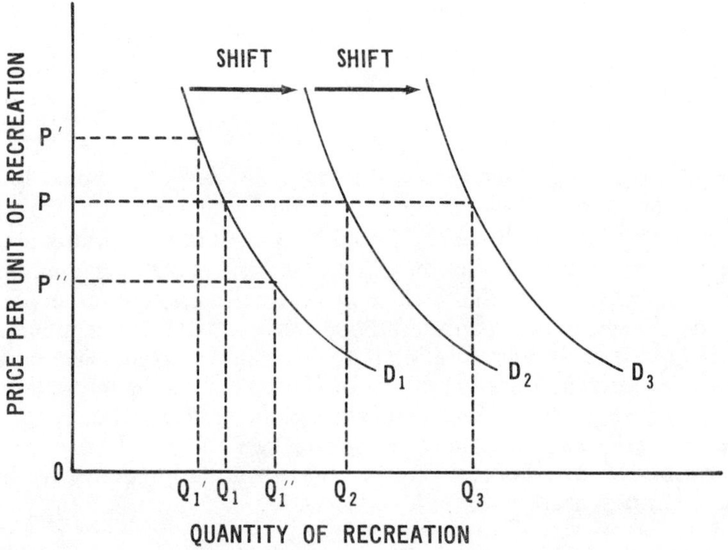

FIGURE 9-2. *Role of Price and of Shifts in Demand on the Quantity of Recreation Consumed*

The concept of economic demand incorporates the important characteristic of price-responsive quantities demanded by individuals and groups of consumers.

Demand does not involve just the quantity of goods consumed, the number of people recreating at a given location, or similarly misused planning concepts as per capita needs or requirements. Such concepts are descriptive measures devoid of economic content and inadequate to explain or to predict consumer behavior beyond the time of observation. They all too frequently have led to erroneous resource planning decisions as market conditions or determinants of consumer demands over time.

When we consider recreation demands within the context of the economic theory of demand, we find that the same types of constraints that influence market-priced consumption operate to constrain recreation consumption. And the same conceptual logic that underlies formal demand theory related to market goods is relevant to the analysis of the demand for nonmarket-priced recreation where no market-determined price exists.

As a surrogate for market price, variable money costs are used in explaining variations in quantities of recreation consumed by recreationists. The logic supporting this substitution is as follows:

As illustrated previously in figure 9-1, utility-maximizing levels of consumption are determined by marginal costs. Therefore, variable costs (those costs which vary with the amount of consumption) incurred in pursuit of recreation experiences constrain or ration actual quantities demanded and logically serve as a substitute for the market price in estimating economic demands. Said another way, the number of trips which maximize a recreationist's utility for a season is determined by variable travel and on-site costs and not by the fixed cost of investments which have no relationship to the level of consumption. The current reliance on variable time costs only as a surrogate for market price indicates our interest in the development of an analytical estimate of time costs for future incorporation into empirical models of recreation demands.

Given these conditions, an individual's recreation demand may be viewed in the formal context of figure 9-2. The number of trips or recreation days he consumes (quantity demanded) is a function of variable use costs (the proxy for market price) and appropriate demand determinants such as his income, his tastes and preferences, and the cost of alternative recreational sites and activities. If the variable use cost is high, he will consume less than if it is lower. Furthermore, income changes or other demand shifters may result in price and quantity adjustments equivalent to those inherent in analyzing market-priced commodities. The equivalent type of formulation can be developed for a specific recreation site such as a hunting or fishing location.

Economists, therefore, see outdoor recreation as having economic characteristics and potentials for demand analysis equivalent to those of other types of economic goods. (The same applies to supply considerations, but time and space preclude a discussion of this increasingly important area of inquiry.) Demand analysis can be useful to decision makers as a tool leading to valuation of alternative nonmarket recreational activities and sites.

DEMAND-ESTIMATING PROCEDURES

We have already argued that the consumption of outdoor recreation is subject to constraints similar to those for market goods and services. This means that both individuals and groups are limited as to the amount they will spend to enjoy recreation experiences. The most relevant measure of value, therefore, is the recreationist's "willingness to pay" for the experience. Values thus derived are conceptually equivalent to those for other commodities, since exchange values throughout the economic system are universally determined by the willingness of consumers to pay for given quantities at various prices.

The procedures for deriving empirical demand estimates for market-priced commodities can be legitimately applied to outdoor recreation with the modifications noted in the previous section. Here we will give a short explanation of the reasoning used in order to disclose the systematic nature of consumer willingness to pay for outdoor recreation.

The object is to develop empirically the functional relationship illustrated in figure 9-2. The demand curve forthcoming from this procedure is an ex post description of consumers' willingness to pay for recreation experiences. In a simplified form, we need to determine the different number of recreation days that recreationists will take at various cost levels (variable travel and on-site expenditures). This assumes common and stable levels of all demand determinants except variable cost, although more advanced methodology can incorporate data for situations not meeting this assumption. Cost variations can be observed either over time (time series) or geographically (cross-sectionally). The latter is the data base for most recreation demand studies, since extended time series data are not usually available.

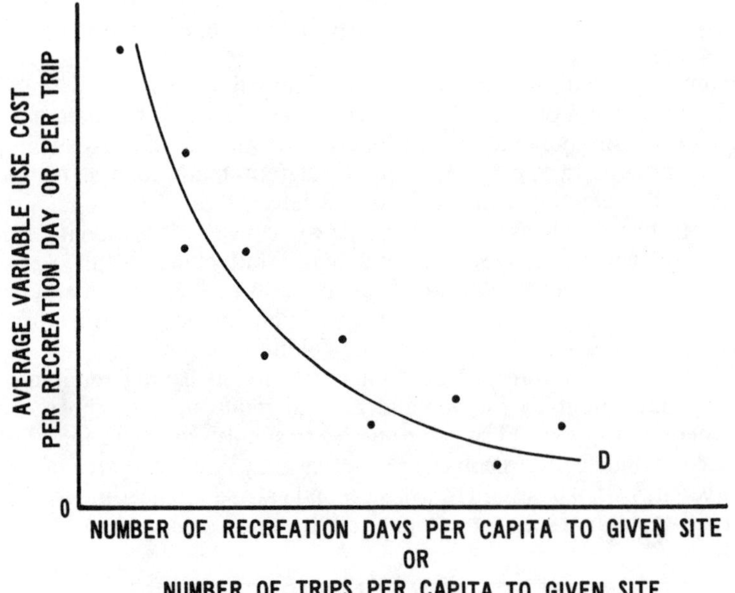

FIGURE 9-3. *Development of a Hypothetical Demand Function (D) for Recreation*

In deriving a demand relationship for a given recreation site, average variable use costs are typically determined for users from different origins and related to the number of recreation days consumed. Each origin represents a point in the scattergram when illustrated graphically (figure 9-3). Origins more proximate to the site with lesser variable costs to users can be expected to demonstrate higher levels of use and, conversely, more distant origins will be characterized by higher user costs and lower levels of use. The points generated from the various cities of origin, which are spatially related to the site, serve as the data base to which a mathematical function is fit as a statistical estimate of demand. The function defines the quantity of recreation days that will be taken by an "average" recreationist (the demand curve is based on averages) at a given site if he or she were subject to the different levels of average variable costs associated with use.

VALUATION CONCEPTS

The development of an empirical demand curve is not an end unto itself but rather should be regarded as a means to obtain information useful for policy purposes to managers, administrators, and other decision makers. One such use is the determination of site value.

The estimation of net recreation value uses the statistical demand curve (the revealed willingness to pay for a recreational experience) in its construct. While several valuation concepts are prevalent in the literature, all logically defensible procedures require the construct of an empirical economic demand curve. One commonly used valuation technique is based upon the premise that the benefits of the experience accrue solely to the individual and that the summation of all net benefits to individuals is the total net value derived from the recreation activity or site under study. This approach uses the concept of consumer surplus as described below.

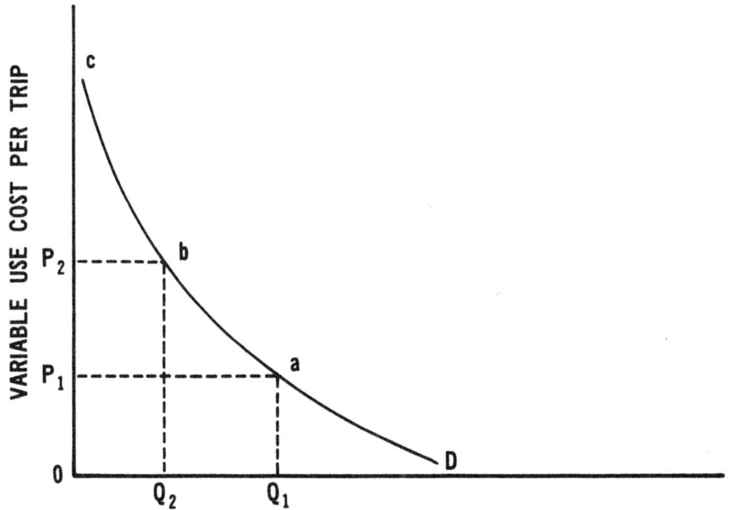

FIGURE 9-4. *Determination of Consumer Surplus*

Consider figure 9-4, where the demand curve, D, expresses the willingness to pay for recreation. The nature of the demand for this recreation experience is such that the recreator consumes some positive quantity (number of trips) so long as the variable use cost is less than c, the point of intersection of the demand curve with the vertical axis. Recall that as an individual rationally allocates his resources to recreation, he will consume or use increasing quantities of recreation up to the point where the marginal cost of the last unit consumed exactly equals the marginal utility of the experience (figure 9-1).

Thus, a recreator with variable use costs of P_1 per unit of recreation will choose Q_1 units. This decision is forthcoming because OP_1 is both the marginal cost of the trip and the marginal benefit or marginal utility of the Q_1^{th} trip to the recreator. At that level of use, his total variable costs are equal to the price per trip (OP_1) times the number of trips (OQ_1) or the area OP_1aQ_1. The total utility (satisfaction) from that quantity of recreation experiences is $OcaQ_1$. We can make this deduction, since the demand curve expresses willingness to pay for quantities, and the area under the demand curve to the intersection of the price line (a) and vertically to the horizontal axis Q_1—i.e., the area $OcaQ_1$—is the total utility from consumption or use. Since total costs are only OP_1aQ_1, the remaining, or surplus, area P_1ca is the surplus value (benefits) to the consumer of the recreational activity. This is equivalent to the concept of consumer surplus which holds for market goods.

Consumer surplus, then, is the excess of the expenditures which a consumer would be willing to pay for the level of commodity use ($OcaQ_1$) over that which he actually does pay (OP_1aQ_1).* ... [T]o summarize the implicit logic of the formulation of surplus value, we note that the demand relationship from real observations of recreationists' behavior provides an ex post statement of their willingness to pay and that it reflects total values (utility, benefits) received from the experience. If a recreationist rationally allocates his individual resources, the net utilities associated with the marginal trip to each site will be zero, since the marginal cost and marginal utility will be equal for that trip. This suggests that recreationists capture surplus utility on all except the marginal trip.

The rationale also suggests that recreationists get more surplus value from sites closer to their points of origin. Again from figure 9-4, recreationists living at the more distant—and, therefore, more expensive—origin with per unit cost of OP_2 will extract a surplus value equal to the area P_2cb. Obviously, this is less than the per capita surplus realized by individual recreationists from lower cost origin with per unit costs of only OP_1, for example.

Site values can be logically estimated from demand curves by adding consumer surpluses for all consumers from each of several origins; that is, multiply the "surplus value" determined for the average recreationist at each origin by the number of recreationists from the origin and add the products for all origins to obtain total site value for the annual observation period.

Lastly, the resulting annual site value can be used with the appropriate discount rate empirically to obtain an estimate of total recreation value either for the site or for sites with similar characteristics with appropriate adjustments

*To enlarge on this example, note that if the per unit cost were OP_2, the recreator would have chosen OQ_2 trips at a total cost of OP_2bQ_2, total benefits of $OcbQ_2$, and a lesser net surplus value of only P_2cb.

for location, quality, etc. The resulting value may then be used by decision makers to compare benefits among competing alternatives. In the face of scarce public investment resources, we suggest that rational decisions consider and favor developments or investments with potentially higher values.

SUMMARY

Our major focus has been directed toward concepts underlying economic demands. Review of a valuation concept introduces the usefulness of demand estimates to that endeavor. More detailed discussion of topics and concepts is merited. . . .

We want to reemphasize our basic postulate that recreation is an economic good that differs from other goods in the economy primarily because recreational activities are not market priced. Our important analytical problems grow out of this deficiency not out of the presence of esthetic properties. Also, the absence of market prices does not mean that outdoor recreation is free. Time and money costs constrain outdoor activities, just as they do the consumption of market goods and services. Consequently, definable demands exist for recreation sites, just as they do for other commodities. By substituting variable use costs for market price, economists can apply the logic and analytical power of demand theory to the analysis of outdoor recreation demand. Demand estimates and value approximations are prerequisites to economically efficient public investment decisions, which, in turn, are basic to efforts to maximize society's returns from public expenditures.

CHAPTER 10

SOME SOCIAL CONCEPTS FOR OUTDOOR RECREATION PLANNING

George H. Stankey

Many recreational values cannot be measured in economic terms, and other approaches developed in the social sciences can be utilized. Seven important social science concepts that strengthen the ability to understand recreation behavior are described by George Stankey in this paper. These concepts are broad and abstract, but they provide recreation planners and policy makers with refined notions and guidelines for evaluating recreation benefits and alternatives.

. . . Competition for money is increasing, and tightening budgets have increased the need for better measures of outdoor recreation's costs and benefits. Efforts to further refine the economic measures of recreation should be continued and strengthened. But it is the premise of this paper that the concepts offered by economics only partially answer the problems recreation managers confront. The concepts of a variety of social sciences will be needed as research attempts to aid decision makers.

The social sciences include many disciplines, ranging from psychology, cultural anthropology, and geography to history as well as economics. The social sciences are joined by a common thread that attempts to explain man—as an individual, as a member of society, and as a resource user. Each individual discipline has developed a unique perspective on man. For instance, economists look at the mechanisms whereby we allocate scarce resources; psychologists are concerned with the processes that influence an individual's behavior with regard to the environment around him.

Each discipline provides important insight on how and why people seek recreation and on how recreation programs can best fulfill human needs. Disciplinary boundaries are foggy at best. For instance, geographers studying recreationists' behavior have drawn heavily on concepts and methods used by psychologists and sociologists. The point is that participation in recreation, like all human behavior, is complex. The greater diversity we bring to bear in examining recreational behavior, the more likely we [are to] develop accurate notions about it.

What concepts can we draw from the social sciences that will aid recreation managers? . . . In the following discussion, I have attempted to organize

Reprinted from *Outdoor Recreation—Advances in Application of Economics,* USDA Forest Service General Technical Report WO-2 (March 1977), pp. 154–61, with permission of the author.

a number of diverse notions and perspectives from the various social science disciplines into a set of concepts for recreation planning. These include: (1) the recreation opportunity spectrum; (2) recreational preference; (3) substitutability; (4) carrying capacity; (5) dependent satisfactions; (6) externalities; and (7) cost effectiveness.

RECREATION OPPORTUNITY SPECTRUM

The basic premise of the recreation spectrum concept is that a variety of environmental settings "from the paved to the primeval" (25) are needed to fulfill the many needs, motivations, and preferences that lead people to participate in outdoor recreation. One of the dominant themes to emerge from recreation research has been the existence of a wide range of tastes and preferences among users. These include such diverse dimensions as socialization and challenge. Different kinds of outdoor settings differ in their ability to satisfy these various dimensions. The opportunity spectrum concept recognizes the existence and legitimacy of these various motivations. The fundamental issue facing planners, then, is not one of "either-or" or even "how much" (19) but, rather, of establishing a dynamic balance across the entire continuum (4).

We can specify four important principles concerning the spectrum:

1. *It is not defined by a quality continuum.* Quality is measured by the extent to which participants are able to experience their desired dimension of satisfaction (26). Providing quality recreation, then, becomes a matter of providing a package of opportunities that permits people to choose alternatives to best provide the satisfactions they seek. For instance, quality camping for some is the opportunity to experience solitude. For others, it is the opportunity to socialize with new friends. In each case, the activity is the same but the product is different.

2. *We can define the spectrum by several criteria.* For instance, one recent paper suggested space requirements, desirable frequency of contacts among users, participant objectives, development required, access, and mode of transportation as criteria for defining the spectrum (19). Although other criteria might be relevant in defining the spectrum, these will emerge from research and experience. The point is, the spectrum is founded upon the presence of a range of conditions within each criterion.

3. *What happens to one part of the spectrum can influence other parts of the system.* For example, we find few instances of programs for providing dispersed recreation opportunities (with the exception of classified wilderness). However, research has shown that many wilderness visitors desire an experience that could be better supplied in other locations (28). Because of the gap in the opportunity spectrum (or in knowledge about other opportunities that do exist), this use and its associated impacts are directed at an opportunity that is relatively scarce and subject to rapid, often irreversible, change.

4. *The opportunity spectrum is dynamic.* The range of activities found along the opportunity spectrum can change over both time and space. However, changes in activities, brought about perhaps by technology (e.g., snow-

mobiling), might simply reflect new outlets for value systems that remain fairly stable.

Data are available that give us some clues on how and why people move about the opportunity spectrum. For instance, the process of learning certain skills (e.g., how to get along in the woods) appears to lead to a shift toward more demanding kinds of opportunities (1; 5; 14). However, such changes might be linked to gradual changes in the environmental conditions on different sites. As conditions change (use levels increase, more facilities are developed, etc.), those aspects of the site that once attracted users are lost. Persons using this site similarly change; new conditions repel former users while attracting new ones. This process of "invasion and succession" (4) may help explain declining participation rates in some recreational activities (15).

The opportunity spectrum should be viewed as an objective for recreation planning; that is, when the programs of the various recreation suppliers (e.g., federal government, state government, private sector, etc.) are considered, we should find a broad, diverse set of alternatives from which people can choose. However, competition for resources from other users and other forms of recreation means that choices about what will be provided, where, and by whom will never be completely free. Given these constraints, coupled with the uncoordinated fashion in which recreation is provided,* the opportunity spectrum will not, in all likelihood, evolve. Other concepts, therefore, must be used to assist recreation planners to provide diversity.

RECREATIONAL PREFERENCE

The Federal Land and Water Conservation Act of 1964 requires states to prepare recreation plans based on use projections derived from demand studies. However, most of these demand studies simply project past consumption. They do not reflect demand.

Demand is a technical term that refers to the quantity that would be consumed at different price levels. However, the typical demand study is based upon an examination of past participation at a set of given opportunities, coupled with an estimate of the future growth rate (2). From these calculations, projections of "demand" are made that, despite their shortcomings, play a dominant role in planning. Because of the failure to recognize participation as a function of the user's opportunity, time, and money, demand studies have contributed little information about the actual preferences of the population.

Recreation participation is linked to what has been called "opportunity theory" (8); i.e., participation depends upon availability. Availability is influenced by a variety of factors: the Bureau of Outdoor Recreation 1965 Outdoor Recreation Survey revealed that the main reason for not participating in an activity *at all* was lack of time followed by lack of opportunity and lack of skill (29). Lack of accurate information about existing opportunities also

*There are over 20 federal agencies with recreation-related programs and over 200 different organizations at the state level. County, municipal, and other public jurisdictions, as well as a growing private sector, further cloud the picture.

restricts availability. For instance, Lime (17) found that one-third of the campers in the Superior National Forest knew only of three or fewer campgrounds, although the area had thirty-six (the average number known about was only eight).

Another problem in relying upon past participation to guide future decisions is that when opportunities are available, particularly at little or no cost, they will be used. But *used* should not lead us automatically to assume people are satisfied with existing opportunities or that alternative opportunities might not have been even more sought after.

Preferences generally are obtained orally or in writing. Actual behavior remains perhaps the ultimate test of preferences. The gap between word and deed is a snarl with which social scientists have long wrestled. Careful attention must be paid to reduce this gap. However, surveys can provide important clues about what people seek and their probable response to different programs.

For instance, carefully designed surveys of preference can help measure the range, mix, and intensity of sentiment for alternative outdoor recreation opportunities. Such surveys also can help establish management goals. Goals describe what should be, and must be, set by an informed citizenry—not technocrats (27). What we often find today, however, are management objectives that reflect the values of managers rather than users (4). Because managerial notions about users and their desires are not always accurate, it is important that policy makers have an objective source of feedback so programs will reflect actual preferences.

Preference surveys also reveal the values people place on alternative outdoor recreation programs and who receives these values. One major role social scientists ought to play in recreation planning is helping to define the nature of the product of recreation programs. Greater attention should be devoted to defining the nature of what we are producing and the basis for its demand.

An understanding of preferences enables planners to balance programs with public desires and to review demand studies. Such review could illustrate gaps in opportunities currently provided (e.g., back country areas, facilities for . . . the handicapped, etc.). Such information is important feedback, particularly with regard to recreation where feedback mechanisms are often absent or inadequate.

SUBSTITUTABILITY

The concept of substitutability refers to the extent to which recreation activities can be interchanged in terms of satisfying user's motives, wishes, and desires (9). It thus has an important bearing on problems of supply because different settings might be capable of providing the same or similar kinds of experiences. This becomes significant when the cost of one location far exceeds another. For instance, many people enjoy sunbathing at the seashore. However, such lands are expensive and becoming increasingly scarce. With a better understanding of substitutability, we might find that we are able to produce the same recreational product on alternative locations that do not require as large an investment as do seashore lands. In turn, we might reserve scarce seashore lands to produce those experiences which cannot be supplied by other settings.

Substitutability is concerned with psychological, sociological, and personality variables that lead to interchange among activities, rather than on the physical characteristics of the activity setting. Cross-country skiing, for instance, would not necessarily represent an appropriate substitute for downhill skiing just because both occur on snow. Very different motives and interests probably exist for these two activities. Cross-country skiing and hiking might be fairly substitutable, however, because they produce very similar experiences, despite the differences in physical setting.

Any recreational activity we might look at probably is substitutable to some degree. A major question before us, then, is to determine which activities show a high degree of substitutability as well as those which exhibit little substitutability. Trying to do this for every recreational activity, however, would be almost impossible. One method of handling this problem would be to group activities into categories with all activities in one category similar to one another in some way.

One such grouping of recreational categories has been proposed by Hendee, Gale, and Catton (11). [See also chapter 14 of this volume.] In a study of recreationists in car campgrounds and national park back country and national forest wilderness in the Pacific Northwest, Hendee et al. (12) asked respondents to select, from a list of twenty-six leisure activities, the six activities they most preferred in descending order of preference. Those activities chosen as "most preferred" were grouped together into five categories called "activity preference types." The categories were named according to the general type of motivation they fulfilled:

1. *Appreciative-symbolic.* Activities such as mountain climbing and seeing natural scenery: The focus here is on appreciation of environmental qualities and preservation.
2. *Extractive-symbolic.* Hunting and fishing are examples. These activities involved the extraction of "trophies" from the environment.
3. *Passive-free play.* This category includes painting, relaxing, and sightseeing. The activities typically require little effort and are generally not limited to a forest environment.
4. *Sociable learning.* This includes such things as nature study, visiting with other campers, and viewing exhibits. The opportunity to interact with others is a primary source of satisfaction.
5. *Active-expressive.* Includes water-skiing, playing games, and driving motorcycles or snowmobiles. As with passive-free play, these activities do not require a forest setting and are largely focused on the activity rather than the setting in which it takes place.

We would generally expect to find greater substitutability among activities within categories than between. As suggested above, one important part of the substitutability problem is determining what activities show little or no substitutability. These probably tend to be found in the appreciative-symbolic category where the setting (e.g., wilderness or white-water river running), is a major component of the participant's experience (9; 10).

Discrepancies between the values held by managers and those held by users can lead to conflict. As an example, we find some campers today who participate in camping for its social rewards (meeting new friends, comparing equipment, etc.) rather than as a source of contact with nature (4; 16). Because contact with other people is an important source of enjoyment, it might be possible to produce similar experiences in different settings. Many people decry the growth of new campgrounds, such as the recently proposed "high-rise" facility near downtown New Orleans, because the activity provided "isn't really camping." Such judgments fail to recognize the diverse nature of the camping experience (15).

Perhaps the primary value of the substitutability concept is that it directs attention to the human experiences produced by activities. Activities are simply a means to an end, and planners must focus attention on the product of their programs not the programs themselves (3). As public preferences shift, the relative priority accorded various outdoor recreation programs will also shift. Failure to identify and respond to these shifts could lead to spending that fails to satisfy public desires and creates conditions that might invite vandalism and other destructive behavior.

CARRYING CAPACITY

Carrying capacity refers to the capability of a recreational opportunity to produce a specified type or set of experiences. The experiences to be produced by any given opportunity are outlined in the management objectives.

A basic principle in carrying capacity is that any use produces change. Small amounts of use can produce significant changes in soil and vegetation (6; 30). Similarly, the various dimensions of the recreational experience are subject to change. Where solitude is a key value in the management objectives, even low levels of use can result in adverse impacts; where socialization with others is important, relatively high levels of use might be permissible (30). The point is, carrying capacity is not a value fixed solely by physical-biological conditions (18).

Change, either ecological or sociological, is defined as undesirable only when it conflicts with the area's management objectives. The objectives, in turn, are a function of various constraints and factors: ecological conditions, public attitudes and existing opportunities, and administrative and budgetary considerations. Thus, the manager's task is to determine the "limits of acceptable change" (6); i.e., How much change will be permitted to occur before taking steps to prevent further change?

The capacity of a site to provide certain human experiences can be expanded through intensive management. The common response when we seem to have too little of something is to add to the supply; for instance, more acres of land for camping. We can also increase supply, however, by making the acres we have more useful. For instance, it might not be possible to increase the acreage of a campground that is experiencing increasing use. Through the use of management tools—such as more efficient design and location of individual units or the use of plant materials more resistant to use—it might be possible to accommodate a significant increase in use. As suggested above, capacity is not a fixed value; it is responsive to management.

DEPENDENT SATISFACTIONS

Recreation resources range from the readily available and common to the scarce and unique. Through a variety of programs, we have tried to protect the unique ones lest they be lost to society for all time, perhaps without a conscious decision.

There is an important difference in the range or continuum of recreation resources that goes beyond mere appearance. On one hand, we have many recreation settings that can be easily duplicated if they are lost. For instance, a picnic ground that is removed because of a freeway can be rebuilt elsewhere, perhaps almost identically to the original. Other settings are much less susceptible to being duplicated. Wild, white-water rivers simply cannot be recreated once they are destroyed; even if we possessed the technology to do so, the cost would be prohibitive. Economists called this difference in susceptibility to reproduction "asymmetry" (14).

Although it is important to understand how opportunities differ regarding our abilities to duplicate them, the major significance of asymmetry is in terms of kinds of experiences these different opportunities produce. On the one hand, we can describe satisfactions [that are] common to many settings and that are not uniquely linked to any one particular setting. Visiting with friends is an example. Because of the broad base from which they can be derived, we might label these relatively easily replaced satisfactions as "generic" (26). Loss of the recreational resource does not necessarily constitute loss of the satisfaction. On the other hand, certain satisfactions, such as challenge, are specifically linked to particular kinds of environments. We would label these satisfactions "dependent." When the setting is lost, the capability to provide such satisfactions is similarly lost. Wilderness and white-water river are settings that might produce such experiences.

Thus we can see that those opportunities which we have the least capability of restoring are also the ones which produce these "dependent" satisfactions. From this one could argue that in allocating resources to different users, those producing "dependent" satisfaction should be reserved if at all possible.

We have little information on the value of the authenticity of recreation opportunity. Certainly, some features of the natural environment can be duplicated, perhaps rather realistically. One can envision engineers hard at work constructing pipes and boilers to create a new "Old Faithful." For many people, the naturalness of their surroundings is of little consequence to the satisfaction they derive (20). "Plastic trees" can be as important as real ones (13). The concept of "dependent satisfactions" is not to be interpreted to mean that one experience is better than another; it merely calls attention to the relative availability of these experiences and to our ability to duplicate the settings capable of producing these experiences.

EXTERNALITIES

When any land management decision is made, there generally is an effort to measure both the benefits and the costs associated with that decision. But commonly, some of these benefits and costs "escape" off the site. Benefits that are not received or costs that are not borne by a decision maker are called "externalities." Air pollution from a factory is perhaps the most easily understood example where a cost (e.g., sulfur dioxide) is not absorbed by a decision maker (i.e., the factory) but rather [is] allowed to become a cost the public must bear.

Many of these external benefits and costs have no direct economic measure; we cannot say how much they cost or benefit us in terms of so-many dollars. Nevertheless, they are real and planners need to account for them. Although the concept of externalities is founded in economics, other social scientists find it useful. As used here, the objective of the concept is to promote beneficial relationships between different resource programs while minimizing costly relationships.

For instance, few efforts have been made to develop positive and aggressive management programs aimed at the dispersed end of the recreation spectrum, with the exception of wilderness (22). At least some present wilderness use could probably be better accommodated elsewhere—persons primarily seeking some forms of dispersed recreation (28). However, virtually no programs exist for such persons; primitive, non-wilderness opportunities generally exist as "leftovers" rather than as the result of any deliberate positive effort. Because of the lack of diverse opportunities, conflicts between user groups holding differing value systems but seeking the same scarce lands have developed. As a result, different clientele groups often are pitted against one another and the pressures for "either-or" (19) have grown.

The general strategy advocated here is that we review the externalities that our resource programs create and, in a sort of "social cost-benefit" analysis, strive to reduce the costs and raise the benefits. To facilitate this, we need to examine the relationships among various programs. For our purpose, let us consider three different types of relationships: (1) complementary relationships; (2) supplementary relationships, where development of one opportunity can provide benefits to another (the development of back country areas for dispersed, nonmechanized recreation and the relationship of such areas to wilderness is an example); and (3) competitive relationships, where changes in one opportunity cause negative impacts on another. Developing roaded recreation opportunities immediately adjacent to wilderness would create such a relationship.

It seems we can draw two principles from this concept for outdoor recreation planners. First, functional planning (i.e., planning for one resource use at a time) probably tends to create competitive relationships and only occasionally leads to complementary or supplementary relationships. Thus, an integrated, multifunctional planning process is called for. Second, planning programs that provide a package of opportunities will generally encourage complementary and supplementary relationships. For instance, placing the more socially oriented forms of outdoor recreation opportunities into areas where access is good, while retaining those opportunities dependent on naturalness and solitude in more remote locations, should provide a more desirable experience for all concerned (7; 21).

COST EFFECTIVENESS

The discussion up to this point has dealt with concepts that social scientists other than economists might recommend to the outdoor recreation planner. The concept of cost effectiveness, however, is a notion that economists commonly use. [The] purpose in including it in this discussion is to consider how the concept might be made more useful with the input of social scientists.

When an administrator decides to spend money for recreational purposes, he would like to know how "good" that decision was. However, because recreation is normally provided free or at only low cost, the normal feedback mechanism, price, is absent. Only rarely are recreation costs met by the consumer; rather, they are subsidized by the public at large on grounds that society benefits because recreation is provided to it (24).

Although we previously argued that economic measures of the recreation value are limited in their usefulness, planners and policy makers still need some notion as to how effectively the money they have invested in some recreation project is being used. Consider the following problem: It has been decided that an area is to be developed as an auto-access campground of moderate size and with standard facilities (e.g., picnic tables, fireplaces, pit toilets, etc.). Given that decision, what kinds of information would an administrator need so that the investment returns the most value to the user?

This is a very common problem facing recreation managers today. Occupancy rates in campgrounds are typically very uneven. For instance, on the Superior National Forest, Lime (17) found that occupancy rates at individual sites ranged from in excess of 100 percent to only about 10 percent over the summer use season. There we can see how a knowledge of user behavior could be very useful in guiding investment decisions. For instance, what are the environmental qualities that make one site more attractive than another? How do people go about choosing a location [at which] to camp? Knowing the answer to these and similar questions could mean the difference in providing campsites that cost $2.50 per night with full occupancy to perhaps a hundredfold that figure at only 10-percent occupancy (23).

The concept of cost effectiveness calls for planners to give greater attention to the product of their recreation programs. Although costs are an important constraint within which we operate, decisions should be guided by concern for what we are buying rather than costs alone. We must also consider the kind of product an opportunity can produce as well as the demand for that product and its relative availability.

CONCLUSIONS

In this paper, we have attempted to describe several social science concepts that have relevance to outdoor recreation planning, particularly when coupled with economic concepts. Because recreation behavior is complex and because there are substantial aspects of it that cannot be easily considered in an economic framework, it seems appropriate that our package of planning concepts be broadly based.

Applying these concepts directly to recreation management problems will be difficult. At the moment, they should be considered broad concerns of which planners must be aware. The pressing task now before social scientists and recreation planners is the translation of these broad, abstract concepts into operational guidelines in the form of specific criteria. Such criteria would allow for increasingly refined notions of the noneconomic trade-offs, costs, and benefits of alternative recreation programs. Coupled with the sophisticated tools and methods of economics, our ability satisfactorily to meet the recreational needs of society should be markedly improved.

REFERENCES

1. Burch, W., and Wenger, W. 1967. The social characteristics in three styles of family camping. Forest Service Resource Paper PNW-48. Portland, Ore.
2. Burdge, R., and Hendee, J. 1972. The demand survey dilemma: Assessing the credibility of state outdoor recreation plans. *Guideline* 2: 65–68.
3. Chappelle, D. E. 1973. The "need" for outdoor recreation: An economic conundrum. *Journal of Leisure Research* 5: 47–53.
4. Clark, R.; Hendee, J. C.; and Campbell, F. 1971. Values, behavior, and conflict in modern camping culture. *Journal of Leisure Research* 3: 143–59.
5. Davidson, P.; Adams, F. G.; and Seneca, J. 1966. The social value of water recreational facilities resulting from an improvement in water quality: The Delaware Estuary. In *Water Research*, pp. 175–211. Baltimore: Johns Hopkins Press.
6. Frissell, S. S., and Stankey, G. H. 1972. Wilderness environmental quality: Search for social and ecological harmony. In *Society of American Foresters National Convention proceedings* (1972), pp. 170–83. Hot Springs, Ark.
7. Hart, W. J. 1966. A systems approach to park planning. IUCN Publications, New Series Supplementary Paper 4. Morges, Switzerland.
8. Hendee, J. C. 1969. Rural-urban differences reflected in outdoor recreation participation. *Journal of Leisure Research* 1: 333–41.
9. Hendee, J. C., and Burdge, R. J. 1974. The substitutability concept: Implications for recreation research and management. *Journal of Leisure Research* 6: 155–62.
10. Hendee, J. C., and Stankey, G. H. 1973. Biocentricity in wilderness management. *Bioscience* 23: 535–38.
11. Hendee, J. C.; Gale, R. P.; and Catton, W. R., Jr. 1971. A typology of outdoor recreation activity preferences. *Journal of Environmental Education* 3, no. 1: 28–34.
12. Hendee, J. C., et al. 1968. Wilderness users in the Pacific Northwest—Their characteristics, values, and management preferences. Forest Service Research Paper PNW-61. Portland, Ore.
13. Krieger, M. H. 1973. What's wrong with plastic trees? *Science* 179: 446–55.
14. Krutilla, J. 1967. Conservation reconsidered. *American Economic Review*, September, pp. 777–86.
15. LaPage, W. F., and Ragain, D. P. 1971. Trends in camping participation. Forest Service Research Paper NE-183. Upper Darby, Pa.
16. ———. 1974. Family camping trends—An eight-year panel study. *Journal of Leisure Research* 6: 101–12.

17. Lime, D. W. 1971. Factors influencing campground use in the Superior National Forest. Forest Service Research Paper NC-60. St. Paul, Minn.
18. Lime, D. W., and Stankey, G. H. 1971. Carrying capacity: Maintaining outdoor recreation quality. In *Recreation Symposium proceedings*, pp. 174–84. Upper Darby, Pa.: Forest Service. Also see chapter 7 of this volume.
19. Lloyd, R. D., and Fischer, V. L. 1972. Dispersed versus concentrated recreation as forest policy. In *Seventh World Forestry Congress proceedings*, p. 176. Buenos Aires.
20. Lowenthal, D. 1962. Not every prospect pleases—What is our criterion for scenic beauty? *Landscape*, winter, pp. 19–23.
21. Lucas, R. C. 1964. Wilderness perception and use: The example of the Boundary Waters Canoe Areas. *Natural Resources Journal* 3: 394–411.
22. Lucas, R. C., and Stankey, G. H. 1973. Social carrying capacity for backcountry recreation. In *Outdoor recreation research: Applying the results*, pp. 14–23. Forest Service General Technical Report NC-9. St. Paul, Minn.
23. Lundgren, A. L. 1973. Economic bases for allocating resources in outdoor recreation. In *Outdoor recreation research: Applying the results*, pp. 7–13. Forest Service General Technical Report NC-9. St. Paul, Minn.
24. Manthy, R. S., and Tucker, T. L. 1972. Supply costs for public forest land recreation. Michigan State University Agricultural Experiment Station Research Paper 158.
25. Nash, R. 1967. *Wilderness and the American mind.* New Haven: Yale University Press.
26. Potter, D.; Hendee, J. C.; and Clark, R. 1973. Hunting satisfaction: Game, guns, or nature? In *Human dimensions in wildlife programs*, pp. 62–71. Washington, D.C.: Wildlife Management Institute.
27. Reich, C. A. 1962. Bureaucracy and the forests. Center for the Study of Democratic Institutions Occasional Paper. Washington, D.C.
28. Stankey, G. H. 1973. Visitor perception of wilderness recreation carrying capacity. Forest Service Research Paper INT-142. Ogden, Utah.
29. U.S. Bureau of Outdoor Recreation. 1967. *1965 survey of outdoor recreation.* Washington, D.C.: Government Printing Office.
30. Wagar, J. A. 1964. The carrying capacity of wildlands for recreation. *Forest Science Monograph* 7.

CHAPTER 11

COMPARISON OF METHODS FOR RECREATION EVALUATION

Jack L. Knetsch
Robert K. Davis

Basic economic concepts as applied to outdoor recreation were presented in chapter 9. In the present chapter Jack Knetsch and Robert Davis compare several different economic methods of measuring the value of recreation. The basic problem is attempting to discover a proxy for a non–market priced service or commodity. The authors examine and reject the notion of using gross expenditures, costs, and market values as means of approaching a recreation value. They demonstrate that interviews and travel costs are valid methods, since they are based on the concept of demand as exhibited by willingness to pay or to travel.

Evaluation of recreation benefits has made significant headway in the past few years. It appears that concern is increasingly focusing on the hard core of relevant issues concerning the economic benefits of recreation and how we can go about making some useful estimates.

The underlying reasons for this sharpening of focus are largely pragmatic. The rapidly increasing demand for recreation, stemming from the often-cited factors of increasing population, leisure, incomes, mobility, and urbanization, calls for continuing adjustments in resource allocations. This is the case with respect to our land and water resources in general; but more specifically it bears on such matters as the establishment of national recreation areas, setting aside or preserving areas for parks and open spaces in and near expanding urban areas, and clearly on questions of justification, location, and operation of water development projects.

Recreation services have only recently been recognized as products of land and water resource use. As such, they offer problems that do not occur when resolving the conflicting uses of most goods and services—for example, steel and lumber. Conflicting demands for commodities such as these are resolved largely in the marketplaces of the private economy, where users bid against each other for the limited supplies.

Outdoor recreation, however, has developed largely as a nonmarket commodity. The reasons for this are quite elaborate, but in essence outdoor recrea-

Reprinted from Allen V. Kneese and Stephen C. Smith, eds., *Water Research* (Baltimore: Johns Hopkins Press, 1966), pp. 125–42, copyright by Johns Hopkins Press and published for Resources for the Future, Inc., by permission of Johns Hopkins Press and the authors.

tion for the most part is produced and distributed in the absence of a market mechanism partly because we prefer it that way and have rejected various market outcomes and partly because many kinds of outdoor recreation experience cannot be packaged and sold by private producers to private consumers. This absence of a market necessitates imputing values to the production of recreation services. Such economic benefits can be taken into account in decisions affecting our use of resources.

MISUNDERSTANDINGS OF RECREATION VALUES

Discussions of values of outdoor recreation have been beset by many misunderstandings. One of these stems from a lack of appreciation that the use of outdoor recreation facilities differs only in kind, but not in principle, from consumption patterns of other goods and services. Another is that the market process takes account of personal and varied consumer satisfactions.

It is, furthermore, the incremental values that are important in making decisions relative to resource allocations. The incremental values of recreation developments of various kinds are a manageable concept which can be used for comparisons in spite of the very great aggregate value that some may want to attribute to recreation. Nothing is gained—and no doubt a great deal has been lost—by what amounts to ascribing the importance of a total supply of recreation to an added increment rather than concentrating on the added costs and the added benefits.

A similar difficulty arises with respect to questions of water supply. That man is entirely dependent upon the existence of water is repeatedly emphasized. While true, the point does not matter. Decisions necessarily focus on increments and therefore on the added costs and benefits that stem from adding small amounts to the existing total.

Further, no goods or services are priceless in the sense of an infinite price. There is an individual and collective limit to how much we will give up to enjoy the services of any outdoor recreation facility or to preserve any scenic resource. The most relevant economic measure of recreation values, therefore, is willingness on the part of consumers to pay for outdoor recreation services. This set of values is comparable to economic values established for other commodities, for it is the willingness to give up on the part of consumers that establishes values throughout the economy.

Failure to understand these value characteristics results in two types of error. The first is the belief that the only values that are worth considering are those accounted for commercially. A second and related source of error is a belief that outdoor recreation experience is outside the framework of economics, that the relevant values have an esthetic, deeply personal, and even mystical nature. We believe both of these to be incorrect. In particular, the notion that economic values do not account for esthetic or personal values is fallacious and misleading. Economically, the use of resources for recreation is fully equivalent to other uses, and the values which are relevant do not necessarily need to be determined in the marketplace. This last condition does indicate that indirect means of supplying relevant measures of the values produced may be necessary. But this is an empirical problem, albeit one of some considerable dimension, and the primary concern of this paper.

The problem of using imputed values for value determination has been met with a considerable degree of success for some products of water resource development. Procedures have been developed to assess the value of the flood protection, irrigation, and power services produced by the projects, even though in many cases a market does not in fact exist or is inadequate for the actual benefit calculations. Without commenting on the adequacy of these methods, it is generally agreed that such measures are useful in evaluating the output of project services.

NATIONAL AND LOCAL BENEFITS

Discussions of these topics have often been further confused by failure to separate two types of economic consequences or benefit. This has led to improper recognition of relevant and legitimate economic interests, and to inferior planning and policy choices.

There are, first, what we may call primary benefits, or national benefits. Second, there are benefits we may refer to as local benefits, or impact benefits. Both sets of values resulting from investment in recreation have economic relevance, but they differ, and they bear differently on decision.

The primary recreation benefits, or values, are in general taken to be expressions of the consumers' willingness to pay for recreation services. These values may or may not register in the commerce of the region or in the commerce of the nation, but this does not make them less real. When appropriately measured, they are useful for guiding social choices at the national level. The other set of accounts is concerned with local expenditure of money for local services associated with recreation. While outdoor recreation is not marketed—in the sense that the services of parks, as such, are not sold to any great extent in any organized market—money does indeed become involved in the form of expenditures for travel, equipment, lodging, and so forth. The amount of money spent in connection with outdoor recreation and tourism is large and growing, making outdoor recreation expenditures of prime concern to localities and regions which may stand to benefit. Our concern is with measuring the more difficult of the two types of benefit just mentioned—national recreation benefits. While these are measured essentially by the consumers' willingness to pay, in some cases the benefits extend to the nonusing general public.

ALTERNATIVE MEASUREMENT METHODS

There are obvious advantages to evaluating recreation benefits by market prices in the same manner as their most important resource competitors. However, as we have indicated, past applications have been hampered by disagreement on what are the meaningful values. In spite of growing recognition that recreation has an important economic value, economists and public administrators have been ill-prepared to include it in the social or public calculus in ways that lead to better allocations of resources.

The benefits of recreation from the social or community viewpoint are alleged to be many and varied. Some of the descriptions of public good externalities arising from recreation consumption are gross overstatements of the real values derived from the production of recreation services. But recreation benefits do in fact exist. Where externalities are real—as in cases of recreation in connection with visits to various historic areas or educational facilities, or where preservation of unique ecological units has cultural and scientific values —they should be recognized in assigning values to the development or preservation of the areas. However, it is our view that, by and large, recreation is a consumption good rather than a factor of production, and the benefits to be enjoyed are largely those accruing to the individual consumer participating. This is even more likely to be the case with recreation provided by water projects. The large bulk of primary recreation benefits can be viewed as the value of the output of the project to those who use them. This view stems from the concept that recreation resources produce an economic product. In this sense they are scarce and capable of yielding satisfaction for which people are willing to pay. Finally, some accounting can be made of this economic demand.

As the desirability of establishing values for recreation use of resources has become more apparent over the past few years, a number of methods for measuring or estimating them have been proposed and to some extent used. Some of the measures are clearly incorrect; others attempt to measure appropriate values but fall short on empirical grounds (3; 7; 9).

Gross Expenditures Method

The gross expenditures method attempts to measure the value of recreation to the recreationist in terms of the total amount spent on recreation by the user. These expenditures usually include travel expenses, equipment costs, and expenses incurred while in the recreation area. Estimates of gross recreation expenditures are very popular in some quarters; for one thing, they are likely to produce large figures. It is argued that persons making such expenditures must have received commensurate value or they would not have made them. The usual contention is that the value of a day's recreation is worth at least the amount of money spent by a person for the use of that recreation.

These values have some usefulness in indicating the amount of money that is spent on a particular type of outdoor recreation, but as justification for public expenditure on recreation or for determining the worth or benefit of the recreation opportunity afforded, they are of little consequence.

The values we seek are those which show not some gross value but the net increase in value over and above what would occur in the absence of a particular recreation opportunity. Gross expenditures do not indicate the value of the losses sustained if the particular recreation opportunity were to disappear, nor do they show the net gain in value from an increase in a particular recreation opportunity.

Market Value of Fish Method

A proposed method for estimating the recreation benefits afforded by fishing imputes to sport fishing a market value of the fish caught. The main objection to this procedure is the implied definition that the fish alone are the primary objective of the activity.

Cost Method

The cost method assumes that the value of outdoor recreation resource use is equal to the cost of generating it or, in some extreme applications, that it is a multiple of these costs. This has the effect of justifying any contemplated recreation project. However, the method offers no guide in the case of contemplated loss of recreation opportunities and allows little or no discrimination between relative values of alternative additions.

Market Value Method

Basic to the market value method measure is a schedule of charges judged to be the market value of the recreation services produced. These charges are multiplied by the actual or expected attendance figures to arrive at a recreation value for the services.

The method is on sound ground in its emphasis on the willingness of users to incur expenses to make choices. However, the market for outdoor recreation is not a commercial one, certainly not for much of the recreation provided publicly and only to a limited extent for private recreation. It is in part because private areas are not fully comparable with public areas that users are willing to pay the fees or charges. It seems, therefore, inappropriate to use charges paid on a private area to estimate the value of recreation on public areas. Also a single value figure or some range of values will be inappropriate for many recreation areas. Physical units of goods and services are not everywhere equally valuable, whether the commodity be sawtimber, grazing, or recreation. Location in the case of recreation affects value greatly. Moreover, differences of quality and attractiveness of recreation areas are not fully comparable or recognized by the unit values.

There are other methods, but few have received much attention. Where does this leave us? The only methods to which we give high marks are based on the concept of willingness to pay for services provided.

METHODS BASED ON WILLINGNESS TO PAY

We have alluded to two kinds of problems we face in measuring the benefits of outdoor recreation: the conceptual problems and the measurement problems.

Conceptually, we wish to measure the willingness to pay by consumers of outdoor recreation services as though these consumers were purchasing the services in an open market. The total willingness of consumers to pay for a given amount and quality of outdoor recreation (that is, the area under the demand curve) is the relevant measure we seek. Our conceptual problems are essentially that any measurement of effective demand in the current time period, or even an attempt to project effective demand in future time periods, must necessarily omit from the computation two kinds of demand which may or may not be important. These are option demand and demand generated by the opportunity effect.*

Option demand is that demand from individuals who are not now consumers or are not now consuming as much as they anticipate consuming, and who therefore would be willing to pay to perpetuate the availability of the commodities. Such a demand is not likely to be measured by observance or simulation of market phenomena. The opportunity effect derives from those unanticipated increases in demand caused by improving the opportunities to engage in a recreational activity and thereby acquainting consumers with new and different sets of opportunities to which they adapt through learning processes. To our knowledge no methods have been proposed which might be used to measure those two kinds of demand for a good.

Notwithstanding the undoubted reality of these kinds of demand, our presumption is that effective demand is likely to be the predominant component of the aggregate demand for outdoor recreation of the abundant and reproducible sorts we have in mind. We further presume that this quantity can be estimated in a useful way, although by fairly indirect means, for we have no market guide of the usual sort. Two methods—a direct interview and an imputation of a demand curve from travel cost data—currently appear to offer reasonable means of obtaining meaningful estimates.

Interview Methods

The essence of the interview method of measuring recreation benefits is that through a properly constructed interview approach one can elicit from recreationists information concerning the maximum price they would pay in order to avoid being deprived of the use of a particular area for whatever use they may make of it. The argument for the existence of something to be measured rests on the conception that the recreationist is engaged in the utility-maximizing process and has made a rational series of allocations of time and money in order to participate in the recreation being evaluated. Since the opportunity itself is available at zero or nominal price, the interview provides the means for discovering the price the person would pay if this opportunity were marketed, other things being equal.

The chief problem to be reckoned with in evaluating interview responses is the degree of reliability that can be attached to the information the respondent provides the interviewer. Particularly on questions dealing with matters of opinion, the responses are subject to many kinds of bias.

One such bias of particular interest to economists stems from the gaming strategy that a consumer of a public good may pursue on the theory that, if he understates his preference for the good, he will escape being charged as much as he is willing to pay without being deprived of the amount of the good he now desires. This may be a false issue, particularly when it comes to

*These concepts are developed by Davidson, Adams, and Seneca in "The Social Value of Water Recreational Facilities Resulting from an Improvement in Water Quality: The Delaware Estuary," in Allen V. Kneese and Stephen C. Smith, eds., *Water Research* (Baltimore: Johns Hopkins University Press, 1966).

pursuing recreation on private lands or waters, because the consumer may be well aware that the owner could, through the exercise of his private property rights, exclude the user from the areas now occupied. An equally good case can be made that, on state and national park lands to which there is limited access, particularly when at the access points the authority of the state is represented by uniformed park patrolmen, recreationists would have no trouble visualizing the existence of the power to exclude them. This being the case, it is not unreasonable to expect the recreationist to be aware of some willingness to pay on his part in order to avoid being excluded from the area he now uses.

Counterbalancing the possibility that the recreationist may purposely understate his willingness to pay in order to escape charges is the possibility that he may wish to bid up his apparent benefits in order to make a case for preserving the area in its current use, a case equally appropriate on private or public lands and waters.

The problem, to continue the argument, is narrowed to one of phrasing the question in such a way that the recreationist is not asked to give his opinion on the propriety of charging for the use of recreation areas.

It has become something of a principle in survey methodology that the less hypothetical the question, the more stable and reliable the response. By this principle, the respondent ought to be a consumer of the product rather than a potential consumer, thus distinguishing the data collected as pertaining to effective demand rather than to option or potential demand. It may also be preferable to impose the conditions on the interview that it occur at a time when the respondent is engaged in the activity. This may contribute to the accuracy of the responses by reducing the requirement that he project from one situation to another. (Admittedly, it is desirable to experiment with the methodology on this question, as well as others, in order to determine its sensitivity to such variations.)

In sum, then, we expect to discover the consumer's willingness to pay through a properly constructed interview; and, further, we expect that this measure will be the same quantity as would be registered in an organized market for the commodity consumed by the respondent. In other words, we hold a deterministic view that something exists to be measured, and is a sufficiently real and stable phenomenon that the measurement is useful.

The interview procedure. The willingness to pay of a sample of users of a forest recreation area in northern Maine was determined in interviews on the site (4). The interviews included a bidding game in which respondents could react to increased costs of visiting the area. Bids were systematically raised or lowered until the user switched his reaction from inclusion to exclusion or vice versa. At the beginning of the interview rapport was established with the respondents largely through objective questions inquiring into their recreation activities on the area, on other areas, and the details of their trips. The bidding questions were interspersed with a series of propositions for which the respondent was to indicate his opinion in the form of a positive, negative, or neutral reaction. His reactions to increased expenses connected with the visit constituted the essence of the bidding game. Personal questions regarding income, education, and the like were confined to the end of the interview.

The sampling procedure amounted to cluster sampling, since the procedure followed was to locate areas of use such as campgrounds and systematically to sample from the available clusters of users. The interviews were conducted from June through November by visiting areas in the privately owned forests of northern Maine and in Baxter State Park.

The data from the interviews is pooled to include hunters, fishermen, and summer campers. This pooling is defended largely on the grounds that no structural differences between identifiable strata were detected in a multiple regression analysis of the responses.

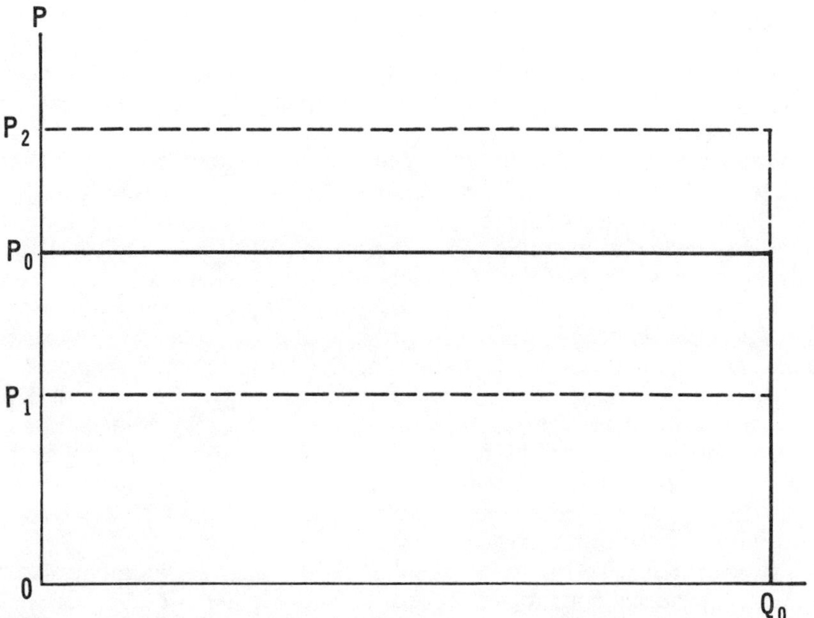

FIGURE 11-1. *Rectangular Demand Curve*

Note: At prices in the range O–P_0, the constant amount Q_0 will be demanded. Above P_0 demand will fall to zero. The individual may be in one of three states depending on the reigning price. Consider three individual cases with market price at P_0: The user paying P_1 is excluded; P_0 is associated with the marginal user; and P_2 is the willingness to pay of the third user, who is included at the reigning price, P_0.

The procedure imputes a discontinuous demand curve to the individual household which may be realistic under the time constraints faced particularly by vacation visitors and other nonrepeating visitors. This rectangular demand curve (see figure 11-1) reflects a disposition either to come at the current level of use or not to come at all if costs rise above a limiting value. Its realism is supported by a number of respondents whose reaction to the excluding bid was precisely that they would not come at all. It seems reasonable to view the use of remote areas such as northern Maine as lumpy commodities which must be consumed in five- or six-day lumps or not at all. Deriving an aggregate demand function from the individual responses so characterized is simply a matter of taking the distribution function of willingness to pay cumulated on a less-than basis. This results in a continuous demand schedule which can be interpreted for the aggregate user population as a conventional demand schedule.

For the sample of 185 interviews, willingness-to-pay-per-household-day ranges from zero to $16.66. Zero willingness to pay was encountered in only three interviews. At the other extreme, one or two respondents were unable to place an upper limit on their willingness to pay. The distribution of willingness to pay shows a marked skewness toward the high values. The modal willingness to pay occurs between $1.00 and $2.00 per day per household.

Sixty percent of the variance of willingness to pay among the interviews is explained in a multiple regression equation with willingness-to-pay-per-household-visit a function of income of the household, years of experience by the household in visiting the area, and the length of the stay in the area (see equation 1). While the large negative intercept of this equation necessitated by its linear form causes some difficulties of interpretation, the exhibited relation between willingness to pay and income, experience, and length of stay appears reasonable. The household income not only reflects an ability to pay but also a positive income elasticity of demand for outdoor recreation as found in other studies. It is also significant that an internal consistency was found in the responses to income-related questions.

$$W = -48.57 + \underset{(1.52)}{2.85Y} + \underset{(0.58)}{2.88E} + \underset{(1.03)}{4.76L} \qquad R^2 = .5925 \qquad (1)$$

$$W = .74\underset{(.13)}{L^{.76}}\ \underset{(.07)}{E^{.20}}\ \underset{(.17)}{Y^{.60}} \qquad .3591\dagger \qquad (2)$$

Standard errors of regression equations: (1) 39.7957; (2) 2.2007.
Standard errors of coefficients are shown in parentheses.

W = household willingness to pay for a visit
E = years of acquaintance with the area visited
Y = income of the household in thousands of dollars
L = length of visit in days
F = Ratios of both equations are highly significant.

†Obtained from arithmetic values of residual and total variances. (R^2 of the logarithmic transformation is .4309.)

The significance of years of experience in returning to the area may be interpreted as the effect of an accumulated consumer capital consisting of knowledge of the area, acquisition of skills which enhance the enjoyment of the area, and in some cases use of permanent or mobile housing on the area.

The significance of length of stay in the regression equations is that it both measures the quantity of goods consumed and also reflects a quality dimension suggesting that longer stays probably reflect a greater degree of preference for the area.

Colinearity among explanatory variables was very low. The general economic consistency and rationality of the responses appear to be high. Respondents' comments indicated they were turning over in their minds the alternatives available in much the same way that a rational shopper considers the price and desirability of different cuts or kinds of meat. Both the success in finding acceptable and significant explanatory variables and a certain amount of internal consistency in the responses suggest that considerable weight can be attached to the interview method.

The simulated demand schedule. While providing an adequate equation for predicting the willingness to pay of any user, the results of the interviews do not serve as direct estimates of willingness to pay of the user population because the income, length of stay, and years' experience of the interviewed sample do not accurately represent the characteristics of the population of users. Fortunately, it was possible to obtain a reliable sample of the users by administering a questionnaire to systematically selected samples of users stopped at the traffic checking stations on the private forest lands. A logarithmic estimating equation, not as well fitting but free of a negative range, was used to compute the willingness to pay for each household in the sample (see equation 2). The observations were then expanded by the sampling fraction to account for the total number of users during the recreation season.

The next step in the analysis consists of arraying the user population by willingness to pay and building a cumulative distribution downward from the upper limit of the distribution. Table 11-1 shows the resulting demand and benefit schedule. The schedule accounts for the total of about 10,300 user households estimated to be the user population in a 450,000-acre area of the Maine woods near Moosehead Lake, known as the Pittston area.

The demand schedule is noticeably elastic from the upper limit of \$60 to about \$6, at which point total revenues are maximized. The interval from \$60 to \$6 accounts for the estimated willingness to pay of nearly half of the using households. Total benefits at \$6 are \$56,000. The price range below \$6 accounts for the other half of the using households but only for \$15,000 in additional benefits. Benefits are estimated as the cumulative willingness to pay or the revenues available to a discriminating monopolist.

Willingness to drive vs willingness to pay. An alternative expression of the willingness of recreationists to incur additional costs in order to continue using an area may be found in their willingness to drive additional distances. This measure was first proposed by Ullman and Volk (10), although in a version different from that used here. (See also reference 8).

Willingness to drive additional distances was elicited from respondents by the same technique used to elicit willingness to pay. If there are biases involving strategies to avoid paying for these recreation areas, then certainly willingness to drive is to be preferred over willingness to pay as an expression of value. Analysis of the willingness to drive responses shows that a partly different set of variables must be used to explain the responses. Equation 3 shows willingness to drive extra miles to be a function of length of stay and miles driven to reach the area.

	Interview Results		Willingness to Drive[b]		Willingness to Drive[c]	
Price ($)	Household Visits	Benefits[a] ($)	Household Visits	Benefits[a] ($)	Household Visits	Benefits[a] ($)
70	0.00	0.00				
60	11.36	747.77				
50	15.35	983.56				
40	44.31	2,281.46				
30	150.22	6,003.19	11.36	384.79	165	3,800
26	215.80	7,829.71				
22	391.07	12,027.89				
20	536.51	15,099.31	76.96	1,890.12	422	12,134
18	757.86	19,275.95				
16	1,069.01	24,607.81				
14	1,497.75	31,027.17	392.29	7,287.06		
12	1,866.41	35,802.70				
10	2,459.70	42,289.68	2,157.91	28,921.93	1,328	26,202
8	3,100.99	48,135.01				
6	4,171.89	55,794.64				
4	5,926.94	64,436.36	5,721.06	53,531.68	3,459	44,760
2	7,866.02	70,222.66				
0	10,333.22	71,460.94	10,339.45	63,689.99	10,333	69,450

TABLE 11-1. *Demand and Benefit Schedules for Pittston Area, Based on Alternative Estimates of Willingness to Pay*

[a] Benefits are computed as the integral of the demand schedule from price maximum to price indicated. Willingness to drive computations are based on an assumed charge of 5 cents per mile for the one-way mileage.

[b] Interview method.

[c] Travel cost method.

$$Wm = 41.85 + \underset{(3.03)}{20.56L} + \underset{(.04)}{.15M} \qquad (R^2 = .3928) \qquad (3)$$

Wm = willingness to drive additional miles
L = length of visit in days
M = miles traveled to area.

The respondents thus expressed a willingness to exert an additional driving effort, just as they expressed a willingness to make an additional money outlay if this became a requisite to using the area. Moreover, there is a significant correspondence between willingness to pay and willingness to drive. The simple correlation coefficient between these two variables is .5. Because of the correlation with length of stay, the reduction in unexplained variance produced by adding either variable to the equation in which the other variable is the dependent one is not very high. However, willingness to pay was found to increase about 5 cents per mile as a function of willingness to drive additional miles. This result gives us a basis for transforming willingness to drive into willingness to pay.

We may now construct a demand schedule for the Pittston area on the basis of willingness to drive and compute a willingness to pay at 5 cents per mile. The resulting demand and benefit schedules appear in table 11-1. The estimated $64,000 of total benefits is very close to that developed from the willingness to pay interview. While one may quibble about the evaluation of a mile of extra driving and about the treatment of one-way versus round-trip distance, the first approximation using the obvious value of 5 cents and one-way mileage as reported by the respondents produces a result so close to the first result that we need look no further for marginal adjustments. The initial result strongly suggests that mileage measures and expenditure measures have equal validity as a measure of benefits in this particular case, at least.

There are some differences worth noting among the respective demand schedules. The much lower price intercept on the willingness to drive schedule reflects the effect of the time constraint in traveling as well as our possibly erroneous constant transformation of miles to dollars when an increasing cost per mile would be more reasonable. The travel schedule is also elastic over more of its range than is the dollar schedule—also perhaps a result of the constant transformation employed.

This initial success with alternative derivations of the benefits schedule now leads us to examine an alternative method for estimating the willingness-to-drive schedule.

Travel-Cost Method of Estimating User-Demand Curve—Application to Pittston Area

The direct interview approach to the estimate of a true price-quantity relationship, or demand curve, for the recreation experience is one approach to the benefit calculations based on willingness to pay. An alternative approach has received some recognition and has been applied in a number of limited instances with at least a fair degree of success. This uses travel-cost data as a proxy for price in imputing a demand curve for recreation facilities (1; 2; 5; 6). As with the direct interview approach, we believe that estimates derived from this approach are relevant and useful for measuring user benefits of outdoor recreation.

The travel-cost method imputes the price-quantity reactions of consumers by examining their actual current spending behavior with respect to travel cost. The method can be shown by using a simple, hypothetical example. Assume a free recreation or park area at varying distances from three centers of population given in table 11-2.

The cost of visiting the area is of major concern and would include such items as transportation, lodging, and food cost above those incurred if the trip were not made. Each cost would vary with the distance from the park to the city involved. Consequently, the number of visits, or rather the rate of visits per unit total population of each city, would also vary.

City	Population	Cost of Visit	Visits Made	Visits/1,000 Pop.
A	1,000	$1	400	400
B	2,000	3	400	200
C	4,000	4	400	100

TABLE 11-2. *Visits to a Hypothetical Recreation Area*

The visits per unit of population, in this case per thousand population, may then be plotted against the cost per visit. A line drawn through the three points of such a plot would have the relationship given by the equation $C = 5 - V$, or perhaps more conveniently $V = 5 - C$, where C is cost of a visit and V is the rate of visits in hundreds per thousand population. This information is taken directly from the tabulation of consumer behavior. The linear relationship assumed here is for convenience. Actual data may very well show, for example, that $1 change in cost might have only a slight effect on visit rate where the visit is already high in cost and a large effect on low-cost visits.

The construction of a demand curve to the recreation area, relating number of visits to varying cost, involves a second step. Essentially, it derives the demand curve from the equation relating visit rates to cost by relating visit rates of each zone to simulated increases in cost and multiplying by the relative populations in each zone. Thus we might first assume a price of $1, which is an added cost of $1 for visits to the area from each of the three different centers used in our hypothetical example. This would have the expected result of reducing the number of visitors coming from each of the centers. The expected reduction is estimated from the visit-cost relationship. The total visits suggested by these calculations for different prices or differing added cost are given in table 11-3. These results may then be taken as the demand curve relating price to visits to the recreation area. While this analysis takes visits as a simple function of cost, in principle there is no difficulty in extending the analysis to other factors important in recreation demand, such as alternative sites available, the inherent attractiveness of the area in question or at least its characteristics in this regard, and possibly even some measure of congestion.

A difficulty with this method of benefit approximation is a consistent bias in the imputed demand curve resulting from the basic assumption that the disutility of overcoming distance is a function only of money cost. Clearly this is not so. The disutility is most likely to be the sum of at least three factors: money cost, time cost, and the utility (plus or minus) of driving, or traveling. The total of these three factors is demonstrably negative, but we do not know enough about the significance of the last two components. In all likelihood their sum—that is, of the utility or disutility of driving and the time cost—imposes costs in addition to money. To the extent that this is true the benefit estimate will be conservatively biased; for, as has been indicated, it is assumed that the only thing causing differences in attendance rates for cities located at different distances to a recreation area will be the differences in money cost. The method then postulates that if money cost changes are affected, the

Price (added cost)	Quantity (total visits)
$0	1,200
1	500
2	200
3	100
4	0

TABLE 11-3. *Suggested Total Visits*

changes in rates will be proportional. What this bias amounts to is, essentially, a failure to establish a complete transformation function relating the three components of overcoming distance to the total effect on visitation rates. The resulting conservative bias must be regarded as an understatement of the recreation benefits which the approach is designed to measure.

The travel-cost method was applied to the same area as that used to illustrate the interview method of recreation benefit estimation. The same data were utilized to allow at least a crude comparison of the methods. In all, 6,678 respondents who said the Pittston area was the main destination of their trip were used in the analysis.

Visit rates of visitors from groups of counties near the area and from some states at greater distances were plotted against distance. The results were fairly consistent, considering the rough nature of the approximations used in estimating distance. A curve was drawn through the points, giving a relationship between visit rates and distance. The demand curve was then calculated, giving a price-quantity relationship based on added distance (or added toll cost) and total visits. It was assumed initially that travel cost would be 5 cents per mile, using one-way distance to conform with our earlier analysis of travel cost by the interview method.

The results at this point were not comparable to the interview method because of a difference in the number of users accounted for. It will be recalled that in the analysis we are now describing only those respondents were used who had specifically stated that the visit to the Pittston area was the main destination of the trip. In order to make this number comparable to the total number of users accounted for in the interview estimate, we counted at half weight the 1,327 respondents who said that Pittston was *not* the primary destination of the trip and also included in this group the nonresponse questionnaires and others with incomplete information. In this way we accounted for the same number of users as in the interview estimate. This very crude approximation points out problems of the multiple-destination visit but perhaps adequately serves the present purpose.

On the basis of these approximations, the benefit estimates on an annual basis were $70,000, assuming 5 cents per mile one-way distance. While the assumptions made throughout this analysis are subject to refinement, the exercise does seem to illustrate that the procedure is feasible from a practical standpoint and does produce results that are economically meaningful.

COMPARISON BETWEEN TRAVEL-COST AND INTERVIEW METHODS

Having demonstrated that fairly close results are obtained from both the interview and imputation methods of estimating recreation benefits on the basis of reactions to travel costs and further that the interview method of directly estimating willingness to pay agrees closely with both estimates based on travel costs, we can now begin to assess the meaning of these results. In some ways the task would be easier if the results had not agreed so closely, for the three methodologies may imply different things about the users' reactions to increased costs. At least, it is not obvious without further probing as to why the agreement is so close.

The interview and imputation methods of estimating benefits on the basis of willingness to incur additional travel costs do not, for example, neatly imply the same relationship between distance traveled and willingness to incur additional travel costs. The estimating equation derived from the interviews (equation 3) suggests that the farther one has traveled, the greater additional distance he will travel. Yet the imputation procedure implies that the willingness to drive by populations in the respective zones does not vary consistently with distance. Furthermore, according to the interviews, responses to the monetary measure of willingness to pay do not attribute any variance in willingness to pay to the distance factor, nor is an indirect relationship obvious. It seems relevant to inquire into the implied effects of these factors to discover why the alternative procedures appear to imply substantially different determinants of willingness to pay.

The superficial agreement in results may be upheld by this kind of further probing, but there are also some methodological issues which should not be overlooked. The travel-cost methods are obviously sensitive to such matters as the weighting given to multiple-destination visits and to the transformation used to derive costs from mileage values. Both methods are sensitive to the usual problems of choosing an appropriately fitting equation for the derivation of the demand schedule. The interview method has a poorly understood sensitivity to the various methodologies that might be employed in its use. Moreover, even the minimal use of interviews in studies of recreation benefits makes the method far more costly than the imputation method based on travel costs.

There are, however, complementarities in the two basic methods which may prove highly useful. In the first place, the two methods may serve as checks on each other in applied situations. One is certainly in a better position from having two methods produce nearly identical answers than if he has to depend on only one. There are also interesting possibilities that interviews may be the best way of resolving the ambiguities in the travel-cost method concerning the treatment of multiple-destination cases and for finding the appropriate valuation for converting distance into dollars. Much can be said for letting the recreationist tell us how to handle these problems.

In sum, we have examined three methods of measuring recreation benefits. All three measure recreationists' willingness to pay. This, we argue, is the appropriate measure of primary, or national benefits. Furthermore, the measures are in rough agreement as to the benefits ascribable to an area of the Maine woods. This may be taken as evidence that we are on the right track. There are, however, some rough spots to be ironed out of each of the methods —an endeavor we believe to be worthy of major research effort if benefit-cost analysis is to contribute its full potential in planning decisions affecting recreation investments in land and water resources.

REFERENCES

1. Brown, W. G.; Singh, A.; and Castle, E. N. 1964. *An economic evaluation of the Oregon salmon and steelhead sport fishery.* Technical Bulletin 78. Oregon State Agricultural Experiment Station, Corvallis.
2. Clawson, M. 1959. *Methods of measuring the demand for and value of outdoor recreation.* Reprint no. 10. Washington, D.C.: Resources for the Future.
3. Crutchfield, J. 1962. Valuation of fishery resources. *Land Economics* 38, no. 2.
4. Davis, R. K. 1963. The value of outdoor recreation: An economic study of the Maine Woods. Ph.D. dissertation, Harvard University.
5. Knetsch, J. L. 1963. Outdoor recreation demands and benefits. *Land Economics* 39, no. 4.
6. ———. 1964. Economics of including recreation as a purpose of water resources projects. *Journal of Farm Economics,* December.
7. Lerner, L. 1962. Quantitative indices of recreational values. In *Water resources and economic development of the West.* Report no. 11. Proceedings, Conference of Committee on the Economics of Water Resources Development of Western Agricultural Economics Research Council with Western Farm Economics Association. Reno: University of Nevada.
8. Meramec Basin Research Project. 1961. *The Meramec Basin.* Vol. 3. St. Louis, Mo.: Washington University. Ch. 5.
9. Merewitz, L. 1965. Recreational benefits of water-resource development. Unpublished paper, Harvard Water Program.
10. Ullman, E., and Volk, D. 1962. An operational model for predicting reservoir attendance and benefits: Implications of a location approach to water recreation. *Papers of the Michigan Academy of Sciences, Arts and Letters.* 1961 meeting.

CHAPTER 12

RECREATIONAL TRAVEL: A REVIEW AND PILOT STUDY

Bryan Thompson

This chapter introduces the importance of determining travel patterns of recreationists. After reviewing a variety of methods for analyzing recreational flows, Bryan Thompson utilizes the traditional method of the gravity model to determine the propensity of campers in Ontario to travel to certain parks within the province.

This paper has a dual purpose: first, to examine the methods that have been used for analyzing patterns of recreational travel and, second, to conduct a pilot study to examine the flow of campers to a sample of Ontario provincial parks.

The models examined are the gravity model, the intervening opportunities model, and the systems theory model. Basically, although there are many variations, the gravity model relates recreational travel to population, attractiveness of the recreational area, and distance (or time). The intervening opportunities model assumes that the traffic generated between a population area and a recreational area is directly related to the number of opportunities closer (in travel time) to the population area than the recreation area. The last model, the systems model, uses theory borrowed from the electrical engineering literature.

Data obtained from a sample survey by the Ontario Department of Lands and Forests were used for analyzing recreational travel patterns to a sample of Ontario parks. The assumption was that camper traffic flow is related to city population (*P*), city-park distance (*D*), and park capacity (*C*), as indicated by the number of campsites. The Department of Highways IBM 7040 Computer was used to calculate the exponents for *P*, *C*, and *D*. A number of tentative conclusions are drawn from an evaluation of the residuals. These conclusions relate to park location, park size, spacing of parks, and the size and socioeconomic structure of cities. Limitations of and suggested refinements in the gravity model are outlined, along with suggestions for experimentation with the intervening opportunities approach and the systems theory approach.

The paper concludes by emphasizing the need for creating and preserving a quality recreational environment.

Man spends his leisure time in many ways. One of the most popular forms

---

Reprinted from "Recreational Travel: A Review and Pilot Study," *Traffic Quarterly*, October 1967, pp. 527–42, copyright 1967 by the Eno Foundation for Transportation and reprinted by permission of the *Traffic Quarterly* of the Eno Foundation for Transportation, Inc., and the author.

involves participation in various types of outdoor recreation. Unquestionably the demand for outdoor recreational facilities will increase as an expanding population enjoys more leisure time while becoming more affluent and more mobile.

The recreational component of vehicular flow has grown enormously ... in Canada, and the jammed roads leading out of and into the Metropolitan Toronto area on a summer weekend attest this fact. One form of outdoor recreation is camping, and this increase in recreational traffic flow has brought with it a commensurate increase in the demand for camping facilities. To meet this demand, the parks branch of the Ontario government has developed numerous parks throughout the province (ninety-one in 1965) to accommodate day-visitor trips, and short- and long-term camping trips. Viewed from the standpoint of a highway department, these parks generate traffic flows which must somehow be incorporated into the highway system. In matters of highway planning, the ability to predict these flows with some degree of confidence is desirable. Further research is needed to provide definitive answers to the following basic questions: How does the demand for recreation at a particular park decrease as distance from the park increases? How can the attraction of a park be evaluated? What socioeconomic factors affect recreational travel habits? When answers to these questions are forthcoming, highway officials will be in a better position to improve existing roads, plan new roads, and locate new parks.

One purpose of this paper is to review some of the techniques that have been used for analyzing recreational travel. A second purpose is to examine one form of recreational travel, that of campers to Ontario provincial parks, and to develop an exploratory and simplified model for simulating the flow of campers between the major centers of population and a sample of Ontario parks.

GRAVITY MODEL

The gravity model has been used successfully for predicting travel between two areas.[1] This model, an analogue of Newton's Law of Gravity, states that the trip volume between area i and area j can be expressed:

$$Tij = KP_iP_jD_{ij}^x$$

where Tij = the number of people traveling between area i and area j
Pi = population of area i
Pj = population of area j
Dij = the distance between area i and area j
K and x are constants.

Volk used the gravity model in his analysis of travel to national parks in the United States.[2] To measure the effect of distance, he computed the per capita visits from each state to each park and plotted the results against distance to the park on a log-log scale.[3] This relationship showed that factors other than distance influence the degree of participation in outdoor recreation.[4] Volk went on to use a multiple regression technique to study the effects of median income, degree of urbanization, and mobility on park attendance.[5] In all cases, distance accounted for at least 60 percent of the total variation, and in some cases the effect was as high as 90 percent. Income and urbanization were so closely linked that they were considered as one variable, and together they explained an additional 3 to 16 percent of the variation.

Schulman, working on a smaller scale than Volk, collected data on visitors to five of the twenty parks in the Indiana state park system.[6] A license plate study provided the necessary origin-destination data, since Indiana license plates are prefixed by the county number. The form of the equation fitted to these data was:

$$Tij = \frac{Ti}{\sum_{j=1}^{n}} \cdot \frac{\frac{Rj}{Dij}^{x}}{\frac{Rj}{Dij}^{x}}$$

where Tij = the corrected number of trips from county j to park i. A correction factor was needed since the model tends either to over- or underestimate the total number of trips attracted to a park. The correction factor for park i, for example, was a ratio of the observed and calculated number of trips to park i from all residential areas

Rj = a measure of the number of recreational trips generated from county j

Ti = the total number of automobile trips attracted to park i from all residential areas

Dij = the road distance between county j and park i

x = the value of the exponent for Dij.

An analysis of the pattern of visits indicated a rapid drop-off in the number of visitors beyond a certain distance.[7] "The trips from in-state counties tend to be undercalculated (greater percentage of positive errors), while the trips from out-of-state counties tend to be overcalculated (greater percentage of negative errors)."[8]

A study by Crevo of weekend recreational travel to two parks in southeastern Connecticut incorporated time-distance into the model.[9] Neither of the parks is used for camping but rather for bathing, boating, and picnicking. Zones were constructed around the parks and the ratio of actual to theoretical trips was calculated for each zone.[10] This figure was then plotted against the travel time in minutes from origin zone centroids to the parks. The resulting scatter of points indicated that a curve of the exponential form was the best fit.

A modified version of the gravity model was used for forecasting traffic growth in the county of Dorset, England.[11] Traffic was measured in two classes: "native," which was related to resident population, and "holiday visiting," which was related to the national records of vehicles licensed. To calculate the percentage of traffic ending in Dorchester, Whitehead modified a formula developed by Tanner.[12] Tanner had proposed that the number of journeys should fall off with increasing distance according to a low inverse power for short distances and a high inverse power for long distances, a function of the form $x^{e-\lambda x}$. The equation used was:

$$Q = \frac{K \cdot P_1 \cdot P_2 e^{-\lambda x}}{n_x}$$

where Q = traffic flow between two population centers
P_1 P_2 are populations of two towns distance x apart
K, λ, and n are constants.

Whitehead modified the $P_1 \cdot P_2$ relationship since he felt that it was unreasonable to assume that if populations are doubled, the traffic will increase fourfold. He also used a time measurement in place of distance.

The gravity model was used to analyze patterns of camper travel in Michigan parks. As Crevo, Van Doren used a time-distance measure but also introduced a measure of park attraction into his model.[13] The assumption was that park attraction is related to the park's physical attributes and the type of recreational activities offered. The general form of the equation was:

$$Nij = K\ Pi\ Aj\ Tij^{a}$$

where Nij = the number of campers at park j from county i
Pi = county population
Tij = time-distance between park j and county i
Aj = measure of park attraction
K and a are constants.

The gravity model has been used successfully in the analysis of recreational travel patterns. Its application can be quickly learned and it is readily adapted to computer programming. However, there are many problems associated with its use. For example, human behavior, involves more complex sets of forces than argument by analogy to a physical law will bring to light. Yet the model may lead to a greater understanding of human behavior, since residual analysis, for example, often will yield insights into behavioral variations.

Another problem arises in assigning an exponent of unity to population. Hauser found that people in large cities have a lower propensity to go camping than do people in small cities.[14] Furthermore, the socioeconomic structure of a city also is related to the degree of activity in outdoor recreation.[15] Problems also arise in measuring the attractiveness of a recreational area. How are factors such as park size, esthetic qualities, and types of facilities to be weighted? Distance poses yet another problem. Measurement is an easy matter, but how well does distance measure the friction effect? A number of studies have substituted a time measure for distance. Furthermore, the distance people will travel is also a function of the availability of alternative recreational opportunities. Under this assumption, the greater the number of alternative and competing opportunities close to the city, the less the need people have to travel large distances for participation in outdoor recreation.

INTERVENING OPPORTUNITIES MODEL

The importance of intervening opportunities has been alluded to in a number of studies of recreational travel, but any rigorous testing is lacking. Adams found that the traffic arriving at Algonquin Park from northern Ontario and Quebec was less than expected; that is, relative to the populations of the areas.[16] An abundance of camping and other outdoor recreational opportunities in northern Ontario and Quebec was proposed as an explanatory factor. Similarly, Volk, in explaining the patterns of visits to Rocky Mountain National Park, submitted that the reason for the disproportionately high number of visits to the park from the Great Plains and the midwestern states compared with the low number from the western states was a function of the greater number of opportunities in the West.[17]

Simply stated, the intervening opportunities model assumes that the probability of a trip originating in area i and terminating in area j will be directly related to the total number of opportunities in area j and inversely related to the number of opportunities closer (in travel time) to area i than area j.[18] Stated mathematically, the model is expressed:

$$Vij = Vi(e^{-LV} - e^{-L(V + Vj)})$$

where Vij = trips originating in zone i and terminating in zone j
Vi = trip origins in zone i
V = number of possible destinations lying closer (travel time) to zone i than to zone j
Vj = number of possible destinations in zone j.
L = empirically derived factor varying with trip type
e = base of natural logarithms.

The intervening opportunities model appears to have potential for the study of recreational travel patterns. There is little doubt, for example, that the number of campers visiting a park from a city in southern Ontario is related to the number of camping facilities located between the park and the city.

SYSTEMS THEORY MODEL

Using theory borrowed from electrical engineering literature, Ellis has developed a method for analyzing flow between population centers and the parks of Michigan.[19]

> The systems theory model ... assumes that each *component* can be modeled separately—the parameters of individual components appear in formulae *specific* to the behavior of the class of component to which it belongs—and it also takes into account the specific interconnection pattern of the system under study. These features, again, are indicative of the strength and weakness of the method. It provides a very satisfying procedure from the behavioral point of view, but also requires specific behavioral knowledge to model the components—or at least good *postulates* regarding behavior. The theory of the system[s] approach appears in the electrical engineering literature, and small-scale applications have been shown to apply to non-physical systems.[20]

The gravity model has been used successfully in the analysis of recreational travel patterns. However, it suffers because of an assumed applicability throughout an entire system. The systems theory model avoids the problem by individual modeling of the system components, and the intervening opportunities model replaces the distance measure with a measure of alternative or competing opportunities.

CAMPERS FROM CITIES IN SOUTHERN ONTARIO: A PILOT STUDY

The densely settled areas of southern Ontario pose major problems in terms of present and future flows of recreational traffic. As an initial phase in the research, ten cities and ten parks were selected for study (see figure 12-1). Randomness was deliberately sacrificed in the selection of cities in order to focus on the major centers of traffic generation (see table 12-1).

The choice of parks also was biased, since most of the parks are located in the southern part of Ontario (see table 12-2). Presumably these parks will generate a higher proportion of short-distance camping trips than will the parks in the northern parts of the province, since long-distance traveling is often precluded by time constraints. Parks in the southern Ontario region probably receive a higher proportion of short-term (weekend) campers than the northern Ontario parks. However, this is by no means certain, since many campers in the north may be stopping overnight en route to other parks. Unfortunately, data limitations ... prevent any detailed breakdown regarding length of park visit and eventual destination. The parks selected ranged in size from 42 acres (Oastler) to 4,333 acres (Pinery). A number of the parks selected were located on the Canadian Shield, an area generally considered more attractive than the Paleozoic areas to the south and west. Some parks were close to large urban centers and presumably would generate a different type of flow than would the parks located in more remote, wilderness-type areas. [See table 12-2 for the parks used in the study.]

Method and Results

The gravity model was used in this, the initial phase of a long-range program of research, despite the previously discussed limitations of using this model. The assumptions were that camper flow is related to city population (P),

FIGURE 12-1. *Approximate Locations of the Cities and Parks Used in the Analysis of Travel Patterns of Southern Ontario Campers*

City	Approximate Population (1963) (in 000s)
Metropolitan Toronto	1,652
Hamilton	376
Ottawa	302
London	171
Windsor	112
Kitchener-Waterloo	104
St. Catharines	86
Sarnia	51
North Bay	42
Guelph	41

TABLE 12-1. *Cities Used in Camper Study*

Park	Size (ac)	Campsites
Pinery	4,333	1,075
Killbear Pt.	2,334	722
Presqu'Ile	2,170	500
Marten River	1,059	240
Outlet	265	350
Rideau River	130	191
Ipperwash	109	268
Black Lake	76	200
Emily	67	88
Oastler	42	120

TABLE 12-2. *Park Campsites, Southern Ontario*

city-park distance (*D*), and park capacity (*C*). The Ontario Department of Highways made up a questionnaire, and surveys carried out by the Department of Lands and Forests provided a sample of origin-destination data. Distances were computed in miles, and park capacity was expressed as the number of campsites multiplied by the average number of campers in a party, in this case four. The general form of the equation was:

$$Nij = K\, P^{x}{}_{i}\, C^{y}{}_{j}\, D^{z}{}_{ij}$$

where Nij = the number of trips from city i to park j
Pi = population of city i, in 000s
Cj = park capacity
Dij = city-park distance in miles
x, y, and z are exponent values.

The department of highways' IBM 7040 Computer was used to calculate the exponents for population, camp capacity, and distance. The resulting equation was:

$$Nij = 20.3\ Pi^{1.11}\ Cj^{0.71}\ Dij^{-1.53} \quad (r = 0.81)\ (r^2 = 0.65)$$

The t-test indicated that all of the variables were significant at the 0.025 level—distance, population, and capacity, in that order. A refinement was made in the model by the incorporation of an adjusted capacity measure (E). This was expressed as the product of capacity and the percentage of available sites that were actually used for camping. The revised equation was:

$$Nij = 3.52\ P_i^{1.12}\ E_j^{1.03}\ D_{ij}^{-1.45} \quad (r = 0.81, r^2 = 0.65)$$

Analysis of Results

Attendance at parks located on the Canadian Shield was in all cases underestimated (see table 12-3).[21] Suggested explanations are in terms of the greater attraction of these parks and a directional bias on the part of people from southern Ontario. There is little doubt that the juxtaposition of forests, lakes, and rock outcrops makes this an area of high scenic quality. Furthermore, Wolfe[22] and Lucas[23] have shown that outdoor recreationists have a directional preference favoring the north.

	Cities (no.)*		Errors (no.)		
Park	Under-estimated	Over-estimated	$\leq$20%	$\geq$50%	Median % Error
Marten River	9	0	1	6	61
Killbear Pt.	7	2	3	5	59
Oastler	9	1	2	7	55
Black Lake	5	2	0	4	53
Rideau River	6	3	0	6	69
Outlet	3	6	4	4	32
Presqu'lle	5	4	2	5	58
Emily	4	4	4	3	27
Ipperwash	5	4	3	4	46
Pinery	7	3	1	5	49

TABLE 12-3. *Residual and Percentage Error Analysis for Sampled Parks in Southern Ontario*

Notes: Data omitted where observed number of visitors to a park was less than five. Percentage error defined as:

$$\frac{\text{Expected} - \text{Observed}}{\text{Observed}} \times 100.$$

*From which visitors were.

Pinery Park, the largest park in the sample, was underestimated. This park has a reputation of being one of the most beautiful in the provincial park system. However, it is also possible that scale effects may be important. A large park may be able to provide more and better facilities and activities than a smaller park, resulting in higher camper attendance.

Parks where the number of visitors was overestimated the greatest number of times included Outlet, Presqu'Ile, Emily, and Ipperwash. Outlet and Presqu'Ile are both located on Lake Ontario to the east of the urban centers of southern Ontario. Another detracting factor may be the extremely cold waters of Lake Ontario. Furthermore, the boundary of the Canadian Shield swings southward in this area, and it is only a short trip from the Lake Ontario shore to the attractive Kawartha Lakes to the north (see figure 12-1). Emily, the smallest park in the sample, is located a few miles to the south of the Canadian Shield. The availability of camping opportunities in an attractive nearby area contributes to the lower-than-expected attendance at this park. Ipperwash, even though attendance was underestimated in some cases and overestimated in others, suffers because it is close to Pinery Park.

There were more campers than expected from the small urban centers and fewer from Hamilton and Toronto, the two largest centers (see table 12-4).

The result supports Hauser's theory of an inverse relationship between city size and camping propensity.[24]

	Parks (no.)*		% Error		
City	Under-estimated	Over-estimated	≤20%	≥50%	Median % Error
Toronto	3	7	3	4	29
Hamilton	4	6	3	6	56
St. Catharines	5	4	1	5	53
Kit.-Waterloo	8	2	3	6	56
Guelph	7	1	0	6	67
London	7	3	3	5	53
Windsor	10	0	2	7	66
Sarnia	8	0	1	5	74
Ottawa	5	5	4	4	35
North Bay	3	1	0	2	

TABLE 12-4. *Residual and Percentage Error Analysis for Sampled Cities of Southern Ontario*

Notes: See table 12-3.

*Where visitors were.

CONCLUSION

A number of conclusions, tentative though they may be, can be drawn from the preceding analysis of camper flow to a sample of southern Ontario parks. The results do indicate possible orientations for further research. The attractiveness of a park relates to its situation. Parks located on the Canadian Shield have greater drawing power than parks located elsewhere. Site characteristics will also determine how attractive a particular park will be. For example, a park with a long stretch of sandy beach will generally be more attractive than a park lacking a beach. Facilities, both type and number, also influence the attractiveness of a park.[25]

When two parks are located close to each other, the tendency is for one to dominate the other. For example, Ipperwash appears to suffer because of its location with respect to Pinery, and Outlet because of its nearness to

Presqu'Ile. This whole question of the spacing of parks requires careful attention and will necessarily demand some consideration of intervening opportunities. A random sample of provincial park visitors was taken over the entire 1966 summer season at each park in Ontario.[26] Each vehicle became a sample vehicle for the duration of the park season and was given a yellow sticker. A questionnaire was completed each time a sample vehicle entered a park. This method had the effect of a "carbon tracer" on the park visitations of sampled vehicles.

There is evidence to indicate that park size and attractiveness are related. Attendance at Pinery Park, the largest park in the sample, was underestimated to a greater degree than any other of the parks. Research needs to be directed to this question of size. Is there an optimal park size from both the managerial standpoint and that of people using the park? Are small parks less attractive than large parks? If so, is it a question of inadequate facilities or are there problems of insufficient space and deficient esthetic qualities?

The volume of camper traffic generated appears to vary with the size of city. Large cities generate proportionately fewer campers than smaller cities. This might be related to the fact that large cities have many recreational activities that are not found in smaller cities. Further refinements could be made by considering the socioeconomic structure of cities, since it has been demonstrated that the probability of a person being a camper increases with income, education, and professional status.[27]

The gravity model appears to have potential for the analysis of recreational travel patterns. In this phase of the research, its use met with limited success. However, refinements can be made by the incorporation of more parks and cities, and by the introduction of additional variables. Other modes of recreational travel—for example, travel to cottages and commercial resorts—also need to be analyzed. And, lastly, there is a need to experiment with other techniques; for example, using the intervening opportunities approach and the systems analysis approach.

However, it is not enough to understand patterns of flow or to relate camping propensity to a number of socioeconomic variables. This type of research needs to be coordinated with research which concerns itself with determining what is meant by quality in the recreational experience. Here the elements are subjective and, furthermore, the standards used to define quality invariably change. Despite the problems involved, it would seem that questions relating to quality should be paramount in the planning of future outdoor recreational activities.

What type of approach should be employed by public agencies in an attempt to preserve and create a quality environment? One approach argues that public policy, in order to improve the quality of the environment and consequently the quality of the recreational experience,

> ... should seek not to maximize beauty but minimize ugliness, these not being bi-polar opposites. It is easier to identify that which is ugly through the misfit and thus make the shared environment more agreeable to the many sensitive people in our midst. But if this were all to such a policy we

> might well have found ourselves in pursuit not of beauty, but widespread mediocrity. Therefore we must seek to provide some accessibility to all for the rare and unique experience. In this we are limited by nature and opportunity but much more so by talent and the lack of a public policy that really desires or knows how to utilize talent.[28]

These ideas could be used as a framework for the planning and design of outdoor recreational activities: elimination of that which is objectionable and reliance on the creative individuals in our society for the esthetically satisfying.

NOTES

1. For a general review of gravity model concepts, see David F. Bramhall, "Gravity Potential, and Spatial Interaction Models," in Walter Isard, ed., *Methods of Regional Analysis* (Cambridge, Mass.: MIT Press, 1960), pp. 493–568.
2. Donald J. Volk, "Factors Affecting Recreational Use of National Parks" (Paper given at the Annual Convention of the Association of American Geographers, Columbus, Ohio, 1965). See also Edward L. Ullman, Ronald R. Boyce, and Donald J. Volk, "The Meramec Basin" (St. Louis, 1961); Edward L. Ullman and Donald J. Volk, "An Operational Model for Predicting Reservoir Attendance and Benefits: Implications of a Location Approach to Water Recreation," *Papers, Michigan Academy of Science, Arts and Letters*, no. 47, 1962 (1961 meeting), pp. 473–84.
3. A similar method was used to analyze the effect of distance on the demand for day use, camping, and interior use in Algonquin Park, Ontario. See Robert L. Adams, "The Demand for Wilderness Recreation in Algonquin Provincial Park" (M.A. thesis, Clark University, 1966).
4. For the effect of urbanization on the degree of participation in outdoor recreational activity, see Philip M. Hauser, "Demographic and Ecological Changes as Factors in Outdoor Recreation," in *Trends in American Living and Outdoor Recreation*, U.S. Outdoor Recreation Resources Review Commission Study Report 22 (Washington, D.C.: Government Printing Office, 1962), pp. 81–100. The relationship between socioeconomic variables and outdoor recreation is described in *National Recreation Survey*, U.S. Outdoor Recreation Resources Review Commission Study Report 19 (Washington, D.C.: Government Printing Office, 1962). Socioeconomic characteristics of campers are described in David A. King, "Characteristics of Family Campers Using the Huron-Manistee National Forests," U.S. Forest Service Research Paper LS-19 (1965), Lake States Forest Experiment Station, St. Paul, Minnesota, 1965; Roy I. Wolfe, "Parameters of Recreational Travel in Ontario: A Progress Report," D.H.O. Report no. RBIII (Paper prepared for presentation at the forty-sixth Annual Convention of the Canadian Good Roads Association, Saskatoon Downsview, Ontario, October 1965).
5. Volk, "Factors Affecting Recreational Use of National Parks."
6. Lawrence Leonard Schulman, "Traffic Generation and Distribution of Weekend Recreational Trips" (M.Sc. thesis, Purdue University, 1964).
7. Adams found a break in slope between the 150- and 220-mile zones in his analysis of recreational visits to Algonquin Park, Ontario. See Adams, "The Demand for Wilderness Recreation. . . ." Similar findings were also obtained by Ullman, Boyce, and Volk. See Ullman, Boyce, and Volk, *The Meramec Basin*, particularly vol. 3, p. 15.
8. Schulman, "Traffic Generation and Distribution of Weekend Recreational Trips," p. 77.
9. Charles C. Crevo, "Characteristics of Summer Weekend Recreational Travel," *Highway Research Record* 41 (1963): 51–60.
10. The theoretical number of trips to park A from zone i was calculated by multiplying the total number of trips to park A by the proportion of the state population in zone i.
11. James Ivor Whitehead, "Road Traffic Growth and Capacity in a Holiday District (Dorset)," *Proceedings of the Institution of Civil Engineers* 31 (May 1965): 589–608.
12. J. C. Tanner, "Relations Between Population, Distance and Traffic—Some Theoretical Considerations," *Research Note RN-2921*, Road Research Laboratory, Harmondsworth, Middlesex, January 1957.

13. Carlton S. Van Doren, "A Recreational Travel Model for Predicting Campers at Michigan State Parks" (Ph.D. diss., Michigan State University, 1965). Also refer to Jack B. Ellis and Carlton S. Van Doren, "A Comparative Evaluation of Gravity and Systems Theory Models for Statewide Recreational Traffic Flows" (Paper presented at the Twelfth U.S. Annual Meeting of the Regional Science Association, Philadelphia, Pennsylvania, November 12–14, 1965).
14. Hauser, U.S. Outdoor Recreation Resources Review Commission Study Report 22, p. 48.
15. Wolfe, "Parameters of Recreational Travel in Ontario."
16. Adams, "The Demand for Wilderness Recreation in Algonquin Provincial Park."
17. Volk, "Factors Affecting Recreational Use of National Parks."
18. For descriptions and evaluations of the intervening opportunities model see Colin Clark and G. H. Peters, "The Intervening Opportunities Method of Traffic Analysis," *Traffic Quarterly* 19, no. 1 (1965): 101–19; Chicago Area Transportation Study, vol. 2, *Data Projections* (1960), pp. 79–86; D. K. Witheford, "Comparisons of Trip Distribution by Opportunity Model and Gravity Model," Pittsburgh Area Transportation Study (1961); Clyde F. Pyers, "Evaluation of the Intervening Opportunities Trip Distribution Model" (Paper presented for the Forty-fourth Annual Meeting of the Highway Research Board, Washington, D.C., 1965).
19. Jack B. Ellis, "Analysis of Socio-economic Systems by Physical Systems Techniques" (Ph.D. diss., Michigan State University, 1965); Ellis and Van Doren, "A Comparative Evaluation of Gravity and Systems Theory Models for Statewide Recreational Traffic Flows."
20. Ellis and Van Doren, "A Comparative Evaluation of Gravity and Systems Theory Models for Statewide Recreational Traffic Flows," pp. 3–4. References to the electrical engineering literature include: Sundaran Seshu and Merrill B. Reed, *Linear Graphs and Electric Networks* (Reading, Mass., 1961); J. B. Ellis and D. N. Millstein, "A Behavior-Specific Component to System Construct for Traffic Flows," *Proceedings, Third International Symposium on Traffic Flow* (New York, June 1965).
21. The total number of visitors to a park was used as a measure of park attendance. A highway department is interested in the number of campers visiting the parks. On the other hand, a parks department probably is more interested in the average length of stay at the parks, and consequently a measure involving camper days would be more appropriate.
22. Wolfe, "Parameters of Recreational Travel in Ontario," p. 5.
23. Robert C. Lucas, "The Recreational Use of the Quetico-Superior Area," U.S. Forest Research Paper LS-8, Lake States Forest Experiment Station, St. Paul, Minnesota, 1966, p. 38.
24. Hauser, U.S. Outdoor Recreation Resources Review Commission Study Report 22, p. 48.
25. A more sophisticated measure of park attraction is possible since the evaluation of 1966 data. A detailed questionnaire sent to rangers in all of the provincial parks in Ontario will provide the necessary data.
26. See note 25.
27. Wolfe, "Parameters of Recreational Travel in Ontario," p. 5.
28. Robert W. Kates, "The Pursuit of Beauty in the Environment," *Landscape* 16, no. 2 (winter 1966–67): 25.

CHAPTER 13

RECREATION SERVICES

Donald M. Fisk
Harry P. Hatry

Many of our leisure and recreation needs are in urbanized areas, and measuring the effectiveness of the services provided there has not been efficient. In this chapter Donald Fisk and Harry Hatry recommend a set of indices to assist in measuring a local government's progress in providing a variety of leisure services. Twenty-four measurement procedures are carefully described, and the specifics of a local government recreation user survey to assess recreation effectiveness provide a fitting conclusion.

Measuring the effectiveness of recreation services is not completely new to most local governments, but current procedures have major deficiencies. Past evaluation of local government park and recreation activities has tended to focus more on inputs such as the number of acres of land, the number of facilities, and the number of arts-and-crafts programs provided rather than on outputs such as the number of persons served and their satisfaction with those services. The park and recreation agencies of most local governments lack information on even the most fundamental facts: What percentage of the population is being served? How satisfied with recreation services are citizens? Who does not use the services and why not? To what extent do factors such as accessibility, dislike of the facility, fear of crime, or lack of knowledge about recreation opportunities affect the use of facilities and programs?

The work reported here builds on earlier efforts, especially in Washington, D.C., to develop better procedures by which local governments can measure the effectiveness of their recreation services. The park and recreation agencies in Nashville, Tennessee, and St. Petersburg, Florida, tested some of the procedures developed in the Washington, D.C., effort. With only limited help from the project team, three other jurisdictions have tested some of the same procedures: Rockford, Illinois, in 1972; Palo Alto, California, in 1973; and Birmingham, Alabama, in 1974. . . .

The objectives, measures, and data collection procedures [here] focus on recreation opportunities for individual citizens. Recreation is considered for the purposes of this report as an end in itself not as a means to some other end

Reprinted from Harry P. Hatry et al., eds., *How Effective Are Your Community Services? Procedures for Monitoring the Effectiveness of Municipal Services* (Washington, D.C.: Urban Institute, 1977), pp. 41–65; 313–14, by permission of the publisher and the authors. This article has been considerably condensed for this volume. Illustrative citizen and user survey questionnaires referred to in the article are contained in the Urban Institute report.

such as reducing juvenile delinquency or improving mental and physical health. . . .

OBJECTIVES AND RELATED EFFECTIVENESS MEASURES

A basic objective for recreation services, one that seems common to most communities, is:

> To provide for all citizens a variety of enjoyable leisure opportunities that are accessible, safe, physically attractive, and uncrowded.

A set of indices to help measure progress toward meeting the various parts of this objective is presented in table 13-1.

The objectives and measures identified in this chapter are intended to assist in evaluating the total recreation system. Most of the procedures can be used to assess recreation effectiveness in major geographic areas of the community. To a more limited degree, these measures can also be used to assess specific agency functions (such as park maintenance or public information about recreation opportunities) or specific activities (such as swimming or arts and crafts). Some of the data collection procedures suggested here, such as the on-site surveys of users, will provide large enough samples to draw conclusions about specific facilities.

Although these measures focus on public facilities and activities, private and quasi-public efforts (such as voluntary youth-serving agencies) indirectly influence some of the measured values. For example, data on the accessibility of swimming opportunities can include the availability of private but nonrestricted facilities. The measure of "households rating neighborhood's recreational opportunities as satisfactory (or unsatisfactory)" reflects both private and public opportunities. As such, the measure can be used to indicate the adequacy of and the need for more or different public facilities.

GROUPING MEASUREMENT DATA BY POPULATION OR CLIENT CHARACTERISTICS

The different perspectives of various population or client groups are very important, and the performance of each group should be distinguished whenever data collection procedures permit. Eight factors seem particularly important to recreation decisions: age, sex, area of residence, income, race, education, existence of handicap, and ownership of or access to an automobile. The last characteristic is important because of potentially important variations in accessibility and, thus, potential differences in the character, variety, and level of satisfaction with recreation experiences between those with and those without access to automobiles or public transportation.

The data collection procedures suggested in this chapter generally permit performance data to be grouped by the characteristics cited above—if not too many categories for any one characteristic are sought. For example, the citizen survey sampling procedures can probably permit a government to distinguish

Objective	Quality Characteristic	Specific Measure*	Data Collection Procedure
Enjoyableness	Citizen satisfaction	1. Percentage of household rating neighborhood park and recreation opportunities as satisfactory.	General citizen survey
	User satisfaction	2. Percentage of those households using community park or recreation facilities who rate them as satisfactory.	General citizen survey or survey of users (of particular facilities)
	Usage—participation rates	3. Percentage of community households using (or not using) a community park or recreation facility at least once over a specific past period, such as three months. (For nonusers, provide the percentage not using facilities for various reasons and distinguish reasons that can be at least partly controlled by the government from those that cannot.)	General citizen survey
	Usage—attendance	4. Number of visits at recreation sites.	Attendance statistics; estimates from general citizen survey
Avoidance of crowdedness	User satisfaction	5. Percentage of user households rating crowdedness of community facilities as unsatisfactory.	General citizen survey or survey of users (of particular facilities)
	Nonuser satisfaction	6. Percentage of nonuser households giving crowded conditions as a reason for nonuse of facilities.	General citizen survey
	Crowding factor	7. Average peak-hour attendance divided by capacity.	Attendance statistics and estimates of carrying capacity

Physical attractiveness	User satisfaction	8. Percentage of user households rating physical attractiveness as satisfactory.	General citizen survey or survey of users (of particular facilities)
	Nonuser satisfaction	9. Percentage of nonuser households giving lack of physical attractiveness as reason for nonuse.	General citizen survey
	Facility cleanliness	10. Percentage of user households rating cleanliness as satisfactory.	General citizen survey or survey of users
	Equipment condition	11. Percentage of user households rating condition of equipment as satisfactory.	General citizen survey or survey of users
Safety	Injuries to participants resulting from accidents	12. Number of serious injuries (for example, those requiring hospitalization) per 10,000 visits.	Accident and attendance statistics
	Criminal incidents	13. Number of criminal incidents per 10,000 visits.	Criminal incident statistics of some park and recreation agencies and most municipal police forces; attendance statistics
	User satisfaction	14. Percentage of user households rating safety of facilities as satisfactory.	General citizen survey or survey of users
	Nonuser satisfaction	15. Percentage of nonuser households giving lack of safety as a reason for nonuse of municipal facilities.	General citizen survey

TABLE 13-1. *Effectiveness Measures for Recreation Services*

Note: Overall objective is to provide for all citizens a variety of enjoyable leisure opportunities that are accessible, safe, physically attractive, and uncrowded.

*Many of the measures inquire into percentages of citizens or users who find conditions "satisfactory." Local officials may wish in some instances to focus more directly on the amount of *dissatisfaction*, in which case the word *satisfactory* would be changed to *unsatisfactory*.

TABLE 13-1—*continued*

Objective	Quality Characteristic	Specific Measure*	Data Collection Procedure
Accessibility	Physical accessibility	16. Percentage of citizens living within (or not within) 15 to 30 minutes' travel time of a community park or recreation facility distinguished by type of facility and principal relevant mode of transportation.	Counts from mapping latest census tract population figures against location of facilities, with appropriate travel time radius drawn around each facility
	Physical accessibility—user satisfaction	17. Percentage of user households rating physical accessibility as satisfactory.	General citizen survey or survey of users
	Physical accessibility—nonuser satisfaction	18. Percentage of nonuser households giving poor physical accessibility as a reason for nonuse.	General citizen survey
	Hours/days of operation—user satisfaction	19. Percentage of user households rating hours of operation as satisfactory.	General citizen survey or survey of users
	Hours/days of operation—nonuser satisfaction	20. Percentage of nonuser households giving unsatisfactory operating hours as a reason for nonuse.	General citizen survey
Variety of interesting activities	User satisfaction	21. Percentage of user households rating the variety of program activities as satisfactory.	General citizen survey or survey of users
	Nonuser satisfaction	22. Percentage of nonuser households giving lack of program variety as a reason for nonuse.	General citizen survey
Helpfulness of staff	Staff helpfulness—user satisfaction	23. Percentage of user households rating staff helpfulness or attitude as satisfactory.	General citizen survey or survey of users
	Staff helpfulness—nonuser satisfaction	24. Percentage of nonuser households giving poor staff attitude as a reason for nonuse.	General citizen survey

perhaps five to ten different geographic areas or age groups within a jurisdiction but would not permit twenty or more to be distinguished with any reasonable precision.

The particular clientele groupings used should be related to the specific characteristics of those groups for which programs and activities are planned and operated by the park and recreation agency. For example, Washington, D.C., used six age groupings—less than 6 years old, 6 to 13, 14 to 19, 20 to 34, 35 to 64, and 65 and over—because it operated programs specifically aimed at these age groups. In selecting age groupings, it also is helpful to choose those for which census information is readily available. This will aid in the calculation of several measurements such as physical accessibility and will facilitate checking the representativeness of sample survey results.

PRINCIPAL RECOMMENDED MEASUREMENT PROCEDURES

1. A major need in measuring the effectiveness of recreation services is to obtain reliable indicators of community satisfaction with available public recreation services. A regular (perhaps annual) survey of a sample of the community's citizens is recommended to obtain information on their satisfaction with recreation services. Reasonably reliable information can be obtained with survey techniques that obtain feedback from a relatively small (a few hundred households) but representative cross-section of the community. Information can be obtained from the survey as to both overall satisfaction with recreation opportunities and ratings of characteristics such as accessibility, cleanliness, safety, helpfulness of personnel, and condition of the equipment.

The same survey can also be used to obtain figures on the percentages of the community using and not using recreation facilities. For those who do not use government recreation services, the survey can also produce estimates of the apparent reasons for nonuse. This will enable recreation planners to distinguish reasons that could be affected by the government (for example, inaccessibility of recreation areas, lack of safety, lack of knowledge about recreational opportunities, and the types of recreational opportunities available) from reasons that, for the most part, cannot be affected by government (such as lack of interest or preference for nongovernmental recreation opportunities).

Data for twenty of the twenty-four measurements of effectiveness proposed in table 13-1 can be collected by the citizen survey. Pilot measurement efforts in Nashville, St. Petersburg, Palo Alto, Birmingham, Rockford, and Washington, D.C., have drawn heavily on that survey to collect information on citizen experiences and perceptions. In each of these six cities, park and recreation agency personnel were heavily involved. In all jurisdictions except Palo Alto, city personnel handled the survey, but with considerable outside technical advice. Each of the surveys except Palo Alto's was conducted by telephone.

The efforts in Nashville and St. Petersburg relied on internal personnel to undertake the surveys because the departments did not feel that the necessary funding (approximately $5,000) could be made available to hire a professional survey firm. Although park and recreation agencies were able to handle the survey, they found it a larger undertaking than they had expected.

Substantial outside assistance ... seems necessary in order for regular surveys of this type to be feasible in most communities. If a jurisdiction is unable to support a full citizen survey on recreation alone, a fallback position is to include a reduced number of recreation questions on a multiservice citizen survey....

2. Annual surveys of *users* of recreation programs and facilities should be considered. These can be conducted on site, and they provide citizen feedback on satisfaction with the specific programs and facilities. Nashville, St. Petersburg, and Palo Alto, which conducted such surveys, found the resulting information to be of particular interest to park and recreation management.

User surveys can produce data on twelve of the measures of effectiveness. Unlike the general citizen survey, user surveys probably can be handled primarily by recreation staff personnel; and because they are administered at recreation sites, they place less [of a] burden on the staff than does the household survey. To avoid pitfalls such as poorly worded questions and sloppy surveying techniques, some outside assistance is recommended....

Although these user surveys probably provide the best way to collect data on users' behavior patterns and perceptions, they do not provide information on nonusers and their reasons for nonuse. For these latter purposes, the general citizen survey discussed in (1) above is necessary.

3. To gauge physical accessibility to facilities—a crucial factor contributing to facility use—a mapping technique is suggested. This technique, which plots a community's population distribution against the location of existing recreation facilities, permits a calculation of the percentages of the population within or beyond a convenient time or distance (such as fifteen minutes) of a neighborhood recreation facility.

4. Basic community records also should be tracked on factors such as attendance (where obtainable), crowding (measured as estimates of average daily attendance divided by carrying capacity), and rates of injuries and criminal incidents. Thus comparisons can be made over time, among various areas, and of particular facilities in the community.

RESOURCE REQUIREMENTS FOR MEASUREMENT PROCEDURES

A local government with a park and recreation department of about 100 full-time employees is estimated to require about one and a half person-years of effort to pursue effectiveness measurement on an ongoing basis. A smaller department with 40 or fewer employees might require one person-year of effort. A large department with 500 or more employees would probably consume two person-years of effort.

Because of the sampling procedures involved, the cost of measuring effectiveness is not directly proportional to the size of the park and recreation department [undertaking the measurements]. Effectiveness measurement is likely to be easier to fund in medium-size and larger departments than in smaller departments simply because the task consumes a smaller percentage of the operating budgets in departments of medium and larger size. However, there are ways to reduce the cost of regular effectiveness measurement; these include using community volunteers and reducing the number of measurements and the frequency with which they are obtained.

INDIVIDUAL MEASURES

This section discusses the rationale for the measures shown in table 13-1 and describes procedures that appear usable in collecting data for each measure. Because most of the measures use data from either general citizen surveys or surveys of recreation users, procedural discussions are kept to a minimum in this section. Subsequent sections of this chapter discuss in more detail each of these two principal data collection approaches.

The measures are arranged in seven groups:

1. enjoyableness (measures 1–4);
2. avoidance of crowdedness (measures 5–7);
3. physical attractiveness (measures 8–11);
4. safety (measures 12–15);
5. physical accessibility (measures 16–20);
6. variety of interesting activities (measures 21 and 22); and
7. helpfulness of staff (measures 23 and 24).

Measures of Enjoyableness—[Data Collection]

. . . This set of measures [see table 13-1] uses two approaches to gauge enjoyableness. Measures 1 and 2 are direct indices of satisfaction; they call for obtaining citizens' ratings of the level of satisfaction with their recreation opportunities. Measures 3 and 4 attempt to get at enjoyableness more indirectly by measuring attendance or usage by citizens.

Measure 1 is the more comprehensive of the direct satisfaction measures. Using the general citizen survey (discussed in detail later), it produces a rating from a representative cross-section of all households in the community. Measure 2 focuses only on those citizens who have actually made use of at least one local government-operated recreation facility during a recent time period. If the data are obtained from a general citizen survey, the findings should be representative of a cross-section of the whole population of users in the community. If feedback from a sample of users of specific facilities is obtained, these individuals will be representative of users of all government facilities to the extent that the user surveys cover all programs and facilities or at least are representative of them.

All measures that inquire into "satisfactory" ratings by citizens or users may be changed to focus on "unsatisfactory" ratings if these would appear more meaningful to a local jurisdiction.

Data for measure 1 can be obtained by surveying a representative sample of households in the community. . . . For ratings by users (measure 2), either a general citizen survey or surveys of users of specific facilities can be employed. . . .

One problem is how to define *user.* [One can] somewhat arbitrarily define a user as "any household which has used a facility at least once in the past month." . . . Measure 3 defines the period as three months. A government may prefer to alter the definition to consider a longer time period (such as twelve months) or to require more uses during the given time before considering the household a "user." Another possibility is to tally responses for households with various amounts of usages.

In the Nashville survey, a period of three months was used as the reference period. Because of seasonal problems, it can be argued that the individual should be asked about the full period between surveys, which might normally be twelve months. However, the longer the time period asked about, the more difficult it may be for some respondents to remember experiences and impressions with sufficient accuracy.

There is little direct evidence on the memory problem. However, the evidence available . . . indicates that even if the survey is taken only at annual intervals, citizens can reasonably by expected to respond to questions covering longer periods of time such as six or twelve months. The memory problem is of less concern for "satisfaction" questions than for questions asking for frequency of usage of recreation facilities.

For measures 3 and 4—estimates of attendance or usage—the assumption is that people "vote with their feet"; that is, by using programs or facilities they indicate their satisfaction with them. Others may argue that citizens, particularly the less affluent, have few choices and in effect are a captive audience. To the extent that this is true, attendance or participation rates will not indicate the degree of enjoyableness of the facilities. Then, too, users of facilities will have different degrees of satisfaction. But usage is clearly important information to government officials and represents an important indicator of the value of recreation activities.

The traditional method for estimating usage is by attendance figures, as in measure 4. Most agencies keep some statistics; [for example,] the numbers of persons attending classes and using facilities with controlled access such as community centers. Generally lacking are attendance counts at open facilities such as city parks and playgrounds. In the latter cases, attendance estimates are sometimes obtained using various formulas often based on counts at peak periods. For example, the National Recreation and Parks Association has offered a "peak count" formula to determine summer playground attendance. This procedure calls for multiplying a factor of 1.8 by the peak-time morning attendance count, 2.5 by the afternoon peak count, and 1.8 by the evening peak count. These figures are then added to produce the estimated daily attendance. Developed in 1938, this formula was retested nationally in 1960 and supported by the test findings.[1]

The general citizen survey provides an additional way to estimate total recreational attendance and to estimate for those few facilities specifically asked about in the survey.[2] The user survey provides a way to collect attendance statistics at several specific facilities. Both Nashville and St. Petersburg found [that] their reported attendance counts differed from estimates based on the general citizen and user surveys. (Drawing on the user data, Nashville held a series of meetings with community center supervisors to improve attendance taking.) At this stage of knowledge, however, there has been too little analysis of the data and probable reasons for differences to make firm conclusions or recommendations as to the most accurate procedures for estimating attendance.

What is clear is that attendance counts do not indicate how many *different* persons or families use the facilities because those attending may be repeat users. The general citizen survey is a better way to obtain participation rates. That is the purpose of measure 3, which provides an estimate of the percentage of households which have (or have not) used community facilities. . . .

As discussed under measure 2, the definition of *use* and *nonuse* is important; but there is no clearcut, preferred definition. [A] one-month recall period . . . may provide for more accurate responses, but it does not seem to cover a large enough period, especially if the surveys are taken only annually. As indicated under measure 2, a six- or even twelve-month period seems more appropriate in order to cover a greater amount of the respondents' recreational experiences. Usage can be defined as "at least one use during the referenced period," but some communities may prefer a higher threshold, such as three uses or more.

Decisions on length of recall period and number of uses will affect the values derived for the measure. As long as the decisions are used consistently, however, any choices should provide adequate information for making comparisons on participation rates from one time period to another, from one geographical section of the community to another, or from one facility to another.

Reasons for nonuse are likely to be critical in measuring the objective of reaching all citizens who desire to be served. Thus it is important that the nonuse rates be broken down by reason for nonuse. . . .

Governments testing these procedures have found it particularly helpful to group the reasons for nonuse into those that are "potentially within government control" and those that are "probably beyond government control." Table 13-2 lists a sample set of reasons grouped by these two categories. In addition, the [table] presents, for illustrative purposes, the frequency of individual reasons given by citizens for nonuse in three surveys.

Most of the reasons for nonuse that are categorized as "potentially within government control" are also used as the basis for subsequent indicators of effectiveness—that is, measures 6 (crowded conditions), 9 (lack of physical attractiveness), 15 (safety problems), 18 (inaccessibility), 20 (inconvenient hours), 22 (lack of interesting programs), and 24 (poor staff). Two other reasons for nonuse also could be added: lack of information or knowledge about the facility or programs and the cost of using facilities or programs. . . .

A note of caution is in order in directing action based on reasons for nonuse. Experiences in other service areas, particularly in the use of public transportation, suggest that actions based primarily on reported reasons for nonuse did not necessarily produce usage. Thus, government officials using these data should be careful to treat them as approximate and tentative, more

Causes	Rockford (%)	St. Petersburg (%)	D.C. (%)
Potentially within government control			
Facility unknown	10	12	26
Too far away	13	5	10
Activities not interesting	3	13	5
Too dangerous	4	4	3
Too crowded	5	2	2
Inconvenient hours	3	1	1
Not attractive	2	0	1
Costs too much	1	1	0
Total	41	38	48
Probably beyond government control*			
Too busy	21	20	18
Poor personal health	1	19	6
Too old	3		5
Don't like other users	4	2	2
Total	29	41	31
No opinion—Won't say	31	21	21

TABLE 13-2. *Reasons Given by Citizens for Nonuse of Recreation Facilities*

Source: Statistics compiled from citizen surveys in Washington, D.C. (June 1972); Rockford, Illinois (August 1972); and St. Petersburg, Florida (September 1973).

*An additional category not used in these surveys could be Satisfied with Nongovernmental Recreation Facilities.

indicative than definitive. Such information does appear on the surface to be useful for guiding government action, but confirming information should be sought.

Measure 3 could be expressed as either household participation rates or individual participation rates, or both. The questions . . . ask about the respondent's own participation and that of each of the other members of the household. With this information, participation rates can be calculated for respondents, households, or both. The accuracy of respondents' reports on usage by other household members is not clear. . . .

In the process of obtaining citizen ratings on overall satisfaction, it seems highly desirable for the government also to obtain ratings on particular aspects of the facilities. These include hours of operation, cleanliness, condition of equipment, helpfulness and attitude of personnel, crowded conditions, safety, accessibility, and parking availability. . . . Most of these ratings are used in subsequent measures and are discussed below.

Measures of Crowded Conditions

. . . These three measures [see table 13-1] cover three perspectives. Measure 5 obtains ratings of crowdedness directly from persons who have used the community facilities, based on either the general citizen survey . . . or user surveys. . . . Measure 6 provides the percentage of nonuser households which give crowded conditions as a reason for nonuse. . . . Because citizen perceptions of crowded conditions may be quite different from actual conditions, the citizen ratings obtained from measures 5 and 6 seem particularly important in assessing crowdedness.

Measure 7 provides a statistic based on actual attendance records; it attempts to relate attendance counts to an estimate of the "capacity" for various recreation sites. For some facilities, such as tennis courts and swimming pools, the capacity can be defined with some precision. However, the problem is more difficult for playgrounds, open space, and multiple-use facilities.

In order to consider all facilities rather than each individually, measure 7 could be transformed into a form calling for the "number of recreational facilities in which average daily attendance exceeded the capacity." However, this measure still reflects the problem that the average figures may hide the specific frequency of occasions when capacity was exceeded. Preferably, there would be an estimate of the number of occasions, perhaps in number of hours, when capacity was exceeded. The feasibility of gathering such information comprehensively, given the current state . . . of attendance measurements, seems questionable. The data collection seems feasible, however, for selected kinds of activities such as swimming, golf, tennis, and various recreation classes, in which attendance counts, waiting times, and possibly the number of turnaways can be feasibly monitored, especially during peak use periods.

Measures of Physical Attractiveness

. . . Similar to the measures for crowdedness, measures 8, 10, and 11 provide ratings—from households which have used recreation facilities—of overall physical attractiveness (measure 8) or such specific aspects as facility cleanliness (measure 10) and equipment condition (measure 11). . . .

Although not explored as part of this investigation, it should be possible to develop "objective" measures of facility cleanliness (measure 10) and equipment condition (measure 11). In both cases, it should be possible to develop a trained observer rating. . . .

Measure 9 provides an estimate of the percentage of nonuser households giving lack of physical attractiveness as the reason for nonuse. . . . The same qualifications already mentioned in the discussion of measure 3 on reasons for nonuse also apply here.

Measures of Safety

. . . Measures 12 and 13 use basic government statistics, whereas measures 14 and 15 employ ratings from the citizen or user surveys.

For legal and administrative reasons, most park and recreation agencies keep detailed statistics on reported injuries (measure 12), and all local police departments keep statistics on criminal incidents (measure 13). Some park and recreation agencies also have their own police forces, which maintain crime statistics. What is lacking in most of these agencies, however, is any attempt to track the statistics through time to see if the situation is changing. . . .

When making comparisons of the number of injuries or criminal incidents over various time periods, among recreation districts, or by facility, it is highly desirable to relate the number of incidents to some indicator of the population at risk. (After all, the playground or swimming pool with the fewest number of injuries would be the one that is not used at all.) An approach that seems appropriate is to divide the number of injuries or incidents in a given time period by the attendance or number of attendance hours during that period.

Although losses because of vandalism are not included in the list of measures in table 13-1, some governments may also want to track the dollar amount of these losses. Vandalism records normally will be kept by most agencies for purposes of reporting to the police, scheduling repairs, and justifying budgets. Again, generally lacking are procedures to track these data through time and across geographic areas. In making comparisons about vandalism losses, it is desirable to relate the amount of loss to the amount of property at risk, such as the total value of the property. Thus, the vandalism loss measure might be expressed as "dollar value of vandalism losses per $1,000 of property value." In making comparisons from one year to the next, adjustments for rising costs would also be appropriate.

Measure 14 estimates the percentage of households using recreation facilities who rate their safety as satisfactory (or unsatisfactory).... Measure 15 provides estimates of the percentage of nonuser households giving lack of safety as a reason for nonuse of municipal facilities....

An additional concern for measures 12 and 13 is that not all injuries resulting from accidents or criminal incidents are likely to be reported. The citizen and user surveys could be employed to ask citizens whether they were involved in any recreation area accidents or criminal incidents that were not reported. Estimates of frequency of unreported incidents could then be added to tallies of the reported incidents. The unreported crimes in recreational areas could be included in the series of questions on victimization.... However, the small number of citizens who both (1) use park and recreation facilities and (2) are victimized means that the estimates ... would provide only a crude approximation of the extent of victimization at those facilities.

Measures of Accessibility

... The concept of accessibility is complicated. It includes factors such as physical accessibility, problems due to various forms of explicit or implicit discrimination, lack of transportation, inconvenient hours of operation, excessive waiting (see crowdedness measures), or inadequate parking space. Measures 16–18 provide indications of physical accessibility, whereas measures 19 and 20 focus on hours of operation. No specific measures of the extent of discrimination or parking problems are included....

Measure 16 focuses on the proximity of the population to recreational facilities and can be obtained by a mapping technique. Measure 17 focuses on ratings by user households, employing a user survey question.... Measure 18 provides an estimate of the percentage of nonuser households which give poor physical accessibility as a reason for nonuse based on a question in a general citizen survey....

Measure 16 requires more discussion. Ease of accessibility is one of the crucial factors contributing to facility use. Two important considerations in examining accessibility are first, how close the individual citizens are to the facilities and second, the extent of the individuals' mobility. For many potential users of recreation facilities, such as youths and others without access to automobiles, mobility is a problem and the geographic distribution of facilities in a community is important. Therefore, the measurement of accessibility will vary somewhat with the mobility characteristics of the intended user group.

One way to measure accessibility is to calculate the percentage of the total population (or of a particular potential user group) residing within a given distance of a facility. These data provide a useful adjunct to citizen perceptions of physical accessibility and a check against them. Specific procedures for the mapping technique . . . are:

1. Obtain appropriate maps, such as those prepared locally or by the U.S. Census Bureau. Census population statistics are keyed to census tracts, with block group and block numbers printed on the maps. Several census map sheets will probably be needed to cover each city, plus a "fringe area" of at least three-fourths of a mile around its political boundary. Calibration marks, such as four "+"s, should be placed on the base map. These marks will guide aligning the map overlays described in succeeding steps.
2. Identify on the maps physical barriers that would affect accessibility to recreation areas. These barriers, including freeways, railroads, industrial zones, and rivers, should be marked on the base maps. An examination of the local transportation planning agency highway map —or even a common street map—[and] government personnel's knowledge of the city are [both] helpful in determining locations of barriers. On-site checks may be desirable in some instances.
3. Plot the population distribution on an overlay. Use the basic population data tabulations (from census statistics or planning information) to prepare population overlays on tracing paper or acetate. Place the population overlay on the base map. Write population data on the overlay for the appropriate census tracts, block groups, or blocks.
4. Plot the location of recreation facilities on an overlay to the base map.
5. Draw an accessibility circle on the facility location overlay around each plotted facility. The radius used for these circles should reflect the mode of transportation persons are assumed to use and the estimated maximum travel time. We suggest fifteen- and thirty-minute travel times, or three-fourths and one and one-half miles. In order to account for the effect of physical barriers and any other identifiable barriers to access, the areas blocked from access to facilities should be eliminated from the circles.
6. Assemble overlays on base map, using the calibration marks on the maps and overlays to permit rapid alignment.
7. Estimate the "number and percentage of people living within" the physical accessibility circles. The proportion of the population in tracts or in blocks that are split by the accessibility circles should be esti-

mated by visually estimating the percentage of the census tract or block group area lying within each physical accessibility circle and then splitting the population proportionately.... This method assumes that the population is evenly distributed throughout the area.

Note that separate sets of overlays will be necessary to distinguish different population segments—for example, to consider accessibility for various age groups. In addition, car-oriented facilities such as golf courses or major city or county parks will require riding-time accessibility circles, whereas neighborhood facilities will require walking-time circles. (For client groups without access to automobiles, transit-time accessibility might be needed to estimate accessibility to major local recreation facilities, with such access plotted around transit stops.... For measure 19, user-household ratings of the hours of operation can be obtained from questions in the general citizen survey and in the recreation user survey. For measure 20, the proportion of nonusers giving hours of operation as a reason for nonuse, data can be obtained from the general citizen survey....

Measures of Variety

... Two perspectives are provided on variety. Measure 21 obtains a rating from households which used the facilities.... For measure 22, the percentage of nonuser households giving lack of program variety as a reason for nonuse, data can be obtained from the general citizen survey.... At the same time, information could be obtained on the particular activities of interest to the nonuser households by asking "What would be interesting?" ...

A measure such as "the average number of different program activities per facility" was considered as an easy way to gauge program variety. However, this appears to measure input more than results, so it has not been included in our list of suggested effectiveness measures.

Measures of Helpfulness of Staff

... In the process of providing recreational services, considerable interaction often occurs between government employees and the clients of recreational activities. Some feedback seems appropriate on the degree to which such government employees are helpful and courteous to clients. Measure 23 provides a perspective on user households.... Measure 24 provides estimates of the percentage of nonuser households giving poor staff attitudes as a reason for nonuse.... This factor seldom appeared in early surveys asking respondents about "other" reasons for nonuse. Such a question, however, could be included.

... GENERAL CITIZEN SURVEYS

These surveys, if properly carried out, produce [data] difficult to obtain in any other way. First, the surveys provide a way to obtain a representative citizen evaluation of facilities and programs. Second, the surveys are probably the most efficient way to gather usage-participation data on urban parks and playgrounds that lack controlled access points. Third, they provide a means for probing the behavior of various classes of recreation users and nonusers, alike.

Problems do exist in using general citizen surveys to assess recreational effectiveness. [Such] surveys require significant resources, and most park and recreation agencies will need outside expertise to set up, conduct, and analyze survey results.

. . . A number of park and recreation agencies in the United States, particularly at the state and federal level, have conducted on-site surveys of persons who use park and recreation facilities. Such surveys are much less common at the local government level, but they have been used by a number of city and county park and recreation agencies. Generally, these surveys have been one-time efforts that focused on the overall satisfaction of users and any modifications they would like made. User surveys have not been employed to collect regular information on the effectiveness of current services, at least not in a systematic way that permits annual comparisons.

The surveys described in this section focus on service effectiveness. They ask about users' recent past experiences and attitudes toward existing facilities and activities. When administered annually, these surveys can be used to provide time-trend information on both program and individual facility effectiveness.

The suggestions presented here are based on on-site user surveys undertaken in 1973 or 1974 in Nashville, St. Petersburg, and Palo Alto. The Nashville survey was restricted to community centers, but the St. Petersburg survey included those centers and selected parks as well. The Palo Alto survey involved only golf course users. . . .

On-site user surveys offer the following advantages over general citizen surveys:

1. They provide an efficient way to collect data directly related to users' actual experiences.
2. They produce, at low cost, sample sizes large enough for statements to be made about the effectiveness of specific facilities or programs. This is in contrast to general citizen surveys, in which, because of cost, it is not usually feasible to have large enough samples to make precise statements about individual facilities and programs.
3. They permit individuals to speak for themselves. In most household surveys, by comparison, time and cost factors mean that one person is asked to speak for the entire household.
4. They seem well within the capability of the average recreation department to conduct on its own.

There are three principal disadvantages to user surveys:

1. They do not permit a department to collect data on nonusers and their reasons for not taking advantage of recreation services.
2. From the information provided by a user survey it is difficult to esti-

mate with any precision the percentage of different users in a community.
3. User surveys are difficult to conduct where the site is large and lacks controlled access (such as a large park).

The user surveys discussed here can produce data for ten of the twenty-four measures shown in table 13-1. Those ten measures are . . .

1. user satisfaction
2. crowded conditions
3. physical attractiveness
4. facility cleanliness
5. equipment condition
6. safety
7. physical accessibility/convenience
8. hours/days of operation
9. variety of interesting activities
10. staff helpfulness.

In addition to client ratings, questions should also be included on the survey to produce demographic and diagnostic data. These data include factors such as age, sex, and income range of respondents; how far the individual traveled to reach the facility; the mode of transportation used; and perhaps the length of time spent in transit. . . .

Interviewing Method [and Length of Interview]

There are two basic interviewing approaches: face-to-face interviewing and self-administered forms. The former requires an interviewer to read each question and record the answer. With self-administered surveys, users complete the questionnaire themselves. Most park and recreation agencies will find a combination of the two procedures to be advisable. Both Nashville and St. Petersburg used such a combination, with face-to-face interviewing used only in the case of young children or others unable to complete the form themselves. The Palo Alto golf survey relied solely on the self-administered questionnaire.

The type of questionnaire suggested should require less than ten minutes to complete. In Palo Alto the average time to complete the questionnaire was six minutes; in St. Petersburg, five minutes; and in Nashville, four minutes.

Special Validity Issues

Essentially the same [question] can be raised with the user survey as with the general citizen survey concerning the validity of citizen responses: Does the survey questionnaire obtain valid information from respondents? . . . However, in several respects, user surveys present less-severe problems than do citizen surveys. First, in user surveys individuals speak only for themselves; they are not asked to respond on behalf of other members of their families as well. Surveys in the health field show that, at least for health-related questions, this factor improves accuracy.[3] Second, sampling is much less of a problem. There should be little or no bias introduced by sampling if fairly simple procedures are followed.[4] Third, the user is more likely to be interested in the survey and as a result to give more accurate answers. . . . Fourth, the questions do not rely heavily on respondent's memories.

Who Should Undertake the Survey Operations?

With only limited outside assistance, government personnel in Nashville, St. Petersburg, and Palo Alto designed their own survey questionnaires, pretested the forms, conducted the surveys, and tabulated the results. Although most governments should have professional advice, particularly for the initial survey and questionnaire design, local governments should be able to handle most aspects of a user survey by themselves.

There is a question as to whether the use of recreation personnel to handle the interviewing produces a bias in the results. There are two sources of potential bias. First, recreation personnel may unintentionally encourage responses that correspond to their own perceptions. Second, if the persons being interviewed felt park and recreation personnel were being rated on the basis of their responses, the interviewees might respond more favorably to facility conditions than they otherwise would. St. Petersburg attempted to overcome this potential problem by assigning its personnel to facilities other than those where they would normally work.

It also may be possible to use interviewers outside the park and recreation agency. Possibilities include other government personnel; volunteers from groups such as the League of Women Voters, Park and Recreation Board, or Health and Welfare Council; or paid outside help. The Palo Alto survey was administered entirely by volunteers of the local golf club and League of Women Voters. Washington, D.C., used Neighborhood Youth Corps personnel to help with a swimming pool survey. When such outside personnel are used, close supervision is particularly important.

Frequency . . . Timing [and Sample Size and Selection]

Since seasonal differences are important in recreation, it may be advisable to conduct a survey at the end of each major recreational season. Governments interested in evaluating a particular program—such as summer activities—may want to conduct the survey at the end of that season. . . .

Sampling is much less of a problem for a user survey than it is for a household survey because the users come to the site and to the interviewer. Hence it is a relatively simple task to select those to be sampled. The factor that primarily determines the cost of the user survey is not the absolute sample size but rather the number of different facilities covered and the number of survey hours and days spent at each facility.

The sample size should be sufficiently large at each site to permit grouping the user responses into desired categories such as age, sex, race, and location or residence. In St. Petersburg, the sample design called for 100 completed interviews from each center. In total, there were 1,207 interviews at fourteen facilities. At some places where the expected attendance was small, everyone was interviewed. At other sites, every other person or every third person was selected; at one busy facility, every fifteenth person was selected to complete a questionnaire. . . .

Interviewing the Users; [Tabulating and Analyzing the Results]

The user surveys in Nashville, Palo Alto, and St. Petersburg were conducted at sites where access was controlled. No surveying took place at open-access parks and playgrounds, sites that introduce a more complicated sampling problem not investigated in the course of this study. . . .

If the survey is larger than several hundred interviews, it is probably advisable to precode the survey questionnaire, keypunch the results directly from the survey forms, and tabulate by computer. Several computer programs facilitate a variety of tabulations and statistical manipulations. Nashville, Palo Alto, and St. Petersburg each used the Statistical Package for Social Sciences (SPSS) in tallying the results of their surveys. Of course, the results can always be hand tabulated, but this is an onerous task and increases the possibility of error. . . .

User Survey Staffing and Timing Requirements

. . . Based on the experiences in Nashville, St. Petersburg, and Palo Alto in 1973 and 1974, it appears that designing the questionnaire, conducting the survey, and tabulating results take about one person-hour for each completed survey questionnaire. The amount of staffing and time will vary, depending mainly on the number of different sites and the number of hours over which the survey is conducted. Less important for user surveys is the number of questionnaires completed at any one facility.

Repeat surveys in future years should cost somewhat—but not much—less, as the only saving would be in the design and pretesting of the questionnaire. Staffing for a survey at ten facilities (seventy survey hours) would probably require one survey leader, one computer programmer, one management analyst, and twenty interviewers. It is possible that a single person [could] handle more than one of these tasks. . . .

COSTS AND STAFFING REQUIREMENTS FOR MEASUREMENT PROCEDURES

Earlier publications have presented the cost and staffing requirements for measuring the effectiveness of recreation services.[5] Based on the experiences in Nashville, Palo Alto, and St. Petersburg, there appears to be no reason to change the earlier overall cost and staffing estimates.[6] . . .

The overall effort needed to collect the data on the measurements outlined in table 13-1 is likely to be a little less than one person-year of effort for a department with an operating budget of $500,000 or less; about one and one-half person-years of effort for a department with a budget of approximately $1 million; and about two person-years for a department with a budget of $10 million or more. . . .

The actual added expenditures in each city were small, less than $1,000. Also, it is not necessary for a jurisdiction to adopt all of the measurement procedures. Government managers may be more interested in certain elements than in others. Finally, the frequency of reporting will have an important impact on the overall cost of the system.

USING THE RECREATION EFFECTIVENESS INFORMATION

... Park and recreation officials with whom we have discussed measures of effectiveness have generally demonstrated a lively interest in information that can be collected through citizen surveys—both the general citizen survey and the on-site user surveys.... However, when presented with information from the general citizen survey, some have expressed disappointment because it did not provide data on individual programs or facilities; the sample sizes were large enough to provide meaningful data only on major districts in the cities or counties. Recreation managers found such information difficult to interpret and insufficiently relevant to their needs. The information they seem to have found most interesting thus far is that collected by the user survey. These data can be tied to specific facilities, programs, and individuals. Thus, the user surveys can provide feedback to individual facility managers as well as higher level officials on the effectiveness of their operations. This feedback provides a way to establish accountability in the park and recreation field.

NOTES

1. See Butler (1) and International City Management Association (3, p. 347). (The latter suggests slightly different factors.)
2. See U.S. Department of the Interior (5, pp. 57–63) for a discussion of this procedure and a fuller discussion of recreation attendance figures.
3. See U.S. HEW (4).
4. Nashville did find that some of its centers failed to complete the survey as instructed. Only 6 centers out of 27 conducted the survey entirely as instructed; another 3 completed the survey with minor errors (e.g., a few interview forms without a date or time); 16 partially completed the survey; and 2 centers did not participate at all. Although St. Petersburg and Palo Alto completed the user survey as planned, supervising personnel in the two cities reported that it was necessary to visit those carrying out the survey frequently—that is, several times a day. Otherwise, interviewers tended to skip individuals and failed to check the completed survey forms properly.
5. See U.S. Department of the Interior (5, pp. 73–79) and Hatry and Dunn (2, pp. 42–44).
6. For a summary of the estimated annual costs for each of the measurement procedures, see U.S. Department of the Interior (5, p. 75, exhibit 32). For the estimates of the total costs for three agency sizes and three measurement levels, see idem (p. 74, exhibit 31).

REFERENCES

1. Butler, George. 1961. Summer playground attendance formula. *Recreation*, April.
2. Hatry, Harry P., and Dunn, Diana R. 1971. *Measuring the effectiveness of local government services: Recreation.* Washington, D.C.: Urban Institute.
3. International City Management Association. 1960. *Municipal recreation administration.* 4th ed. Chicago.
4. U.S. Department of Health, Education, and Welfare (HEW), Public Health Service. 1965. *Reporting of hospitalization in the health interview survey.* July.
5. U.S. Department of the Interior, Bureau of Outdoor Recreation. 1973. *How effective are your community recreation services?* Ed. Donald M. Fisk. Washington, D.C.: Government Printing Office.

CHAPTER 14

RECREATION ACTIVITY PACKAGES AT WATER-BASED RESOURCES

Stephen F. McCool

Here we review the concept of recreational activity packages and the fact that behavior at a recreation site is dependent on a visitor's definition of the site as a locale for various recreational activities. Professor McCool also points out the difficulties and weaknesses of some past research using activity packages that limited the utility of the concept for planning and management purposes. Suggesting the use of a previously proposed activity package typology, he presents the results of a study using data collected in Utah state parks.

The importance of water in the provision and enhancement of wildland recreation opportunities has been noted by both researchers and managers (5; 16; 8). Studies have suggested that visitors to campgrounds and picnic areas often prefer sites located near to, or with a view of, a water surface (4). Other researchers have suggested that the availability of water-based recreation is often an important component of the visitor's decision process when choosing a locale for a wildland recreation experience (15; 14). Finally, the presence of a water surface has been cited to "explain" differential use rates among various recreation sites (20).

The particular patterns of participation in various recreational activities may also hold significant implications for managers of wildland water-based resources. Users of these areas often participate in several recreation activities during their visit. For example, a visitor's decision to engage in recreational boating at a reservoir may be accompanied by decisions to participate in swimming, picnicking, sunbathing, and water-skiing. The various activity participation patterns in which the visitor may engage can result in differences in site impact and in the number of demands upon managers for site maintenance, law enforcement, and visitor contact programs. And, as suggested by Shafer (19), conflicts among visitors may arise when two or more user groups with dissimilar interests compete for the same water surface and related shoreline.

The decisions of visitors to engage in various recreation activity patterns at water-based resources is a result of a complex process involving site or

---

Reprinted from *Leisure Sciences* 1, no. 2 (1978): 163–73, by permission of Crane Russak & Co. and the author.

The research on which this paper is based was conducted while the author was a faculty member of Utah State University, Logan.

supply characteristics and variables, the visitors' dispositions and attitudes, interactions with other persons having similar social characteristics, and experience. Frequently, research on activity participation at lakes and reservoirs has focused on supply variables for explanation of different participation rates or has been conducted from the viewpoint that recreation activities occur singly rather than in distinctive patterns or "packages" (for example, see reference 10). A central purpose of this paper is to identify the patterns of recreation activity participation (in terms of activity packages) at water-based resources and to assess the influence of a particular social characteristic—location of residence—on those patterns.

RECREATIONAL ACTIVITY PACKAGES

Lee (13) has suggested that human behavior at outdoor sites is influenced by the visitor's definition of the site as a locale for recreational activity. Definition of the site as a recreational place influences visitors to participate in distinctive activities, which have social meanings congruent with that definition. Lee demonstrated that a particular recreational place, such as a water-based resource, may assume several definitions depending upon the sociocultural group, or area of residence, of the users visiting the site. In other terms, Burch (2) has stated that behavior at the recreational place is "structured by a set of collective goals" agreed to by the visiting group.

The set of activities in which the visiting group engages at a water-based recreation area may be termed an *activity package.* Visitors can be observed participating in a "similar set of actions at a similar time and place" (3). In Burch's early study of activity participation at forested campgrounds in the Pacific Northwest, four packages were identified: family fishing camps, nature study camps, family water-skiing camps, and overnight transient tourist groups. Each of the four packages displayed a unique set of human activity. Importantly, Burch noted that none of the campgrounds had been specifically designed for any of the packages assigned to it by visiting groups; and each package apparently had different requirements for campsite spacing, comfort facilities, screening, and spatial movement. Grouping activities into packages by their meaning may thus help managers and planners (1) to understand better the kinds of opportunities visitors are seeking, and their consequent behavior; (2) to develop facilities and visitor contact programs to enhance those opportunities; and (3) to identify those packages which may conflict with other packages in the use of a recreation site.

Researchers concerned with recreation activity participation have become more and more cognizant of the activity package concept. Such recognition, however, has been shown primarily through the use of empirical methodologies rather than through the development and testing of conceptual frameworks. Many studies have used factor or cluster analytical techniques to derive activity packages. Beginning with Proctor (17) and continuing with (among others) Bishop (1), Witt (21), and Romsa (18), a number of activity factors or clusters for several subject populations have been determined. These studies have identified from three to eight activity packages for each population examined, but they have several weaknesses that may limit their utility for planning and management.

First, researchers employing factor and cluster analysis methods generally use frequencies of participation of a particular population or sample in recreational activities to form the resulting groupings. It is possible that correlations among these activities may be spurious. For example, a high correlation between swimming and snow skiing may not necessarily represent participation in an activity package in the sense that this term has been defined here. Such clustering procedures also fail to take into account the locationally dependent nature of activity packages. Because particular types of recreational places hold particular meanings for the users, use of general population participation frequencies ignores the definitions assigned by subpopulations to specific recreational places. Thus, data from studies employing a factor or clustering technique would be of little assistance to the managers of a particular water-based recreational place.

Second, because the packages are derived from empirical data, the activities comprising each package may change over time. While Bishop and Witt in their investigations found their factors stable across the cities they studied, they derived a different set of factors for the adult and the youth samples engaging in the same activities. Since the individual recreation activities comprising each factor are subject to change, it is difficult to determine not only the underlying meaning of each factor but also how the various social, economic, and situational factors influence participation in the activity package.

Some of these problems can be overcome by developing an a priori taxonomic system which defines packages in terms of social meanings. Recreational activities would be placed within an activity group based on similarities in meaning to the participant. This would allow researchers to test the effects of psychological, sociological, and situational factors on participation in any given package.

Such a system has been proposed by Hendee, Gale, and Catton (9). This system was originally designed to group preferences for recreational activity into a few classes, based on perceived similarities in the underlying meanings of the activities to the participant. Their categories and definitions (somewhat abbreviated) of the five conceptually linked activity packages may be stated as follows:

1. *Appreciative-symbolic.* Activities directed toward appreciation of features of the natural environment. The recreationist's focus is on appreciation of material items in the environment rather than on their extraction in the form of "trophies," although areas visited and mountains climbed are surely considered as trophies in a symbolic sense.
2. *Extractive-symbolic.* Activities characterized by the quest for trophies extracted from the natural environment.
3. *Passive-free play.* Activities requiring little effort and not confined to the forest environment.
4. *Sociable-learning.* Clearly social activities such as visiting, looking around camp, and singing, combined with learning activities such as nature study, hearing nature talks, and visiting exhibits.

5. *Active-expressive.* Activities not requiring use of a forest setting and which, in fact, sometimes interfere with other activities at the same site.

Since this typology is based on the similarity in meanings of activities, it is especially useful in describing the visitor's definition of the recreation place.

What variables affect the visitor's decision to select participation in the above activity packages at particular types of recreational places? Several authors have suggested or observed that out-of-state tourists and local (in-state) residents appear to define similar resources differently. For example, it has been noted that "while on vacation, the tourist is more interested in seeing and learning new things than in doing the same things he does at other times" (11; 12). The same authors also felt that the local (resident) user is more active in a "physical relationship" to the resource than the nonresident vacationer. In terms of the Hendee, Gale and Catton taxonomy, local (in-state) residents would be expected to show a greater frequency of participation in extractive-symbolic and active-expressive packages than nonresident tourists. On the other hand, nonresidents would display greater participation in appreciative-symbolic and sociable-learning packages than local residents. The time available for engaging in recreational activities may act as an intervening variable on the visitor's definition of *place.* It is logical to assume that the day user has a more constrained time budget than the camper. The more limited time budget of the former would be reflected in a greater concentration of activity in any given activity package.

THE STUDY

The purpose of the present effort is to explore participation in activity packages by visitors to water-based wildland recreation resources and to test the hypotheses concerning the influence of resident status on that participation. In cooperation with the Utah Outdoor Recreational Agency and the Utah Division of Parks and Recreation, visitors to sixteen water-based units of the state park system were asked about their recreation activity participation during the summer of 1974. All sixteen units recorded a minimum of 6,500 visits during the May/September sampling period, and all are similar in terms of resource characteristics and developed recreational opportunities available. Random groups of visitors entering each unit on preselected days were given mail-return questionnaires and were asked to record their participation in twenty-eight recreational activities during their visit. These activities were then classified according to the Hendee, Gale and Catton (9) scheme. . . . [T]he activities that were assigned to each of the five packages [are:]

1. Appreciative-symbolic: sightseeing, hiking, backpacking, exploring, photography, and other natural environment activities;
2. Extractive-symbolic: fishing, hunting;
3. Passive-free play: driving for pleasure, picnicking;
4. Sociable-learning: nature study, visiting historic sites, visiting museums, interpretive trail hikes;

5. Active-expressive: golf, softball, volleyball and other team games, trail biking, motorcycling, dune buggying, jogging, bicycling, water-skiing, swimming, boating, sailing, horseback riding.

The data are based on a total of 834 questionnaires returned, or a return rate of about 30 percent.

Visitors were grouped into day users and campers. Campers stayed overnight in the park, while the day users had some other type of lodging outside the park—whether their own home, a motel, or another campground. Each group was also identified either as Utah resident or as nonresident.

STUDY RESULTS

The intervening effect of length of stay is shown in table 14-1. The high X^2 value indicates that day users and campers do display different rates of participation in the indicated activity packages. Thus to test the hypothesis that residents and nonresidents define water-based resources differently, length of stay must be controlled.

Activity Package	Day Use (N)	(%)	Camping (N)	(%)
Active-expressive	489	53.6	666	41.1
Appreciative-symbolic	129	14.1	308	19.1
Extractive-symbolic	93	10.2	231	14.2
Passive-free play	167	18.3	237	14.6
Sociable-learning	35	3.8	179	11.0
Total	913	100.0	1,621	100.0

TABLE 14-1. *Number and Percentage of Activity Occasions, by Activity Package and Type of Use, Utah State Park Visitor Study, 1974*
Note: X^2 = 76.40, P < .005.

Table 14-2 compares camper activity package participation for both residents and nonresidents, while table 14-3 shows this information for day users. Participation in the activity packages was found to be dependent upon residence in both cases. Residents participated most frequently in active-expressive activities, whether or not their visit included an overnight stay in the park. Resident day users' next most frequent choice was passive-free play activities, while the resident campers' next most frequent choice was extractive-symbolic activities. Participation in sociable-learning activities was chosen least frequently by both resident day and overnight users.

Nonresidents demonstrated significantly different activity package participation patterns than residents. Nonresident campers tended to show a more uniform distribution of activity occasions across packages than resident campers. Most occasions were in the appreciative-symbolic category. While the day users displayed a more uneven distribution of activity occasions, the modal category of participation was the same as the campers'. The second most

Activity Package	Utah Resident (N)	Utah Resident (%)	Nonresident (N)	Nonresident (%)
Active-expressive	506	51.7	160	24.9
Appreciative-symbolic	137	14.0	171	26.5
Extractive-symbolic	174	17.8	57	8.9
Passive-free play	135	13.8	102	15.9
Sociable-learning	26	2.7	153	23.8
Total	978	100.0	643	100.0

TABLE 14-2. *Number and Percentage of Activity Occasions, by Activity Package and Residence of Campers, Utah State Park Visitor Study, Summer 1974*
Note: $X^2 = 280.203$, $P < .005$.

Activity Package	Utah Resident (N)	Utah Resident (%)	Nonresident (N)	Nonresident (%)
Active-expressive	441	58.0	44	29.6
Appreciative-symbolic	82	10.8	47	31.5
Extractive-symbolic	78	10.3	15	10.0
Passive-free play	132	17.4	35	23.5
Sociable-learning	27	3.5	8	5.4
Total	760	100.0	149	100.0

TABLE 14-3. *Number and Percentage of Activity Occasions, by Activity Package and Residence of Day Users, Utah State Park Visitor Study, Summer 1974*
Note: $X^2 = 60.384$, $P < .005$.

frequent category was found to be active-expressive among both campers and day users. Beyond that point, there is little similarity between nonresident campers and day users. Campers exhibit a relatively high amount of participation in sociable-learning experiences that is not shown by the day users. Day users, on the other hand, demonstrate a fairly high frequency of participation in passive-free play. Analysis of the camper X^2 test shows that over half the total X^2 value was contributed by participation in the sociable-learning package; another fourth by participation in the active-expressive package. Among the day users, nearly 63 percent of the contribution to the total X^2 was from the appreciative-symbolic category; an additional 31 percent can be attributed to participation in the active-expressive package.

DISCUSSION

Apparently residents and nonresidents are defining the wildland water-based resources covered in this study differently. These definitions are influenced by length of stay. Residents are using these recreational places principally as opportunities for active and extractive sets of activities, while the nonresidents focus on participation in appreciative and learning experiences. Definitions of the recreation place as locale for passive-free play activities apparently was similar for both user groups, although the author's study did not include many of the activities comprising the original classification of Hendee, Gale and Catton (9).

Another explanation of the data suggests that it is inconvenient for tourists on long trips to bring specialized equipment needed for boating and water-skiing. Both activities represent a large component of the active-expressive package. A subsequent analysis of the study data, with boating, water-skiing and sailing activity removed, still supports the relationships shown in tables 14-2 and 14-3.

Management programs aimed at providing active-expressive opportunities—beaches, boat ramps, play fields—are relatively capital intensive, compared to the facility requirements for appreciative-symbolic activities—principally trails and interpretive facilities. Visitor contact programs also have a different emphasis. Active-expressive and extractive-symbolic packages require more in the way of rules, supervision, and enforcement than appreciative-symbolic or sociable-learning packages. These latter groups suggest visitor contact programs with the thrust of information, education, and interpretive learning. This all means that the manager must look closely at his user populations in determining how personnel and facility resources are to be allocated most effectively.

It is important to note that apparent definitions of place and consequent activity participation are not necessarily dependent upon facilities provided at the site. Few facilities exist at the sites included in this study to support and enhance sociable-learning experiences. Yet a sizable proportion of the nonresident campers reported participation in those activities. This finding is similar to that noted earlier by Field and Cheek (6). Their study of activity participation in water-based recreation demonstrated that "human action observed was not related to or dependent upon the recreational activity for which the area might have been designed."

Such a conclusion does have major implications for management of these resources. Development of water-based recreation resources and the provision of supporting facilities reflect the appropriateness of certain activities and the planner's definition of the area (and he has varying degrees of sensitivity to user definitions). Visiting groups, however, may or may not define the same resource in a similar manner. Thus their participation in certain activity packages may be unanticipated. In a sense, a single resource becomes several recreational "places" because of the varying visitor definitions of the resource. In certain situations, these activity packages could conflict with the major recreation opportunity objectives established for the development.

While no data on conflict were collected in the present study, one may speculate that under conditions of high use there could be conflicts between residents and nonresidents visiting the same recreation place during the same time period. Of course, user choice of unanticipated activity packages could also lead to unacceptable degradation of the resource. The differences in resident and nonresident participation in the various activity packages also have implications for local tourism policies. If an objective of management is to attract nonresidents to the site—say, for economic reasons—development of facilities and programs to enhance appreciative-symbolic and sociable-learning experiences would seem to be imperative to achievement of such an objective. The program would of course need to be coupled with an effective marketing strategy.

The search for explanation of why residents and nonresidents choose participation in different activity packages at water-based resources is important for students of wildland recreation. Answers to this question may lie in an analysis of social group influence rather than in studies of social aggregate variables. It has been shown that examining leisure behavior from the perspective of social group typology is a more effective approach to explaining differences in participation rates than socioeconomic variables (7). Further research on the interrelationships among social groups' definitions of recreation place and activity packages would be appropriate.

The activity package typology included here was developed in another situation for a slightly different purpose. However, it does appear to be a viable tool for describing participation at water-based recreation resources in terms of the meaning of the activities to the visitor. Other methods of grouping recreational activities—such as time involved or spatial requirements—may also offer appropriate descriptions but will serve substantially different purposes. However, identifying participation in activities on the basis of their underlying meanings may help managers increase their understanding of the recreational opportunities they are providing.

REFERENCES

1. Bishop, D. W. 1970. Stability of factor structure of leisure behavior: Analysis of four communities. *Journal of Leisure Research* 2: 160–70.
2. Burch, W. R., Jr. 1964. Two concepts for guiding recreation management decisions. *Journal of Forestry* 62: 707–12.
3. ———. 1969. The social circles of leisure: Competing explanations. *Journal of Leisure Research* 1: 125–47.
4. Cordell, H. K., and Sykes, C. K. 1969. User preferences for developed site camping. USDA Forest Service Research Note SE-122, Southeastern Forest Experiment Station. Asheville, N.C.
5. Dougal, M. D. 1970. Developing water areas for outdoor recreation. *Iowa Farm Science* 24, no. 12: 6–9.
6. Field, D. R., and Cheek, N. H., Jr. 1974. A basis for assessing differential participation in water-based recreation. *Water Resources Bulletin* 10: 1218–27.
7. Field, D. R., and O'Leary, J. T. 1973. Social groups as a basis for assessing participation in selected water activities. *Journal of Leisure Research* 5: 16–25.
8. Green, B. L., and Wadsworth, H. A. 1966. Campers: What affects participation and what do they want: Purdue University Agricultural Experiment Station Research Bulletin no. 823. Lafayette, Ind.
9. Hendee, J. C.; Gale, R. P.; and Catton, W. R., Jr. 1971. A typology of outdoor recreation activity preferences. *Journal of Environmental Education* 3, no. 1: 28–34.
10. Holman, M. A., and Bennett, J. T. 1973. Determinants of use of water-based recreational facilities. *Water Resources Bulletin* 9, no. 5: 1208–18.
11. Hunt, J. D. 1968. Tourist vacations—Planning and patterns. 1968. Utah State University Agricultural Experiment Station Bulletin 474. Logan.
12. Hunt, J. D., and Black, D. H. 1964. Prehistoric and historic Bear Lake area. *Utah Science* 25, no. 3: 68–71; 85–86.
13. Lee, R. G. 1972. The social definition of outdoor recreational places. In *Social behavior, natural resources, and the environment*, pp. 68–84. New York: Harper & Row.

14. Lime, D. W. 1971. Factors influencing campground use in the Superior National Forest of Minnesota. USDA Forest Service Research Paper NC-60, North Central Forest Experiment Station. St. Paul, Minn.
15. Lime, D. W., and Cushwa, C. T. 1969. Wildlife aesthetics and auto campers in the Superior National Forest. USDA Forest Service Research Paper NC-32, North Central Forest Experiment Station. St. Paul, Minn.
16. Myles, G. A. 1970. Effect of quality factors on water-based recreation in western Nevada. University of Nevada-Reno Agricultural Experiment Station Bulletin 24. Reno.
17. Proctor, C. 1962. Dependence of recreation participation on background characteristics of sample persons in the September 1960 National Recreation Survey. In *National recreation survey*, pp. 77–94, (appendix A). Washington, D.C.: Outdoor Recreation Resources Review Commission.
18. Romsa, G. H. 1973. A method of deriving outdoor recreational activity packages. *Journal of Leisure Research* 5: 34–46.
19. Shafer E. L., Jr. 1968. The demand for water-oriented outdoor recreation: Suggestions for handling its increasing managerial problems. *Parks and Recreation* 8 (February): 23–25; 57.
20. Shafer, E. L., Jr., and Thompson, R. C. 1968. Models that describe use of Adirondack campgrounds. *Forest Science* 14: 383–91.
21. Witt, P. A. 1970. Factor structure of leisure behavior for high school age youth in three communities. *Journal of Leisure Research* 3: 213–19.

FURTHER READING

Methods of Recreation Use Evaluation

Aldskogius, Hans. 1977. A conceptual framework and a Swedish case study of recreational behavior and environmental cognition. *Economic Geography*, April, pp. 163–83.

Berelson, B., and Steiner, G. A. 1964. *Human behavior.* New York: Harcourt, Brace & World.

Burton, T. L. 1971. *Experiments in recreation research.* Totowa, N.J.: Rowman & Littlefield.

Burton, T. L., ed. 1970. *Recreation research and planning.* London: Allen & Unwin.

Burton, T. L., and Cherry, G. E. 1970. *Social research: Techniques for planners.* London: Allen & Unwin.

Burton, T. L., and Noad, P. A. 1968. *Recreation research methods.* University of Birmingham Center for Urban and Regional Studies Occasional Paper no. 3. Edinburgh, England: R & R Clark.

Coomber, N. H., and Biswas, A. K. 1972. Evaluation of environmental intangibles: Review of techniques. *Environment Canada,* Ottawa, June.

Ellis, J. B. 1967. *A systems model for recreational travel in Ontario: A progress report.* Report no. RR126. Ontario: Department of Highways.

Ellis, J. B., and Van Doren, C. S. 1966. A comparative evaluation of gravity and system theory models for statewide traffic flows. *Journal of Regional Science* 6, no. 2: 57–70.

Kerlinger, F. W. 1973. *Foundations of behavioral research.* New York: Holt, Rinehart & Winston.

Knetsch, J. L. 1963. Outdoor recreation demands and benefits. *Land Economics* 39, no. 4 (November).

Litton, R. Burton, Jr. 1972. Aesthetic dimensions of the landscape. In *Natural environments—Studies in theoretical and applied analysis.* Ed. John V. Krutilla. Baltimore: Johns Hopkins Press.

Maw, R. 1972. Analyzing demand for leisure facilities. *Built Environment,* November, pp. 519–22.

Mercer, D. 1971. The role of perception in the recreation experience: A review and discussion. *Journal of Leisure Research* 3 (fall): 261–76.

Ontario Research Council on Leisure. 1976. *Canadian outdoor recreation demand study.* 3 vols. Ottawa: Parks Canada.

———. 1977. *Analysis methods and techniques for recreation research and leisure studies.* Outdoor Recreation—Open Space Division, Lands Directorate. Environment Canada, Ottawa.

Romsa, G. 1973. A method of deriving recreational activity packages. *Journal of Leisure Research* 6 (fall): 35–46.

Searle, G. A., ed. 1975. *Recreation economics and analysis.* New York: Longman.

Smith, R. J. 1971. The evaluation of recreation benefits: The Clawson method in practice. *Urban Studies* 8, no. 2.

Smith, Stephen, et al. 1976. *Survey research for community recreation services.* Michigan State University Agricultural Experiment Station Research Report 291. February.

Smith, V. Kerry, and Krutilla, John V. 1975. *A simulation model for the management of low density recreation areas.* Resources for the Future Reprint no. 119. September.

U.S. Department of Agriculture. Northeastern Forest Experiment Station. 1971. *Recreation symposium proceedings 1971.* Washington, D.C.: Government Printing Office.

______. Department of Interior. Bureau of Outdoor Recreation. 1975. *Assessing demand for outdoor recreation.* Washington, D.C.: Government Printing Office.

Vickerman, R. W. 1975. *The economics of leisure and recreation.* New York: Mac Millan.

Wilkinson, P. 1973. Neighborhood parks and their use. *Bulletin of the Conservation Council of Ontario* 20, no. 1 (January): 7.

Part Four

PROVISION OF RESOURCES: PUBLIC & PRIVATE

OVERVIEW

The U.S. Open Tennis Championships were held in the summer of 1978 at the $10 million National Tennis Center at Flushing Meadow Park, New York. This was a significant departure from tennis tradition. The U.S. Open had always been held at the stately and exclusive West Side Tennis Club in Forest Hills. The significance of these facts, which are not news to tennis enthusiasts, is that the sixteen-acre National Tennis Center is an excellent example of a public/private joint venture between the U.S. Tennis Association and the city of New York, and it may serve as a model for future partnerships between a city and private enterprise. The chapters that follow in part 4 are more conceptual than practical, but they will serve to alert the serious student to the philosophy and general guidelines inherent in making recreation pay its own way. As one author states: "It is not important who provides these [recreation] opportunities," so long as adequate opportunities exist for the community.

With a declining tax base and a reduction in services due to inflation, public recreation agencies are beginning to engage in more profit-making recreational activities and also are beginning to contract some services to private firms. Future recreational professionals will probably have to have better training and experience working jointly with private enterprise in measuring the quality control of private services on public resources. To that end, this section, which is new to the second edition of *Land & Leisure*, presents purposefully selected chapters that introduce and demonstrate new and imaginative thinking about the supply of recreation/leisure services.

CHAPTER 15

PUBLIC-PRIVATE INTERFACE

C. A. Gunn

The private and public sectors have separate, conflicting, but sometimes overlapping roles in recreation. In this essay Professor Gunn shows that the public and private sectors do not have to be in conflict because, in reality, they already have a strong functional interface. He reviews the historical precedents of the private and public sectors' relationships to recreational resources and facilities and discusses three major ideologies—conservation, tourism, and recreation—that have inhibited collaboration between industry and government.

Along with unprecedented growth of recreational opportunity has come an alarming amount of misunderstanding and conflict between the public and private sectors. As greater demand has stimulated more intensive use and more extensive development for outdoor recreation, the number and intensity of controversies over many issues of policy, development, management, and service have multiplied greatly.

The purpose of this discussion is neither to be comprehensive nor to offer solution, but to examine some fundamentals of the public-private relationship as a basis for resolution of the issues, particularly for the federal role. It will be seen that there is historic precedent for each sector to perform as it does today—that the apparent overlap, confusion, and conflict is a logical outcome. Furthermore, all outdoor recreational development has been and continues to be heavily influenced by penetrating ideologies, especially those of conservation, recreation, and tourism. Deeper examination shows a much stronger functional symbiosis between and among the elements of both the private and the public sector than is carried over into either organization or policy. Therefore, when the entire outdoor recreational phenomenon is given an overall systems approach, many avenues of collaboration and cooperation appear to be possible.

DEVELOPMENT OF THE PRIVATE SECTOR

The private sector in resource development for recreation has grown to become a huge and unintegrated complex of separate establishments and programs that are supported primarily by nongovernment sources. This support

This article was prepared as a contribution to Task Force V, Federal Role in the Private Sector 1978, Nationwide Outdoor Recreation Plan, Heritage Conservation and Recreation Service. It appears with permission of the author.

comes mostly from fees and charges as well as from foundations, gifts, and nonprofit organizations. Although many private establishments are *subsidized* by government in various ways, they are not *operated* by government. The scope ranges from airlines to river-running tour operators, from Boy Scout camps to historic sites, and from resorts to amusement parks. Such a vast and complicated array almost defies enumeration and definition but represents a volume of activity of vital importance. It is important to society, to the economy, and to the environment, and it has been since the beginning of the nation.

Although the strain of the frontier and the demands on survival forced emphasis on work for all of the able-bodied population, recreation activity, especially that provided by the private sector, was a vital part of the country's evolution. The corn huskings and barn-raising bees, the hoe-down fiddler dances, as well as card playing, theatrical skits, and sports and amusements took place primarily on private grounds in private buildings and were sponsored by private interests.

With the coming of steamboats and railroads in the late 1800s, largely through private initiative and investment, came also the development of private resorts with their many indoor and outdoor recreations. Boating, fishing, hunting, riding, promenading, and indoor sports were popular recreations. The pursuit of health was a strong motivation and provided a market for mountain, lake front, seaside, mineral spring, and cool northern summer fun sports. Intellectual and religious programs were also involved at many locations. The electric trolley of interurban railway provided access to nearby waterfronts and stimulated the development of private amusement parks for a great many U.S. cities.

But it took the automobile, a private development, to produce an explosion in the opportunity to recreate—greater variety of activities, greater expansion of locations, and greater mass use. Mass outdoor recreation seems to have paralleled the expansion of automobile ownership and use. The "tin can" tourists of the late 1920s and the 1930s became the butt of cartoons and editorials, as these new travel recreationists picnicked and camped everywhere including city lawns and country farmyards. The first commercial reaction was the building of service stations and hot dog and pop stands along the roadside. This was followed by the only segment of the building industry to expand during the depression—"tourist cabins." Then came "tourist courts," followed by "motels." During the same period, vacation homes began to increase in popularity especially around lakes newly accessible on a weekend drive from home.

In recent years additional factors have spurred the growth of the private sector into a sprawling, diverse, and extremely productive mass of services and facilities, catering to millions—approximately 8 million Americans traveling for business or pleasure at any one time. Among important factors have been higher incomes, expressways, air conditioning, and greater mobility of friends and relatives. Certainly the massive development of thousands of private services and facilities has increasingly provided for enrichment, entertainment, relaxation, physical renewal, and general leisure pursuit of millions of Americans.

The policies (objectives) of the private sector for outdoor recreation are difficult to generalize. They vary greatly even in the degree of profit making. Generally, they fall into the following categories:

a. major profit making: e.g., hotels, motels, gift shops, airlines, theme parks;
b. supportive or partial profit making: part-time farm vacation resorts, seasonal motels, hunting guides, industrial tours;
c. social welfare and education: youth camps, children's camps, church camps;
d. activity oriented: sports clubs, trail clubs, hunt clubs;
e. preservation, protection: historic buildings, historic sites, events, pageants;
f. business protection: business and professional organizations;
g. personal: private vacation homes, recreation vehicle owners.

Therefore, when we speak of the private sector in only a commercial context, we are only partially correct. Many other purposes are equally strong. The private sector thrives on freedom to organize, to acquire property, and to develop and manage it for stated private sector objectives. Generally, the least constraint by laws and regulations is preferred by the private sector. Commercial operations are willing to take risks of possible financial loss at the same time they hope to succeed. The rewards from being creative and innovative and accepting their own probabilities of being successful financially are prime motivators. Competition is accepted on the premise that selectivity of the market and quality of management will eventually demonstrate success of the viable and failure of the weak or unproductive enterprises. The nonprofit sector "succeeds" on its ability to identify specific organizational goals and work toward them with programs and physical development.

The private sector sets its own policies regarding what to provide and the standards of design and quality of such services or products, but within certain limits set by governments. For example, a restaurateur can identify his own market, create his own menu, set his own standards of food service and products, and build to his own design at a location of his own selection. Although health departments may require certain standards of sanitation and building departments, certain minimum standards of construction, generally private interests set their own standards. Those in the nonprofit sector—such as organization camps and historical societies—are equally free to develop their own outdoor recreation facilities and programs within government constraint.

The major influence on the number, quality, and class of product or service is the market. Each private enterprise must show concern over a public's acceptance of its standards, or it cannot survive for long. What may be criticized as "poor," "trashy," "overcommercial," or even "posh" and "exclusive" may in fact be serving a vital demand by some segment of the public. Increasingly recreation businesses, like all private enterprise, are becoming more sensitive to markets and consumer behavior. Increased research is demonstrating the need for refinement of consumer preferences and consumer decision making.

Collectively, the private sector of recreation has responded to mass recreation demand with a variety of development and programs that include social welfare as well as profit-making objectives.

DEVELOPMENT OF THE PUBLIC SECTOR

At the same time, governments at all levels have increasingly become directly and indirectly involved in recreation. This involvement has been expressed basically two ways—as a *regulator* and as a *competitive developer.* As a regulator, much legislation and many agencies control aspects of private sector land acquisition, planning and management of resources, facilities, services, and programs. As a competitor, governments own and manage extensive land areas, facilities, and services, and they direct programs for the recreating public. While there may have been logical rationale and public support for the establishment of each of the many segments of recreation over the history of development—both private sector and governmental—there is now an increasing number of policy questions that deserve attention and resolution.

The entrance of government, at all levels in the United States, into recreation development had several and quite disparate beginnings. What now is generalized as the public sector is not at all singular and is not easily understood unless its background is traced. The complicated maze of agency involvement today may appear to be overlapping and even unnecessarily proliferated. It has this composition because of its past growth pattern. For example, the contemporary definition of a governmentally owned and managed urban park is far from uniform. It may be merely open space with lawns, trees, and natural streams or ponds. Or, it may be a football stadium, a zoo, a swimming pool, a playground, or an outdoor theater. This is the result of a variety of different policy and agency origins. The original urban park concept, borrowed from England, was that of a pleasant natural setting for rest and contemplation. The purpose was to provide a social welfare antidote to the ills of industrialization, especially bad working conditions and unhealthful housing, but not necessarily recreation as physical activity.

It is surprising to learn that even though some 85 percent of all outdoor recreation land in the United States is owned by the federal government, no federal recreation agency, exclusively created for recreation, administers these lands. Even the Heritage, Conservation, and Recreation Service is not a landowner-manager but a catalyst and banker for public outdoor recreation development. Many agencies with other-than-recreation original legislative mandates, have, over the years, assumed recreational functions.

For example, the U.S. Forest Service (155 national forests with 822 million recreation days a year) was not established for recreation. The purpose of this agency, according to its organic act of 1897, was to protect and improve forest reserves for continued supply of timber and for watershed control. Incidental to this purpose, it discovered that these forest lands often contained physical assets, including favorable location, desired by outdoor recreationists. Since most of the reserves contained usable waters, game, and esthetic assets, they were in demand by increasing numbers of visitors. In order to reduce fire hazard, erosion, and stream pollution and even to protect the users against themselves, the Forest Service began to provide development and programs for recreation, especially camping and outdoor sports such as hunting and fishing. And, as was discovered by highway departments, development of services and facilities even further induced use.

A similar sequence was experienced by the U.S. Fish and Wildlife Service. Its main purpose was to assure the protection and perpetuation of fish and wildlife. When this was necessarily translated into landholdings, the public became aware of their recreational assets and demanded access.

The U.S. Army Corps of Engineers, now manager of some 3,080 recreational sites with nearly 391 million recreation days a year, was originally concerned with engineering solutions to navigation and flood control. Because one technique was the building of dams, the resulting reservoirs became of even greater economic, social, and political importance for recreational purposes.

When created in 1933, the Tennessee Valley Authority had the purpose of reclaiming an entire region that had been socially and economically eroded through overexploitation of forests, soils, and minerals. Because electrical power was fundamental to economic growth, emphasis was placed on hydroelectric plants. Again, the recreational potential of the resulting reservoirs was exploited; and now the 600,000 acres of water and 11,000 miles of shoreline support millions of dollars of private development as well as some 108 state, county, and municipal parks, 2 national wildlife refuges, and 22 state fish and game wildlife management areas.

The Bureau of Indian Affairs, conceived as a management agency for protection of the hunting and settlement land for Indians, has backed into equal concern over tourism and recreation. The lands often happened to contain many elements of scenic, historic, and ethnic interest to visitors. To exploit these resources or not has caused considerable controversy within Indian tribal councils.

The Bureau of Land Management, an outgrowth of the General Land Office, now manages some 203 sites for 91 million recreational visits a year—quite outside its original purposes. Instead of exclusive concern over the disposal of public lands and later the regulation of privately owned livestock on public lands, recreation is now one of several multiple-use management responsibilities.

Perhaps these illustrations are sufficient to dramatize the point that today's recreational involvement of many federal agencies was more an accident of history than an act of purpose. Much of this history has been public pressure (user, visitor, recreationist) supported by political commitment to make recreational use of public lands no matter who has custody. It should be emphasized, however, that agency reaction to this pressure has varied greatly. Even the National Park Service, originally created to protect certain resource assets and provide for public use, has not consistently supported recreation as a major function.

Throughout the country, state agencies have experienced similar shifts into recreational activity even though not mandated originally. Therefore, it is not unusual for the recreating public to experience the same services and facilities by governments as by private enterprise. For example, the resorts, marinas, and camping areas of the Kentucky state park system outrank in quality and level of service many private enterprise operations of similar kinds.

INFLUENTIAL IDEOLOGIES

Running through these developments of both the private and public sector have been several ideological themes that have further complicated recreation roles. Expanded land development, exploding recreational use, and increased awareness of environmental issues now suggest reassessment of at least the three ideologies of *conservation*, *tourism*, and *recreation*.

Conservation

The North American concept of conservation grew from several independent and even conflicting roots. Modern mutations of conservation emerged from these roots.

Often associate with conservation are parks. Actually, the park movement, especially that of urban parks, grew out of *social concern*. The ills of expanding industrialization and industrial cities, first in England and then in the United States and Canada, gave rise to a demand for park and open space. The dedication of public land was (and still is) seen as an antidote to delinquency, crime, illness and the drudgery of work. Moral and ethical values were and continue to be strong elements of conservation in the eyes of many.

Early conservation efforts, both in the United States and Canada, also were expressions of *efficiency* of resource use. It was less "wasteful" of resources to consider long-range programs, especially those for renewable resources such as timber. But the emphasis was on utilization not preservation. Water resources were to be harnessed and soils were to be made more productive. Much of modern agricultural production is based upon this concept of conservation.

The idea of land conservation in an *esthetic* sense historically came relatively late. The defense of conservation areas today on the grounds of scenic beauty is a complete capitulation of the frontier: mastery of nature. The most popular recreation activity today, sightseeing, depends heavily upon a strong contemporary definition of conservation. Wilderness beauty is described as timeless, dimensionless, all encompassing, dynamic, uncluttered by the artist's conception and a form of beauty that gratifies all the senses.

Another contemporary concept of conservation is that of *science and ecology*. The premise is that of man-environmental balance. The only way of striking this balance is to define conservation in terms of resource protection. This must prevent habitat destruction, habitat homogenization, reduction of species, and natural resource pollution.

Conservation, in the sense of preservation and redevelopment of the *cultural heritage*, is increasingly supported today. Many man-made artifacts have a scarcity value that becomes as important to society's well-being as do the natural resources. Therefore, conservation means their protection, restoration, and interpretation.

In summary, the three sectors of outdoor recreation—profit-making enterprise, nonprofit organizations, and the federal government—now carry out conservation roles but in varying degrees. Profit-making enterprise capitalizes upon natural and cultural resources for its own profit-making goals and for its immediate functions (hotels, parking, product sales). However, at the same time, its profit making depends upon the conservation of these resources for repeated and continuing enjoyment and participation by visitors. Nonprofit organizations, likewise, must meet their individual goals but frequently depend upon resource conservation in order to continue meeting them. Most of the historic sites of this country are owned, restored, and interpreted by nonprofit organizations. Many federal government agencies and programs are oriented toward conservation.

Tourism

Currently well accepted into the language is a term that grew out of the nineteenth-century society and technology: *tourism.* Although definitions vary, most include elements such as pleasure travel, expenditures of money at a place other than where earned, and more than a short stay.

Tourism development dominantly has economic motivations. Proponents support tourism development locally, nationally, and internationally primarily for economic reasons. States, provinces, and nations cherish the tourism economy they now possess, and undeveloped nations seek its economic rewards. Economic inputs cited most frequently are those of incomes, jobs, and taxes—derived primarily from an export-type of business enterprise. In the United States, travel is reported to account for approximately $100.4 billion and 4.0 million jobs annually (15).

Because of its economic emphasis, profit-making segments dominate tourism. Those most directly involved provide lodging, food service, transportation, and recreation activities.

Profit making, like conservation, has many colored meanings. For some persons, particularly those outside tourism, it means excessive exploitation of resources and lack of social sensitivity for the sake of personal money rewards. For others, it means the provision of services and facilities on a creative free-enterprise basis that supports national economic health.

Certainly, in tourism, the profit-making sector is important and is represented by several levels: small, independent businesses, chain and franchise corporations, and lease or concession arrangements on public lands. Research has shown that profit motives vary with different business types, especially among the small outdoor recreation owner-managers. Some do not wish to maximize financial returns but are in business because of beliefs in conservation or because of recreational values for family members. Some wish to keep retirees busy. Others seek only supplementary incomes for unemployed or underemployed family labor. Others seek the more traditional goals of gaining revenues that will cover all capital and operating costs including return on investment (1, p. 3). While some criticism is levied toward profit-making enterprise because of its apparent lack of sensitivity to social welfare issues, Drucker insists that

> There is no conflict between "profit" and "social responsibility." To earn enough to cover the genuine costs which only the so called "profit" can cover, is economic and social responsibility—indeed it is the specific social and economic responsibility of business. It is not the business that earns a profit adequate to its genuine cost of capital, to the risks of tomorrow and to the needs of tomorrow's worker and pensioner, that "rips off" society. It is the business that fails to do so (5).

By and large, tourist businesses would not be in business if it were not for attractions that lure people to travel and participate in a variety of recreation activities. And the bulk of the ownership and management of attractions in the United States is by the public and nonprofit sectors. Hence, a major role of tourism is played by the not-for-profit sector, especially the federal government agencies that have custody of special scenic, historic, and recreational resources.

Typical of profit-making enterprise, tourism businesses engage heavily in marketing and promotional activities, individually and collectively. From the standpoint of marketing, tourists are seen as consumers of tourism "products": enjoyable activities related to pleasure travel. Segments of tourist businesses therefore engage in consumer behavior studies in order to understand better the characteristics of people and their interests. For example, Plog (12, p. 57) divided flyers and nonflyers into classifications of "psychocentrics" versus "allocentrics," based upon their individual habits and interests. Another study indicated that tourists are not always sure of their plans when they leave home—many engage in "impulse" travel (8, p. 8).

Government involvement in tourism varies. At the state level, governments generally provide regulation and control, heavy inputs for promotion, functions of support through highways, airports, and the provision of public lands that actually serve as attractions. At the federal level the greatest involvement has been the provision of attractions, assistance to transportation, and the promotion of foreign visitors to the United States.

In promotion, businesses are assisted greatly by state and federal involvement. For example, forty-eight state tourism offices, together with those in U.S. territories and possessions, spend approximately $62 million a year (16, p. 3). In addition, the U.S. Travel Service budget is $14.5 million a year, most of which is spent on promoting travel to the United States (14, p. 5).

In summary, tourism is primarily involved with profit-making businesses that relate to pleasure travel. These businesses are largely of four categories: lodging, food service, transportation, and other items, especially entertainment and the purchase of goods. The goals are dominantly profit making but these are met only by the provision of goods and services desired by consumers.

Recreation

Recreation, as a pleasurable diversionary activity, has been practiced for centuries. Although it has met with varying social acceptance throughout history, it has been practiced by all people everywhere. For example, Sunday games were decreed by King James I in 1618 but prohibited by colonists (6, p.10).

Recreation is defined in many ways, but most definitions include such terms as: activity engaged in during leisure; the acquisition of skills and better physical, mental, and emotional health; activity for pleasure and enjoyment or activity that enriches the lives of people (9; 10; 4). But in many countries the word does not exist. Instead, the several segments—such as sports, physical training, dance, hunting, and fishing—are actively engaged in but are not under control of recreation agencies.

In North America, as soon as recreation became a role of government, definitions became more important. As it was formalized and institutionalized, recreation was defined in whatever terms the proponents created as policy.

Some recreation professionals, especially those supporting government-sponsored recreation, draw a strong distinction between that which is an end in itself and that which is purposeful. They say that the former is negative while the latter is positive. Leisure, engaged in for its own sake, provides no focus, whereas those recreation activities accepted by society as wholesome, creative, and uplifting are worthy of public support (13, p. 4).

Although interpretations vary, recreation is generally agreed to mean human activity associated with leisure (3, p. 222). It is social in context because it is part of society's cultural class structure, status groupings, and temporal patterning and because it generally follows the rules laid down by society. At this same time, it is individual. In spite of group pressure and conformity with social norms, in recent years there has been in recreation a strong

> . . . social need for the individual to be his own master and to please himself, to enjoy the time formerly taken up by activities which were in part imposed by the firm, the family, and socio-spiritual or socio-political activities (7, p. 40).

Recreation agencies having land, facilities, and programs are now well institutionalized at all levels of government in both Canada and the United States. They vary from those that are resource oriented (extensive parks that accept a minimum of people-use) to those that are user oriented (marinas, beaches, picnic areas, and playgrounds).

The prime justification for public agency and nonprofit entrance into recreation programs is that of social welfare: for the good of the individual and society. The federal role is seen as a responsible acceptance of the need for fostering the development of lands, facilities, and programs that provide for recreation participation. It is on this basis—not on economics or resource protection—that recreational policies of many federal agencies—such as the Corps of Engineers, National Park Service, and the Forest Service—are founded.

At the same time, the private sector has also assumed a heavy responsibility for the provision of recreation lands, facilities, and programs. Even though the primary motivation for entrance—profit making—may have varied from that of the federal government, by and large the private sector must also provide for the social welfare. There is little evidence to prove that the gains—either to the individual or to society as a whole—are any the less from participation in the recreation at Disneyland (profit-making enterprise) or Williamsburg (nonprofit organization) than from participation in the recreation at Padre Island National Seashore (National Park Service).

Recreation therefore is an ideology that is dominantly social and personal—promoted and supported for its value to the participants within society. Although custom and law have supported strong recreational programs by government, both profit-making and nonprofit organizations support recreation as a social welfare good.

RELATIONSHIPS

Coexistence

For many years, the three separate forces, with their three separate leaderships and followings, functioned independently and without much conflict. Recreation exponents were preoccupied with program emphasis and were busy promoting the establishment of playgrounds, parks, and their staffs. Recreation programs and development were associated with governments because of their sponsorship. Recreation became a motherhood goal that never failed for public support.

Conservation, even with its many meanings, retained its popularity and support primarily from its soil erosion control and reforestation origins. It also was associated primarily with governments and government programs.

Tourism was seen strictly as promotional efforts by business for economic objectives. It appeared that greater enticement was the only element lacking for the development and support of tourism. Therefore, the first expression was that of providing moneys for advertising.

During this stage, there was little contact among the agencies, organizations, and individuals from these three groups. Whatever contact that did take place was casual and polite, and it tended to support their independence. Each saw his role as well defined and clearly separate from the others. In many countries and in some states, that is true today.

Conflict

As all three forces—conservation, tourism, recreation—grew in stature, and in total public awareness, the next expression was that of conflict. Park departments in cities saw their roles as clearly separate from those of recreation departments and opposed overtures toward amalgamation. Each saw the other as competing for public funds and public support and, in some instances, as competing for the same lands.

Federal agencies that had declared or were induced to accept recreational roles began to define recreation according to their own values. These, particularly in the 1960s, were not wholly acceptable to the visiting publics; and increasing conflict between managers and users developed, even to rioting and property destruction.

As mass recreation expanded and congestion at campground and beaches became the rule in parks, conservation interests cried "rape." In spite of the fact that early park policies in both Canada and the United States supported and promoted visitor use and visitor facilities, the exponents of conservation (meaning resource protection) believed people were ruining the parks. Excessive erosion, wear and tear at certain intensively used sites supported this belief.

With the promotion and increased growth of tourist travel, parks began to function as attractions. As the masses of recreation participants and tourists increased, the need for commercial tourist facilities and services increased. The manner in which these were located, built, and managed were not always to the liking of those who created and managed the parks. Within national parks those profit-making tourism segments—primarily concessions—became the target for much criticism from conservation protection organizations.

Park and conservation exponents couched their goals in social welfare terms and justified as "for the good of society" land condemnation and entrance into commercial-type operations such as concessions and campgrounds. Tourism exponents, as champions of private enterprise, often called this unfair competition.

Further conflict came between all three of these forces and outside interests. Competition for land occurred between tourism-recreation-conservation forces and other developers, such as those involved in manufacturing, housing, and agriculture. Sometimes tourism, with the use of "outside" capital and labor, disrupted both the social and economic order of the locality.

Symbiosis

In spite of continuing issues of conflict, the three forces of tourism, conservation, and recreation have developed many symbiotic characteristics: mutual benefit by functioning together (2).

As natural and cultural resources are put in public and nonprofit ownership and management for resource protection and *conservation* programs, they increase in popularity. Millions of people take greater interest in these assets of the nation and wish to see them, photograph them, enjoy them, and become enriched by them: functions commonly labeled *recreation.* In the process of doing so, they demand lodging, transportation, food service, and a variety of products (camera film, hiking gear, boats) and services (guides, travel agents): functions easily labeled *tourism.*

As *recreation* virtues are promoted—both by agencies and organizations as well as society itself—millions more people are interested in gaining the rewards of such recreational activities. Although the majority of this leisure activity takes place indoors, the outdoor segment has mounted to unprecedented magnitude in recent years. Outdoor recreation takes place on lands frequently brought into the identification and management sphere of *conservation.* At the same time, recreation in the out-of-doors frequently demands lodging, transportation, food service, and a variety of products and services, easily identified as *tourism.*

As businesses and agencies promote *tourism,* a very important component of their "product" is the outdoor natural and cultural resources that were dedicated to *conservation* purposes. An equally important "product" is that of *outdoor recreation:* boating, fishing, swimming, skiing, hunting, photography.

Synergism

Although proponents of each force would deny it, tourism, recreation, and conservation are abstractions that have greater total impact and interdependencies than their sums would imply; hence, strong synergistic characteristics.

Tourism, for example, is not only completed by the addition of commercialism to recreation and conservation, but it is made different, stronger, and more penetrating because of the conservation and recreational components within its makeup. It could not survive without them and the result is greater than the sum of the several parts.

Recreation is more than social concern over physical fitness or mental enrichment. Much of the participation would not take place if it were not for the components of tourism, such as travel, lodging, food service, and the sale of products. Furthermore, elements of conservation, such as esthetics, resource protection, environmental education, and heritage interpretation are included in definitions of recreation.

A national park such as Yosemite is not a conservation area—it is a complex that has elements of conservation (protection of many natural and historic resource assets), of recreation (hiking, horseback riding, photography, camping), and of tourism (convention lodging, food services, souvenir sales).

CONCLUSIONS

It is clear that both the private and the public sector have separate, conflicting, and overlapping roles in recreation in this country. It is likely that these roles will continue. It is also likely that these roles will continue to be influenced by the ideologies of conservation, tourism, and recreation.

The main issue today seems to be one of rising above polarization and of improving the functioning of both the public and private sectors to meet desirable goals. While each segment of each sector may appear to have divergent objectives, there seem to be at least three goals common to both sectors:

1. The goal of improving the quality of life through leisure is a very pervasive one for both sectors. There is a constant desire to improve the means for more people to obtain greater enrichment from a variety of recreational opportunity. Governments establish new areas and new programs; the private sector responds to markets.
2. Both sectors, as they develop land and provide programs for recreation, increasingly strive toward improving their own rewards. Private recreational business seeks greater freedom to create and to produce in order to obtain greater financial stability and less constraint in

performing its role. Nonprofit organizations hope for greater realization of their organizational objectives. And the public sector seeks ways of gaining better support for its public service.

3. Finally, both sectors now must assume the national goal of greater environmental sensitivity and responsibility.

It is not a question of choice between these goals but one of reaching toward all three at the same time. But with the great number and diversity of decision makers in recreation, the process of reaching toward these goals is neither easy nor simple.

On the surface, it would seem that much progress could be made if communication and even collaboration between the sectors and the many elements of each sector could be accomplished. However, several obstacles tend to keep them apart. There are semantic obstacles. To tourism developers the concept of conservation is interpreted to be antidevelopment. Park managers readily accept visitors but resent tourists, in the belief that they are different. In spite of the fact that both public and private recreation interests provide for many of the same activities, government-supported recreation seems purer and more wholesome, whereas commercially supported recreation is less desirable. Institutions, both public and private, tend to foster boundary protection of their own agencies and organizations and resist contact with others, particularly those who might compete. The land-taking ability of governments tends to alienate the private sector. And lack of understanding of each one's role in recreation planning, development, and management for recreation tends to keep the sectors apart.

Even so, it seems that recently a trend has begun toward more open relations and greater understanding of each sector's role. Perhaps this has been brought about by greater participation by citizen groups in public agency decision making. Maybe it has been fostered by the many pieces of land use and environmental legislation in recent years. Perhaps the higher levels of education and better awareness of environmental issues are fostering better understanding. It is possible that the "social reversals" of the late 1960s (11, p. 266) have introduced a new era of cultural determinism rather than blind faith in economic and technical growth. Whatever the causes, there is room for great optimism. The political climate now suggests greater opportunity for clarifying federal roles toward the private sector. It is possible that some government agency operations can be returned to private enterprise. It is possible that the public welfare in recreation is better served by government assistance and programs than by government landownership, development, and management. It is possible that government constraint of private recreation can be relieved. It is possible that private institutions can take on even greater responsibility for social welfare such as safety, land use, ethics, and public satisfaction from leisure.

In conclusion, it appears that single acts of the public sector—such as major federal legislation—have much greater impact upon the public-private interface of recreation than do decisions of the private sector. It is for this reason that each federal and state act must be researched in depth before enactment. Furthermore, the private sector, in order to compete on the basis of social and environmental as well as economic reasons, must develop a stronger commitment to all acts of government that might affect it. At the same time, it must take on a greater social consciousness to avoid additional governmental control.

REFERENCES

1. Bevins, Malcolm I. 1971. Private recreation enterprise economics. Paper presented at the Forest Recreation Symposium. Pinchot Institute Consortium for Environmental Forestry Research.
2. Budowski, Gerardo. 1973. Tourism and the conservation of nature: Conflict, coexistence or symbiosis. Paper presented at the Pacific Area Travel Association. Morges, Switzerland: International Union for Conservation of Nature and Natural Resources.
3. Cheek, Neil H., Jr., and Burch, William R., Jr. 1976. *The social organization of leisure in human society.* New York: Harper & Row.
4. Doell, Charles E., and Twardzik, Louis F. 1973. *Elements of park and recreation administration.* Minneapolis, Minn.: Burgess.
5. Drucker, Peter F. 1975. The delusion of "profits." *Wall Street Journal,* February.
6. Dulles, Foster Rhea. 1965. *A history of recreation.* New York: Appleton-Century-Crofts.
7. Dumazedier, Joffre. 1974. *Sociology of leisure.* New York: Elsevier.
8. Guinee, B. T. 1970. *Impulse travel: Changing trends in auto vacation travel.* Arog, Ill.: National Advertising.
9. Hormachea, Marion N., and Hormachea, Carroll R. 1972. *Recreation in modern society.* Boston: Holbrook Press.
10. Meyer, Harold; Brightbill, Charles K.; and Sessoms, H. Douglas. 1969. *Community recreation.* Englewood Cliffs, N.J.: Prentice-Hall.
11. Platt, John. 1975. The future of social crisis. *The Futurist,* October.
12. Plog, Stanley C. 1974. Why destination areas rise and fall in popularity. *Cornell H.R.A. Quarterly,* February.
13. Rodney, Lynn S. 1964. *Administration of public recreation.* New York: Ronald Press.
14. U.S. Department of Commerce, Travel Service. 1976. *International tourism: 1976, the Bicentennial Year—A record breaker.* Washington, D.C.: USTS Media Services Division.
15. U.S. Department of Commerce, Travel Service, Office of Research and Analysis. 1975. *Tourism Landmarks in 1974.* Washington, D.C.
16. U.S. Travel Data Center. 1976. *Survey of state travel offices, 1976–77.* Washington, D.C.

CHAPTER 16

THE PUBLIC-COMMERCIAL JOINT VENTURE

John L. Crompton

As competition for the public tax dollar increases, bold and imaginative recreation and parks departments will seek new ways for public-private cooperation. As John Crompton emphasizes here, it is really not important who provides leisure services, so long as the leisure opportunities are available at an equitable price. He advocates cooperation between public agencies and private industry in providing leisure services and discusses three major qualifying conditions—attitude, agency policy, and user fees—and also the pragmatic hurdles that must be understood by both sectors before joint working arrangements can be implemented.

The increasing difficulty recreation and park departments are experiencing in securing adequate financial resources from traditional tax base sources has been well documented.[1] Agencies have begun to explore more seriously the potential of a whole range of working formulas for cooperating with private and commercial organizations to provide programs and facilities.[2]

The raison d'être of leisure service delivery systems is to insure adequate opportunities exist through the provision of recreation activities and programs for members of the community to enjoy. It is not important who provides these opportunities, although public agencies have in the past largely preempted the field. A more pragmatic approach may be to regard the function of municipal agencies not to provide directly but rather to serve as catalysts whose function is to stimulate others to provide. Thus if the level of leisure services is to be sustained, the public sector, recognizing its own financial constraints, should adopt as a primary goal encouragement of the private and commercial sectors to provide leisure opportunities.

This would involve a philosophical shift from the traditional position, but anxiety caused by the shift should be lessened by increasing awareness of the falseness of the public/commercial dichotomy. *Public* refers to government-operated facilities and *commercial*, to profit enterprises; but these are complementary rather than mutually exclusive institutions [and their] goals are increasingly in alignment. Federal and most state laws insist that commercial recreation facilities be open to the general public, making them as "public" as facilities built with government funds. At the same time governments are

Reprinted from *Parks and Recreation*, July 1977, pp. 20–23; 69, by permission of the National Recreation and Parks Association and the author.

engaging more and more in profit-making recreational activities—for example, indoor tennis facilities, golf courses, and amusement parks.

Traditionally, public agency philosophy has led to the provision of facilities aimed at catering to self-oriented recreation, self-improvement, self-expression, or social interaction.[3] However, individuals' leisure preferences have tended towards involvement in role playing, fantasy, or escapism, as reflected in the popularity of television, spectator sports, and theme parks. Public agencies are beginning to recognize this disparity between their objectives and the user's objectives. The commercial sector has had considerable experience at developing and operating this kind of facility, and its participation in public agency projects is likely to be an asset in providing people with what they want. In addition, the prevailing political climate of "less government involvement is better" would seem accommodating to such involvement.

While there are many examples of successful commercial leisure enterprises, capital investment made by the commercial sector in leisure and recreation developments is small when compared to investment in other segments of the economy. An important contributing factor to this has been that government is often in competition. Government subsidy of many recreation facilities and programs necessarily limits the role of commercial enterprise. In addition, experience has shown that such investments are relatively high risk.[4] The risk has been compounded recently by high real estate costs, interest rates, and tighter zoning and permit regulations. Much of the recreation supply base which exists today in the commercial sector would not exist if it had to be developed at today's prices.

The public agency and commercial enterprise bring complementary strengths to a joint working arrangement. The public agency may have a substantial land bank; low-cost capital and tax shelter availability; control over zoning and permit processes and consequent ability to expedite them; and credit worthiness secured by its tax base. The commercial enterprise has the ability to pledge significant assets to raise large amounts of capital, provided the investment shows potential of an adequate return on investment; it has considerably greater legal flexibility in what it is empowered to do; and it is free of the lengthy bureaucratic decision-making structure characteristic of public agencies. With goals which are increasingly compatible and with complementary strengths, both institutions potentially have much to gain from cooperation.

Although the rationale for cooperation between the two sectors is persuasive, there are a number of qualifying conditions which must be recognized and accepted by both sides before any benefits can be realized. These conditions may be viewed as counter-influences to cooperation and are the product of both historical and contemporary circumstances. They fall into two categories. First, there are three major conditions which may require fundamental shifts in philosophical position. Unless these three conditions are confronted and reconciled, contrasting perspectives and values—together with different styles of working and different aspirations for future development—will insure that divisiveness prevails and joint working efforts are frustrated. Second, there are a variety of lesser, though not inconsequential, conditions which represent pragmatic hurdles to be surmounted before a joint working arrangement can be implemented. These hurdles present potential pitfalls to one side or the other; and, until they are fully understood, resolved, and interests consequently safeguarded, they will cause the affected party to hesitate before entering into joint arrangements.

[Below] are discussions of the three major qualifying conditions—attitude, agency policy, and user fees—together with a subsequent discussion of the lesser pragmatic hurdles to be surmounted.

ATTITUDE

The most serious obstacle working against greater cooperation in recreation projects is frequently the attitude of one side towards the other. Adherence to stereotypes and outmoded prejudices is a problem that both sides must address. Although the public agency frequently appears to encourage commercial development in recreation, often there seems a desire for this to occur without involvement of the commercial developer, who is viewed with distrust and suspicion. At the same time the commercial operator often views public agencies negatively: as incompetent bureaucracies bent on frustrating the legitimate goals of the businessman. Concern in [the present] article is primarily with cooperation from a public agency perspective, hence the problem of attitude is addressed only from that viewpoint.

Suspicion of commercial motives is not unique to agencies in the field of recreation and parks but is, rather, endemic through all of society. It has been recently pointed out, for example, that public opinion polls reveal that the ordinary man or woman today has far less favorable attitudes towards business than was the case twenty or thirty years ago.[5] Much of the negative attitude towards commercial enterprise arises from misunderstanding of the emotive word *profit* with its traditional connotations of onerous exploitation. Drucker has stated that there is no such thing as profit, only costs.[6] If government offers the particular recreation service rather than commercial enterprise, it still must incur these costs albeit by another name.

The profit element reported in company accounts consists of three categories of costs. First, profit is the genuine cost of a major resource; namely, capital. Very few businesses actually earn enough to cover this basic cost. Second, profit is a necessary insurance cost for the real, and again largely quantifiable, risks and uncertainties of all economic activity. Johnson found that "Probably 3 out of 5 recreation enterprises will fail financially or go out of business for some other reason, within 5 years after they start. And probably not half of the remainder will ever be really financially successful."[7] The risks of natural events such as fire have long been considered normal business costs. Economic, technological, and social risks and uncertainties are no less real. They too require an adequate insurance premium, and it is the function of profit to supply this cover. Third, it is the cost of investment for tomorrow's jobs and the cost of insuring employee pensions, since the major shareholders of large companies are pension funds, which rely on a level of return on their investment sufficient to guarantee satisfactory pensions.

Thus before joint working can occur, public agencies need to agree that there is no inherent conflict between profit and social responsibility. The profit motive is not incompatible with providing a public service. Drucker stresses that to earn enough to cover these genuine costs demonstrates social responsibility.[8] [The business] that "rips off" society is not the [one] that earns a profit appropriate to its genuine costs of capital, to the risks of tomorrow, and to the needs of tomorrow's worker and pensioner; rather, it is the business that fails to do so.

AGENCY POLICY

A public agency must adopt a clear philosophical position from the outset on what it hopes to gain and what it is prepared to risk in any cooperative agreement. Only when this policy statement has been established and [when] the parameters within which the agency is prepared to negotiate [is] understood, is it in a position actively to solicit involvement from the commercial sector. To proceed without this policy statement may lead to internal confusion and contradiction: an insecure foundation on which to enter into long-term commitments with a commercial operator. The ultimate result may be frustration, loss of good will, and economic loss, at least in the form of person-hours and opportunity cost, to both parties. There are at least three policy positions, not necessarily mutually exclusive, which agencies may adopt.

Minimum Investment Risk

Given this criterion, the agency would be prepared to support facilities such as golf courses, where the high real estate content provides relatively good security in the event of any subsequent failure. At the other end of the continuum, facilities such as theme parks would be excluded from consideration. Their highly specialized equipment is likely to represent up to half the total development cost, and in the event of failure this investment could not be recouped.

Maximum Revenue Return

This criterion may be measured in terms of income to the local authority through direct dollars or through the economic impact of new dollars in the community. For example, in establishing Seven Seas Marine Park in Arlington, Texas, the city mayor stated, "Cities are going to have to look for new sources of revenue . . . citizens will enjoy helping raise revenue in this fashion."[9] Since high return is synonymous with high risk, adoption of this criterion is likely to be controversial. A good example of adoption of this criterion is Marina Del Rey on the California coast.[10] The public agencies involved promoted the project primarily because of the estimated increases in revenues and taxes from anticipated marina businesses and associated property development which would result.

Maximum Feasible Participation

Under this criterion, facilities such as swimming pools, parks, or playgrounds would be acceptable. However, the public agency would not invest resources in cooperative facilities which were used only by a limited segment of the community.

USER FEES

A public agency decision to seek commercial involvement in a recreation project may, as a corollary, require a philosophic shift by necessitating an increase in user charges on similar facilities which the agency operates. Commercial involvement is likely to preclude the public providing any subsidized services which may be perceived as being in competition with a project involving commercial enterprise. Diamond has stated, "... we cannot give away cake and expect people to rush into the bakery business at the same time."[11]

A lead editorial in the *Wall Street Journal* described a predicament which illustrated this problem.[12] Gore Mountain Ski Center, a public facility operated by New York State, receives an annual tax subsidy of $50,000 a year and was constructed with tax-free bonds. It applied for $264,000 in federal grants to help in funding a $2.87 million capital extension that involves installing snowmaking machinery and other equipment. The balance of the capital will be raised by issuing tax-free bonds. With these advantages, Gore Mountain charged $400 for a family season pass in 1975, while commercial resorts in the area charged an average of $1,125, reflecting their requirement (1) to pay commercial prices for investment capital without any assistance from federal grants and (2) to show a return on their investment. Thus, the publicly operated state project is gradually forcing the commercial operations out of business. The editorial comments, "By a sort of Gresham's law of competition, we have noticed that state enterprises in the mixed economy tend to drive out private enterprise."[13]

PRAGMATIC CONDITIONS

If the necessary philosophic adjustments or compromises are forthcoming, there are still a number of pragmatic problems which must be addressed. They include lease length, control, liability, budget synchronization, and labor policies.

In most cases where cooperation is considered, a long-term lease is essential. The commercial operator requires sufficient time to recoup his investment. Public agencies are frequently reluctant to grant long leases, and this forestalls the possibility of major capital investment. But perhaps the public agency should demand a long lease, since it provides some evidence of long-term commitment to the project. Many companies are motivated to enter into recreational projects primarily by cash-flow considerations. For example, the Six Flags Over Texas theme park, as originally conceived in 1962, was created with the specific intention of its having a limited five-year life span, during which time it would generate considerable cash flow to assist the financing of a large industrial estate which the parent company was developing in the area. Commercial operators motivated by such considerations are likely to seek a swift return on capital invested but then may withdraw from the project, even though it continues to provide a profit margin which would be acceptable to a public agency.

However, there are situations in which a short-term lease may be acceptable. Dunn discovered that open-space acquisition dramatically exceeded the loss of parkland in many cities between 1965 and 1970.[14] However, there may be reluctance by either the public agency or commercial operator to commit any of this land, which is under their control, on a long lease because it may represent a state of transition between the demise of old structures and the construction of new improvements. Nevertheless, by the use of inflatable buildings, for example, some open space could be transformed into a useful recreation resource and be a viable proposition on a short lease instead of remaining sterile open space.

Any successful formula for cooperation must address the problem of control. If a public agency solicits involvement of the commercial sector in a partnership venture, then it must be willing to compromise the degree of control it can exercise over the project. Control is part of the incentive needed to encourage commercial participation. Such an incentive involves a trade-off. The public agency is mandated to insure that public benefits are commensurate with public costs. The dilemma is to find the optimum balance point for compromise. Much of the problem—and its solution—again revolves around the question of mutual trust. The control issue is perhaps exemplified by long-standing and well-documented problems in the relationship between concessionaires and the National Park Service in national parks.[15] Having granted the concessionaires' leases, the public agency also must give them sufficient control and rights in the park to enable them to convince bankers to loan the long-term capital needed to provide facilities.

To make cooperation with commercial enterprise palatable on either a mandatory or voluntary basis, especially in situations involving the donation of real property or services, the public agency has to safeguard the liability position of the commercial operator by insuring that it falls under the city's liability coverage. A real difficulty exists in determining how to exclude from this coverage that which is obviously the result of negligence by the commercial operators. The knowledge that errors by their own personnel or facility defects may lead to damage suits is clearly a deterring factor in soliciting commercial cooperation. In mandatory situations there is a danger to the public agency of inheriting liability problems at some later date as a result of initial actions by the developer; for example, inferior equipment specifications. To avoid this situation, public agency input before those decisions are made is clearly important. As a point of law the lessee should assume the tort liability to the public, but the lessee in some cases may not have the legal power to assume such liability.[16]

Difficulties experienced by a public agency in synchronizing its budget to take advantage of an imminent opportunity for cooperation may constitute a further hurdle. Budgets are frequently decided years ahead of their implementation date, but an opportunity may not remain available over that period of time.

If a commercial enterprise enters into a cooperative arrangement with a public agency, it may also have to accept labor policies which apply in the public sector. For example, loans from the Economic Development Administration are conditional upon project contractors paying prevailing wages to meet requirements of the Davis-Bacon Act, and employment in the construction of the project and operation of the new or expanded business must comply with the nondiscrimination provisions of the Civil Rights Act of 1964.

Throughout [the above] discussion there is an implicit assumption that the public agency has enabling legislation which permits it to enter cooperative ventures with the commercial sector. In some instances it is possible that narrowly conceived and inflexible legislation forces agency personnel to confine their operations to the traditional role. Even given the necessary legislative flexibility, cooperation with commercial enterprise demands a new orientation. Public agency personnel whose training and outlook have been geared to regarding parks and recreation exclusively as a tax-funded service now face a new and very different proposition. Laurance Rockefeller, when discussing cooperative ventures, commented that ". . . sometimes bureaucratic inertia has blinded us to these opportunities because they seemed like too much trouble or simply because they had never before been used."[17] Pervasive throughout these qualifying conditions for cooperation is the assumed willingness and capability of public agency personnel to adapt to a changed situation.

NOTES

1. Richard Kraus, *Urban Parks and Recreation: Challenge of the 1970s* (New York: Community Council of Greater New York, 1972); Diana Dunn, *Open Space and Recreation Opportunity in America's Inner Cities* (Springfield, Va.: National Technical Information Services, 1974); John L. Crompton and Carlton S. Van Doren, "Changes in Fundamental Status of Leisure Services in 30 Major Cities 1964–1974," *Journal of Leisure Research* 10, no. 1 (March 1978).
2. John L. Crompton, "Commercial and Public Provision of Recreational Facilities through Cooperation: United States and Europe," *Leisure Today*, November/December 1975.
3. Seymour M. Gold, *Urban Recreation Planning* (Philadelphia: Lea & Febiger, 1973).
4. Malcolm I. Bevins, "Private Recreation Enterprise Economics," in *Forest Recreation Symposium Proceedings: Syracuse, New York 1971* (Washington, D.C.: Government Printing Office, 1971). See also chapter 17 of this volume.
5. Irving Kristol, "On 'Economic Education,'" *Wall Street Journal*, 8 February 1976, p. 20.
6. Peter F. Drucker, "The Delusion of 'Profits,'" *Wall Street Journal*, 5 February 1975, p. 10.
7. Hugh Johnson, *Opportunities and Limitations in Private Recreation Development* (Washington, D.C.: USDA, Economic Research Service, 1966).
8. Drucker, "Delusion."
9. "Seven Seas Marine Park," *Dallas Morning News*, 16 May 1971.
10. Marsha V. Rood and Robert Warren, *The Urban Marina: Managing and Developing Marina Del Rey*, University of Southern California Center for Urban Studies Sea Grant Program (1974).
11. H. L. Diamond, "The Private Role in the Provision of Large-Scale Outdoor Recreation," *Elements of Outdoor Recreation Planning*, ed. B. L. Driver (Ann Arbor, Mich.: University Microfilms, 1970).
12. "Mike Brandt's Competitors," *Wall Street Journal*, 12 September 1975.
13. Ibid.
14. Dunn, *Open Space*.

15. U.S. House, Select Committee on Small Business, Subcommittee on Environmental Problems Affecting Small Business, *Small Business Enterprises in Outdoor Recreation and Tourism* (Washington, D.C.: Government Printing Office, 1974).
16. Kenneth Lounsberry, "From Springboards to Roadblocks," in *Proceedings of the First Annual Institute on Inter-agency Recreation and Leisure Services* (South Lake Tahoe, Calif., 1975).
17. Ernest J. Hodges, "Private Enterprise Reacts to Recreation Demands," *Parks and Recreation*, January 1970.

CHAPTER 17

PRIVATE RECREATION ENTERPRISE ECONOMICS

Malcolm I. Bevins

Private recreational enterprises will play an important future role. This short article provides an excellent overview of some factors—poor location, small size, short seasons—that may limit their success. At the same time, Malcolm Bevins points out that project maximization is not always the prime entrepreneurial goal: personal and noneconomic considerations or long-run capital gain may have an overriding effect.

Public law 88-29, passed by Congress in 1963, called for a coordinated effort among all levels of government and private interests to assure adequate outdoor recreation resources for present and future generations. This law stimulated numerous studies of the economics of the private recreation firm. As a rule, these studies indicated relatively limited opportunity for financial success in the outdoor recreation business.

This report reviews a number of these studies and analyzes those factors associated with poor returns. Some of the goals of recreation entrepreneurs are reviewed, and the appropriateness of current financial analysis techniques is evaluated.

PROFITABILITY OF THE RECREATION FIRM

Most economists agree on procedures for determining annual returns to labor and management. In simple terms, the commonly accepted procedure is to deduct actual cash expenses from gross income and subtract from this amount an allowance for depreciation and return on capital investment. The residual is the return to labor and management. Further deduction of an allowance for unpaid family labor yields a residual that is called "return to the operator for his labor and management."

In general, returns to labor and management have been extremely low for firms engaged in providing outdoor recreation. Addressing a recreation workshop in Pennsylvania, Johnson (4) said, "Probably three out of five recreation enterprises will fail financially, or go out of business for some other reason, within 5 years after they start. And, probably not more than half of the remainder will ever be really financially successful."

In a study of rural recreation enterprises in New England, Moore (7) found that low returns to labor and management characterized a wide variety

Reprinted from *Recreation Symposium Proceedings,* Northeastern Forest Experiment Station, USDA Forest Service (1971), pp. 33–39, with permission of the author.

of recreational firms. His report was based on detailed case studies of thirty operations. The specific findings shed important light on enterprise profitability.

In a study of the private campground industry in Vermont (1), I found that 47 percent of the campground operators were operating at a loss. To make matters worse, they had no return on their equity. In another study of campground businesses in New York, Loomis and Wilkins (6) concluded, "Incomes derived from the campground operations studied were extremely modest." Actually, net cash income less depreciation averaged only $83 for the season (before any allowance was made for interest on investment). The authors suggested that many campground operators need to look for nonmonetary returns to derive satisfaction from such operations.

Several factors are associated with income level in the outdoor recreation field. Among the more important are location of enterprise, scale of operation, business volume, length of season, and price level.

Location of Enterprise

Johnson (3) emphasized the importance of a good location: "Awesome scenery, salubrious climate, spectacular fishing, and other natural resources are economically sterile without the well-beaten path along which the necessary services can afford to cluster." Location is critical when one is estimating demand for outdoor recreation. Any good text in business management stresses the importance of studying the business site in great detail before making a final selection. But many recreation entrepreneurs never take this critical step. They commonly start with a specific location and then attempt to select a recreation enterprise to fit it. In some cases, the property has been in the family for years. In other cases, it is purchased for personal pleasure rather than business potential. Quite possibly the owner has fond memories of the area as a boy and desires to "return home" to relive these memories. This is fine for personal satisfaction but makes poor business sense.

Scale of Operation; Business Volume

Johnson (4) concluded that two major causes for low returns from recreational ventures were small size of enterprise and too few customers. Citing a report prepared for the Appalachian Regional Commission, . . . Johnson (3) noted that fewer than 6 percent of all recreation enterprises employ five or more persons on a year-round basis. Even during the peak of the season, fewer than 16 percent have five or more employees.

According to Loomis and Wilkins (6), "It is difficult to operate businesses profitably without sufficient volume over which to spread fixed costs." A campground swimming pool with the necessary filtration and cleaning equipment may cost $6,000. The cost for providing this type of recreation service is excessive for the operator who is small or fails to reach fairly high occupancy rates. Loomis and Wilkins correlated campground size with net cash income less depreciation. They found that, for the campgrounds studied, those with fewer than 100 sites averaged a minus $1,043; those with 100 to 199 sites, a minus $451; and those with 200 or more sites, a plus $1,818. On the basis of occupancy, the New York study indicated that those firms with less than 40-percent occupancy had a net return of minus $2,273; those with 40- to 60-percent occupancy had a positive return of $758; and those with occupancy exceeding 60 percent had a positive return averaging $4,289.

Length of Season; [Price Level] ...

The Bureau of Outdoor Recreation surveyed more than 2,000 financial institutions in a nationwide attitude study of lending practices (10). Bankers and lenders were asked if outdoor recreation enterprises were more risky than other business ventures and, if so, why. Nearly two-thirds of the respondents answered yes and cited the limited length of season.

The major recreation market is the family unit. The family travels when children are on vacation from school, so most family recreation trips are limited to the summer months. One might legitimately question how a business firm can succeed when full-scale operations are restricted to ten weeks of the year.

Loomis and Wilkins (6) indicated that fees currently charged in New York campgrounds may be inadequate in terms of generating realistic levels of income. The entrepreneur who establishes price levels on the basis of operational cost is a rare person indeed. Observation indicates that pricing is more typically based on prevailing rates in the area than on operating costs.

Recreation is a service that the customer expects to receive at a minimal price. This attitude has been conditioned over the years where public facilities have been made available at less than full-cost pricing. At a ... congressional hearing to restore the Golden Eagle program (9), testimony revealed that 73 percent of the respondents in a general population survey felt entrance fees at public areas should cover half or less of the total operational cost. Only 8 percent of respondents felt all costs should be borne by the recreationist.

Recreational services available at a subsidized rate impose serious restrictions on the private sector to price according to actual cost of operation. Recreation is a service for which the consumer will do comparison shopping if significant price differentials are apparent.

With low returns so prevalent in the outdoor recreation industry, we must question how the industry stays alive. The answer lies in an analysis of entrepreneurial goals.

ENTREPRENEURIAL FINANCIAL GOALS

Johnson (5) classified recreation enterprises into three groups: the windfall or social operation, the supplemental operation, and the major enterprise. He describes the *windfall* or *social operation* as a business in which the operator does not necessarily want to maximize cash returns from recreation. He will operate his facilities if returns cover cash costs because he believes in conservation, because members of the family want to partake in recreation, or because this is one way for a gregarious, retired person to keep active and have people around. Johnson describes the *supplemental enterprise* as a business that provides work for unemployed or underemployed family labor. Cash returns usually are more important than in the first instance, but noncash benefits still can be of major importance. Where recreation is a *major enterprise*, all cash costs and most fixed costs associated with the operation must be covered.

Few data are available to indicate the relative importance of each of these classes of recreation business. However, it is apparent, after reviewing studies of enterprise net returns, that many firms may not look upon profit maximization as the primary enterprise goal. This creates a real problem for the operator who is vitally concerned with maximum net returns. He cannot use economic logic to predict the action of his competitors—a far different situation than exists in other commercial areas.

Uvacek and Schmedemann (12) noted a similar situation in an analysis of Texas cattle operations. They divide cattlemen into three categories—traditional, transitional, and contemporary. The *traditional* cattleman receives most of his income from livestock production. His actions are based upon rational farm management thinking. He buys and sells according to market conditions. His primary goal is profit maximization. The *transitional* cattleman is primarily a "land stocker." His primary goal is to hold land. Grazing is really a side consideration. Profits may not be large; but to this person a cattle operation provides an enjoyable use of free time and makes some contribution to total family income. The third type, the *contemporary* cattleman, owns a ranch for many reasons—recreation, prestige, health, a basic desire for landownership, land value appreciation, or tax benefits.

The Texas study concluded that most transitional cattlemen and practically all contemporary cattlemen fail to increase or decrease business operations in response to price changes. Paradoxically, these cattlemen have an important effect on cattle prices, yet their buy-and-sell decisions are not greatly affected by price. The traditional cattleman who attempts to analyze local market conditions and follow rational economic thinking in predicting market changes is frustrated when faced with such competition.

In analyzing these three types of cattlemen, Uvacek and Schmedemann maintained that under these circumstances it is unreasonable to assess all land costs against the cattle operation. Some value must be placed on the indirect benefits associated with the operation. Only by some revision of management-analysis techniques can we realistically project future growth of these types of operations.

Traditional labor income analysis rarely considers changing land values. Increases in land values are apparent only through a year-by-year comparative balance sheet, and then only if land values are adjusted annually. In the Northeast, values of land with high recreational attributes are increasing phenomenally. Sinclair (8) reports more than a fivefold increase in the weighted average price per acre of unimproved land sold in thirty-one typical Vermont towns between 1958 and 1968. Such an appreciation in land value can offset many years of low labor returns whether it be from farming, recreation, or other activity.

A smaller, though significant, increase in land values was noted in [a]

Bureau of Outdoor Recreation report (11) . . . [which] showed that land values are rising from 5 to 10 percent per year throughout the nation.

RESEARCH IMPLICATIONS

If entrepreneurial goals are distinctly different, then the researcher who groups all firms together in an analysis of business operations is presenting a confused picture. This problem goes back to the initial collection of research data. At that time, he must ask the right questions, so that each firm can be properly classified according to the operator's true goals. Firms must be so classified in any descriptive analysis of business operations if these analyses are to be meaningful. Following this procedure makes possible more realistic projections of recreational industry growth.

Negative returns to labor and management might be expected for the social entrepreneur (described by Johnson—see references) or the contemporary entrepreneur (12). . . . A prolonged period of low returns might be possible where recreation is only a supplementary enterprise. Separation of these groups, in any analysis, permits a more direct focus on enterprises where recreation is the primary business activity or where profit maximization is the desired goal.

Extension workers and others who advise the recreation firm would benefit immeasurably from such a business analysis. Lenders would get a more realistic appraisal, and loan applications might be more favorably received. Lenders freely admit ignorance of the economics of the outdoor recreation enterprise (11). . . . And this ignorance is magnified when researchers group firms with unlike goals together for analytical purposes.

And if we are to gain insight into the likely tenure of recreation business operations, we must look beyond returns to labor and management. We must build into our analytical framework consideration for increasing land values. This may have as much or more bearing on tenure than actual business profits.

IMPLICATIONS FOR EXTENSION WORK

The recreation firm adviser should first determine the true personal and business goals of the landowner before making specific recommendations. Johnson (4) said, "If profits are not the major concern, we have no business trying to justify their success or flay their failure by use of economic measures."

Perhaps this means that we . . . should establish some values to reflect these noneconomic considerations and incorporate these values into formulas used to judge business decisions. Time-tested decision-making procedures should not be dropped. Every business operator, regardless of his motivation, should at least be aware of how his operation deviates from the optimum situation dictated by rigid economic analysis. Ideas that might be discarded for the entrepreneur whose primary goal is profit maximization might not be discarded for the entrepreneur with other goals.

Consider, for example, the retired plumber who fondly remembers bobsledding as a boy and wishes to establish a commercial bobsled run on his property. His prime motivation is personal recreation. Perhaps he should not be discouraged from such an operation, even though market analysis indicates that the odds for success are low. He must mentally equate his total personal gains and financial losses in arriving at a final decision.

All business operators should be made aware of the break-even concept and its application. Campground operators might use this tool to project cost-revenue data and to determine the occupancy level at which revenue from campsites will cover specific expenses. From such an analysis, proper decisions might be made concerning an economically sound rate structure. If an operator chooses to deviate from such a rate structure, he does so in full recognition of the economic consequences.

Capital budgeting should become common practice in evaluating alternatives. Recognition of the time value and opportunity cost of money must be impressed upon individuals making financial decisions, whether they be personal or business motivated. We should not fear the use of sophisticated and complex tools in educational programs, even though some of our clients may hold other values higher than profit maximization.

Time and motion study and work simplification techniques are needed in the recreation field. Every effort should be made to reduce labor requirements associated with daily operations. This type of analysis would be appropriate for all classes of entrepreneurs, irrespective of motivation. No one likes to work harder than is absolutely necessary. Substantial improvements in work methods have been accomplished through time and motion studies in agriculture and forestry. These same techniques need to be applied in the recreation field—in both public and private sectors.

PROPERTY TAXATION: A MAJOR PROBLEM

In the Northeast, property taxation is a major emerging problem that could have a pronounced impact on all private recreation development. The problem is acute in areas where the fair market value of land is rising unchecked in response to an urban interest in a rural retreat.

In Vermont I studied taxation of youth camps and attitudes of operators (2). In 1966 only 15 percent of the youth camp operators felt that they might be taxed out of business. By 1969 the number had risen to 38 percent. The youth camp industry is a victim of circumstances. Land and water resources, which are absolutely necessary effectively to operate a youth camp, carry a high value for seasonal-home development. The camp operator will receive a significant capital gain if and when property is sold for seasonal homes. But some operators would prefer to continue a camp operation and would do so if property taxes were realistically aligned with camp revenue.

A parallel situation may be emerging with other recreational firms. It would indeed be unfortunate to see all types of private outdoor recreation resources sold for seasonal-home development. Yet such a situation could be triggered by unchecked increases in property taxation.

THE SHORTER WORKWEEK: A MAJOR OPPORTUNITY

On the brighter side of the picture, the recent movement toward the ten-hour workday and four-day workweek is encouraging for the outdoor recreation enterprise. If this transition should become widespread, recreation enterprises located relatively near northeastern urban population centers might be greatly affected. The extra day off might provide a much-needed addition to weekday business volume—currently a severely limiting factor to business success. Moore (7) noted that in New England, except for summer camps and vacation farms, weekend business accounted for 70 to 90 percent of total weekly receipts.

If the ten-hour day becomes acceptable, we might very logically move to a situation where each of two crews works three days a week, ten hours a day. This would make economic sense, as industrial firms could use their equipment far more efficiently. Consider the impact that this might have upon the recreation industry. What does this mean in terms of primary residence? Is it not conceivable that the seasonal home might become the permanent home if the urban apartment is needed only two nights a week? Recreation planners should seriously consider this possibility if urban pressures continue to increase and more industries reduce the length of the workweek.

PROFITS TO THE INNOVATOR

The innovator in American industry is usually well rewarded. In the recreation field, this opportunity is not diminished in the least. An innovator must have imagination; a superior knowledge of people, their interests, and [their] attitudes; and a constant awareness of changing technology.

Accurate prediction of changing recreation interests is not easy. People change and their interests change over time. Consider the gross inaccuracy had we projected 1930 recreation interests into the 1970s on the basis of population increases alone. Our failure to recognize man's increasing mobility would have led to the construction of an oversupply of large country inns, many of which would be abandoned today. A similar overbuilding would have occurred had we developed youth camps on the basis of population projections alone.

One cannot project recreation demand too far with any degree of reliability. Specific activity interest may come, go, and later return. Witness the changing interest in cross-country skiing. At one time this was a highly popular activity. Later it was overshadowed by downhill skiing, and now it is again an expanding activity.

The innovating entrepreneur is a gambler in a sense. He will not be satisfied adhering to the security of a currently acceptable recreation mode. He will question his customers thoroughly to determine their true recreation interests and their unsatisfied goals. He will critically observe their actions to determine how he might modify his operation to yield greater customer satisfaction. He will experiment with new ideas. Some of these ideas will prove worthless, but his ultimate success may hinge upon the early development of just one ingenious idea. The lightweight boat was developed in response to man's interest in mobility, while the quick-release ski binding was the outcome of man's interest in increased safety.

The aggressive entrepreneur will study our mathematical projections of demographic data and apply his personal knowledge of people, their interests, and [their] attitudes. He will conceive a development program that will yield far greater returns than the operation planned in accordance with a stereotyped set of recommendations. Entrepreneurial gain is still very much a matter of individual initiative and perseverance.

SUMMARY AND DISCUSSION

As a rule the returns to the labor and management input in private outdoor recreation enterprises are low. Improper location is a major factor associated with low returns. Other factors include insufficient size of operation and too short a business season. We cannot assume that these limiting factors and low returns will discourage landowners from entering and continuing in the private outdoor recreation field. In many instances the decision to operate an outdoor recreation enterprise is more related to personal and noneconomic considerations than to profit maximization. If, however, low returns are coupled with high property taxation over a prolonged period, the ultimate effect may be an overbalancing of these personal and noneconomic considerations and an end to recreation business activities.

The traditional methods of measuring enterprise profitability are unrealistic unless we consider land value appreciation. This factor may be a far greater determinant of enterprise tenure than actual cash returns to labor and management. Any realistic projection of the role of private enterprise in outdoor recreation must consider: (1) cash enterprise returns, (2) land value appreciation, (3) land taxation, and (4) noneconomic entrepreneurial goals. Failure to consider any one of these factors could lead to a grossly inaccurate projection.

Outdoor recreation researchers can clear some muddy waters if they will properly classify outdoor recreation enterprises according to entrepreneurial goals. Research results so classified will be far more useful to field advisers, bankers, and others than any information now available. Recreation field advisers must tailor their advice to the product of rational economic analysis coupled with full consideration of personal landowner desires.

A major problem of the recreation firm is underutilization of facilities on weekdays. Improvement may be on the horizon if the four-day workweek should become common. At some point in the future, a three-day workweek with two crews may become common. Such action would have a profound impact on the outdoor recreation industry.

The private outdoor recreation firm has an important role to play in years ahead. The highest degree of success will accrue to the entrepreneur who uses ingenuity and imagination and becomes an innovator among recreation firms. Researchers and field advisers are challenged to help guide the private sector to minimize mistakes in judgment and to maximize benefits, both monetary and nonmonetary.

REFERENCES

1. Bevins, Malcolm I. 1967. *The private campground industry in Vermont.* University of Vermont Department of Resource Economics Pamphlet 67-4.
2. ———. 1970. *Youth camps in Vermont.* University of Vermont Agricultural Experiment Station Bulletin 662.
3. Johnson, Hugh A. 1962. *Private enterprise in the development of outdoor recreation.* USDA Economic Research Service.
4. ———. 1966. *Opportunities and limitations in private recreation development.* USDA Economic Research Service.
5. ———. 1968. *The enterprise analysis.* USDA Economic Research Service.
6. Loomis, Clifton W., and Wilkins, Bruce T. 1970. *A study of campground businesses in New York State.* Cornell University Agricultural Experiment Station Agricultural Economics Research Pamphlet 315.
7. Moore, Elmer J. 1964. *Rural recreation enterprises in New England.* USDA Economic Research Service Research Report 56.
8. Sinclair, Robert O. 1969. *Trends in rural land prices in Vermont.* University of Vermont Agricultural Experiment Station Bulletin 659.
9. U.S. Congress, Subcommittee on National Parks and Recreation. 1970. *Golden Eagle program.* Washington, D.C.: Government Printing Office.
10. U.S. Department of the Interior, Bureau of Outdoor Recreation. 1966. *Financing of outdoor recreation.* Washington, D.C.
11. ———. 1967. *Recreation land price escalation.* Washington, D.C.
12. Uvacek, Edward, Jr., and Schmedemann, Ivan W. 1968. The cattle business—Agricultural enterprise or outdoor recreation? *Texas Agricultural Progress* 14, no. 1. Texas A&M University.

CHAPTER 18

THE LOCAL ECONOMIC IMPACT OF OUTDOOR RECREATION FACILITIES

Frank W. Millerd
David W. Fischer

Public tax dollar investment in a recreational facility may depend on the perceived social and economic benefits that will accrue to the local populace. This chapter by Frank Millerd and David Fischer describes how a theoretical and empirically based analysis of the local economic impact of a recreational facility can be accomplished. The authors discuss the relevant concepts involved, define *economic impact,* outline the empirical problems, and provide appropriate measurement techniques.

Part of the debate on the provision or expansion of outdoor recreation facilities has focused on the local economic impact of these facilities. Those in favor of increased spending on recreation projects or preservation of recreational areas from competing uses seek to reinforce their arguments by demonstrating the regional development benefits which parks bring through increased local income and employment. It is the feeling of others, however, that the true local economic impact is very small, if not negative, due to low levels of visitor expenditures and the significant costs imposed on a local area by the development of an outdoor recreation facility.

One result has been a demand for careful and complete analyses of the local economic impacts of such facilities. This paper suggests how a theoretically and empirically sound study may be carried out.

DEFINING ECONOMIC IMPACT

The local economic impact of an outdoor recreation facility measures the economic consequences to an area due to the establishment of an outdoor recreation facility, excluding the benefits which accrue to local users of the project. More specifically, *economic impact* may be defined as the net secondary benefits of the outdoor recreation facility or the secondary benefits less any costs associated with the generation of these benefits.

The most common view of secondary benefits is that of Marglin (21), who defines secondary benefits under the redistribution objective of public expenditures. Primary redistribution benefits are the consumption gains of particular

This paper was developed from consulting work done by the authors for the Ontario provincial government. It appears with permission of the authors.

groups or regions where the gains are measured as the difference between the willingness to pay of a particular group for the direct outputs of a project and the actual charge levied upon that group. Secondary benefits under the redistribution objective would be any contributions from the project to regional income or consumption not due to direct increased consumption of the goods and services produced by the project. They are those income and consumption gains which stem from or are induced by a project or activity. They are not the value of the project to the primary users of the project but rather are the value of the project to those who are involved in ancillary activities such as supplying the primary users.

Secondary benefits are specific to a region and will usually exist only in that particular region or area, since—assuming no differences in the economic characteristics of local areas (such as unemployment rates)—most secondary benefit gains in a particular area will be offset by actual or potential losses elsewhere. The supplying of services to a project's users which takes place in a particular region is a gain to that region but a loss to some other region which would have had the activity otherwise. From a national or possibly even a regional point of view, the secondary impacts associated with many projects will cancel themselves out, and an analysis using a national viewpoint will usually ignore them. Only if the economic impact is viewed over a limited area can secondary benefits be said to exist.

Certain secondary benefits, however, may represent a benefit to the national economy if special circumstances exist in a particular region so that income and consumption gains are greater in that region than they would be with comparable development in another region. For example, if the presence of the project in a region means that unemployed or underemployed local resources will be more fully employed, economies of scale will be captured by local producers, exports by local producers will be increased, or a wider range of goods and services will be made available to resident consumers, then there will be legitimate gains to the national economy.

Although this discussion has dwelt on the definition of secondary benefits, computation of the local economic impact requires that all local costs to the region of the outdoor recreation facility be subtracted from secondary benefits. It should also be noted that residents of the region may be users of an outdoor recreation project and thus be recipients of the primary benefits of the project.[1] This paper, however, concentrates on discussing the net secondary benefits.

WHAT TO MEASURE

Having defined economic impact, it is now appropriate to outline a procedure for its calculation. Mentioned first are guidelines for establishing the area over which the impact is to be measured. Then the sources of local benefits and costs and their roles in the calculation of economic impact are discussed.

Establishing the Area of Economic Impact

Before any calculation of economic impact may proceed, the geographic area over which the impact is to be calculated must be carefully defined, since the magnitude of the economic impact will usually increase as the size of the region expands. Ideally, the area chosen for study should be that in which the outdoor recreation facility exerts an economic influence which is both meaningful and measurable. Indicators such as travel patterns, population groupings, and the location of complementary tourist facilities could be used to outline the area of economic impact.

Regional delineation, however, will often be influenced by practical considerations. In many cases the area to be studied will be defined by the area of the administrative unit or agency for which the analysis is being done. In other instances the availability of data and the overall objectives of the study may decide the impact area.

Sources of Secondary Benefits

There are several ways secondary benefits can arise from outdoor recreation projects. First, public expenditures for the initial construction or preparation of the facility and its continuing operation will cause income increases in the local area. Employment in construction and maintenance and in local firms supplying inputs during construction and operation will be stimulated. Similar effects will occur if other local public expenditures are induced by the outdoor recreation project.

Secondary benefits also stem from the expenditures of the primary beneficiaries or users of the outdoor recreation project. The expenditures in question are not the user fees for the facility but rather the expenditures which take place locally and are associated with participation in the outdoor recreation experience. Included are expenditures on transportation, meals, and accommodation. All are potential sources of income and employment in the local area.

The secondary benefits of an outdoor recreation facility may also be manifested by increased private investment because of the facility. This investment will be for revenue-generating facilities such as stores and motels and non–revenue generating facilities such as cottages. Employment and income benefits will come from those involved in construction and supplying of building materials.

The general expansion of recreation-related economic activity may have effects on other sectors of the local economy. For example, the development of better transportation facilities or the provision of a wider range of goods and services to local residents could occur as a result of the establishment of a nearby outdoor recreation facility. These are termed *external effects* and are properly included in secondary benefits.[2]

Users of outdoor recreation facilities also incur expenses which do not directly depend on the amount of time spent participating in outdoor recreation. Expenditures on outboard motors, camping equipment, and recreation vehicles are examples. The local income and employment effects of this type of expenditure, to the extent they may be categorized as being due to a particular outdoor recreation facility, are difficult to determine. Most of these expenditures take place in and have effects on areas well removed from the site of any outdoor recreation facility. It is practically impossible to develop a direct relationship between a particular outdoor recreation facility and this type of secondary benefit.

Multiplier Effects

Secondary benefits which increase income have a direct and an indirect component. The direct part is income generated by those who receive payments directly from the recreationists or the outdoor recreation agency. This is the first round of effects. The indirect component is the local income resulting from spending by the first-round recipients and the further rounds of effects as the expenditures circulate through the area. Each time this income circulates, however, it is subject to leakages. Only part of the sales of local businesses is paid out as income to local employees and employers. The remainder leaves the area to purchase inputs from other areas or as returns to nonresident owners of factors of production. Furthermore, only part of the income earned by residents is respent locally. The remainder is saved, taxed away, or spent outside the area.

The total effect on income may be measured by the use of a multiplier formula, such as the following[3]:

$$Y = Y_1 \frac{1}{1 - K_1 K_2}$$

where:

Y = total income effect of income payments to local residents
Y_1 = first-round income payments
K_1 = proportion of income earned by residents that is respent locally
K_2 = proportion of sales to local residents that is paid out as income to employees and employers
$\frac{1}{1 - K_1 K_2}$ = income multiplier.

Local Costs of Outdoor Recreation Facilities

The outdoor recreation facility may also impose local costs which must be subtracted from secondary benefits to arrive at net secondary benefits or the true economic impact of the outdoor recreation facility. The costs can occur as lost income opportunities for local residents, increased local government expenditures, and various external costs imposed on residents.

Development of the outdoor recreation facility probably means that the natural resources used for the facility cannot be used for other purposes such as agriculture and forestry. These lost opportunities mean foregone local income and employment, both directly and indirectly. Any opportunity income lost must be included as a cost in net terms. That is, the costs to the local community of obtaining that income and the net costs of the local externalities arising out of the proposed alternative use of the resources must be subtracted from any possible opportunity income.

Income opportunities may also be lost by changes in the pattern of recreation expenditures by local residents. The outdoor recreation facility will act as a substitute source of recreation for local residents, and the expenditures they make to enter the facility may mean a reduction in their spending on other forms of local recreation.

Increases in local taxes may be necessary to provide medical, fire protection, and police services to the tourists attracted to the area. If the outdoor recreation facility stimulates nonresident recreational home development, however, the effects on local government finances may be offset or even positive. In this case the local tax base would be enhanced considerably, while the recreation home owners would use local public facilities only on a part-time basis.

Externalities imposed on the local residents may take market and non-market forms. Market-type external effects directly affect prices. For example, the markets for locally produced agricultural products, private recreation land, and transportation facilities will be affected by the presence of tourists. These goods and services may be available at higher prices and in more limited amounts than would be the case if tourists were not present. The type and quality of goods and services available could also be affected as, for example, imported goods are substituted for locally produced goods. Increased demand by visitors for recreational facilities may result in higher fees being imposed: another increased cost to local residents.

Nonmarket external effects do not directly change prices but indirectly impose additional costs, inconvenience, or discomfort on local residents. The outdoor recreation facility can result in increased environmental deterioration and traffic congestion in the region, both of which cause a certain amount of discomfort to local residents. More generally, the influx of large numbers of visitors may undermine and adversely alter local lifestyles, particularly in more remote areas.

It should be noted that for certain individuals the benefits and costs associated with the outdoor recreation facility may not be offsetting. Those affected most by higher rents, more congestion, and poorer public services are not necessarily the ones who benefit from employment opportunities, higher sales, rising property values, and larger profits.

Calculation of the Local Economic Impact

The various benefits and costs may now be brought together to estimate the local economic impact of an outdoor recreation facility. The following is an outline of this calculation:

I. Benefits
   A. Local income generated by
      1. Construction of the outdoor recreation facility
      2. Other public investment generated by the facility
      3. Local private investment induced by the facility
   B. Present value of the local income generated by
      1. Annual maintenance of the outdoor recreation facility and other public investments

2. Expenditures in the local area by facility users

C. Other local benefits (positive externalities)

II. Costs

A. Present value of the net opportunity income lost

B. Present value of cost of local services provided for recreationists

C. Other local costs (negative externalities)

III. Difference: Local economic impact of the outdoor recreation facility

A distinction is made between those benefits and costs which occur only once and those which are continuing. Construction and investment expenditures usually occur only when the facility is started, while maintenance and user expenditures will continue over the lifetime of the project. The value of continuing benefits or costs is determined by calculating the present value of these streams of future benefits and costs. The present value of a stream of future benefits shows what a person would be willing to receive today instead of the stream of future benefits, while the present value of a stream of future costs shows what outlay today is equivalent to the stream of future costs.

The positive items in the calculation of local economic impact are the local income generated by construction and investment expenditures, the present value of the local income generated by maintenance expenditures and user expenditures, and positive externalities which occur as a result of the development and use of the outdoor recreation facility. The negative items are the present value of local income lost, the present value of the cost of local services provided for recreationists by local residents, and negative externalities resulting from the project. All income data are the total or multiplied values of income.[4]

It is unlikely that the positive and negative externalities can be expressed in income terms. Thus the items in the outline are not additive because they will not be expressed in similar units. This does not mean that externalities should be ignored, but several "accounts" may have to be established to include properly all items in the calculation of the local economic impact.

HOW TO MEASURE

The problem now is to measure the benefits and costs which have been defined and classified. Some benefits and costs, such as those due to the expenditures of public agencies, may be easily quantified; while others, such as external effects, are extremely difficult to quantify. A review of the measurement problems and techniques available for each of the major categories of benefits and costs is carried out below.

Public Agency Expenditures

The income and employment effects which result from the actions of public authorities can be gathered by contacting the appropriate public agencies. Public expenditures from outside the area used for construction and operation of the park and associated facilities will provide income and employment benefits (see outline items A1, A2, and A3 under Benefits). Local expenditures for services to recreationists will be a negative economic impact (item B under Costs).

Opportunity Incomes

The opportunity income lost to the area as a result of the facility, if any (item A under Costs), could be estimated by using information from similar areas which have used their resources for non–recreation development. If the recreation facility is being planned or is a recent development, opportunity income data is available from actual experience in the area.

If an economic model of the region has been constructed, such as an input-output model discussed below, the effects of alternative developments of the natural resources of an area could be simulated. Brown (3) has done this for agricultural development in the Interlake area of Manitoba.

External Effects

Most of the external effects (item C under both Benefits and Costs in the outline) are usually not subject to monetary valuation. They do exist, however, and should be included in any complete analysis. If it is impossible to provide quantitative information, then qualitative or descriptive information should be presented. Attempts to measure environmental costs are being made (10).

One of the external effects which will probably occur as a result of the development of the outdoor recreation facility is an increase in the price of nearby land. This is an external cost which may be measured. Knetsch (18) has estimated the relationship between land values and proximity to a reservoir project; and Conner, Gibbs, and Reynolds (7) have studied the relationship between water frontage and property values.

Private Investment Expenditures

Information on private investment induced by the outdoor recreation facility (item A3 under Benefits in the outline) will have to be gathered by contacting, at least on a sample basis, those directly involved. This will usually mean surveying local construction companies to obtain the business and income resulting from this private investment. Care should be taken to insure that only those investment expenditures occurring as a result of the outdoor recreation facility are included.

User Expenditures

Several techniques have been developed to measure the annual user expenditures due to a recreation facility (item B2 under Benefits). They may be classified as direct (principally survey methods) or indirect (using secondary sources of information). These techniques usually calculate only first-round or direct effects. The total effects have to be calculated by estimating and using a multiplier.

Direct Measurement Methods. Direct measurement methods are those which gather information directly from the individuals involved, often using survey techniques. The objective of these surveys is to determine the level and type of annual local expenditures by the users of the outdoor recreation facility. The survey may be carried out from the demand side or the supply side; that is, the estimation of tourist expenditures may be derived by asking the tourists themselves or the recipients of these expenditures.

One of the problems in this type of survey is the need first to identify exactly who is a user of the outdoor recreation facility. Usually, in a particular area, the tourists and facility users are one and the same. Those who travel to the area do so for a particular purpose: to use the outdoor recreation facility. In some cases it may however be necessary to separate tourists from other types of travelers such as migrants, commercial travelers, and persons visiting the area for family reasons or even for other recreational pursuits. The problem becomes more complex when there is more than one outdoor recreation facility in the area. Some fraction of their expenditures then has to be assigned to each facility visited, perhaps on the basis of the time spent in each facility. One further complication should be mentioned. It is not necessary that a person come from outside the area to use the facility in order that his expenditures be counted as part of the economic impact. All that is necessary is that some of his expenditures would not have been made in the area if the particular facility was not located there.

Tourist surveys commonly gather information on the tourists' origin and destination, the number of days they have spent in the area, their type and amount of expenditures, socioeconomic characteristics of the tourist and his family, etc. The survey is usually done on a sample basis. Much of the information gathered is useful for park planning and tourist promotion.[5] Examples of studies where user surveys have been used are those by Brown (3) and Dean et al. (8).

As with any type of consumer survey there are some real and potential administrative problems. The cost of gathering the information, the necessity of having a truly unbiased sample, and the difficulty of expanding the sample when estimates of the total population may be difficult to obtain are the types of problems inherent in the survey method.[6] Also, such surveys contain the usual difficulties associated with asking a person to recall how much he has spent in a specific area and requiring him to compartmentalize his expenditures into categories suddenly thrust upon him by the interviewer.

A variation on the user survey is to have visitors complete a daily diary of their expenditures. Mak, Moncur, and Yonamine (20), in comparing a diary method with a survey of visitors after their return home, found much lower response rates for those using the diary but significantly higher average daily expenditures per capita from the diary results, suggesting that many visitors may not fully recall all expenditures.

The same expenditure information can be obtained by direct observation at the retail and service outlets doing business with tourists.[7] Usually the outlets are sampled, either on an establishment basis, a time period basis, or both. The establishments are asked to record their sales to tourists for the total season or for particular time periods. Cost, sampling, and recall problems will again occur with this technique. Additionally, there will be the problem of obtaining the cooperation of a sufficiently large number of establishments to make the sample meaningful and the difficulty of separating tourist expenditures from nontourist expenditures. Bird and Miller (2), Dean et al. (8), and Meyer (22) used local business surveys in their studies.

A local business survey can also provide data useful in the calculation of the multiplier. One of the values necessary in multiplier computation is the proportion of sales to local residents that is paid out as income to employees or employers. It should be possible to obtain estimates of this value through questions asked during the local business survey.

Indirect Measurement Methods. Indirect methods are those that use information which has already been collected, usually for other purposes. Most of these methods are related to economic base theory.[8] The essence of this theory is the proposition that the rate and growth of a region is determined by its function as an exporter to the rest of the world. These export activities make up the economic base or basic sector of the region. Supporting these activities is the nonbasic sector, which does not export outside the region. In most economic base studies the basic sector is made up of primary or secondary agriculture, industry, and manufacturing, with the retail and service sectors making up the nonbasic sector. If tourism in the area is regarded as an export industry, however, then that part of the retail and service sectors selling to tourists makes up the basic sector. These indirect measurement methods attempt to measure that proportion of retail and service sector sales made to tourists.

Among the techniques suggested are the following:

1. Estimate the expenditures of local residents on retail goods and services using, for example, national averages. The excess of the total retail goods and services over local consumption can then be attributed to export consumption and tourist spending (19). The estimates of local resident expenditures can be adjusted for such factors as varying propensities to consume among local residents and consumer mobility.
2. Compare the region under study to one having similar disposable income and propensities to consume by the residents, but not dependent on tourism. The differences in retail and service sector sales may then be attributed to tourism.
3. Compare the region under study to a number of regions each having similar characteristics. The region with the lowest per capita retail and service sector sales may be assumed to have the minimum necessary to fulfill local needs. Any excess in the region under study may then be attributed to tourism or other sources of demand from outside the area. This technique is often termed the "minimum requirements" approach (1).

The advantages of indirect methods center on their inexpensiveness and ease of implementation. The necessary data are usually already published and are completely accurate. Detailed information is usually available on the types and operations of retail and service establishments by community, and calculations of this type should probably be used to cross-check other impact studies.

The disadvantages have to do with the assumption necessary. Variations in the level of per capita retail and service sector sales in an area could take place for a variety of reasons other than changes in the level of tourist activity. It would appear that the larger the area the more accurate this type of study would be, as local variations may be cancelled out.

Summary of Data Sources for Private and Public Expenditures

Table 18-1 summarizes the types of expenditure information which should be considered and the primary and secondary data sources for each, assuming no detailed model of the area's economy, such as an input-output table, is carried out. The data sources listed in table 18-1 will usually give only expenditure data which must be transformed into total local income generated by the outdoor recreation facility. To use the multiplier suggested above it is necessary to calculate the proportion of first-round expenditures which are income payments to local residents, the proportion of sales to local residents that is paid out as income to employees and employers, and the proportion of income earned by local residents that is respent locally. The first two values, proportions of sales which are income payments, may be obtained from the local business survey, surveys of similar businesses, or published statistics on retail and service businesses. The proportion of income earned by local residents that is respent locally will have to be estimated from local sales and income data or obtained from a survey of local residents. These values are then substituted into the multiplier formula, and the total multiplied effects of the expenditures can be calculated. The total annual local incomes generated by the outdoor recreation facility will then have been computed.

Input-Output Analysis

An alternative procedure for measuring expenditure impacts is provided by input-output analysis. This technique presents detailed information on the production and distribution characteristics of individual sectors of the local economy and the nature of the monetary relationships between sectors. For showing the general interdependence of the economy of a region input-output analysis is the most powerful tool available.

Although the completeness of the technique is its greatest advantage, it also leads to its greatest drawback. Input-output analysis requires the construction of a transactions table showing the sales and purchase allocations of each local industry, including outdoor recreation, in relation to other local industries, local consumers, and the outside world. Construction of such a table is an expensive and time-consuming process. The information available from this table, however, allows the researcher to calculate precisely the direct impact of tourist expenditures on the local economy and the multiplier effects. There is no need for side calculations of multiplier effects. Input-output tables have been constructed for the purpose of measuring recreational impacts by Hinman (15), Hiser and Fisher (16), and Strang (26).

It should be noted that the input-output table is a picture of the average interrelationships among the sectors of an area at one point in time which may not be representative of marginal changes. Also, as the economy of an area

Expenditure	Principle Source	Alternative Source(s)
Construction and maintenance of outdoor recreation facility	Outdoor recreation agency	
Public investment induced by the facility	Relevant public agencies	
Expenditures in local area by users of the facility	User survey	Local business survey Published retail and service trade statistics
Local private investment induced by the outdoor recreation facility	Local business survey	Published retail and service trade statistics

TABLE 18-1. *Data Sources for Expenditure Information*

changes, the previous coefficients will no longer perfectly reflect the interrelationships among the sectors of an area. Brown (3) and Tung, MacMillan, and Framingham (27) have used a dynamic input-output model to overcome the problem of fixed interrelationships between sectors. In the dynamic model input requirements are adjusted to allow for the influence of technical change and the relaxation of resource constraints.

Several studies have used adaptations of the input-output method in order to reduce data requirements. Kalter and Lord (17) and Stevens and Kalter (24) used a from-to model. This model retains the characteristics of an interindustry model but reduces the data necessary by following output flows, only. Morrison and Smith (23) examined the possibility of eliminating regional data collection entirely by using national interrelationships for a regional model. They feel, however, that these methods can produce only an approximation of a proper regional model.

Other Models

Other forms of economic models could be adapted for the measurement of local economic impact. Econometric models such as the Tourism Expenditure Model and the Tourism Impact Model developed by the Canadian Office of Tourism, although currently applicable only at the provincial level, provide a framework which can be developed for use at a local level. With the Tourism Expenditure Model a particular tourism visitation pattern can be translated into total tourist expenditures by sector. The Tourism Impact Model uses these expenditure estimates to produce the total provincial tourism—induced economic impact.

Choosing a Technique

The type of study undertaken will depend on the objectives of the study and the resources available. The objectives should determine the scope of the study and the desirable degree of accuracy, detail, and flexibility; while the resources available, when coupled with these factors, will decide the appropriate methodology to use. The detail and accuracy of the study should normally increase when the more costly techniques such as input-output analysis are used. Once the study has been completed some form of sensitivity analysis may be appropriate to see the amount by which the results are altered with changes in the assumptions or methods of analysis.

RESULTS

No attempt will be made to summarize previous impact studies. The variety of situations encountered makes any comparison difficult. Several recent studies, however, have found the public and private expenditure effects associated with outdoor recreation facilities to be relatively small. Brown (3), Frick and Ching (12), Garrison (13), and Stoevener, Retting, and Reiling (25)—all found recreation's contribution to the local economy to have a low value. The initial reason for this is the low levels of daily spending by most recreationists. In reviewing a number of studies, Woods, Gordon, and Co. (28) found average daily expenditure estimates for park visitors to vary between $13 and $61. It appears that many view participation in outdoor recreation as a way to have an inexpensive holiday.

Additionally, low multiplier effects has been found in most areas. Harvey, Foster, and McNutt (14), for example, reported a multiplier of 1.108; Stoevener, Retting, and Reiling (25) calculated multiplier values of approximately 2; and Woods, Gordon, and Co. (28) found multipliers of less than 1.2. The "leakages" out of most local economies are very high. This is no doubt due to the fact that most outdoor recreation facilities are scattered in relatively isolated areas with only smaller communities in close proximity. Neither the outdoor recreation facility nor the local community provides the economies of scale and other conditions necessary for the development of extensive local business activity.

Those examining employment effects have found similarly low impact values. Garrison (13) suggests that the small employment effect is due to the tendency, in small rural or small-town communities which have been growing slowly, for the work force in trade, services, and finance to be underutilized. Additionally, many of the jobs are seasonal or poorly paying.

This suggests that most outdoor recreation facilities, unless extremely large, cannot be looked at as the primary stimulant for the economic growth of a region. The Canadian Council for Rural Development (5) suggests that tourism and recreation development should be viewed as a method of expanding the variety of income and job opportunities in an area rather than the main source of economic activity. An outdoor recreation facility can be an important supplement to the existing local economy but is rarely capable of supporting a sizable community itself. Only the larger national parks generate sufficient economic activity to provide the basis for significant regional development.

One role an impact study could play is that of examining the conditions necessary for increasing the local economic impact. Brown (3) suggests that the magnitude of local expenditures depends on the type of development (day use or camping), type of visitor (particularly income level), length of stay, and availability of goods and services. Dean et al. (8) found the largest impact to be generated by parks not completely self-sufficient but developed sufficiently to attract nonlocal visitors to the area. Brownigg and Grieg (4) and Strang (26) disaggregated regional multipliers to provide income and employment multipliers by tourist and development type. These suggest the forms of tourist development most likely to have the strongest impact on an area.

SUMMARY AND CONCLUSIONS

This paper has attempted to outline and clarify some of the theoretical and methodological issues involved in calculating the local economic impacts of outdoor recreation facilities. Local economic impact may be defined as net secondary benefits or secondary benefits minus the costs associated with receiving these benefits. Although secondary benefits may not exist from a national point of view or may occur independently of primary benefits, they do exist on a local level. The costs are those incurred by the local area because of the proximity of the outdoor recreation facility.

A range of techniques is available for measuring secondary benefits, from the use of published data to input-output analysis. Generally, the greater the effort expended on data collection and analysis, the more accurate and comprehensive the results. The type of study undertaken should depend on the objectives of the study and the resources available.

A proper economic impact study must be complete and sound in its analysis. There must be a search for and an accounting of the positive and negative aspects of an outdoor recreation facility, particularly the social and environmental effects. Although this may be time consuming and expensive, it is only in this way that the economic viewpoint will be given its proper weight.

NOTES

1. See Fischer and Millerd (11) for a discussion of primary benefit measurement techniques.
2. External effects occur when parties outside a transaction are affected. In this case improved transportation facilities are provided for recreationists, but others benefit when they take advantage of them. External effects, or externalities, may be positive or negative.
3. This formula is adapted from Harvey et al. (14) and Clawson and Knetsch (6).
4. Although income data are used here, employment data could also be generated. This could most easily be done by dividing the income data by the average annual income for this type of employment.
5. This type of survey may be combined with one showing the primary benefits or the willingness to pay for the recreational resource. See Fischer (9) for a critique of these techniques.
6. Brown (3) lowered the cost of data gathering by using a self-administered questionnaire.
7. Dean et al. (8) in carrying out surveys of both users and local businesses found the overall order of magnitude of park impact on local business employment to be about the same.
8. For a summary of this theory and methods of analysis see Bendavid (1).

REFERENCES

1. Bendavid, Avrom. 1974. *Regional economic analysis for practitioners.* New York: Praeger.
2. Bird, Ronald, and Miller, Frank. 1962. *Where Ozark tourists come from and their impact on the local economy.* Columbia: University of Missouri College of Agriculture.
3. Brown, W. A. N. 1977. The role of outdoor recreation in regional development: A study of Hecla Provincial Park. Ph.D. dissertation, University of Manitoba.
4. Brownigg, M., and Grieg, M. A. 1975. Differential multipliers for tourism. *Scottish Journal of Political Economy* 22: 261–75.
5. Canadian Council for Rural Development. 1975. *Economic significance of tourism and outdoor recreation for rural development.* Ottawa.
6. Clawson, M., and Knetsch, J. 1966. *Economics of outdoor recreation.* Baltimore: Johns Hopkins Press.
7. Conner, J. R.; Gibbs, K. C.; and Reynolds, J. E. The effect of water frontage on recreational property values. *Journal of Leisure Research* 5: 26–38.
8. Dean, Gillian; Getz, Malcolm; Nelson, Larry; and Siegfried, John. 1978. The local economic impact of state parks. *Journal of Leisure Research* 10: 98–112.
9. Fischer, David W. 1975. Willingness to pay as a behavioural criterion for environmental decision-making. *Journal of Environmental Management* 3: 29–41.
10. Fischer, David W., and Davies, Gordon S. 1973. An approach to assessing environmental impacts. *Journal of Environmental Management* 1: 207–27.
11. Fischer, David W., and Millerd, Frank W. 1976. Methods for allocating public recreational and tourism benefits: A review. *Tourist Review* 31: 10–15.
12. Frick, G. E., and Ching, C. T. K. 1970. Generation of local income from users of a rural public park. *Journal of Leisure Research* 2: 260–63.
13. Garrison, C. B. 1974. A case study of the local economic impact of reservoir recreation. *Journal of Leisure Research* 6: 7–19.
14. Harvey, A.; Foster, M.; and McNutt, T. 1974. *Kejimkujik Park socio-economic impact study.* Halifax: Regional and Urban Studies Center, Dalhousie University.
15. Hinman, R. C. 1969. *The impact of reservoir recreation on the Whitney Point microregion of New York State.* Ithaca, N.Y.: Department of Agricultural Economics, Cornell University.
16. Hiser, Michel, and Fisher, Dennis U. 1977. *An interindustry analysis of Clinton County, New York.* Ithaca, N.Y.: Department of Agricultural Economics, Cornell University.
17. Kalter, Robert J., and Lord, William B. 1968. Measurement of the impact of recreation investments on a local economy. *American Journal of Agricultural Economics* 50: 243–56.
18. Knetsch, J. R. 1964. The influence of reservoir projects on land values. *Journal of Farm Economics* 46: 231–43.
19. Kreutzwiser, R. D. 1973. A methodology for estimating tourist spending in Ontario counties. M.A. thesis, University of Waterloo.
20. Mak, James; Moncur, James; and Yonamine, David. 1977. How or how not to measure visitor expenditures. *Journal of Travel Research* 14: 1–4.
21. Marglin, S. A. 1967. *Public investment criteria.* London: Allen & Unwin.
22. Meyer, Gary C. 1975. The role of tourism-recreation in regional economic development: A case study of northern Minnesota. Ph.D. dissertation, University of Minnesota.
23. Morrison, W. I., and Smith, P. 1974. Nonsurvey input-output techniques at the small area level: An evaluation. *Journal of Regional Science* 14: 1–14.
24. Stevens, T. H., and Kalter, R. J. 1970. *Technological externalities, outdoor recreation and the regional economic impact of Cayuga Lake.* Ithaca, N.Y.: Department of Agricultural Economics, Cornell University.
25. Stoevener, H. H.; Retting, R. B.; and Reiling, S. D. 1974. Economic impact of outdoor recreation: What have we learned? In D. R. Field, J. C. Barron, and B. F. Long, eds. *Water and community development: Social and economic perspectives.* Ann Arbor, Mich.: Ann Arbor Science Publishers.
26. Strang, W. G. 1971. Recreation and the local economy: Implications for economic and resource planning. *Marine Technology Society Proceedings,* pp. 509–21.

27. Tung, F. L.; MacMillan, J. A.; and Framingham, C. F. 1976. A dynamic regional model for evaluating resource development programs. *American Journal of Agricultural Economics* 58: 403–14.
28. Woods, Gordon, and Co. 1978. *St. Lawrence Islands National Park economic impact study.* Toronto.

CHAPTER 19

MARKET ANALYSIS FOR RECREATION MANAGERS

W. F. LaPage

One of the barriers to effective communication between economists and administrators in outdoor recreation may be a six-letter word: *demand.* For the economist, "demand" is a concept of simple elegance and almost unlimited use. For the recreation manager, "demand" is the less-than-elegant—but equally unlimited—herd knocking down the gate. W. F. LaPage in this paper suggests that there is a middle ground—market analysis—where economic theory and the realities of administration can meet.

MARKET RESEARCH QUESTIONS

... The size of the camping market is a function of some uncontrollable factors, like weather, and some potentially controllable ones, like advertising and supply. The amount of camping people do is largely determined by individual decision-making processes.

The questions I usually hear being asked by public park managers and private investors alike are not questions of how much recreation at what price; they are questions of what kinds of recreation and for how long. Questions such as, Should we build more campgrounds? How many of the 100 new campsites that we are planning should have full utility connections? and What caused last year's slump in attendance?—all indicate doubt about the market. They are readily translated into market research questions: What growth stage is the camping market in? Has growth peaked for awhile, or should we get ready to accommodate more? How many more? How stable is the market; that is, will attendance be roughly constant despite minor changes in the economy? Is it a fad? Are there style trends within the market that will require changes in the design of facilities or in the location of facilities, such as more primitive campsites or more convenience campsites?

Despite their relevant interests and training, economists have not been inclined to address themselves to the very important tasks of describing recreation markets, measuring their trends, and building models of how markets grow and respond to changes in their environment. The tasks have not grown easier while they were neglected; and the dynamic nature of markets has probably contributed to their neglect. Descriptive research is too often of transitory value; trends are difficult to distinguish from normal fluctuations in

Reprinted from *Outdoor Recreation—Advances in Application of Economics,* USDA Forest Service General Technical Report WO-2 (March 1977), pp. 77–81, with permission of the author.

the short run; and the complexities of modeling markets apparently whimsically responsive to a great variety of social, political, economic, cultural, and meteorological forces are immense. However, the question, [Will the demand for camping be higher next year?] . . . and its related budgeting, planning, and land allocation considerations is sufficiently important that we should make an effort to find the answer.

Recreation Markets

Complex phenomena are sometimes best approached through analogy. The market for automobiles is an appropriate point of departure for understanding many of today's recreation markets. Parallel growth in the automobile industry and in the availability of roads and highway services was not a masterpiece of public-private cooperation as much as it was the result of fortunate coincidences of public policy.

Long before the arrival of the first motor car, improved transportation was a matter of considerable concern to government. Incentives for developing improved transportation routes, canals, highways, and railways had emerged generations earlier. The growth of the highway industry paralleled that of the auto industry, with new automobile technology requiring more and better roads, until finally both industries reached a size where their influence on the economy made them subject to public policy as "ends," as major sources of employment, rather than just as the "means" of improved commerce.

Recreation markets have rarely been recognized as deserving of special treatment because of their contribution to the economy, but they are no less dependent upon favorable public policy, changes in technology, and an element of good luck, so that related industries will just happen to grow in step with each other. For example, continued growth in the sales of recreation vehicles by the several hundred manufacturers of truck campers, motor homes, and trailers depends on the uncoordinated policies of more than 100 federal, state, and local parks agencies toward providing campsites. It also depends upon the availability of investment capital to thousands of private campsite developers and on the ability of all of these developers to "read the market," or understand what people want.

Certainly the equipment manufacturers can market their products with no concern for where their equipment will be used. But, if they oversell their equipment beyond the existing capacity availability and variety of campsites, their customers will become dissatisfied with camping conditions and will use their equipment less and less. Rather than see that equipment standing idle week after week, many owners will lend or rent it to their friends and neighbors. If they, too, find quality campsites lacking, they will become lost to the market as potential buyers of new equipment. Eventually, a second-hand market for camping equipment emerges, with the result that production of new equipment declines even further and some manufacturers may go out of the business. A few years ago, the Recreational Vehicle Institute estimated the number of manufacturers of mobile camping equipment at 800; last winter, the figure was down to 650; and today, it may be under 600 (8; 7).

How Markets Work

The sequence of events that I have just described is not simply an illustration of the complex interdependence of industries serving a market, it is also a crude attempt at modeling how a market works. And, as such, it contains a number of "index points" for examining how well the market is performing.

Performance, in the case of the recreational vehicle camping market, implies compatibility between: (1) the vehicle manufacturers, who must match their production capabilities and their marketing efforts with the needs of 23,000 dealerships; (2) the commercial campground industry, which must develop attractive, well-located campsites to accommodate the new types of vehicles being produced each year; (3) the camping information industry, which must provide directories, reservation services, and ideas to the traveling public; (4) public agencies that contribute to the supply of alternative campsites; (5) more public agencies that provide highways and access to public lands; and (6) still more public agencies that regulate such things as the supply of gasoline and the licensing of vehicles.

Peaks and dips in the sales of recreational vehicles provide one kind of "barometer" to measure how well each segment of the market is reading, and responding to, the signals of all the other segments. But sales curves, like stock indexes, are supersensitive to the political economy in which they operate. The Camping/Recreational Vehicle Stock Index, a composite of fifteen major stocks, dropped 33 percent from November of 1973 to November of 1974, while the Dow Jones dropped 36 percent. And sales curves fail to distinguish replacements from market expansion. If sales of equipment to new campers dropped to zero, it would still be possible to have a stable, and perhaps growing, market for camping equipment and campsite rentals. Growth, if it occurred, would come not from the addition of new campers to the market but from increased participation among active campers and renewed participation by former campers.

Obviously, then, [a] parks administrator must be concerned with two types of growth in the camping market: numbers of campers and average participation rates; that is, both "campers" and "days" rather than the usual "camper-days." He will plan differently if he expects 12,000 campers averaging 21 days per visit than for 21,000 campers averaging 12 days, even though both combinations produce a total of 252,000 camper-days. In the former case, he will have only about half as many permits to write, questions to answer, explanations of rules and regulations to give; and there will be important differences in trash collection procedures, traffic, supervision, and maintenance.

Components of Demand

It is through this kind of examination of the components of demand and their interrelationships that the market analyst can provide important insights both to the economist studying demand and to the park planner or administrator.

Let's examine briefly what we know about these two components—people and their participation—in the field of camping. And ... [with regard to] the emphasis on campers, ... [here are] some findings of a recent study by the NEM-42 research group. It indicates that campers and excampers, nationally, are responsible for about 52 percent of the reported picnicking, 56 percent of the swimming, 62 percent of the fishing, 70 percent of the boating, 73 percent of the hunting, 78 percent of the hiking and skiing, and 95 percent of the backpacking (2). And [other] studies have shown that the more active campers are also the more frequent participants in other outdoor activities (5).

The number of people who have tried camping has increased by about 230 percent over the estimated 4.3 million households found to be campers by the Outdoor Recreation Resources Review Commission (ORRRC) in 1960 (6). A study sponsored by the Bureau of Outdoor Recreation in 1965 found an estimated 6.0 million camping households. In 1971, a study sponsored jointly by the Forest Service and the industry reported 12.6 million camping households (3). And last year, the NEM-42 study, which was also sponsored by selected camping industries and the Forest Service, found 14.3 million camping households (2). The growth rate is slowing from an average of 18 percent per year in the late 1960s to 6.5 percent annually in the early 1970s.

The number of active camping households is only a small part of the total market picture. Not only has the number of active campers been growing, but the number of persons who have tried camping and have given it up either temporarily or permanently has increased even faster. Unfortunately, statistics on inactive campers were not collected before 1971. However, their numbers increased by almost 50 percent, from 9.1 million households to 13.6 million households, from 1971 to 1973.

And while the numbers of campers and excampers have been swelling, the number of potential campers has been declining. The ORRRC study in 1960 identified an estimated 9 million households where respondents said they would like to try camping in the future. Roughly comparable survey techniques in 1973 found only 6 million households that were potential additions to the camping market.

What is immediately apparent from these statistics is that the camping market's potential for expansion has, itself, been expanded by the camping industry's promotional efforts since 1960, which have been exposing more people to the idea of camping and getting them to think about trying it. But that potential is now being depleted by a camping industry that apparently cannot hold onto its campers, and the number of former campers rivals the number in the active camping market. To a large degree, the key to future camping market growth appears to be this already large, and still growing, group of excampers.

At this time, possible ways the industry could stimulate growth in the camping market are, in order:

1. encourage more participation by active campers—and slow down their transition from active to inactive;
2. reactivate former campers;
3. activate potential campers.

Each of these strategies suggests some real marketing challenges for the camping and recreational vehicle industry. Our data suggest that before the current energy situation, the rate of transition from active to inactive status was accelerating and that a growing number of active campers were camping less each year. In 1971 the ratio of inactive to active campers was 3:4. By 1973, it was 1:1. In 1971, one out of five active campers reported declining participation; in 1973 one out of every four active campers was camping less each year. In 1971 one out of every four households with high or moderate potential for camping was seriously planning its first camping trip. By 1973 only one in nine of these potential camping families was planning its first trip.

Clearly not all consumers' intentions are fulfilled, so something less than 1 percent of the population might readily be encouraged to try camping for the first time; larger gains in camping market activity can probably be realized by working with the 21 percent of the population who are active and the 20 percent who are inactive campers. And this is just as true for the camping equipment industries as it is for the campground industry. A survey of recreational vehicle owners . . . indicates that nearly two out of three owners are on their second, third, or fourth camping vehicle (1). So more than one out of three owners may be in the market for their first replacement vehicle—or approximately 1.5 million potential customers, not counting those who are in the market for a third or fourth replacement or those making a move from tents to vehicles for the first time.

As for reactivating excampers, the NEM-42 National Survey of 1973 indicates that approximately four out of ten excampers are out of the market only temporarily for a variety of personal reasons. Of those, 28 percent still own their equipment and 40 percent never owned any . . . , having rented or borrowed it previously. However, our own panel studies of camping participation have demonstrated how temporary inactivity can easily lead to permanent withdrawal from the market. In 79 percent of the cases we studied, we found that a single inactive year led either to further inactivity or to a return at a lower-than-average level of camping activity (5).

MARKET RESEARCH POTENTIAL

The challenge to the entire camping and recreational vehicle industry at this time is to understand and correct, where possible, the causes of declining participation and the rapid increase in the numbers of excampers. And it is here that market research finds its greatest potential for delivering hard answers to managers as well as providing a testing ground for economic theories. Surveys of the causes of camper dissatisfaction, the effects of campground crowding, the effects of differential fees on attendance, the differences in perceptions of camping held by campers, excampers, and potential campers, and trends in camping style and frequency are just a few of the current studies aimed at better understanding participation decline and market dropout.

In short, market research in outdoor recreation is increasingly being grounded both in economic theory and in the practical needs of investors, managers, and planners. For example, recent studies in both Massachusetts and New Hampshire examined the effects of differential campsite pricing on attendance, visit lengths, and shifting patterns of use. The New Hampshire study showed that a substantial increase in campground revenues could be realized by charging premium rates for waterfront campsites, with no political repercussions and no effect upon use levels (4).

Recent studies of the public's image of camping demonstrate how easily a shift in marketing emphasis might swell the "demand" for camping. Among potential campers, the favorable image of camping's attraction and its environment are offset by negative ideas of camping's difficulty and complexity (2). If marketing were to focus on reducing the complexity and inconvenience of camping, a major barrier to market expansion might be removed.

In conclusion, I have been suggesting that recreation economists and parks administrators are essentially concerned about recreation market behavior. And, I would further suggest that past research on demand-supply relationships, prices versus quantity purchased, elasticity coefficients, and rates of substitution was largely undertaken in order to provide surrogate measures of, or at least partial insights into, the more difficult concepts of market systems and market performance.

As I mentioned before, most questions of recreation demand can realistically be framed in terms of doubts about the strength of recreation markets in the face of rising costs and changing social and individual priorities. When dealing with broad-appeal, heavily invested markets such as camping, I would argue that these questions are directly researchable.

Finally, I hope that I have at least hinted that market analysis is a largely untapped research field for both administrators and economists. The cooperative research on fee differentials by the New Hampshire Division of State Parks and the Forest Service is one small example of the highly useful research that can be developed at low cost by simply monitoring changing administrative practices from available data. And economists should be playing a much stronger role in data collection and primary study formulation instead of lamenting the poor quality of available secondary data. Had they been doing so, it is doubtful that we would have seen the repeated failure of national recreation surveys, over the past decade or more, to collect data on the inactive and potential segments of the recreation market.

The public has a right to expect professionals to work together and to do a better job than we have done to date in understanding recreation markets and planning for their orderly development. And I suggest that this goal can be achieved, at least in part, by recognizing the severe limitations of conventional supply-demand approaches to planning and substituting a practical understanding of recreation markets and marketing. Further, let's declare a moratorium on the repeated attempts to look into the future until we have a better understanding of how recreation markets are working now.

REFERENCES

1. Consumer Communications Corporation. 1973. *Woodall's keys to the RV market, 1973.* Chicago, Ill.: Consumer Communications Corporation.

2. Kottle, M. W., et al. 1975. A perspective on the camping involvement cycle. Forest Service Research Paper NE-322.
3. LaPage, W. F. 1973. Growth potential of the family camping market. Forest Service Research Paper NE-252.
4. LaPage, W. F., et al. 1975. Differential campsite pricing and campground attendance. Forest Service Research Paper NE-330.
5. LaPage, W. F., and Ragain, D. P. 1974. Family camping trends—An 8-year panel study. *Journal of Leisure Research* 6, no. 2: 101–12.
6. Outdoor Recreation Resources Review Commission (ORRRC). 1962. *Participation in outdoor recreation: Factors affecting demand among American adults.* Washington, D.C.: Government Printing Office.
7. Recreational Vehicle Institute (RVI). 1974. Position paper on the energy crisis. Mimeographed. Des Plaines, Ill.: RVI.
8. Stout, G. E. 1972. The recreational vehicle industry. *Proceedings of the Second Annual Camping Congress.* Martinsville, Ind.: Family Camping Federation.

FURTHER READING

Provision of Resources: Public & Private

Beardsley, W. G. 1971. The economic impact of recreation development. In *Recreation symposium proceedings.* Upper Darby, Pa.: Northeastern Forest Experiment Station, USDA Forest Service.

Bohlin, K. M., and Ironside, R. G. 1976. Recreation expenditures and sales in Pigeon Lake area of Alberta: A case of trickle-up? *Journal of Leisure Research* 8, no. 4: 275–88.

Dalton, Michael J. 1978. Outdoor recreation development within the private sector. *Utah Tourism and Recreation Review* 7, no. 1 (January).

Destination U.S.A. 1973. Report of the National Tourism Resources Review Commission. 6 vols. Washington, D.C.: Government Printing Office.

Epperson, A. 1977. *Private and commercial recreation: A text and reference.* New York: Wiley.

Field, Richard C., and Convey, Frank J. 1976. Estimating local economic impacts in land use planning. *Journal of Forestry* 74: 155–56.

Gunn, C. A. 1972. *Vacationscape—Designing tourist regions.* Austin: University of Texas Bureau of Business Research.

Kalter, R. J., and Gosse, L. E. 1970. Recreation demand functions and the identification problem. *Journal of Leisure Research* 2, no. 1 (winter): 43–53.

Kalter, R. J., and Lord, W. B. 1968. Measurement of the impact of recreation investments. *American Journal of Agricultural Economics* 50, no. 2 (May).

Ladany, Shaul P., ed. 1975. *Management science applications to leisure—Time operations.* New York: American Elsevier.

LaPage, Wilbur F.; Cormier, Paula L.; Hamilton, George T.; and Cormier, Alan D. 1975. Differential campsite pricing and campground attendance. USDA Forest Service Research Paper NE-330. Upper Darby, Pa.: Northeastern Forest Experiment Station.

U.S. Congress. Committee on Commerce, Science and Transportation. 1978. *National tourism policy study, final report.* Washington, D.C.: Government Printing Office.

Part Five
RECREATION, RESOURCES & DECISIONS

OVERVIEW

The concluding part of the second edition of *Land & Leisure* contains chapters that integrate the salient goals listed in the introduction. Recreation in the urban milieu, public/private recreation services, systems thinking, and the value of the recreation experiences to the individual—all are discussed in part 5. The chapter on amenity resources in an urban context systematically and masterfully discusses the nature and function of the quality of the environment not only for recreational experiences but as a part of our total urban living space. This chapter centers on the intangible values inherent in the landscape that can add or detract from our daily experiences. It is presented in a form that will be useful in the planning decision process.

The second chapter provides an example of the balance necessary in order to plan for regional development and at the same time integrate individual needs and resource values. It clearly illustrates the steps involved; how to gather the data necessary for the process of decision making; how to measure the capacity of the resources; how to consider the relations between man and resources and the economics of the public and private components at issue; how to provide for a process that permits input by all persons involved; and how to create a focus for comparison, choice, and compromise.

The first selection in this volume asked us to take stock of our strengths and weaknesses as professionals in recreation. The final chapter brings us full circle from the first, giving us a framework for guiding the professional to listen to and to involve the public in the decision-making process.

CHAPTER 20

AMENITY RESOURCES FOR URBAN LIVING

Arthur A. Atkisson
Ira M. Robinson

In this chapter Arthur Atkisson and Ira Robinson make a plea for a system to plan and manage urban amenities as an integral part of the public investment decision process. The article includes a great many thoughts and techniques relevant to recreational space and associated amenity values in the urban landscape. It also suggests how behavioral data can be used in the planning process and in municipal decision making.

As more and more people cluster into urban regions, what happens to the natural environment increasingly becomes a matter for public policy interest. Much of this interest is centered on the idea of "amenity resources," although the concept of these highly valued resources remains vague. With growth in population, income, and leisure, pressures on such amenity resources can increase precipitously. Under such circumstances, the "management" of amenities becomes quite complex and can be extremely costly. Clarification of the concept of amenities and a better understanding of what might be called the "amenity management process" can contribute to public policy in this area.

It is helpful in this respect to conceive of the urban environment as a system with certain inputs and outputs and a set of conversion processes. Thus, if the outputs somehow fall short of our expectations, it becomes evident that we must look both at the quantity and quality of the inputs and at the processes by which they are being transformed, utilized, and related to the end states desired of the system. It also becomes clear that we must define the outputs we desire and the functions they are to perform.

It has been argued that such a coldly calculating approach to the design of systems which so deeply touch the quality of man's life does violence to man's very spirit and to the values of human freedom which underpin our society. To this, former Secretary of Defense McNamara has replied:

> To undermanage reality is not to keep it free. It is simply to let some force other than reason shape reality. That force may be unbridled emotion; it may be greed; it may be aggressiveness; it may be hatred; it may be ignorance; it may be inertia; it may be anything other than reason.[1]

Reprinted from Harvey S. Perloff, ed., *The Quality of the Urban Environment* (Washington, D.C.: Resources for the Future, Inc., by the Johns Hopkins Press, 1969), pp. 179–201, by permission of Resources for the Future, Inc., and the authors. This article has been extensively edited for this volume and the notes renumbered.

In this paper we suggest that responses to amenities make up one of the outputs derived from man's environmental system; that these outputs can be "managed"; and that decisional criteria and management systems can be developed to accomplish this task in a rational and socially responsible manner. . . .

AMENITY-RESPONSE SYSTEM

Some basic concepts from psychology are useful here. We are told that all that man learns throughout his lifetime is dependent on the effective operation of his five senses. As he moves from situation to situation he carries with him the cumulative experience derived from the operation of his five senses in other and earlier situations. Influenced by that experience, he reacts to the environmental stimuli which occur in each situation to which he is exposed. The perceived reaction of an adult to the environmental stimuli occurring at any point in time and space can therefore be viewed as a result of the operation of his senses in that circumstance as modified by his cumulative lifetime experience.

In a typical stimulus-response model, the five senses are shown as providing for human reception of environmental stimuli and as being responsible for the consequent experience of human sensations. Based on the sensitivity of the individual to the quality, intensity, extensity, and duration of the sensations evoked by the stimulus, the human organism experiences certain feelings which lead to the establishment of an *affective value* for the experience. Feelings involve such states as unpleasantness, pleasantness, tension, relaxation, excitement, or quiet. Of these, the feelings of unpleasantness and pleasantness characterize the "hedonic tone," or degree of satisfaction obtained from the subjective experience, and are the basis for establishment of affective value.

The affective value of sensations derived from a variety of stimuli have been measured through a number of techniques, including: (1) the scaler method, in which the observer judges the affective value of a stimulus on a subjective scale, extending from very unpleasant through indifferent to very pleasant, and usually involving five or more steps; (2) the serial method, in which the observer establishes the rank order to a set of stimuli with respect to affective value; and (3) the paired comparison method, in which the observer judges the relative pleasantness of all possible paired combinations of a set of stimuli. The frequency with which a stimulus is preferred when paired successively with all others is considered a measure of its affective value.

Over time, the individual's feelings about particular sensations lead to the formation of *attitudes*, *motives*, and *habits*. Every attitude has an object as its focus and involves a feeling about that object. An attitude may therefore be defined as "a readiness to become motivated with respect to an object."[2]

Motives, drives, and attitudes involve some human valuing process by which appreciation or interest is expressed toward the quality of an object or phenomenon within the individual's sensory field or which can somehow be related to that field. Value theorists suggest that *value* and the *feeling of value* are the same thing. Whether expressed in the economic marketplace or in some other way, they have their roots in the feelings people express toward particular sensations. Because of this, feelings are studied experimentally as determinants of preference among various objects or events in the environment of human beings. Since the satisfaction of drives (motives) is usually pleasant, while frustration of them is unpleasant, feelings thus are related to motivation and to the whole field of economic behavior. Thus, the value a human being places on an experience, an object, or a phenomenon is based on: the attitudes he holds toward the commodity; the objects or goals which are motivating him; his preferential ordering of these goals in terms of past feelings about different sensations; and the other learning situations through which he has been processed.

Maslow has suggested that man's motives fall into an ascending hierarchy beginning with those oriented around his needs for survival, safety, and security and ending with those related to self-actualization, which involve the maximum use of all his resources. The satisfaction of lower level needs leads to a loss or reduction in their motivational power and to a reorientation of motives around the achievement of higher level satisfactions. Thus, as the simple requirements for survival, safety, and security are satisfied, higher level satisfactions are increasingly valued and become the basis of an individual's value and behavioral orientation.[3]

Drawing on these basic concepts, it can be said that *those stimuli which lead to feelings of comfort, pleasure, or joy may be referred to as "amenities."* Since these feelings may be manifest in situations in which more basic, lower order human needs are also being satisfied, a system or scale for classifying responses is needed. Because of this, it seems useful to conceive of a scale of human responses which are ordered around man's discernible hierarchy of motives and values, extending from survival at one end to self-actualization, comfort, and joy at the other. Since such a response scale has relevance to stimuli generated by environmental circumstances, it may also be appropriate for the measurement of environmental quality.

In similar terms, Stead has suggested a scale involving four criteria by which environmental quality can be judged: First, does it insure survival? Second, does it prevent disease and accidents? Third, does it help promote efficient or unusual human performance? Fourth, does it promote comfort, pleasure, or joy?[4] In this chapter we will view Stead's fourth criterion in terms of an "amenity scale" along which might be ordered the several types of responses man makes to those circumstances in his environment which generate feelings of comfort, pleasure, or joy. Some of these responses may lead to heightened productivity or to such a relaxation of pressure, tension, and stress that they may be found to increase man's longevity or health. Other responses may be said to have economic value, since they motivate the human being to purchase private amenity goods or to support community investments in public amenity goods. Still other higher order responses may be psychologically valued by the individual but result in no clearly discernible behavioral manifestation, either economic or political (table 20-1).

The example makes clear the several components that are involved in any amenity-response system. The stimulus generator, which we shall call the

Model	Factors
Amenity stimulus generator (or precipitant)	Hilltop bordering on an urban park
Respondent	Family in hilltop residence
Amenity	View of park View of hill contours Sound of breezes in hilltop trees and shrubs Smell of vegetation Quiet Privacy
Amenity response	Purchase of hilltop home Frequent walks on hilltop Potential support for zoning in surrounding area
Potential disamenities	Visually insulting introduction of highway through park Visibility-obscuring smog Noise-generating traffic routes Privacy-destroying developments on hilltop

TABLE 20-1. *A Simple Amenity-Response System*

"precipitant" (the park), generates a stimulus (a view of the park) which in turn provokes a sensation having affective value (pleasure, joy) to a respondent receiving the stimulus. For the sensation to occur, a respondent having sensitivity to and value for the stimulus must be brought into effective proximity (the hilltop) to the precipitant. In the model, it seems clear that the *view*, not the park or the hilltop, is the amenity. Factors, such as smog, which can interfere with the reception of the amenity (or stimulus) or which affect the capability of the precipitant to give rise to the amenity are here called "disamenities."

In the model, the willingness of the hilltop resident to pay a higher price for his home there than for one in alternate locations can be viewed in three ways: as a measure of the intensity of his response to the amenities converging on that site; as an expression of his preference for that particular package of amenities versus others purchasable through a comparable investment; and as an indication of his ability to pay for amenity values in his environment. However, these expressions are simply indicators of his favorable response to this set of amenity stimuli and are not to be confused with the amenity response itself; viz., the feeling of pleasure evoked by the view.

Since a variety of circumstances can lead to amenity responses or can interfere with the generation and reception of amenity stimuli, an amenity-precipitant typology must include not only disamenities as well as amenities but should also cover several types of precipitants in each case (table 20-2.) In this paper, the principal focus is on natural amenities and the disamenities which threaten enjoyment of them, although from time to time other types of amenities will be brought in for illustrative purposes.

Precipitant	Amenity	Disamenity
Sociocultural	Interactive[1] Artistic Community services	Interactive[3] Esthetic "insults" Lack of community services
Physical	Man-made[2] Natural Basic environmental variables Amenity resource areas (ARAs)	Man-made[4] Natural[5]

TABLE 20-2. *Amenities and Disamenities, with Precipitants*

[1]For example, group activities.
[2]For example, architectural artifacts.
[3]"Not our kind of people."
[4]For example, junkyards.
[5]For example, smog, noise, dust.

In our view, then, the amenity value of any environmental configuration is determined by the human responses which it engenders. Thus, the concept of amenities relates to an entire system of stimulus-response variables; to the conditions which influence the occurrence of the stimuli—their intensity, extensity, and duration; and to the significance of these stimuli to human beings exposed to them.

In these terms, it becomes necessary to conceptualize the existence of both an "amenity-response system" and a "disamenity-response system." In one case, the stimulus is an amenity, while in the other it is a disamenity. Each has a systemic reference and cannot be defined outside the context of a system consisting of a precipitant, a stimulus, and a respondent.

AMENITY RESPONSES AND RESPONDENTS

Within the context of the concept of the human stimulus-response system presented above, it is important to recognize that any measurable response attribute may have a wide range of variations. People differ in their response to music and drama, just as they differ widely in their response to the eye-irritating properties of photochemical smog. Where mixed cultural and biological factors are at play, as in the case of human responses to noise, similar wide variations in response patterns are observed. The threshold of amenity or disamenity experience may therefore be hypothesized to vary widely throughout a population, as may the intensity or significance of the experience. The process of socialization to which an individual has been exposed and the values of his family, his region, and his country can be viewed as factors important to the pattern of response he exhibits toward any environmental stimuli. Consequently, an understanding of these variations in human response patterns is a key aspect of urban amenity planning and management.

Since an amenity is measured by the response it evokes from human beings, the values, standards, and tastes of a population must necessarily influence the characterization, as amenities, of those environmental variables which impinge on the life space of that population. Since human perceptions are critical to the root concept, the amenity characteristics of an environmental variable, singly or in combination, may therefore vary from population group to population group, from place to place, and from time to time.

Response curves indicating the distribution of reaction of various population groups to amenity and disamenity precipitants would be helpful for environmental planning and management. However, we have found little hard data which could be used to construct such curves at this time. The task of developing scales of human response to environmental stimuli seems to us to be a most important and challenging one.

The factor of differences in response to amenity stimuli of individuals, groups, and communities might conceivably be measured by:

1. the proportion of exposed population experiencing a response;
2. the distribution of response intensity within the respondent group; and
3. the willingness and capability of the respondent group to pay for any given level of the amenity value as a private good. . . .

AMENITIES, DISAMENITIES, AND THEIR PRECIPITANTS

As noted earlier (and as detailed in table 20-3), it is necessary to distinguish between precipitants (which extend over very many natural and man-made features) and amenities (or stimuli).

Amenity planning and management should be concerned both with the amenity values of the basic natural resources (air, water, and so on) and with those *areas* in which a special juxtaposition of resource endowments and environmental quality characteristics converge at some point in time and space to result in the quality of "being pleasant and agreeable."

The qualitative properties of any basic natural resource, such as water, may be judged, at least conceptually, by an amenity scale. Similarly, some of the public concern over air pollution is directed at the visibility-reducing characteristics of a polluted air mass, characteristics which are esthetically offensive to a substantial fraction of the population.

In contrast, the concept of an amenity resource *area* (ARA) is intended to refer to some point in time and space at which a special juxtaposition of environmental amenity precipitants occurs and which exhibits a complex pattern of amenity stimuli and response. Such a complex system is presented in table 20-3, which deals with a hypothesized area consisting of a major precipi-

Precipitant(s)	Supporting Precipitants	Function/Uses	Amenity	Respondent(s)	Potential Disamenities	Amenity Infrastructure Required[1]
Hilltop bordering on a large park	Congenial climate and weather	Site for residential or commercial and/or industrial development	Views, vistas, panoramas, perspectives of park	Residents of and visitors to hilltop and park	Fumes, odors, smog	Clear trees
	"Pure" air	Viewpoint and natural landmark for residents and visitors to the park	View of hill contours	Bird watchers, viewers, walkers, hikers, nature lovers, tourists	Excessive wind	Build roads / tramway
	Vegetation, soils, wildlife[2]	Open area; limited development and use	The delight of natural sights, sounds, and smells; breezes through trees and song of birds	Campers	Foreground interference from roofs, walls, overhead wires, cars, backyards, trees, structures, signs, poles obstructing or distorting view of park	Install sewers and drainage systems
	Unique geological formations[3]	Camping and active recreation	Natural Quiet		Visibility-obscuring smog	Eliminate disamenities where possible
			Privacy and repose		Noise-generating traffic	Minor roads to hilltop
			Natural landmark		Privacy-destroying developments elsewhere on hilltop	Hiking, riding, bicycling trails
			Communion with nature		Leveling and denuding of hilltop	Viewpoints
			Educational values		Any development as required for residential, commercial, or industrial use	Campsites
			Flora, fauna, wildlife, etc.			Stores, car parks, picnic areas
			Being able to get away from it all			
			Active recreation			

TABLE 20-3. *Amenity-Response Patterns Within an ARA*

[1] If any.
[2] For example, trees, wild flowers, birds.
[3] For example, cliffs, promontories, natural bridges.

tant, a hilltop bordered by a park. Within the area, a variety of supporting amenity precipitants are also discernible, each influencing detectable respondent groups. The population exposed to these precipitants responds to both single amenity variables and to combinations of those variables. The boundaries of any amenity resource area may be difficult to draw, but nevertheless they seem to be prescribed by the pattern of stimuli and human reactions to them exhibited within the system.

Referring back to the question of measurement, these concepts suggest that for any amenity resource area and for any level of amenity quality there is a discoverable

1. exposure group;
2. respondent group;
3. distribution of response intensity within that group;
4. economic demand (value) for the amenity;
5. cost for protecting and/or developing the amenity; and
6. economic gain or loss for protecting and/or developing the amenity.

THE AMENITY DECISION SYSTEM

Clearly, any environmental policy strategy for urban communities must be based on the fact of continued urbanization and urban growth and not simply on current situations. The massive city-building effort that yet lies ahead provides us with numerous opportunities to readjust our traditional decisional practices and undeniably would be enhanced by new sets of criteria concerned with the range of consequences to environmental quality and lifestyles—optional patterns of land use, urban design, population distribution, and other factors. One of the primary virtues of the systems approach is the new visibility it may give to these consequences.

If the approach is to be made operational, however, attention must be given to correction of the most grievous deficiencies of the present decisional system. If the information fed back into the system is confined only to economic criteria rather than being concerned with the full range of human responses to environmental quality conditions, then it seems likely that the system will behave in the future much as it has behaved in the past, at least with respect to the protection and/or development of natural amenities within our cities. The "social-accounting" movement seeks to correct this deficiency.

Also exerting pressure on the existing system is an increasing volume of citizen protestation about the current quality of the urban environment and the lack of public policy concern for our natural amenities. Throughout the country citizen groups have risen in recent years to promote changes in traditional business and public policy practices. Attacks on service station architecture, billboard jungles, esthetically offensive commercial strips, junkyards, the bulldozer rape of the cityscape, overhead utility lines, and unlandscaped freeways have been mounted by citizen groups throughout the United States and are generating new demands for the public policy system to concern itself with the amenity values of urban natural resources.

Each of these several forces is a part of the "decisional reality" within which the amenity planners will function in the future.

THE PHYSICAL CONTEXT OF AMENITY DECISIONS

It is our view that urban amenity planning and management must focus on the environmental subsystems, or "cells," which comprise the urban or metropolitan community. This follows Perloff[5] and others who argue that the urban community may be viewed as a set of interacting subsystems. We see man as an environmentally mobile creature who moves from subenvironment to subenvironment (from cell to cell) throughout the course of the day, the week, the year, and his lifetime within the metropolitan community. We have identified the following subenvironments which interface with a metropolitan community: (1) the *residential* environment, including the dwelling unit, its surrounding space, and the agglomeration of other dwelling places comprising any particular cell; (2) the *occupational* environment, including the work place and its surrounding service facilities, both interior and exterior to the structure or site within which the work is performed; (3) the *service* environment, including the institutions, organizations, commercial establishments, and other facilities which dispense commodities to urban man as he performs one or another of the functions associated with the other environmental cells; (4) the *leisure* or *recreational* environment, including all the places, facilities, and areas to which urban man transports himself for pleasure seeking, rest, and respite—both within the urban environment and outside the urban complex itself, the latter comprising part of what Perloff refers to as "the environment of the urbanite"; (5) the *commuter* environment, including all the pathways followed by the urbanite in transporting himself from his residential environment to other environments within the metropolitan complex and to places such as leisure or recreational areas outside the metropolitan complex itself; and (6) the *background* environment. Each subenvironment is a "setting" for people's lives. The objective of environmental planning and management must be to enhance each of these settings, to bring out and heighten—not to submerge—the character of each subenvironment. The challenge is to produce delight in the whole fabric of the entire metropolitan landscape not merely to pick out the highlights in the fabric.

The available literature suggests that the intensity and extensity of amenity responses within an urban population vary as a function of the subenvironment in which the response is measured. Thus, Wilson suggests that people place more value on the environmental quality of their immediate neighborhood than on environmental quality variables which occur at the scale of the entire community.[6] Since his study focused on two comparatively small communities, these findings may be inapplicable to the giant metropolis; they nevertheless suggest the relevance (1) of examining the significance of amenities as a function of the subenvironment in which they occur and the functions which that subenvironment is to serve and (2) of manipulating environmental variables on the scale of the subenvironment rather than of the whole city in any effort to increase its livability for most people.

A MANAGEMENT SYSTEM FOR URBAN NATURAL AMENITIES

As suggested above, the amenity planner/manager must concern himself with certain key factors: the amenity precipitants, the pattern of amenity responses, the subenvironments in which they occur, and the decisional system within which amenity decisions are made.

The information collected and processed by the planner must meet more than some abstract standard of need; it must conform to the requirements of the decisional system in which the planner resides and the appetite of that system for various kinds and quantities of information.

We are currently engaged in a study of decision chains which impinge on environmental quality in several major sections of Southern California. One aspect of that study has been the decision chain through which proposals are processed for the subdivision of raw land, the subsequent development of physical facilities, and other improvements on the land. Results to date suggest that the people within the system have failed to perceive the "systemic" nature of their actions and the broad spectrum of environmental goals to which they might address themselves. Individually, they judge the quality of their decisions in terms of a very limited set of criteria—such as structural safety—and do not customarily concern themselves with other qualitative considerations, which they see as the function of "other professionals" or "other departments."

In view of the low amenity value of residential developments within Los Angeles County, the study suggests that something more is necessary than the insertion of new criteria into the system. If natural amenities are to receive attention and if the competitive processes of our present decisional system are to act rationally with respect to urban amenities, then it may be necessary to build professional "amenity advocates" into the system. For example, Great Britain utilizes amenity planners whose professional task is to protect and/or develop amenities within the geographic zone of their concern. A similar step may be necessary in the United States if amenities are to receive the attention they deserve.

Operationally, it may be useful to adopt such practices as the conduct of amenity precipitant inventories, amenity demand surveys, attitudinal and opinion surveys of selected groups within the urban population, and research pointed at the development of predictive criteria appropriate for use by amenity planners and decision makers.

INVENTORY OF NATURAL AMENITY PRECIPITANTS

Before beginning any management system for urban natural amenities it is necessary to obtain information on the features that now exist in the urban or metropolitan community that may be considered potential amenities—in short, the nature, characteristics, and location of the amenity precipitants.

Because natural amenity precipitants are place bound (since they are a function of the natural environment) and are not ubiquitous in the metropolitan community, and because they perform different functions and evoke different human responses depending on their location within the urban community, it would be helpful to inventory them for various subunits of the whole. Two localized differentiations should be considered: (1) within each of the subenvironments noted earlier and (2) within different geographic settings or scales; e.g., at the scale of the home, neighborhood, community, county, and metropolitan region.

That the function of natural amenity precipitants varies at different geographic scales is most clearly seen in the case of open space. Table 20-4 illustrates various types of open space amenity precipitants typically found at various geographical scales within a metropolitan region.

The open spaces under (1) are intensively used man-made spaces; those under (2a) and (2b) and some of those under (3) are semideveloped areas; and part of those under (3) and practically all of those listed under (4) are basically natural areas and features.

In short, while open space at the street scale is uniquely man-made, regional open space is the opposite; you can take it only the way it comes and that is the chief justification for its preservation. Therefore, it is not possible to specify standards for open space at the regional level. Some regions—e.g., New York, San Francisco, and Los Angeles—have a great variety of natural open spaces at the regional level; in Washington and Philadelphia, nature was somewhat less generous; Indianapolis and the Dallas-Fort Worth area, to cite but two examples, will have to be more inventive.

The open space immediately associated with homes and work places—i.e., at the street scale—is experienced more than all other open space. This is open space in microcosm. It is with us day in and day out. This dominance suggests that it has an impact on the role of other levels of open space. Open space at the street scale is also unique because it is the most man-made, both in its quantity and design. Nature can be of some help here—for instance, a few trees in a subdivision may save it from barrenness, or a location on a hillside certainly has many benefits—but for the most part street-scale urban open space is a creation of man. In particular, it is the creation of our architects, urban designers, and city planners, working within the framework and limitations of municipal zoning and subdivision regulations, and thus it poses a challenge to these specialists.

AMENITY DEMAND CURVES

As Parr and others have suggested,[7] we need to plot the "behavioral topographies" associated with environmental quality variables, both singly and in the aggregate. More objective information is needed on how people actually respond to amenity and disamenity precipitants within the urban community. Can research instruments be developed and utilized by planners to detect changing response patterns? Can predictive criteria be developed by which planners may more precisely determine amenity demand levels, perhaps through inspection of such readily obtainable information as discretionary income levels?

Scale or Level	Examples of Open Space Amenity Resources (land)	(water)
1. Street scale		
a. Building site	Yards; courts; gardens (i.e., sites less buildings)	
b. Group of buildings	Rights-of-way, streets, pedestrian ways, piazzas, plazas, residential commons, tot lots	
2. Community		
a. Neighborhood	School grounds; playgrounds; small parks (up to 10 ac); hillsides; shopping centers; squares	Small lakes (natural or man-made), ponds, streams, lagoons
b. Municipality	Parks up to 100 ac, play fields; civic center and other public squares; recreation roads and bicycling, riding, and hiking trails	
3. County	Mountain and valley floor parks—100–1,000 ac; shore line parks; streamside preserves; golf courses; minor conservation areas (flood plains, watersheds, wild flower / bird / game preserves); scenic roads (driving, hiking, etc,); reservoir parks	Large lakes, rivers, bays, inlets, water conservation reservoirs, islands
4. Metropolitan region	Mountain and valley floor parks over 1,000 ac; wilderness areas; large conservation areas; private farms, greenbelts, woodland and other land on the urban fringe; coastlines and seacoasts; mountain ranges; milksheds; large institutional open spaces (e.g., university, college, hospital, sports arena, music center); scenic highways; historic natural landmarks	Major water bodies; e.g., oceans, great rivers, major lakes; marine parks; harbors; islands; tidelands; marshland

TABLE 20-4. *Classification of Urban Open Space Amenity Resources by Geographic Scale*
Source: Adapted from Stanley B. Tankel, "The Importance of Open Space in the Urban Pattern," in Lowdon Wingo, Jr., ed., *Cities and Space: The Future of Use of Urban Land* (Johns Hopkins Press for Resources for the Future, 1963), p. 61, tab. 1.

We believe that it is possible to accomplish all this, although a good deal of hard work will have to be done before these planning tools will become available. Specific targets seem appropriate for such an effort.

Human Response Curves

These may be thought of as human value or response scales. They should reveal the fraction of the population which responds to any environmental quality variable or aggregation of such variables (i.e., amenity resources area); the social, economic, and other characteristics of that population fraction; and the distribution of response type and intensity within the respondent group. For example, a *disamenity-amenity* response scale might be constructed for a single environmental quality variable, such as the loading of suspended particulate matter in a cubic meter of air. At the disamenity end of the scale, human respiratory discomfort and ill health would be measured by a particular range of particulate loadings for a specified respondent group. By relating such loadings to ambient visibility conditions, still further responses could be measured, in terms of human values toward optional conditions of visibility (10, 5, or 3 miles, and so on). Through application of paired-comparison methods and other techniques, the utility function of responses to optional visibility conditions might be predicted for specific respondent groups. The intensity of public support for such specific environmental improvement measures as billboard removal, freeway landscaping, protection of primitive areas, and so on might be measured by these techniques and fitted into the response scales.

Economic Demand Criteria

As a special aspect of human responses to amenities, the economic behavior of urban populations with respect to amenity values deserves much more study. It seems clear that a substantial fraction of the public is willing to pay for amenity values as private goods and that substantial citizen support exists for public programs of investment in protecting amenity values and amenity resource areas. Nevertheless, at present it is difficult to compose precise statements that have predictive value to planners and managers in the public and private sector. For example, how much are people willing to pay to protect views now marred by outdoor advertising and overhead utility lines? Of what value to the purchasers in a subdivision is the protection of an adjacent open area, a hiking and riding trail, or a landscaped traffic collector route? Without new or unusual systems of public intervention into the private economic marketplace, the development of answers to these and similar questions would contribute much toward a more rational and socially responsible system of urban amenity management. Gutheim has pointed out:

> In housing economics we have been able to attribute specific values to apartments with balconies, houses with fireplaces, and other design features having little to do with the raw facts of space and structure but much to do with amenity. We know that certain tenants will pay more for these features, and we know how much more they will pay. We also know that location has a specific value, one not always attributable to economic factors, but frequently linked to design. Here we tread more uncertainly; but it should be possible, for example, to compare a house in Georgetown with an identical house in the adjoining community of Foggy Bottom, and to disentangle what parts of the extra value of the Georgetown house are due to its location in a community with definite boundaries, quiet streets, shade trees, ample gardens, historical associations and architectural homogeneity, and what parts are due to its location in a community of high-income families, high property values and accessibility. We can also determine just which families will pay these premiums. Studies of aesthetic value can be usefully pursued at the point of decision when families move in or out, when they buy or sell. They should have a priority second only to experiments and demonstrations in the design of the urban environment itself.[8]

RESEARCH INTO DECISION-MAKING CRITERIA

Of course, the development of amenity-precipitant inventories, measurement scales, response curves, and predictive economic criteria will not alone provide an improvement in amenity abundance and distribution which many now demand. For such an improvement we must look also at our traditional approach to the "unit" amenity decision. How have we traditionally decided on the allocation of land among competing user groups? How valid are these criteria in the modern urban community?

It is probable that much of the erosion in the amenity value of our urban communities has been produced by our orientation to goals related to short-term economic gains and losses. Given a tidal flat having potential for development either as a small-boat marina and waterfront residential development or as a petrochemical complex, we often retreat into a "parochial" cost-benefit analysis. If the greatest economic gain accrues to the petrochemical development, we argue with scientific pride that this is the "preferred" pattern of development. But is this really so?

In John Steinbeck's famous and still unspoiled Monterey-Salinas Valley in California, a recent public conflict focused on this very question. The Humboldt Oil Company desired to locate a major petroleum refinery at Moss Landing, which is located on a small bay at the upper northwestern end of the valley. Construction of the refinery would have resulted in a large economic gain to a limited group of landowners and might have presaged the migration of heavy industry into the valley. In terms of the typical complex of petrochemical establishments which frequently surrounds refineries, one can predict that construction of the refinery might well have resulted in an enlarged pattern of industrial development throughout the area. Escalating land values, an expanded tax base, enlarged employment opportunities, and a higher level of income for the valley would have been the inevitable result. However, this pattern of development would have destroyed one of the last remaining unpolluted airsheds in California and one of the most scenically rich resources of the entire state. The valley, and the Monterey Peninsula to which it is linked, are scenic favorites of many Californians residing hundreds of miles from the site. The area has value to these casual users, yet the dollars they leave behind after their infrequent visits probably amount to a sum much smaller than the possible economic gains from industrial, commercial, and intensive residential development of the area. If this area is finally developed, Californians, as well as tourists from the rest of the United States, will have lost a precious resource whose social value simply cannot be measured on an economic scale.

This case suggests that a community of interest may be identified and measurable with respect to any given amenity resource area and that the discoverable community may include nonresidents as well as residents, and casual visitors as well as habitual and frequent nonresident visitors; that, in some cases, the community may even include persons whose life space is touched by the amenity even though they remain physically remote from it and who would bemoan their loss although they never have and never will, personally and directly, experience it (in short, they represent an "option demand").

In the Moss Landing case, there was a clear need for examination of the broad range of potential costs, benefits, and optional solutions for a variety of groups. Excluding the consideration that this location had an undisputed amenity value for a large group of Californians, how many other sites within the state were appropriate for a refinery complex, and at what incremental costs or benefits? Given the loss of this amenity area, what could be done to replace it? What impact would the loss have on the "quality of lives" of the respondent groups?

These considerations suggest to us that the following dictum might be useful to environmental planners and managers: *Given equivalence in the economic potential of resource areas competing for development, such development should occur last in that area which exhibits the greatest amenity potential and in which the projected pattern of development would most adversely affect the area's amenity potential.*

Assuming that adequate inventories of potential amenity resource areas exist, the adoption of such a precept might permit incremental decision making without a gross dysfunction to amenity values.

Similarly, we suggest that a range of information is available to amenity planners, managers, and decision makers that can help with respect to the two broad clusters of decisional problems they face: (1) those dealing with public investments and (2) those concerned with the public regulation of environmental quality and/or the allocation of amenity resources among competing

Public Investment Decisions	**Allocative and Regulatory Decisions**
I. Cost of acquiring, developing, and/or protecting the ARA in question A. Present (T^1) B. Future (T^n)	I. Reproducibility of ARA A. Cost of ARA B. Cost of reproducing ARA at another location (ARA)
II. Cost of operating the ARA, T^1 to T^n	II. Nonamenity use demands for ARA
III. Size of potential respondent group A. Present (T^1) B. Future (T^n)	III. Availability of alternative sites for nonamenity uses A. Cost of ARA site B. Cost of alternative sites
IV. Expected exposure duration frequency distribution of potential respondent group	IV. Size of ARA potential respondent group A. Present (T^1) B. Future (T^n)
V. Capital costs per respondent and per respondent exposure (T^1) to (T^n)	V. Several of the items under Public Investment Decisions also relevant here
VI. Operating costs per respondent and per respondent exposure (T^1 to T^n)	
VII. Comparative value of ARA to respondent group	
VIII. Distribution of economic valuation of ARA, per unit of exposure, within respondent group	
IX. Distribution of ability to pay within respondent group	
X. Absolute cost of developing and operating ARA	

TABLE 20-5. *Information for Decision Making in ARA Planning and Management*
Note: The table represents only a partial listing.

users. Although it does not lead to any mathematical model appropriate for judging the final end-state decision, such information would expand our understanding of some of the consequences of our decisions. (See table 20-5 for a preliminary classification.)

A more rational and socially rewarding system for the planning and management of urban amenities is sorely needed. The main intention of this paper is to emphasize that the development of such a system may be promoted through increased attention to the nature, functions, and systemic qualities of amenities.

NOTES

1. McNamara, as quoted in "A Changing City: Government," *Progressive Architecture,* August 1967, p. 123.
2. Aaron Quinn Sartain et al., *Understanding Human Behavior* (New York: McGraw-Hill, 1958), p. 81.
3. A. H. Maslow, *Motivation and Personality* (New York: Harper, 1964).
4. Frank Stead, "Levels of Environmental Health," *American Journal of Public Health* 50, no. 3 (1960).
5. Harvey S. Perloff, ed., *The Quality of the Urban Environment* (Washington, D.C.: Resources for the Future, 1969), ch. 1.
6. Robert L. Wilson, "Livability of the City: Attitudes and Urban Development," in F. Stuart Chapin, Jr., and Shirley F. Weiss, eds., *Urban Growth Dynamics* (New York: Wiley, 1962).
7. H. E. Parr, "Mind and Milieu," *Sociological Inquiry* 33 (winter 1963); Raymond C. Studer and David Stea, "Architectural Programming, Environmental Design, and Human Behavior," *Journal of Social Issues* 22, no. 4 (1966).
8. Frederick Gutheim, "Urban Space and Urban Design," in Lowdon Wingo, Jr., ed., *Cities and Space: The Future Use of Urban Land* (Baltimore: Johns Hopkins Press for Resources for the Future, 1963), p. 130.

CHAPTER 21

PLANNING FOR CONSERVATION AND DEVELOPMENT—AN EXERCISE IN THE PROCESS OF DECISION MAKING

Patrick E. McCarthy
Michael Dower

Reconciling recreation/leisure development and conservation depends on skillful selection of goals and values, both public and private. Using Ireland's Donegal County as a setting, Patrick McCarthy and Michael Dower here describe a process designed to help gather material needed for decision making when considering local recreation amenities.

The project from which this article springs is based in Ireland. But we believe it has a much wider significance as a contribution to a theme of growing moment in every western country: the development of tourism and leisure opportunities, coupled with the conservation of natural resources.

Almost every country is seeing dramatic growth and change in the pattern of leisure and recreation among its own people. Almost every country is seeking to increase the number of visitors from abroad. At the same time, country after country is showing more and more active concern with the conservation of its scenic and cultural heritage, a heritage threatened not only by the general pace of development but notably by the very leisure, tourism, and recreation for which it is the prime resource.

The paradox and link between development and conservation, between visitors and resources, between access and beauty, are seen very clearly in both North America and Europe. In the United States, growing controversy centers on the amount and type of recreation facility which should be provided in the national parks. In Britain, the National Park Authorities struggle to keep in balance their two objects, the protection of natural beauty and the encouragement of public access.

The struggle for the countryside, in fact, is becoming everywhere more complex. The tourist, the farmer, the sportsman, and the resident himself—all claim title to its use. Each has his own activity for which he can make a good case. Each, if given the chance, would exclude one or all of the others.

In this circumstance, the emotion of a Ruskin or William Morris, even the

---

Reprinted from the *Journal of the Town Planning Institute* 53, no. 3 (March 1967): 99–105, by permission of the Royal Town Planning Institute and the authors.

Note: The views expressed in this article are those of the authors and do not necessarily represent those of the United Nations.

insight of a Thoreau, are not enough. The system of [making] decisions must match the new complexity and scale of pressures. Who shall determine the manner and method? In the Western world, it is not clear that this can be done by either government alone or private enterprise alone. Each has a large but not a complete stake.

Thus much of the resources, both of land and of enterprise, lies in private hands. But large-scale private development may demand public investment in support services on the same large scale. One thousand new hotel beds may imply heavy public cost in new water, sewerage, and road systems and may place heavy new pressures upon beaches and park lands which the public bodies maintain. Yet the public authority may feel that these costs and pressures are not balanced by the benefits of new income for its rate payers.

Reconciling development and conservation thus depends upon a skillful sorting out of goals and values, both public and private. The tool increasingly used in many countries to do this is the physical development or land use plan. But the nature of this plan is critical. Too often it is a rigid statement of views by the public authority, reflecting *its* goals only, responsive neither to the legitimate values of the private landowner or the citizen nor to the fact of rapid change and wide range of opportunity.

As we see it, a planning system concerned to reconcile development and conservation must have a framework to bring together all parties, public and private, concerned with both themes. Notably, this must include the public bodies that are responsible for spending public money and for protecting public values such as the scenic heritage; the commercial interests whose concern is to exploit resources and promote development; and the private groups who seek to protect private rights or minority values. This bringing together of people demands [both] a common language or understanding of problems and [also] a process for resolving differences and making decisions.

The planning system must also be flexible in time and in scale. There is no absolute or all-time best use of a resource or a piece of land. The pattern of demand changes over the years. A beach once used only by local people may prove, with changing access patterns, to be a regional asset of the first importance. It must be possible to make and remake decisions—but to do so within a system that shows up clearly the consequences of considered changes by measuring them against standards of performance and in terms of benefit and cost. It was the object of the Irish project to formulate such a system.

THE PROJECT IN IRELAND

Ireland has a magnificent heritage of scenery, historic sites, and wildlife —a heritage virtually unaffected by industrialization. With a population that has fallen from 9 million in 1840 to about 3 million now, it has not suffered the pressures of despoilation which have afflicted both America and much of Europe. But the Irish government is keen to boost income from tourism as part of its general drive to improve Ireland's economy. They know that their main tourist asset is the scenic and cultural heritage; and they realize that this heritage must be protected as development grows.

To this end, the government in 1963 passed the Local Government (Planning and Development) Act, which for the first time required local authorities in Ireland to prepare development plans. To assist the authorities in carrying out this new and unfamiliar function, the minister for local government set up the National Institute for Physical Planning and Construction Research. This institute is assisted by experts supplied by the United Nations Special Fund. One of the first projects was the launching of a model amenity-tourism study for the beautiful county of Donegal ... by a team including officers of the National Institute and of Donegal County Council ... [and the present authors] as United Nations advisers.

The object of the Donegal exercise was not so much to produce a plan for the county as to create a thought process which could be pursued by all the local planning authorities in Ireland. These authorities are multipurpose bodies, responsible *inter alia* for the roads, water and sewerage services, and public housing in their areas. The planning function is new to them, and very few of them have a qualified planning staff. It was therefore necessary to create a thought process which could be used at once by small and untrained staffs but which could grow in sophistication as their information and expertise increased.

At the same time, Ireland has many other bodies, public and private, involved in her general process of development; a rapidly growing tourist industry based almost wholly upon private enterprise but assisted by a central Tourist Board; and a small number of amenity and other heritage-protecting bodies [that] are able and willing to help the conservation effort. It was therefore vital to involve them not only in the plan-making process but also in whatever system of decision making was to be proposed.

THE THOUGHT PROCESS

After some trial and error, a simple six-step thought process was evolved on these lines:

1. survey of amenity and tourism resources;
2. survey of client groups;
3. measurement of capacity;
4. statement of options;
5. amenity budget;
6. policy implications.

The first two steps are traditional surveys carried out by the planning staff with information and help from other bodies. That of resources covers a fairly wide range, including the broad patterns of land use and landscape character; the main scenic resources; the potential for shooting, fishing, hill walking, pony trekking, and water sports; man-made recreational facilities such as golf courses; the cultural, historic, and scientific heritage; communications; and the accommodation and services which the county could offer to the tourist. The only unfamiliar thing here was the use of a comprehensive survey data sheet showing all the resource items for which field survey was needed on a standard sheet which could be readily used as an office record.

The form of the survey of client groups was dictated by the material available, which was more national than local in application. It did permit reasonably accurate estimates of the numbers of visitors in each of several national groups coming to the county; the season in which they came; their length of stay and expenditure. Information on the occupancy of hotels and other accommodation permitted a rough estimate of where the visitors stayed within the county. The numbers of local people present and likely to be using leisure resources was also calculated.

CAPACITY—THE KEY

The third step in the thought process is the critical one. When the resources and the clients have been surveyed, one must find a way to compare them directly with each other, in order

a. to see how far the resources are, or are not, adequate for the present use of the clients;
b. to judge what surplus resources there are which might entertain or serve more people and what new resources would be needed if more people came; and
c. to insure that the resources are not damaged by an excessive growth in the number and activity of people.

The last point is critical when one is dealing with conservation *and* development. On the one hand, amenity resources must be protected: on the other, tourism and recreation must be encouraged. A way must be found to balance goals of conservation with goals of development.

The key to this problem is the idea of capacity. Each resource—hotels, beaches, golf courses, cafés, water supplies, roads, and so on—has a measurable capacity in terms of people. The capacity of each resource must be kept in balance with the people using it. If the people exceed the capacity, the result may be discomfort, danger, or damage to the resource.

The theme, in fact, is not unlike the Buchanan formula for towns—that a given area of countryside has a measurable capacity to take people: this capacity cannot be exceeded without congestion and damage to the resources unless the capacity is increased by physical works. Such works might include provision of access to beaches or improved antipollution measures on reservoirs used for sport.

In order to measure capacity, and so to compare resources and clients directly, we pursued a simple sequence of thought. First, we divided the county into "planning areas," each of a size such that the people living within or visiting it could be expected to have the bulk of their activity and, hence, of their demand upon resources within that area. This was necessary because the measurement of capacity cannot usefully be done at county scale: a beach at one end of Donegal could not be regarded as useful to a tourist fifty miles away at the other end of the county.

Then we identified a "resource base"; i.e., those resources which were critical to the development of tourism and recreation. Ten resource items were chosen: night accommodation (noncasual); night accommodation (casual); day resources; wet-weather facilities; meal facilities; evening facilities; water supply; sewerage; road capacity; and public transport. These explain themselves except for the two types of night accommodation. "Casual" includes caravan and campsites plus youth hostels, since these tend to serve a different type of visitor [than] the "noncasual" (hotel, guest house, and other types).

We then assessed the "existing capacity" of the surveyed resource in each of the ten categories for each planning area. This was a straightforward matter for most categories, the basis being the beds or bed spaces in night accommodation; seats in wet-weather, meal, and evening facilities, and in public transport; gallons a day in water supply and sewerage schemes; and passenger car units per day of "tolerable capacity" on main roads, estimated on formulas similar to those in the *U.S. Highway Manual.* The one category on which existing capacity was not so readily estimated was day resources. This includes natural resources such as beaches and mountains; items of heritage such as historic sites and nature reserves; as well as man-made day facilities such as golf courses. Day resources are thus the meeting point of conservation and development. For them, the estimate of capacity must serve not only to show how much of the resource is needed by a given number of people but also how many people the resource can take without physical or ecological damage to the resource and without change to the character which people expect the area to have—unless that change is deliberate.

CAPACITY OF DAY RESOURCES

We therefore made a provisional estimate (informed guess, if you like) of the capacity of each type of day resource to take people at any one time in the context of Donegal. This is a quiet and remote county with slim resources. The county council cannot devote much manpower or money to maintenance: nor do visitors expect to find Coney Island or Brighton densities on the beaches. The capacity estimates were therefore set at a level calculated to minimize the risk of physical or ecological damage and to match the sense of quietness and remoteness which people might seek in Donegal.

The estimates of notional capacity include low basic marks for all enclosed rural land (5 people per square mile), rough or hill land (1 person per square mile), coast and lake shore (40 people per mile), plus additional marks for specific activities such as shooting, fishing, and hill walking or for special qualities of attraction and accessibility. To give one example, an attractive and accessible beach, one mile long, might be marked as having the following capacity:

Basic mark for coast	40 persons
Attractive and accessible coast	+200
Beach	+200
	440 persons

This total estimated capacity of 440 persons to the mile of beach can be used as a guide to the number of people who might be happily occupied on the beach without crowding; to the level of human use beyond which physical or ecological damage might occur to the beach or its surroundings; and to the scale of roads, [parking lots], etc., which would go with or provide access to the beach.

The next step is to estimate the demand that the people present in each planning area at any one time place upon the resources which make up the resource base of that area. To do this, we split the people into three main groups, each with a different pattern of demand upon resources: (a) night visitors, (b) day visitors, and (c) local people. so: [W]e then estimated what that demand might be. Again, for some resources this was easy. For example, for water supply the following basic formula was well established in the county:

$$\text{Demand for water} = 70a + 10b + 100c \text{ [gal./day]}$$

i.e., 70 gallons a day would be needed for each night visitor present, 10 for each day visitor, 100 for each local resident (including industrial and agricultural as well as domestic consumption).

But for some resources, new formulas had to be evolved. Thus we estimated the demand for day resources as follows:

$$\text{Demand for day resources} = \frac{5}{4}\left(a+b+\frac{c}{4}\right) \text{ people-units}$$

i.e., the total day resources should be sufficient to entertain all the night visitors, all the day visitors, and up to one-quarter of the local population (e.g., children on holiday) at any one time, *plus* a one-quater margin to allow for a bad match between the types of resource available and the desire of people to use them.

These calculations of demand for each resource allowed us to express a "necessary capacity" for these resources arising from a given number and mix of clients. This necessary capacity could then be directly compared with the existing capacity to show how far that existing capacity was adequate for present demand or what surpluses or shortfalls there might be.

A graphic example of this comparison is given in figure 21-1, which shows the existing capacity of one resource category, day resources, compared with the use of those resources by clients at present. Each circle refers to one planning area. Several striking things at once emerge:

a. the strong dominance of the coastal areas in existing resource capacity (as shown in most cases by the outer circles);
b. the uneven pattern of use or demand upon these resources, strongest in the east of the county (as shown by the three-part circles);
c. the large part which the local population plays in this demand (as shown by the white part of the three-part circles);

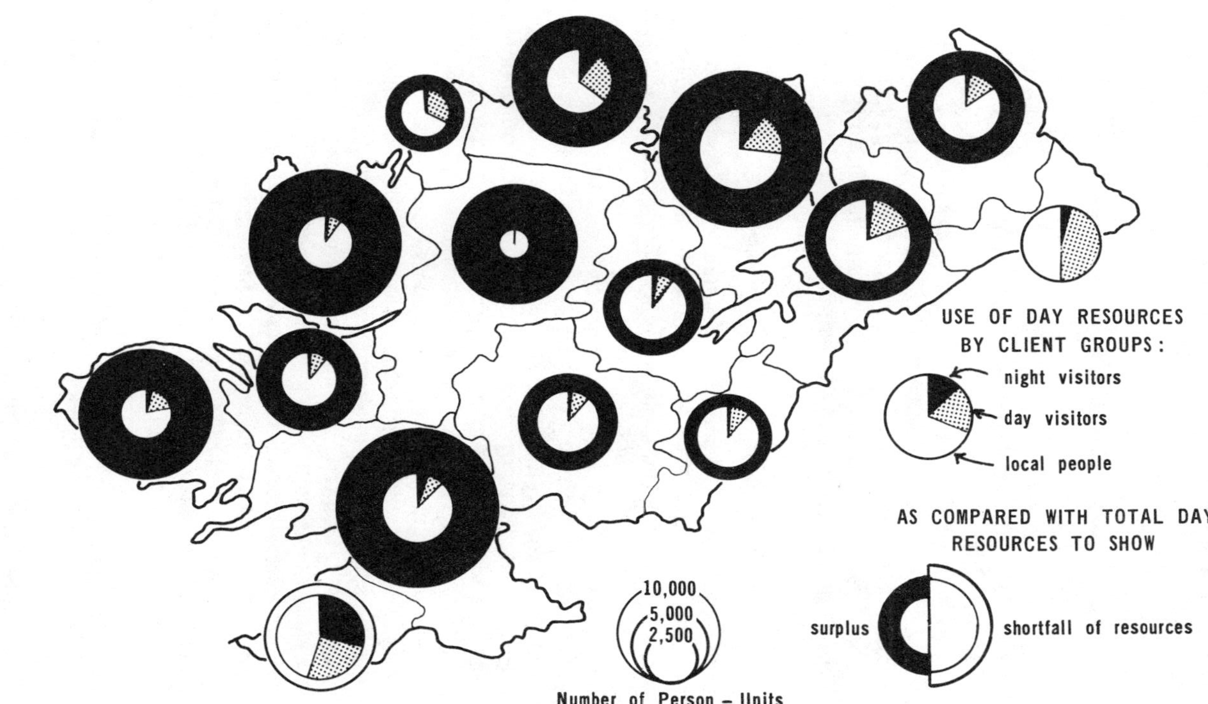

FIGURE 21-1. *Existing Capacity of Day Resources Compared with Actual Use*

d. the fact that two planning areas at the northeast and southwest corners of the county have a shortfall in resource capacity; i.e., demand is already above the level estimated as consistent with character and avoidance of damage. This is confirmed by actual experience in these areas;
e. all the other planning areas have a (generally handsome) surplus of day resources not now used.

In a county of such marked scenic and cultural heritage, known for its beauty and quietness, the presence of this surplus of day resources (largely, in fact, natural resources) is the main reassurance that further development can be made compatible with conservation. If the existing capacity were already exhausted (as may well be the case in large parts of, say, the Lake District National Park in Britain), one would know that further development could not take place without *either* accepting overuse and, hence, damage to the natural resources *or* changing the character of the county by the introduction of man-made day resources such as holiday camps.

STATEMENT OF OPTIONS

The estimates of capacity, no longer merely qualitative but based on direct and refinable measurements, thus become the ground for the consideration of future policy. This is approached, as the fourth main step in the thought process, by the statement of options.

No county has a single, all-time, obvious course of development. There are always choices, each reflecting a different set of goals or values. To weigh the choices against each other, it is necessary to pose them as distinct options. Each option is a simplified goal or aim, different from the other options. This does not mean that only one goal or aim can be pursued at the same time or that one option could not complement or follow the other. It is simply a method of showing the implications of various possible policies in a way such that one can judge their relative merits and see whether they could be usefully applied together, in sequence or as alternatives.

Each option must take into account both development and conservation. This is done by arguing straight on from the earlier steps in the thought process, with its emphasis on clients and resources. Each option has an element of both, by answering two questions: (a) How might a group, or groups, of clients grow or change? and (b) If so, how might their growth or change be disposed to have the best impact on resources? Each option is based, in fact, upon either (1) a notional change in client groups and their effect on resources or (2) a notional change in impact on resources and its implications for change in client groups. Each option chosen must be relevant and reasonable for the county, based upon appraisal of its resources and of its present or potential clients.

In the Donegal exercise, the options chosen for analysis were:

1. An increase in "holiday-makers"; i.e., those staying for the bulk of their

holiday at one place in the county, made up in terms of national groups and types of people according to the share which the county might reasonably expect of the increases in holiday-makers foreseen by the Irish Tourist Board.

2. An increase in "tourists"; i.e., those moving through or within the county on tour, with their make-up estimated as for holiday-makers but distinguished from holiday-makers because of their different pattern of pressure on resources. Both tourists and holiday-makers fall within the general group of night visitors.
3. An increase in day visitors from outside the county, mostly coming across the international border from Northern Ireland.
4. An increase in all three groups at the same time. (No increase in the other main client group, local population, was projected in Donegal at this stage because the other sections of the development plan were not at that time available.)

The "client mix" implied by each option was based on the projection of estimates up to 1985. But this date was not taken as binding for the reason that one element of choice, or of response to circumstances, will be to go faster or slower than a given projection. We decided it was more realistic to talk about units of clients, growth by one unit being a notional target, than to set a number-at-a-given-date as a target.

Each option became expressed as an increase in clients of a given mix, by units of a given size. Thus the unit in the first option might be 1,000 persons, all holiday-makers: that for the fourth option might also be 1,000 persons of which 500 would be holiday-makers, 200 tourists, 300 day visitors. No limit was placed on the speed of development; and each option was taken, for purpose of analysis, up to the point where all the day resources (here taken as the major limiting factor, for reasons stated above) would be fully used.

Once each option was expressed as a client mix in stated units, the impact of each such unit upon resources could be assessed. It was easy to calculate how much of each resource in the resource base would be required by each unit in that mix, using the formulas for necessary capacity described earlier. This new necessary capacity could then be compared with the existing capacity to see what new shortfalls were created and what surplus capacity remained.

AMENITY BUDGET

Most of the material was thus ready for the final stage in the analysis, the preparation of the amenity budget. This was seen not only as a straight capital budget in the traditional sense, with financial costs and benefits set out and compared, but also as a chance to take stock of nonfinancial resources, notably those limited and perishable natural resources which formed the character and prime asset of the county. The amenity budget is in fact the point at which all the foregoing analysis crystallizes into a single statement.

The basic tool used for this purpose was a budget diagram, of which figure

CLOGHANEELY OPTION 1 – Increase in Night Visitors

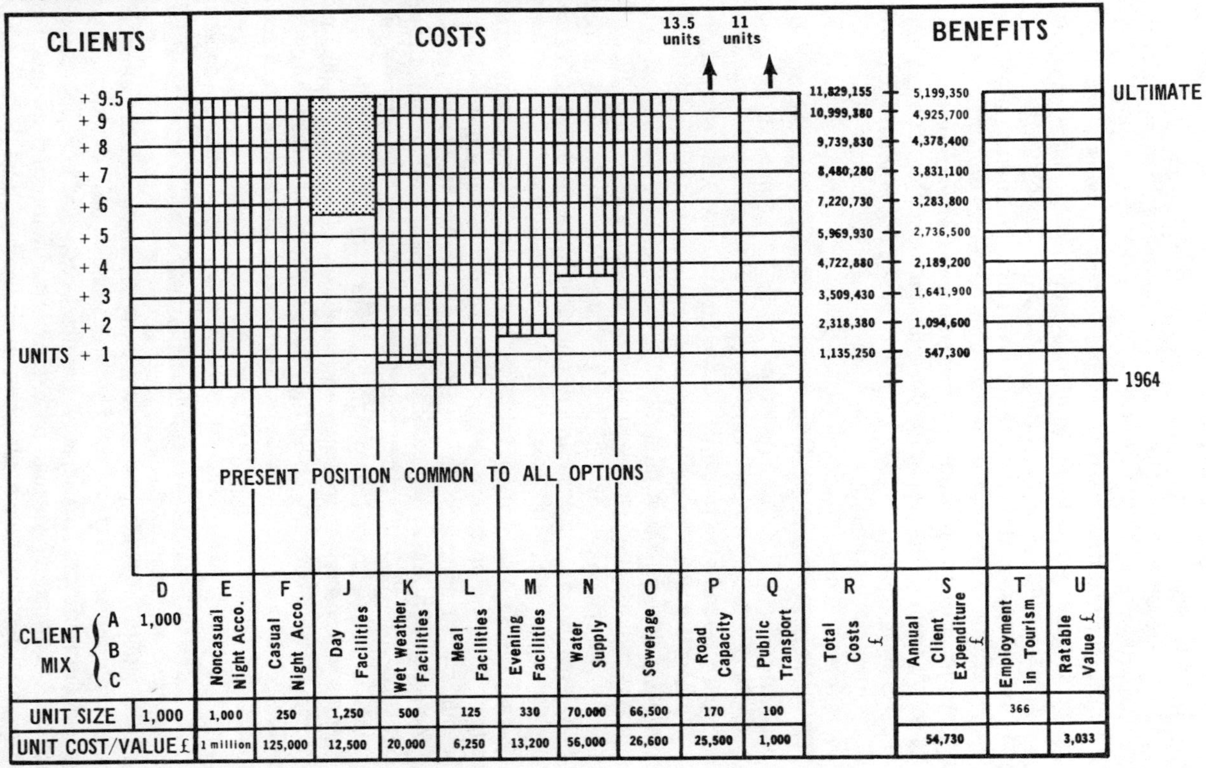

CLIENTS | COSTS | BENEFITS

13.5 units ↑ (P) 11 units ↑ (Q)

UNITS	R Total Costs £	S Annual Client Expenditure £	
+ 9.5	11,829,155	5,199,350	ULTIMATE
+ 9	10,999,380	4,925,700	
+ 8	9,739,830	4,378,400	
+ 7	8,480,280	3,831,100	
+ 6	7,220,730	3,283,800	
+ 5	5,969,930	2,736,500	
+ 4	4,722,880	2,189,200	
+ 3	3,509,430	1,641,900	
+ 2	2,318,380	1,094,600	
+ 1	1,135,250	547,300	
			1964

PRESENT POSITION COMMON TO ALL OPTIONS

	D	E	F	J	K	L	M	N	O	P	Q	R	S	T	U
CLIENT MIX { A B C	1,000	Noncasual Night Acco.	Casual Night Acco.	Day Facilities	Wet Weather Facilities	Meal Facilities	Evening Facilities	Water Supply	Sewerage	Road Capacity	Public Transport	Total Costs £	Annual Client Expenditure £	Employment in Tourism	Ratable Value £
UNIT SIZE	1,000	1,000	250	1,250	500	125	330	70,000	66,500	170	100			366	
UNIT COST/VALUE £		1 million	125,000	12,500	20,000	6,250	13,200	56,000	26,600	25,500	1,000		54,730		3,033

FIGURE 21-2. *Budget Summary*

21-2 is an example. It shows the impact of option 1 (increase in the night visitors) upon the resources of one planning area in Donegal. The main elements in it are as follows:

1. the total number of clients present in 1964, represented by column D up to the first strong horizontal line;
2. ten columns, from E to Q, representing the resource base;
3. the present use of these resources, shown by the strong horizontal line marked 1964, which is also the base line for the options;
4. the upward extension of column D, showing the possible future growth of clients by units of 1,000 up to the line labeled "ultimate," which represents the full use of day resources in column J;
5. the boxes at the base of the diagram, show[ing] the amount of each resource which is needed by each unit of 1,000 clients and also the cost of providing the unit of resource, if this is necessary;
6. the white columns above the 1964 line in columns J to Q, show[ing] the surplus existing capacity in these resources, scaled by the unit size mentioned above;
7. thus the horizontal line opposite each unit number (+1, +2, etc.), show[ing] the extent to which each unit of increase in clients will eat into surplus resources (white columns) or create shortfalls (vertical hatching). These shortfalls represent the need for new investment, assessed according to the unit costs shown below. (The upper part of column J is shown hatched because beyond a certain point, investment —e.g., in access roads—is needed to realize the capacity of the day resources.
8. The combined costs of making good all shortfalls can then be calculated for each unit of increase in clients. These combined costs are shown in column R.
9. These total costs can then be compared with the benefits shown in columns S, T and U, which represent:
   - S Total client expenditure. This is the estimated annual expenditure represented by each unit of clients in column D.
   - T Employment in tourism. This is an estimate of the number of people directly employed in tourism during the summer as a result of the presence of each unit of clients in column D.
   - U Ratable value. This is an estimate of the total ratable value of properties wholly used for tourism by each unit of clients in column D. It is based upon average ratable values per bed in hotels and guest houses and per seat in evening facilities.

In columns R and S, the actual amounts of total cost and total client expenditure involved by each unit of increase in clients are shown. This represents the first step toward a direct cost-benefit analysis. This analysis can show at once not only the scale of the cost or benefit but also the incidence of it—for example, to public bodies where road or water supply investment is needed, to private enterprise largely where hotel investment is involved. However, we emphasize that the budget diagram is a *neutral* document. It does not make decisions: it merely shows, in a clear and comparative way, the implications of a given course of action.

PLAN-BUDGET PROCESS

We envisage that one such diagram would be prepared for each option in each planning area. This would, of course, be only part of a complete plan-budget process. Clearly the main strategic options would be formulated at county scale. It would then be necessary to express and examine them at each planning area and then to proceed to more exact physical and financial appraisal at the scale of the individual resource. We therefore posed a formal plan-budget process, illustrated in figure 21-3. This process is suitable not only for the preparation of the initial plan and its regular review but also for the preparation of annual budgets. There are three levels in the process—county, planning area, [specific] resource. The plan-budget process moves from one level to the next during the sequence of thought.

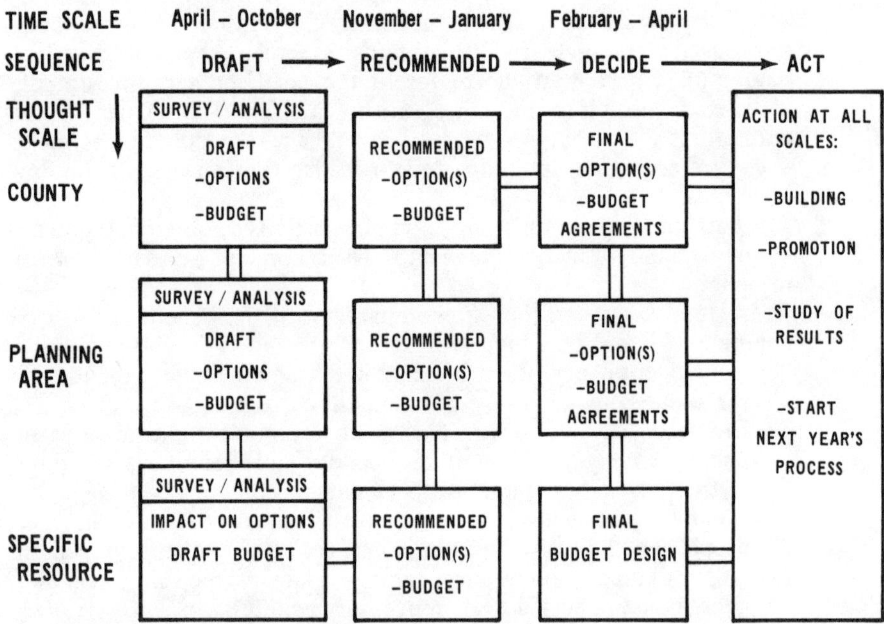

FIGURE 21-3. *Annual Plan—Budget Process*

For the initial plan or review, the process starts with the full stages of survey and analysis stated earlier at county scale. The draft options are stated for the county; and a tentative budget is proposed, mainly in the sense of the capital which the county [feels] that [it] and other bodies might make available.

These options and draft budget are examined at planning area scale, and a set of budget diagrams are produced on the lines shown in figure 21-2. A plan is then prepared to show the possible impact of each option on the specific resources of the planning area. If necessary, detailed study is done at resource scale to decide what this impact might be and what consequent costs might occur.

It may be very clear from this study of specific resources that one option would be preferred. The recommendation might therefore come from the level of a specific resource to the planning area. From the planning area then comes a recommended option and budget to be put together at county level with the recommendations from other planning areas. At the county level, the sets of material from the planning areas are put together to form recommended options and budget, upon which final decisions are then made. These final decisions form the basis not only for the county council's own action but also for discussion and agreement with other bodies [that] may be involved. This is the moment when contact between public and private bodies is most forcefully needed.

When the decisions and agreements have been reached, their implications for each planning area are expressed. This is then reflected in the final budgets and design briefs for each resource. Action then follows at all three levels, not only in the form of building and promotion but also in ongoing study which can provide a continual checking and refinement of the decisions which have been made.

ANNUAL BUDGETING

To assist the annual budgeting, the process is repeated each year following the approval of the initial development plan, and [the process] follows the same series of steps. Thus each year it is necessary to check at county scale the impact of previous decisions and of any other changes that have occurred in the resources or the clients and, hence, in the options which are available. [It is also necessary] to state draft options and budgets for that year. A check is then made of similar changes at the planning area scale, and draft options and budget are prepared for each planning area. Any changes in the capacity or usage of specific resources are then noted, and the implications of the proposed options in terms of cost are calculated.

Recommendations are then made for specific changes in resources and, hence, for options and budgets for each planning area; and these options and budgets are brought together at county scale. The county can then (1) decide the final options and budget for that year—and possibly the draft options and budgets for an ongoing period of five years—at the county scale and (2) make agreements with other bodies accordingly. These decisions and agreements for action are expressed at planning area scale, and design work on specific resources is put in hand. Action is then pursued at all scales, including a start on the plan-budget process for the following year.

The process is deliberately a merry-go-round, with the end of each year's work being simply the start of the next. Planning is a continual process, depending upon the constant refinement of information and constant checking of decisions as the years go by. Planners often take years to gather the information that will satisfy their desire for accuracy. But the world will not wait for years; and many a chance may be lost or resource, destroyed while the search for fact is being carried out.

The plan-budget process allows for action to start with tentative information. But it also provides for the checking and improvement of this information which must be done if large-scale action is to be safely launched. Annual planning and budgeting with careful back checking and feedback will make the budget process a more-and-more-accurate tool for making decisions. Using it in this manner will soon eliminate a large portion of the guesswork in both the public and private pursuit of conservation and development.

POLICY IMPLICATIONS

Most of the policy implications arising from the Donegal study were straightforward and predictable. The most important of these were the emphasis upon the need for constant refinement of information over the years; for careful relating of the amenity-tourism material to other sections of the County Development Plan and to the more local plans for towns in the county; and for the protection of the county's heritage and resources either because they are already in use or because they are the raw material for future development.

But the most profound implication which emerges quite clearly from the study, indeed from the very premises set out in the introduction to this article, is the need not only for a thought process which can involve all the many interested bodies, public and private, but also for an organizational focus for those interests.

The amenity-tourism study has convinced us that there must be, at county scale, an organization capable of:

a. insuring the collection and collation of information and its gradual refinement over the years;
b. insuring a steady progress on the preparation of the County Development Plan and of local studies;
c. coordinating the protection of amenity and tourism resources; and
d. insuring the coordination of action and investment programs by the whole range of bodies, public and private, involved in conservation and development.

The last of these points is perhaps the most important. Conservation and development, like urban renewal in America, need coordination of action and investment by multiple interests. There must be an acceptable focus for both strategic and annual agreements—if necessary, of formal or contractual type—between these interests.

For example, an important (and possibly a dominant) element of investment in a tourism plan may be new hotels, built by private enterprise. The building of hotels may demand new public investment in water supplies, sewerage schemes, and roads. The private interests will wish to be assured that these services will be created: the public interests will need to be satisfied that the hotels will be built to justify their investment. Each side may therefore seek formal agreement from the other and from any other parties involved.

This implies the creation of a new body, or the extension of some existing body, at county scale, [one] consisting of representatives of the county planning authority, other public bodies concerned with amenity and tourism, and private enterprise interests.

This body would have a liaison rather than [an] executive function but would have the main responsibility for pushing forward the full range of programs necessary for the coherent pursuit of policies for the development and conservation in the county.

We further believe that this county body must be complemented by a similar, though less-powerful, body in each planning area. This would be responsible for the collecting of necessary information in the planning area and for focusing interest and enterprise relevant to conservation and development within that area. It might take the form of a formalized and strengthened local development association.

CONCLUSION

We believe that the success of either conservation or development objectives depends upon striking a balance between them. This balance must recognize the effect which actions taken by either the public or the private sector will have on the well-being of people and of their heritage and resources. The thought process described in this article is therefore designed to do five things: to gather the material needed for the process of decision making in this field; to measure the capacity of the raw and processed resources; to state the relationships between the human, physical, and economic components involved; to set a clear process that permits regular overview to the public and private actors in both conservation and development; and to create a focus for comparison, compromise, and choice by all parties. We very much hope that other people may take whatever opportunity they have to use and improve upon these ideas.

CHAPTER 22

A FRAMEWORK FOR AGENCY USE OF PUBLIC INPUT IN RESOURCES DECISION MAKING

John C. Hendee
Roger N. Clark
George H. Stankey

Public involvement provides a vital forum for the public effectively to voice its role as a goal-setting body; but to obtain and effectively use public input in making resource management decisions is a problem for agency administrators at every level of government. In this chapter John Hendee, Roger Clark, and George Stankey describe five integral processes necessary for public involvement and elaborate some of the controversial issues involved.

Public agencies have changed the way they make decisions about the use of natural resources. The stress now is on incorporating public input. The basic concept is that agencies serve the people—what do the people want?

Public involvement has become a major policy objective of several resource agencies. The Forest Service, for example, has formally committed itself to "seek out and obtain local and national views in the process of policy and program formulation" (16). Public participation in decision making is the way that federal resource agencies now seek to be responsive and representative, although other alternatives (reorganization, decentralization, politicizing, etc.) have been proposed to achieve these goals (10).

The search for public participation is not new. Resource managers traditionally have turned to advisory boards, ad hoc committees, and contacts with key people. But some feel that past contacts often were selective, limited, and interest group oriented with a tendency to reflect the whims of industry, conservation organizations, and local political figures.

The increasing tendency for citizens to challenge resource decisions at public meetings, in court cases, and through legislative proposals indicates that some segments of the public feel excluded from policy making. A study of management problems on Montana's Bitterroot National Forest concluded, "They [local people] felt left out of any policy or decision-making and resort to protest as the only available means of being heard" (5). And as O'Riordan (12) pointed out, "Though the majority might be 'silent,' they are not necessarily indifferent.... That silence may be as much a function of political

---

Reprinted from the *Journal of Soil and Water Conservation* 29, no. 2 (March/April 1974): 60–66, by permission of the publisher and the authors.

inefficacy and limited information as it may be to the holding of mild preferences."

There is a growing body of literature about public participation—its policy implications and its significance as a research problem (1; 2; 3; 4; 6; 7; 13; 14; 15; 17). Our concern is how public participation is linked to resource management decision making. We have spent the past two years studying the public involvement process and developing new methods for analyzing public input to Forest Service decisions (8; 9). The subtle complexities and influences surrounding public involvement impress us. Just how issues are defined; how public input is collected, analyzed, and evaluated; and how the resulting decisions are implemented are particularly important in dealing with these inherent complexities and influences.

As a basic structure for making use of public inputs in resource decision making, we propose the following framework.

A MEANS TO AN END

The major objective of public resource management is to provide people with a sustained flow of the benefits they desire. Some of these benefits are material, such as low-cost lumber for housing and adequate quantity and quality of water. Others are less tangible, such as people's happiness by virtue of the recreational opportunities and environmental quality they enjoy.

In devising programs to provide the desired mix of benefits, resource managers must consider many factors, technical as well as social-political. These include, among other things, resource inventory and capability data on soil, water, timber, forage, and scenery; legal and budgetary constraints; and potential economic impacts. Public sentiment, expressed and gathered as citizens participate in decision processes, is a particularly important input because it helps identify the values that people attach to the alternative goods and services that national forests might provide. Sentiment serves as a necessary guide to achieving more acceptable resource decisions. In addition, public participation in decision making is a source of satisfaction, meaning, and identity for the citizens involved.

The overriding objective of public involvement must be to arrive at more acceptable resource management decisions. Public input is not an end in itself but a means to better decisions.

FIVE PROCESSES IN DECISION MAKING

From the resource manager's perspective, public involvement has five integral processes: issue definition, collection, analysis, evaluation, and decision implementation. Problems requiring public involvement must first be defined. Then input must be collected, analyzed. . . , and evaluated to determine what it means and how it is important to the decision. Finally, the decision must be translated into a program of action.

If oversimplified, these processes might be viewed as subsequent stages.

But this is not necessarily true because all land use planning efforts take a variety of approaches and sequences in involving the public. Figure 22-1 shows how these processes relate to public participation in a resource issue, how they relate to other decision factors, and how they combine in leading to a decision. It is important for resource managers to keep these processes separate. Mixing them can seriously affect the usefulness of public input.

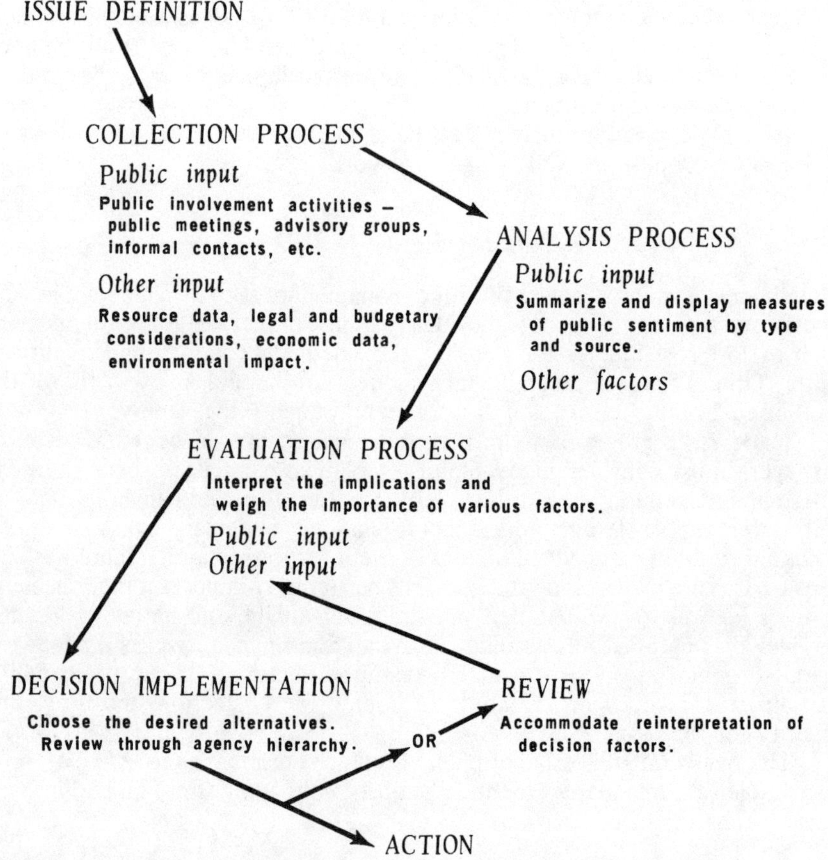

FIGURE 22-1. *Processes for Using Public Input in Resource Decision Making*

Issue Definition

This is the process or stage in resource planning during which managers, working within legal, fiscal, political, resource capability, and environmental constraints, identify the range of alternatives that might require additional public input. The resource base is studied. Environmental and resource-capability data are integrated within broad legal and fiscal constraints. Viable management alternatives are identified.

Advice from key members of the public at this stage can assure that no interests or reasonable alternatives are overlooked. But major public input is yet to be collected, and managers must not become locked into any one alternative.

Collection

The collection process includes all the varied techniques that yield citizen input. The objective of the process is to secure the full range of views from all who are interested or affected. It often begins with efforts to inform the public about issues, alternatives, and consequences. It also includes efforts to solicit and record citizens' views about what courses of action they prefer.

A wide range of activities is involved. Advisory boards, ad hoc committees, public meetings, opinion leaders, professional contacts, workshops, letters, editorials, opinion polls, petitions, and surveys are possible sources of public views. There is no single, best way to obtain public input. All collection methods have advantages and weaknesses, and too much reliance on one can distort the range of input (9).

The input must be collected in a form that can be analyzed and evaluated. Collection methods should involve some record of the input to facilitate its use.

Analysis

Analysis describes . . . the nature, content, and extent of public input so the input reflects public ideas, opinion, and values. Wherever possible, analysis should be systematic, objective, and quantitative. It should use processes that can be replicated by independent analysis.

Analysis should focus on questions about the content of input. What was said? By whom? Where did the input originate? How did it vary? How many people provided input? What views did they express? Wh[ich] interests were represented and wh[ich] ones were not? What were the prevailing opinions and views about management alternatives, general issues, and specific areas? What reasons were given to support the views expressed? What additional issues were raised?

With this information, responsible managers can subjectively evaluate its meaning and implications. But [one] must . . . stress that analysis merely describes public input. It makes no attempt to evaluate the importance of that input. Serious biases result when judgments of importance or "quality" are made in the process of analysis, thereby prematurely screening out certain kinds of input.

Evaluation

Evaluation is the interpretation and weighing of all data collected and analyzed —relative to a decision or recommendation. The process is necessarily subjective. No set formula exists to guide it. But when the resource manager presents his decision, he should clearly state the relative importance he placed on the kinds of public input received and why [he so placed them]. For example, where local, regional, and national inputs differ, he should specify the importance attached to each in arriving at the decision and his criteria for such judgments. Likewise, he should clarify the importance he attached to factors other than public opinion (such as resource capability and legal and budgetary constraints).

It is in the evaluation process that resource managers serve most directly as para-politicians. Decision makers at several levels usually are involved. With a more accurate understanding of public opinion and values, coupled with the other decision factors, decision makers can be better para-politicians. They can justify decisions and recommendations both to the public and to the agency hierarchy. If each decision maker clearly states how he weighed the various public inputs and the relationship of [these] inputs to other factors, his judgment can be reviewed more easily by those who question his decision. In time, guidelines for evaluation will evolve from decisions that are accepted and those that are not.

Decision Implementation

Here decision makers must consider processes such as providing feedback to the public, providing review when necessary, and taking whatever steps are required to translate a decision into an action program. Successfully implementing a public resource decision is not a spontaneous event, particularly when there has been controversy.

It is important to give the public time to react. Reaction to a decision depends on what the public thought the agency would do. When that decision runs counter to public sentiment, untapped opinions can surface again. The "silent majority" suddenly can make itself heard.

Decision implementation should facilitate rather than stymie review when the decision or factors leading to it are seriously questioned. For example, subjective matters such as the importance placed on various factors and input in reaching a decision are legitimate matters for public review and debate. Patience, tolerance, and a good job on the previous processes are the manager's best assets at this stage.

INTERDEPENDENCE OF PROCESSES

Resource managers must understand the interdependence of the five decision-making processes. The way any one is conducted can dramatically affect the others. The ability of decision makers to evaluate data obtained from analysis will be greatly affected by the extent to which issues were defined at the outset of the planning effort, the collection techniques used to tap public sentiment, and the analytical system used to describe and display public input. The ability to implement decisions, with public understanding and support, depends largely on the decision maker's ability to evaluate rationally the factors affecting the decision. Like the proverbial chain and its weakest link, the interdependence of the decision-making processes requires that each be designed rigorously and in full recognition of its relationship to the others.

SOME CONTROVERSIAL ISSUES

Certain complexities, issues, and subtle implications are important to those who need to understand and use the framework we propose.

Criteria for Effective Participation

Many people welcome efforts by resource management agencies to secure public participation. Nevertheless, accusations still prevail that such efforts merely represent lip service. Public involvement must become an explicit, visible part of decision making at the local, regional, and national levels. It must be a process that both administrators and the public expect and recognize as fundamental to decision making, just as resource inventories are recognized as a necessary and fundamental component. The range of public sentiment on any issue should be available for review by administrators and public groups alike.

Public involvement must also be traceable so that an independent second party can determine how input was collected, analyzed, and evaluated. For instance, the party might want to examine how public input influenced development of alternatives, decisions, and overall management direction. Administrators should be able to demonstrate how the input related to their decision. Decisions based on some intuitive "feel" for public sentiment are unacceptable because they are not susceptible to public review.

The demand for public scrutiny no doubt will lead to requests for formal inspection and review of how an agency used public input in making a decision. This pressure for accountability will require public agencies to develop systems for public input analysis that are not only visible and traceable but also objective and reliable, so that agency interpretation of public input can be validated by independent observers.

Professionalism and Public Involvement

Skillful handling of public participation requires considerable professional skill on the part of a resource manager. He must identify those issues and problems that have consequences significant enough to [require] public knowledge, advice, and consent before taking action.

He must define a reasonable range of feasible alternatives within legal, fiscal, political, environmental, and resource limitations . . . and . . . define the probable consequences of each alternative, . . . identify[ing] the trade-offs between them. He must clearly communicate this information to the public; face critical scrutiny; and, using a variety of collection techniques, acquire public input. [Then] he must analyze public input to identify public opinion and values from a variety of public comments that often are emotional in nature and not offered in resource management terms; he must learn the public's language.

[Further, the resource manager] . . . must evaluate the importance of public input in relation to other decision factors and devise resource programs balanced against all of them. He must face the public with his recommendations and decision, explain how he arrived at them, defend them, or, if conditions warrant, call for additional review of the decision factors and offer appropriate revisions. He must then implement decisions through effective, efficient action programs under greater public scrutiny than ever before.

What Kind of Input is Best?

The public expresses its views in many forms, all of which are important in determining the balance of public sentiment. But whether input comes in letters, statements from public meetings, ad hoc committee reports, opinion polls, petitions, or some other form, objective analysis requires that the input be recorded accurately. To insure effective use of public input, an enduring record should be kept. The input must be written or otherwise recorded if it is to be summarized objectively.

Open meetings and publicly solicited written input best exemplify the democratic tradition in which an agency opens its channels to public opinion and, in turn, commits itself to respond to public desires. Open meetings also help insure that segments of the public not represented through other channels have the chance to hear the issues and be heard.

Written inputs can be particularly significant. They represent a deliberate commitment to action on the part of respondents and are influenced less by the spontaneous atmosphere of public meetings—an environment that often precipitates oral input that differs from the more thoughtful, written input received later. The anonymity of written input also helps avoid the influence of peer group pressure at meetings, which can be enormously intense in small, close-knit communities. Most importantly, written input is in a form that resource managers can thoughtfully study and analyze.

Weighing Public Input

Many things prompt public input. Employers urge employees to write letters. Students respond at the suggestion or request of teachers. Special-interest groups spur form letters, coupons, and signed petitions. Voluntary organizations and industrial groups file formal position statements on behalf of their members.

Both the philosophy underlying public involvement in decision making and the techniques used to secure input are important when combining and evaluating such diverse forms of input. The major question, of course, is, What importance should be attached to each when evaluating [its] implications for a pending decision? Judging the importance of different kinds of public input is difficult and sometimes controversial. The task is necessarily subjective and must be done by officials within their political-administrative structure, as is the case with the assignment of priorities in other areas where differing demands compete.

But if the nature of all public input is clearly described as the result of traceable collection and analytical procedures, the proper weights to be assigned will soon become apparent from the degree to which decisions are accepted and from the review of unacceptable decisions. For example, public input can be summarized and displayed in the analytical process as so many letters, statements, petitions, etc., for or against a given alternative. In the evaluation process, administrators must weigh the relative importance of these measures of public values and other factors when ruling for or against an alternative. If the data used are visible and traceable, the relative importance assigned will be either sanctioned by public acceptance of the decision or reassigned in any review leading to a reversal or modification of the decision.

Two important considerations must guide the weighing of public input: (a) It is the responsibility of decision makers—officially responsible line officers—and not their staffs or analysts; (b) effective evaluation depends on a previous analytical process that clearly describes the content of all input received.

WEIGHING CANNOT BE AVOIDED

We have encountered a spectrum of attitudes among resource managers ranging from "we need formulas and guidelines telling us how to weigh various kinds of input" to suspicion and mistrust because "anyone seeking to systematize the handling of public input must advocate weighing it."

In no way can or should formulas guide the weighing of public input. But whenever a line officer makes a decision or recommendation in the evaluation process, he implicitly places varying degrees of importance on all the input he has. There is no way to escape this kind of weighing. For example, a decision favoring a resource development alternative might implicitly place more importance on local opinion than on urban response favoring a preservation alternative. Similarly, a decision contrary to numerous petition signatures implicitly discounts them in favor of other public input, evidence, and/or criteria.

The point is that any time a decision is made, varying degrees of importance are implicitly or explicitly assigned to all available input. Debate over the importance assigned to various inputs is an appropriate matter for public concern, and the public involvement process should facilitate it. If resource managers are not accountable for how they use public input, their tendency to be responsible to it will be limited.

DIRECT VS INDIRECT INPUT; ASSUMPTIONS AND JUDGMENTS

One might argue that if an agency is to respond to all segments of society, then that agency should weigh equally all public expressions of sentiment regardless of their form or apparent motivation. But managers usually assign more importance to a personal letter than to each signature on a petition, form letter or coupon.

Public input can be distinguished as "direct"—generated principally by the independent action of a citizen—and "indirect"—principally the result of group influences. Statements made at meetings and personal letters are direct input. Petitions, form letters, coupons, and questionnaires are indirect. Likewise, the positions of organized groups on behalf of "*x*" number of members should be identified in a way . . . [so] that decision makers can evaluate their relative importance.

How public input will be evaluated must be clarified because it will seriously affect the kind of input that will result. If indirect input will be considered less important than direct input, then administrators must let the public know so they can act accordingly.

A frequent complaint of citizen groups is that the rationale behind a decision is unclear. There is uncertainty about how public input and other factors were evaluated and related to one another (9). We feel it is absolutely necessary that the importance attached to public input be indicated, as well as the relative value placed on other factors such as legal, fiscal, and political constraints; resource capability; environment; etc. If the decision maker states what importance he will or must place on each factor, his judgment can more easily be reviewed by those who question his decision.

QUALITY VS QUANTITY

Resource managers want "quality" input—well-reasoned, site- or issue-specific, . . . couched in appropriate management terminology. Such input is valuable, but too much emphasis on the quality of input can restrict the quantity of input. Whether well-reasoned and detailed or not, all input expresses values, and definition of these values is the overriding objective of public involvement. That citizens must support their opinions with reasons runs contrary to the intangible and emotional values that many people place on forest resources.

It can be difficult to articulate feelings and beliefs about resource development, wilderness, scenery, wildlife, environmental quality, or multiple use and much more difficult to cite reasons that fully explain them. Reasons offered in support of an opinion add depth and meaning to a citizen's input, but their absence should not detract from the fact that his statement represents an important expression of values.

There also is a hazard in trying to identify what constitutes quality or substantive input. Input that decision makers do not support or understand may be tossed out inadvertently or purposely. Their ideas of good or substantive reasons reflect personal values or opinions. This can jeopardize credibility in public involvement, and it certainly can reduce the usefulness of public input as a means to better, more acceptable decisions.

An involved public will continue to express conflicting opinions about public resources management. The relative merits of these views, along with other considerations, must be examined so that decisions reflect the public's best long-term interests. Therefore, it is dangerous to overstress substantive input at the expense of quantity of input. But it is just as dangerous simply to emphasize the number of opinions for or against an alternative. Both quality and quantity of input are important dimensions of public involvement. Both identify public values, preferences, and possible trade-offs.

REPRESENTATIVENESS

Many people become concerned about the representativeness of public input. They are anxious to have the views of the full cross-section of the public on resource management issues. This is an admirable objective but a difficult one to achieve. Despite the best efforts to involve the public, not everyone will respond. Care must be taken in the collection process to assure that anyone wanting to give his opinion has the chance to do so. But resource managers cannot hide behind the "silent majority." Silence may reflect lack of interest. It may also reflect a lack of information on the part of a potentially interested client.

Here it is useful to distinguish between demographic representation of sex, age, residence groups, etc., and interest representation. It is important to see that everyone known to be interested or affected has had an opportunity to make his views known. If groups known to be affected have not responded, there is a responsibility to solicit their views before making a decision. This has important practical implications. If input is not obtained before the decision, it may come later when unsuspecting interests feel they have been ignored or victimized.

VOTE COUNTING

Another concern to resource managers and the public is "vote counting." Some professionals fear that public participation means abdicating responsibility and letting the public dictate a final decision. This is what voting usually means in a democracy. And the public appears equally confused. Are they voting or not?

Public input does not dictate the decision. It is useful and proper to determine the balance of opinion by questioning organizations and individuals, but the search is not for an either/or solution dictated by votes. The goal is an approximate measure of public opinion and values that can be weighed against other decision-making factors.

Tabulation of opinions is not new. Administrators in the past have defended decisions on the amount of support or opposition voiced. The concept of soliciting public input rests on the premise that public participation enables a more accurate measure of public opinion and values. The objective of counting input is to determine more systematically and objectively how all the various segments of the public and affected interests feel about the issue and why they feel as they do. This knowledge leads to decisions that are based on a better understanding of the balance of values expressed.

The balance of opinion about an issue should be supplemented with qualitative information, such as supporting reasons. Reasons given in support of various opinions hold significant clues to their meaning and provide additional information. They may indicate a unique feature that may be lost or how a minority interest would suffer if a particular decision is made. In such a situation the decision maker could logically decide to protect that feature whether or not the balance of opinion favored that alternative. In the absence of such qualitative information, disastrous mistakes can be made simply by ruling in favor of the majority.

CONTINUING INPUT

Public input affecting resource management decisions generally is solicited during a critical period prior to the decision. However, many inputs precede or follow the formal gathering process, in some cases by several years. The balance of opinion can change as more people become involved, as more and better information is obtained, and as public attitudes shift in response to changing situations as decisions and management programs are implemented. It should be possible for managers to consider all input, even that ... not coincid[ing] with a special appeal for response.

It is essential, therefore, that the analysis of public sentiment reflect input made prior to any special appeal for response and that continuing input be recorded for subsequent retrieval when needed; for example, when significant shifts in opinion and values are suspected. Interested persons should not be required to resubmit their views time and again to coincide with administrative convenience.

THE NEED FOR ANALYSIS

Techniques for analyzing and summarizing public input are particularly needed (8; 9; 11). This is important because evaluation of input depends on adequate data, clearly described and summarized. And this is no easy matter when thousands of public inputs are received.

Systematic, objective, and reliable systems for analysis are needed to (a) efficiently summarize and display various kinds of public input using methods that can be validated by independent observers; (b) describe the extent and nature of public expression surrounding a given issue—i.e., all opinions supporting reasons; (c) reveal the sources of input by location of respondent and particular interest in the issues; (d) record both direct and indirect input; (e) provide [both] for continuity in recording input before and after any formal period of collection and [for] the ability to summarize input as needed; and (f) respond sensitively to general expressions of value as well as to specific management suggestions. If analysis provides a clear summary of public input, the decision maker can evaluate its implications more effectively. Table 22-1 illustrates one way input can be displayed as a result of analysis.

CONCLUSION

Failure to solicit public participation aggressively and innovatively—and [to] respond to it—can result in [1] the loss of agency stature, [2] damaging public criticism of agency policies and programs, and [3] continued antagonistic situations between the agency and some of its clientele. Public participation is unlikely to eliminate confrontations with polarized constituents, but it can bring out and focus the conflict well in advance of the deadline for making a decision.

Pressures to secure better public input are, in part, a response to the public's demands for a greater voice in land management. By increasing public

	Forms of Input				
Alternative 1	**Letters**[a]	**Petitions**	**Reports**[a]	**Form Letters**	**Total**
For[b]					
Inputs (no.)	82	2	3	82	169
Signatures (no.)	90	83	3	86	262
Against[c]					
Inputs (no.)	31	18	4	21	74
Signatures (no.)	35	645	5	21	706

TABLE 22-1. *A Hypothetical Example Showing Balance of Opinion According to Form of Input and Supporting Reasons*

[a] A list of organizations submitting letters and reports is provided for every opinion discussed.

[b] Reasons *for*: best for economy (151); provide jobs (111); provide mass recreation (61); other alternatives too restrictive (43); restricts intensive recreation (26); restricts roads (19); impact on local economy (9); restricts timber harvest (4); enough already (1).

[c] Reasons *against*: already too many roads (72); need more wilderness (65); preserve for posterity (47); protect areas from development (31); protect areas from timber harvest (22); protect areas from general misuse (12); last chance (8); wildlife values (3).

participation in decision making, public agencies should avert disastrous mistakes and diminish ex post facto confrontations.

But the issue is a broader one. Public involvement provides a forum in which the public can effectively exert its rightful role as a goal-setting body. On the other hand, with a more accurate assessment of public desires, professional managers can better fulfill their role as achievers of those goals.

REFERENCES

1. Alston, Richard M. 1972. Forest-goals and decision-making in the Forest Service. Forest Service Research Paper INT-128. Ogden, Utah: Intermountain Forest and Range Experiment Station.
2. Behan, R. W. 1966. The myth of the omnipotent forester. *Journal of Forestry* 64: 398–407.
3. Bishop, Bruce A. 1970. *Public participation in water resources planning.* Washington, D.C.: Corps of Engineers, U.S. Department of the Army.
4. Bleiker, Hans. 1971. *Community interaction as an integral part of the highway decision-making process.* Cambridge, Mass.: MIT Press.
5. Bolle, Arnold W. 1971. Public participation and environmental quality. *Natural Resources Journal* 11, no. 3: 497–505.
6. Bultena, Gordon; Rogers, David; and Webb, Vince. 1973. *Public response to planned environmental change—A study of citizen views and actions on the proposed Ames Reservoir.* Iowa State University Soc. Report 106. Ames.
7. Campion, Thomas B., Jr. 1972. *Public involvement in decision-making on the Shoshone National Forest.* Boulder: University of Colorado.
8. Clark, Roger; Stankey, George H.; and Hendee, John C. 1974. *Codinvolve: A system for coding, summarizing, storing, retrieving, and analyzing public input to resource decisions.* Portland, Ore.: Pacific N.W. Forest and Range Experiment Station.
9. Hendee, John C., et. al. 1973. *Public involvement and the Forest Service: Experience, effectiveness, and suggested direction.* Washington, D.C.: USDA Forest Service.
10. Kaufman, Herbert. 1969. Administrative decentralization and political power. *Public Administration Review* 29, no. 1: 3–15.
11. Lundblad, Dennis. 1972. Community workshop—An experiment in public involvement. In

Linda McKenzie, ed. *The grass roots and water resource management*, pp. 41–45. Pullman: Washington State University Press.

12. O'Riordan, Timothy. 1971. Public opinion and environmental quality: A reappraisal. *Environment and Behavior* 3, no. 2: 191–214.
13. Reno, Arlee T. 1972. *Interaction procedures in the transportation systems planning process.* Cambridge, Mass: MIT Press.
14. Sewell, W. R., and Burton, Ian. 1971. *Perceptions and attitudes in resource management.* Ottawa: Department of Energy, Mines, and Resources.
15. Stankey, George H. 1972. The use of content analysis in resource decision-making. *Journal of Forestry* 70, no. 3: 148–51.
16. U.S. Department of Agriculture, Forest Service. 1970. *Framework for the future, Forest Service objectives and policy guides.* Washington, D.C.
17. Warner, Katharine P. 1971. *Public participation in water resources planning.* Ann Arbor: University of Michigan Press.

FURTHER READING

Recreation, Resources & Decisions

Chapin, F. S. 1971. Free time activities and the quality of urban life. *Journal of the American Institute of Planners*, pp. 411–17.

Cheek, N. H., Jr.; Field, D. R.; and Burdge, R. J. 1976. *Leisure and recreation places.* Ann Arbor, Mich.: Ann Arbor Science.

Clark, Roger N., et al. 1974. An introduction to Codinvolve: A system for analyzing, storing, and retrieving public input to resource decisions. USDA Forest Service Report, PNW-223. April.

Mills, A. S.; Merriam, L. C., Jr.; and Ramsey, C. E. 1976. Public opinion and park development. University of Minnesota Agricultural Experiment Station, Station Bulletin 516, Forestry Series 22. July.

Soil Conservation Society of America. 1977. *Land use: Tough choices in today's world.* Proceedings of a national symposium, March 21–24, 1977, Omaha, Neb.

Stankey, G. H. 1972. The use of content analysis in resource decision making. *Journal of Forestry* 70: 148–51.

GENERAL READING AND BIBLIOGRAPHIES

Both students and professionals find it difficult to keep abreast of recreation/leisure literature. The first edition of *Land & Leisure*, for example, had many excellent listings in its recreation bibliographies; but since its publication, reports and scholarly writings in the field have become increasingly specialized, making it even more difficult to maintain a broad knowledge of the literature.

For the purposes of the second edition, therefore, several steps have been taken to facilitate recreation/leisure research. Specialized bibliographies appear after each part division. In addition, a general reading list and bibliography are provided below. The information that immediately follows is presented as a guide to further literature search, much of it by computer.

Guide to Literature Search

The Smithsonian Science Information Exchange (SSIE) provides a national source of information on research progress in the United States. Listings of available research information packages are published in each issue of the *SSIE Science Newsletter*. The SSIE also offers on-line data base search service for those that have access to a computer terminal. For more information, write SSIE, Room 300, 1730 M St., N.W., Washington, DC 20036.

Librarians will be able to assist in computer search from other data banks such as Current Agriculture Information (CAIN), National Technical Information Service (NTIS), and the Indexes of Social Science and Psychological Science Citations.

An additional source for informational bibliographies is the Council of Planning Librarians, P.O. Box 229, Monticello, IL 61856. The council is a nationally organized group of librarians, faculty, professional planners, public and private planning organizations, and others interested both in problems of library organization and research and also in the dissemination of information about city and regional planning. Exchange bibliographies are published by the council and may be ordered through the above address.

The Library of Congress operates the National Referral Center for Science and Technology. The center answers who, what, and where questions without charge; it does not answer scientific or technical inquiries directly, nor does it furnish bibliography assistance.

The editor's knowledge of bibliography sources outside the United States is limited; I would however be remiss not to mention the *Rural Recreation and Tourism Abstracts*, published by the Commonwealth Agricultural Bureaux in Great Britain. This international abstracting service could be a useful source for additional information.

General Reading

Appleton, Ian, ed. 1974. *Leisure research and policy*. Edinburgh: Scottish Academic Press.

Bannon, J. 1976. *Leisure resources*. Englewood Cliffs, N.J.: Prentice-Hall.

Brockman, C. Frank, and Merriam, L. C., Jr. 1973. *Recreation use of wild lands.* New York: McGraw-Hill.

Carlson, Edgar Reynold; MacLean, Janet R.; Deppe, Theodore R.; and Peterson, James A. 1979. *Recreation and leisure—The changing scene.* Belmont, Calif.: Wadsworth.

Coppock, J. T., and Duffield, B. S. 1975. *Recreation in the countryside.* New York: St. Martin's Press.

First Canadian Congress on Leisure Research. 1975. Quebec: Université Laval. October.

Godbey, G. 1978. *Recreation, park and leisure services: Foundations, organizations, administration.* Philadelphia: Saunders.

Godbey, G., and Parker, S. 1976. *Leisure studies and services: An overview.* Philadelphia: Saunders.

Gold, S. M. 1973. *Urban recreation planning.* Philadelphia: Lea & Febiger.

Haworth, J. T., and Smith, M. A., eds. 1976. *Work and leisure.* Princeton, N.J.: Princeton.

Kando, T. M. 1975. *Leisure and popular culture in transition.* St. Louis: Mosby.

Kraus, Richard. 1978. *Recreation and leisure in modern society.* Santa Monica, Calif.: Goodyear.

Lavery, Patrick, ed. 1974. *Recreational geography.* New York: Halsted Press.

Mercer, D., ed. 1977. *Leisure and recreation in Australia.* Malvern, Australia: Sorrett.

Murphy, James F., and Howard, Dennis R. 1977. *Delivery of community leisure services: An holistic approach.* Philadelphia: Lea & Febiger.

Roberts, K. 1970. *Leisure.* London: Longman.

Sage, George H., ed. 1974. *Sport and American society: Selected readings.* Reading, Mass.: Addison-Wesley.

Sessoms, H. Douglas, et al. 1975. *Leisure services—The organized recreation and park system.* Englewood Cliffs, N.J.: Prentice-Hall.

Simmons, I. G. 1975. *Rural recreation in the industrial world.* New York: Halsted Press.

Statistics Canada. 1978. *Travel, tourism and outdoor recreation: A statistical digest* (1975, 1976). Ottawa: Industry, Trade and Commerce.

U.S. Department of Agriculture, Forest Service. 1977. Proceedings, *River recreation management and research symposium.* Minneapolis, Minn.: North Central Forest Experiment Station. January.

Bibliography

Anderson, D. H.; Leatherberry, E. C.; and Lime, D. W. 1978. *An annotated bibliography on river recreation.* St. Paul, Minn.: USDA Forest Service.

Anderson, D. M., and Munro, W. 1970. An initial bibliography on outdoor recreation studies in Canada with selected United States references. Canada Land Inventory, Department of Regional Economic Expansion. Ottawa.

Arthur, Louise M., and Boster, Ron S. 1976. Measuring scenic beauty: A selected annotated bibliography. Rocky Mountain Forest and Range Experiment Station, USDA Forest Service General Technical Report RM-25. Fort Collins, Colo. May.

Canadian Government Travel Bureau. 1970. *Bibliography of tourism research studies.* Ottawa: Information Canada.

Carroll, M. A. 1965. *Open space planning: A selected bibliography.* Department of Urban Planning, Bureau of Community Planning. University of Illinois, Urbana.

Ditton, Robert B. 1970. *Water-based recreation: Access, water quality, and incompatible use consideration.* Council of Planning Librarians Exchange Bibliography no. 159.

BIBLIOGRAPHY

Harker, G. R. 1978. *Bibliography of selected literature on river recreation.* Western Illinois University Department of Recreation and Park Administration. Macomb.

Lime, David W., and Stankey, George H. 1971. *A selected bibliography of literature related to recreational carrying capacity decision-making.* Prepared for the Forest Recreation Symposium, Syracuse, N.Y.

Meyersohn, R. 1969. The sociology of leisure in the United States: Introduction and bibliography, 1945–1965. *Journal of Leisure Research* 1 (winter): 53–68.

Pinkerton, James R., and Pinkerton, Marjorie J. 1969. *Outdoor recreation and leisure: A reference guide and selected bibliography.* University of Missouri School of Business and Public Administration Research Center. Columbia.

U.S. Department of Agriculture, Forest Service, Division of Forest Environment Research. 1972. *Forest recreation research publications, 1942–1966,* and supplements to 1972. Washington, D.C.: Government Printing Office.

———. Department of Commerce, Office of Regional Economic Development. 1966. *Tourism and recreation: A state-of-the-art study.* Washington, D.C.: Government Printing Office.

———. Department of the Interior, Bureau of Outdoor Recreation. 1971. *Outdoor recreation research, a reference catalog* (1970). Washington, D.C.: Government Printing Office.

———. Outdoor Recreation Resources Review Commission. 1962. *Outdoor recreation literature: A survey.* Study Report 27. Washington, D.C.: Government Printing Office.

van der Smissen, Betty, and Joyce, Donald J. 1970. *Bibliography of theses and dissertations in recreation, parks, camping, and outdoor education.* Washington, D.C.: National Recreation and Parks Association.